Translating by Factors

SUNY Series in Linguistics

Mark Aronoff, Editor

TRANSLATING
BY
FACTORS

Christoph Gutknecht
and
Lutz J. Rölle

State University of New York Press

Published by
State University of New York Press, Albany

© 1996 State University of New York

For information, address State University of New York
Press, State University Plaza, Albany, N.Y., 12246

Production by E. Moore
Marketing by Fran Keneston

Library of Congress Cataloging-in-Publication Data

Gutknecht, Christoph.
    Translating by factors / Christoph Gutknecht and Lutz J. Rölle.
       p.   cm. — (SUNY series in linguistics)
    Includes bibliographical references (p.) and index.
    ISBN 0-7914-2957-1. — ISBN 0-7914-2958-X (pbk.)
    1. Translating and interpreting. 2. English language—Translating
into German. I. Rölle, Lutz J., 1952–   . II. Title.
III. Series.
P306.G87   1996
418′.02—dc20
                                        95-32086
                                          CIP

CONTENTS

ACKNOWLEDGMENTS

Our thanks are due to Bernard Wall, Anthony Gawlikowski, and Dieter Bromberg for their advice regarding acceptability in British English, and to Dennis George Russell for consultation regarding American English. We are also grateful to Jo Dawes and Professor Emeritus Yngve Bertil Olsson (London) for their comments on earlier versions of the manuscript.

We also extend our appreciation to Christine E. Worden, SUNY Press acquisitions editor, and to Elizabeth Moore, SUNY Press production editor, for their assistance during the period of this book's preparation. In addition, we would like to thank Gnomi Schrift Goulden, our copyeditor, for her scrupulous and diligent work.

Moreover, it has been a privilege to have the support and advice of Joseph L. Malone, professor of linguistics and departmental chair at Barnard College, Columbia University.

Above all, the writers find themselves indebted to Professor Mark Aronoff (SUNY, Stony Brook), for including this study in his *SUNY Series in Linguistics*. His encouragement has been essential to the realization of this book.

Obligations are thankfully acknowledged to the following persons and agencies for permission to use copyrighted materials (fuller publication data are provided under indicated items in the References): R. Clive Meredith for extracts of Meredith, 1979 (see Chapter 6); Walter de Gruyter & Co. for portions of Shoshana Blum-Kulka, 1985 (see Chapter 4); Jennifer Coates and Croom Helm Ltd. for figures and extracts from Coates, 1983 (see Chapters 3, 4, and 5); Roger Chriss for a portion of Chriss, 1994 (see Chapter 6); Gunter Narr Verlag for a passage from Albrecht Neubert, 1991 (see Chapter 6); Cassell Academic and Michael R. Perkins for a portion of Perkins, 1983 (see Chapter 3); the Chicago Linguistic Society for a diagram from Panther, 1981 (see Chapter 4); and William Hollins & Company for the Viyella House advertisement (see Chapter 8).

FIGURES

TABLES

KEY TO SYMBOLS

SL source language
TL target language
F   factor
*   unacceptable or ill-formed
!   not acceptable in the relevant sense
?   questionable in the relevant sense
→   is rendered as
↔   is rendered as . . . and vice versa
≠   is not rendered as
=   is synonymous with
( ) for introduction of new examples
[ ] for reintroduction of former examples

Capitals for lexemes and fixed expressions such as CAN, MAY/MIGHT (JUST) AS WELL, KÖNNEN, and SOLLEN

Italics

1. for forms (*can't, soll*)
2. for metalinguistic use (or mention) of expressions, including the citation of (parts of) sentences not given an extra line
3. for emphasis
4. for titles of books

Double quotation marks

1. for meanings, such as "ability," "permission"
2. for quotations

Single quotation marks

1. for terms used in a semi-technical sense or terms whose validity is questioned

2. for titles of papers

In quotations from other authors the typographical conventions, numbering of examples, etc. have been adapted to fit ours.

Prosodic notation

1. Stress marks
 | the bar indicates that the following syllable is stressed
 ‖ the double bar indicates stronger or main stress
 /   onset (first prominent syllable in a tone unit)
 !   booster (syllable articulated slightly higher than preceding one)
2. Intonation marks
 ˋ   falling intonation
 ˊ   rising intonation
 ˇ   fall-plus-rise intonation
 ˆ   rise-fall intonation
 # mark for end of tone unit

1. INTRODUCTION

1.1 TRANSLATING BY FACTORS

Translating by factors—this may sound familiar and novel at the same time. Everyone knows what factors are, and everyone knows the preposition *by* in expressions such as *judging by actions, singing by ear, acting by instinct*. In all of these examples *by* precedes the means or the yardstick used to perform an action. And this is exactly what we mean when we say *translating by factors*—translating by means of factors, going by factors to perform translations.

1.1.1 Factors in Translation Studies

To make the idea of translation factors a little bit more concrete let us have a look at the way(s) translatologists have used the notion of "factor" in some of their publications.[1]

- K. Bales (1976), 'Factors Determining the Translation of American Belles-Lettres into Hungarian . . .';
- R. de Beaugrande (1978), *Factors in a Theory of Poetic Translating*;
- M. Bowen (1980), 'Bilingualism as a Factor in the Training of Interpreters';
- B. Hlebec (1989), 'Factors and Steps in Translating';
- J. S. Holmes (1972), 'The Cross-Temporal Factor in Verse Translation';
- O. Kade (1964), 'Subjektive und objektive Faktoren im Übersetzungsprozess. Ein Beitrag zur Ermittlung objektiver Kriterien des Übersetzens als Voraussetzung für eine wissenschaftliche Lösung des Übersetzungsproblems';

- J. Skov-Larsen (1980), 'On the Establishment of Formalized Transfer Rules Based on Cotextual and Contextual Factors';
- K. Soomere (1989), 'A Statistical Analysis of Rhythm as One of the Key Factors of Adequacy of Literary Translation of Prose (from English into Estonian)';
- H. S. Straight (1975), 'Translation: Some Anthropological and Psycholinguistic Factors';
- W. Walther (1990), 'Faktoren für die Übersetzung von Metaphern (Englisch-Deutsch)';
- W. Wilss (1992), 'Was ist Übersetzungsdidaktik? Versuch einer Faktorenanalyse.'

Even this small eclectic list of titles enables us to distinguish several kinds of factors. These are

1. factors in the training of translators and interpreters (Bowen, Wilss);
2. factors for the assessment of quality and adequacy of translation (Soomere, Straight[2]);
3. factors determining the translation of certain text classes (Bales, de Beaugrande, Holmes), other linguistic phenomena (Walther), or translation in general (Hlebec, Kade, Skov-Larsen).

It is only common sense to say that the very same factors determining translation (3) may also be drawn upon as criteria for judging the adequacy of translation (2). And, again, the same factors are expedient to be imparted in the training of translators and interpreters (1).[3] So we can see unity in diversity, which actually facilitates our presentation, because for our purposes it is not ultimately necessary to distinguish among the three areas of application of translation factors.

The various factors themselves, however, do have to be distinguished for an overview—as, for instance, is done by Wilss in describing the situation of the translator who

> can choose from among several more or less equally acceptable TL [target language] versions. The translator's singling out of a specific variant may depend on various factors:
>
> 1. the type of text to be translated,
> 2. the extent to which the SL [source language] text bears stylistic markings,
> 3. the intended TL audience,
> 4. the extent to which the translator can comprehend the SL text and identify himself with it,
> 5. the translator's stylistic preferences and his ability to recognize and handle stylistic registers. (1982: 105)

These, of course, are not the only translation factors existing. Sager (1989: 93 ff.) elaborates on "the considerable number of variables which affect the translation process," including situational factors, the awareness factor, user factor, textual factor, research factor, and revision factor.

Many more factors could be enumerated. In fact, their number is so large that S. D. Ross of SUNY, Binghamton, sums up the whole situation by stating: "The complexity of translation, the number of factors involved, is enormous" (1981: 11).

Capitulate to this complexity? No translator can afford this if he or she wants to stick to that profession. As a way out we propose to make complexity transparent by systematizing translation factors.[4] This is in line with Wilss's (1988: 14) insight that "the more or less *complex* textual situation the translator is faced with consists of a bundle of *factors*, among which the translator sorts out those factors that are relevant to one's decisions in the translation process" (our translation and emphasis).

Systematizing translation factors would first involve pointing out factor dimensions and then finding out the individual factors and their effects. This is exactly what we propose to do in this book, chapter headings indicating factor dimensions. Chapters 2–4 will feature the classical semiotic dimensions of syntax, semantics, and pragmatics. In Chapter 5 we will discuss factors relating to spoken and written language. Chapter 6 will show different translation units as relevant factors. Chapter 7 will be devoted to the influence of factors that are essential elements of any translation situation. Finally, we will examine more theoretical issues such as the distinction between *translation* and *adaptation* in the light of the notion of "factor."

The idea of translation factors, giving an overview of them and setting up a system is nothing new. It was expressed as a desideratum by Senn saying:

> But some better help they would deserve indeed, the translators. . . . What experts could practically contribute would quite simply be a synopsis of *all* aspects recognized. . . . The list would have to be open-ended and continually enlarged. It could at the most be clearly arranged, possibly be fit into a system. In this way it would, after all, outline what matters for an ideal translation . . . , what *else* would *also* have to be taken into account. This would be apt to open several eyes, and a mere glimpse into the very variety of competing criteria could even easily check the dogmatically arrogant peacocking of (some of us) critics. (1986: 83; our translation; emphasis as in the original)[5]

To date there are several synopses as desired by Senn. To begin with, the very volume containing his appeal offers an answer to his quest. Snell-Hornby (1986a: 16 ff.), who is aware of the "multiperspectiveness of language and text" (p. 16; our translation), sets up a layer model of aspects relevant to translation. Within the limits of her introductory remarks, however, she cannot offer much more than an enumeration of factors. Other authors go more deeply into each translation factor. In Chapter 3 of her 1991 publication, Nord lists "the factors of source text analysis," dealing with nine *extratextual factors*,[6] nine *intratextual factors*, as well as the factor *effect* (pp. 35–140). Similarly Stolze (1992) sets up *categories of reception* (pp. 89–194), which she supplements by *categories of production* (pp. 195–264), going into a wide range of factors in each of them.[7] Both authors amply illustrate the factors referred to by means of various sample texts and renditions of various kinds. Last but not least, Wilss (1989: 133) mentions the "multifactor approach as, e.g., developed by Newmark (1981)."

Acknowledging these detailed analyses we venture to add another study in this field. Its justification is twofold: Its first speciality lies in illustrating the factor approach with reference to *one single* linguistic phenomenon—the English and German modals (see Section 1.2). The advantage of this unified perspective is obvious. Each translator is repeatedly faced with translating specific linguistic items. Focusing on a small group of items occurring frequently enables us to point out the many and multifarious factors relevant to their translation. This publication can thus be seen as a guide for translating that group of expressions.

The second speciality about this book is that the kinds of factors referred to above will be presented in their respective functions. Translating by factors does not mean taking factors into account 'as such' but with reference to their specific roles or functions. An example will make this point clear.

Indefinitely many English combinations of the form *adjective plus noun* can safely be transferred into German; such as,

blue sky	blauer Himmel
expensive book	teures Buch
beautiful picture	schönes Bild
small house	kleines Haus

In English, also the expression *medical student* may be added to the list but in German the structurally corresponding construction *medizinischer Student* is just not possible. The reason is that it would suggest that the student himself is medical. In German the rule is that for an adjective to premodify a noun it must denote a characteristic of the referent of that noun; otherwise the syntagma will be ungrammatical. So in the case of the SL expression *medical student* a semantic factor (viz., the information that "medical" is no characteristic of "student") will act or function as a blocking factor to the TL rendition **medizinischer Student*.

This example has shown that we may distinguish between two phenomena:

- kinds of factors (e.g., SL and TL semantic factors, pragmatic factors);
- functions of these factors (e.g., that of blocking renditions, giving rise to blocking factors).

Now the blocking of renditions is, of course, not the only function factors can fulfill. We want, after all, to arrive at possible and actual renditions (such as *Medizinstudent*), so there must also be something like 'enabling factors.' In fact, the factors to be presented in Chapters 2 and so forth may fulfill so many functions that it is possible to come up with a taxonomy of factor functions. To indicate what awaits the reader, here is a small glossary featuring factor functions.

1.1.2 Glossary of Factor Functions

Factor may be defined as "any of the circumstances, conditions, etc. that bring about a result; element or constituent that makes a thing what it is" (*Webster's New Twentieth Century Dictionary of the English Language*, 1983: 656, s.v. *factor* 2).

The result brought about by translation is renditions. The factors bringing about renditions or making them what they are may therefore be referred to as *translation factors*.

So the basic function of translation factors is to bring about renditions. What is involved in detail may be indicated with reference to more specific factor functions, giving rise to corresponding classes of translation factors such as the following ones:

- *invariance factors* make an SL feature reappear in the TL rendition;
- *change factors* make an SL feature disappear or a new or additional feature appear in the TL rendition;
- *partial change factors* make an SL feature appear partially different in the TL rendition;
- *bidirectional factors* operate in both translation directions (for instance, German-English and English-German);
- *unidirectional factors* operate in only one of two translation directions;
- *blocking factors* make a specific TL rendition impossible;
- *incompatibility factors* are blocking factors due to the incompatibility of features;
- *compensation factors* compensate for the effect of blocking factors, of indeterminacy of SL features, and so on;
- *identification factors* identify SL characteristics;
- *disambiguation factors* reduce or eliminate ambiguity in SL items;
- *production factors* contribute to creating the TL version;
- *target factors* relate to the target of the translation as determined by the client;
- *optimizing factors* bring about renditions that are more adequate with respect to specific needs;
- *revision factors* revise otherwise standard translation formulas and other seeming SL-TL correspondences;

- *ellipsis* or *elliptical factors* allow for omission of (a) certain element(s);
- *divergence factors* give rise to a number of TL forms that is greater than that of the SL forms;
- *convergence factors* give rise to a number of TL forms that is smaller than that of the SL forms;
- *transposition factors* bring about transpositions (i.e., changes in word class);
- *modulation factors* bring about modulations (i.e., changes in perspective);
- *relevant factors* are those factors that are functional in a given case;
- finally, according to their 'strength,' factors may be *obligatory* or *optional*. So there are obligatory transposition factors, optional change factors, and so on.

All these functions can be fulfilled by the kinds of factors referred to before (in Section 1.1.1). This gives rise to combinations such as semantic invariance factors as well as semantic change factors, pragmatic identification factors, and so on. What this means in practice will be discussed and illustrated in later chapters. Before doing so, however, we should have a look at the linguistic area that will supply our examples: the modals.

1.2 THE MODALS FOR A CASE STUDY

The English and German modals are a field of study on which much has been published during the past two decades. As the bibliographies by Kątny (1987; 1989a; 1990a) show, however, most of the publications have focused on the modals of one of the two languages only. So in adding another contrastive or translational study of the modals there is not so much danger of repeating others, particularly if translating the modals is expressly considered in the light of a fresh approach—translating by factors.

1.2.1 Status of the Modals

If one's aim is to demonstrate the working of a great variety of factors molding renditions, it would not make much sense to choose as examples pairs of SL-TL expressions that tend to be invariable—for the simple reason that not many, if any, translation factors will be involved.

But what can be expected of words such as WILL, WOULD; SHALL, SHOULD; CAN, COULD; MAY, MIGHT, and MUST? They look so simple, they are constantly being used by everyone; so why should anyone (including translators) be particularly concerned about these *modal auxiliaries,* or *modals* for short?

"There is, perhaps, no area of English grammar that is both more important and more difficult than the system of the modals," Palmer (1979a: v) explains, maybe surprisingly. Palmer, as the author of two books and many articles on modality, will know what he says.

Now if the system of the English modals is that intricate, what can—or even must—be expected of a translation study involving one more language! Will the English modals and the German ones—MÜSSEN, SOLLEN, KÖN-NEN, DÜRFEN, MÖGEN, and WOLLEN—not be a promising object of a translation factor analysis? We contend they will,[8] and in presenting such an analysis, we are reminded of Potter's (1974: 4) words, "Here is a chance for someone. So far as I know, no qualified linguist has yet made a competent and comprehensive investigation of English and German auxiliary verbs."

Eight months after this desideratum was published, Lodge (1974) submitted his Ph.D. thesis on exactly this topic. It was preceded by Schmid (1966), who confined his thesis to the translation of *(nicht) müssen* and *(nicht) dürfen*, however. And it was followed by a few other theses that were also restricted in scope in different ways:

- In Matthews's (1979) study, "German . . . took something of a back seat" (Matthews 1991: 11);
- Buelens (1981) is devoted to KÖNNEN, DÜRFEN, MÖGEN, and their translations into English;
- Temmerman (1981) is a contrastive study of MÜSSEN, SOLLEN, and WOLLEN and their English equivalents.

The drawback of all these studies is that they are not published. Nehls (1986), however, presents in published form a comprehensive contrastive analysis of the English and German modals. As in his 1979 thesis, Matthews (1991) does include the German modals, but again "the discussion mainly concerns English, with occasional side-glances at German" (*Lingua* 85, 1991: 374). In Palmer (1986) English and German are just two of a wide range of languages considered from the point of view of modality.

All these book-length accounts are complemented by a number of papers either giving a short overview of the systems of the English and German modals (Butler 1972, Bouma 1975, Lodge 1977, Standwell 1979), or going into specific linguistic aspects (Townson 1981, Doherty 1982) and aspects of language learning (Kufner 1977).

Because the systems of the modals in English and German differ, it will soon become apparent to anyone dealing with this field of language that, for rendering modals, also expressions other than modals have to be employed. Many of them are referred to as *modal expressions*.

Remembering the time of writing his thesis, Matthews (1993c: 113) observes that "the range of means, both lexical and syntactic, that languages have to express modal concepts . . . received too little attention at the time [of writing this thesis] in the standard English and German works on modality, including reference grammars, and, in my opinion, still receives too little attention . . ."

The present work will cover this "range of means" from the perspective of the modals of the English-German language pair; that is, we will ask, Given an SL modal, which TL modal(s) or other expression(s) can be used to render it? and, vice versa, Given an SL expression, is there a TL modal to render it?

In dealing with these questions we will focus mainly on the *factors* motivating the choice of particular TL renditions. Before presenting these translation factors, one by one, it will be useful to list the criteria that define our object of study.

1.2.2 Defining Criteria of the Modals

Many attempts at defining the term *modality* are based on semantic or pragmatic criteria (see Section 3.2.2 and so forth). For the definition of the class of modals, however, usually syntactic and morphological criteria are given. The following two lists summarize the formal characteristics of the English and German modals as stated by Nehls (1986: 12 ff.).

1.2.2.1 The English Modals

1. No −*s* morpheme in 3rd pers. sg. present tense.
(1) She can speak English.

2. No imperative mood.
(2) *Can! (* [asterisk] indicates that a sentence, utterance, and so on is unacceptable or ill-formed).

3. Modals are linked to an infinitive without TO (a flat or bare infinitive; see example (1)).

4. No DO periphrasis is possible in interrogative clauses (including tag questions) and in negative clauses.[9]
(3) Can she speak English?
(4) She can speak English, can't she?
(5) She cannot/can't speak English.

5. No infinite forms; suppletives or suppletive forms (see examples under a and c) must be used for infinitives, present and past participles, and gerunds.
a. For this reason, it is impossible to form a complex tense with a modal:
(6) *She has never can/could write long letters.
(7) She has never been able to write long letters.

b. Due to lack of past participle, no passive voice may be formed.
(8) *This is could done by her.

c. Modals do not usually combine with each other; hence,
(9) *She must can come.
(10) She must be able to come.

6. Modals precede all other verb forms.
(11) She could have been speaking English.

Criteria 1–6 are applicable to the verbs listed below. As a subsystem of the English verb system, these verbs are thereby formally clearly defined as modals:

WILL	WOULD
SHALL	SHOULD
CAN	COULD
MAY	MIGHT
MUST	

1.2.2.2 The German Modals

1. No verb endings in 1st and 3rd pers. sg. present tense.
(12) Ich/Er kann/darf/muss/ . . .

2. No imperative mood.
(13) *Kann!

3. The infinitive is linked without ZU.
(14) Er kann fahren.

4. Present perfect and past perfect are formed with the infinitive.
(15) Er hat(te) fahren können/dürfen/müssen/ . . .

These four criteria are applicable to MÜSSEN, SOLLEN, KÖNNEN, DÜRFEN, MÖGEN, and WOLLEN, which thus qualify as the German modal verbs proper.

Interestingly, the English and German modals share some characteristics: criteria 1–3 in both languages correspond to each other.

1.3 GOAL OF THIS STUDY

As stated in Section 1.2.1, it is our aim to focus on the factors motivating the choice of particular TL renditions. But neither is it our ambition to cover all possible translation factors existing nor do we intend to deal with all aspects relating to each modal. In view of the complexity of our subject matter we will have to be eclectic and illustrate a number of translation factors by way of some examples. Our presentation is geared more toward inspiring further research in this field than toward compiling an encyclopedia of translation factors.

This eclectic perspective is also reflected in our reference to previous studies. Whenever appropriate we will draw upon others' insights; but it is not our intention to give a full overview of the hundreds of publications on modality or of those in the field of translation studies, which may well be said to run into the thousands. Especially the German modals will be treated largely on the basis of the competence of the authors as native speakers of German.

As indicated in Section 1.1.1, this study is geared toward making the complexity of the translation situation transparent by presenting translation factors in a systematic way. We would consider reading this book an exercise for becoming familiar with what might be called *factor thinking*; that is, the habit of breaking up a complex (translation) task into its smaller, more manageable units—its factors. Naturally, this factor approach will be most useful to those who have not yet acquired full translation competence. Hence our target group is students of translating and interpreting, as well as intermediate and advanced learners of German or English. We hope they will enjoy reading this book not just because it is expected to facilitate and improve their translating, but also because its field of illustration, modality, has an inherent attraction to it: "To seek to understand modality is to set out on a fascinating voyage of discovery in the human mind" (Fawcett 1983: ix). This statement may be explained in terms of the fact that use of the modals presupposes a specific worldview (see Gutknecht 1971): whatever someone may or must (be) do(ing), for instance, depends upon the kind of (physical, social, rational) world he or she lives in. Worldviews in turn exist in consciousness. So study of modality is indeed a voyage of discovery in the human mind.

At the same time every native speaker will agree that modality, especially the modal verbs, are all-pervasive in our world of daily communication and action. This experience is nicely captured in a couplet by Rückert (1882: 335, quotation from section *Fünfte Abtheilung: Weisheit des Brahmanen. Siebente Stufe: Erkenntnis*):

Sechs Wörtchen nehmen mich in Anspruch jeden Tag:
Ich soll, ich muss, ich kann, ich will, ich darf, ich mag.

2. FORMAL FACTORS: SYNTAX AND MORPHOLOGY

It is interesting to see how the defining criteria for the English and German modals as listed in Section 1.2.2 come to act as translation factors. This will be demonstrated in Sections 2.1–2.6, followed by the topics of ellipsis (2.7), word class (2.8), and selection restrictions (2.9).

2.1 CONJUGATION AND SUFFIXATION

The English and German modals are alike in that they do not take a suffix when forming the first and third person singular present tense in the indicative mood:

(16) I/he/she/it can—ich/er/sie/es kann

Whereas in English this applies invariably to the categories of person and number, in German different morphological markers are required in the remaining cases; that is,

(17) du kannst; ihr könnt; wir/Sie/sie können

Here, the need for suffixes and vowel change are among the German change factors.[10]

Also the present subjunctive forms are more divers:

(18) ich/er/sie/es könne
du könnest
ihr könnet
wir/Sie/sie können

11

This variety of forms shows that a word form is the first translation factor; it acts as an identification factor. Here are some examples in which the function of German modals is unambiguously identified by their form.

- *Wollest* can be only the second person singular present subjunctive of WOLLEN;
- *mögt* can be only the second person plural present indicative.

Therefore, for the German modals, recognition of function via correct identification of form is an important factor. Of course, for the identification of instances of multifunctional forms such as *können*, additional factors such as personal pronouns must be taken into account.

But, generally speaking, the need of conjugation in German is an important divergence factor when moving from English to German, resulting in a great variety of forms; see (19) where the arrow → stands for "is rendered as":

(19) CAN → kann, kannst, können, könnt, könne, könnest, könnet.

As for the opposite translation direction, the nonvariability of CAN is a unidirectional convergence factor.[11]

2.2 NO IMPERATIVE MOOD

Because, in principle, the modals do not function as imperatives in English and German (*kann/könne! *können Sie!—*can!), the question of translating them in this function does not arise. As an exception, WOLLEN can form an imperative that, however, sounds a bit old-fashioned, as Nehls (1986: 19, n. 5) observes:

(20) Wolle nur, dann schaffst du es auch!

Nehls states that in contemporary German

(21) Du musst nur wollen.

would be preferred. If *wolle* as in (20) is used, the nonexistence of the English imperative of WANT acts as a change factor, and we would have to resort to a modal-verb construction analogous to (21).

(22) You only have to want it.

2.3 DIRECT LINKAGE TO A FULL VERB

A third defining criterion common to both the English and the German modals is that they are linked to the flat or bare infinitive (i.e., an infinitive [of a full/lexical/main verb] lacking TO/ZU); for example,

(23) He tries to go. *But*
(24) He must go.
(25) Er versucht zu gehen. *But*
(26) Er muss gehen.

This sameness holds for both translation directions, so it constitutes a bidirectional invariance factor (see Section 7.6.1). Occasionally one might be baffled by apparent exceptions, such as

(27) Er tat es freiwillig, d. h. ohne es tun zu müssen.

But note that ZU here comes before the *modal's* infinitive, not before that of the full verb *tun*. The paraphrase

(28) Er tat es freiwillig—er musste es nicht tun.

shows that the positioning of ZU before the modal in (27) is due to the preposition OHNE. Hammer (1991: 256), who deals with this *ohne . . . zu* construction (without reference to the modals) mentions "*without* followed by an *ing*-form" as its English equivalent. So (27) may be translated as

(29) He did it voluntarily; that is, without having to do it.

Sentence (27) touches upon another phenomenon that is of our immediate concern: the final position of the German modal (to be taken up in Section 2.6). Its equivalent, sentence (29), illustrates that there is no present participle of the English modal verb (see Section 2.5).

2.4 NO DO PERIPHRASIS

The fourth defining criterion of the English modals—no DO periphrasis in interrogative clauses and negative clauses—distinguishes them from full verbs. The German modals share this characteristic; but because it is common to full verbs as well, it was not included among their defining criteria. For example,

(30) Does he go there? *But*
(31) Can he go there?
(32) Geht er dorthin?
(33) Kann er dorthin gehen?

(34) He doesn't go there. *But*
(35) He can't go there.
(36) Er geht nicht dorthin.
(37) Er kann nicht dorthin gehen.

The two overall verb systems may then differ, but as far as the modals are concerned, *no periphrasis* can safely be taken to be a bidirectional invariance factor in translation.

Differences arise only with nonperiphrasis in English tag questions, which are rendered in an altogether different manner in German (see further Section 6.6.3):

(**38**) He can go there, can't he?
(**39**) Er kann doch dorthin gehen, oder (etwa nicht)?

2.5 NO NONFINITE FORMS

Major interlingual differences result from the fifth criterion of the English modals—their lack of nonfinite forms. It represents an important change factor necessitating the use of suppletive forms for a variety of functions. In German, modals can be used throughout. In English, nonfinite forms and their associated functions include

(**a**) lack of present infinitive (*to can)
(**aa**) present infinitive as subject
(**40**) *To can ride a horse was Peter's wish.
(**41**) To be able to ride a horse was Peter's wish.
(**42**) Reiten (zu) können war Peters Wunsch.

(**ab**) present infinitive as object
(**43**) *He wished to can play the guitar.
(**44**) He wished to be able to play the guitar.
(**45**) Er wünschte sich, Gitarre spielen zu können.

(**ac**) combinations of modals (double modals, see Section 3.3.5.1)
(**46**) *He must can come.
(**47**) He must be able to come.
(**48**) Er muss kommen können.

(**b**) lack of present participle (*canning)
(**ba**) gerund as subject
(**49**) *Canning sit for an exam is wonderful.
(**50**) Being able to sit for an exam is wonderful.
(**51**) An einer Prüfung teilnehmen (zu) können ist wunderbar.

(**bb**) gerund as part of subject
(**52**) *His canning sit for the exam made him happy.

(53) His being able to sit for the exam made him happy.
(54) Dass er an der Prüfung teilnehmen konnte, machte ihn glücklich.

(bc) gerund as object
(55) *He liked canning demonstrate his strength.
(56) He liked being able to demonstrate his strength.
(57) Es gefiel ihm, seine Stärke zeigen zu können.

(bd) gerund as part of object
(58) *He appreciated my canning visit him.
(59) He appreciated my being able to visit him.
(60) Er schätzte es, dass ich ihn besuchen konnte.

(be) gerund in lieu of an adverbial clause
(61) *Canning speak English fluently, he understood me well.
(62) Being able to speak English fluently, he understood me well.
(63) Da er fliessend Englisch sprechen konnte, verstand er mich gut.

(c) lack of past participle (*canned/could—COULD can be used only for past tense, the subjunctive, and for expressing tentativity)
(ca) complex tenses
(64) *He has/had must work.
(65) He has/had had to work.
(66) Er hat/hatte arbeiten müssen.

(cb) passive voice
(67) *This was could done well by him.
(68) This was done well by him.
(69) Das wurde von ihm gekonnt.

(d) lack of past infinitive
(da) past infinitive as subject
(70) *To have could sit the exam is wonderful.
(71) To have been able to sit the exam is wonderful.
(72) An der Prüfung teilgenommen haben zu können/?haben teilnehmen können ist wunderbar.

In (69), *gekonnt* is used as a past participle of KÖNNEN. Note that, in active sentences with a full verb infinitive, the complex tenses are usually formed with the infinitive—this being the fourth and final defining criterion of the German modals; for example,[12]

(73) He has/had been able to/been allowed to/had to/ . . . go
(74) Er hat(te) gehen können/dürfen/müssen/ . . .

2.6 WORD ORDER

The sixth criterion of the English modals is that they always precede all other verb forms.

This behavior can also be found in German, note the following sentence pair:

(75) He must have been playing the guitar.
(76) Er muss Gitarre gespielt haben.

But a number of syntactic change factors necessitate a move on to a different word order in German. These factors include (see Hammer 1991: 328 ff., 454 ff.)

(a) nonfinite forms in compound tenses
(aa) in main clauses
(77) Er wird gehen müssen.
(78) He will have to go.

(ab) in subordinate clauses
(79) Es war klar, dass er sich würde anstrengen müssen.
(80) It was evident that he would have to make an effort.

(ac) in infinitive clauses with ZU (see (27))
(81) Er erklärte, bald kommen zu wollen.
(82) He declared he wanted to come soon.

(b) finite forms
(ba) in subordinate clauses
(83) Wenn du das machen willst, . . .
(84) If you want to do that . . .

(bb) in relative clauses
(85) Das Haus, das sie verkaufen sollte, . . .
(86) The house she was (supposed) to sell . . .

2.7 ELLIPSIS

In the cotext (the preceding or following words) of the English and German modals, full verbs may be omitted if certain conditions or ellipsis factors come to bear (with elliptical change, partial change, or nonchange [invariance] factors as variants). We would like to mention just a few of them (see also Hammer 1991: 330 f.); F stands for factor.

F1. As an elliptical invariance factor a full verb just mentioned previously may be omitted in both languages:

(87) Must you read this letter? Of course I must.
(88) Musst Du diesen Brief lesen? Natürlich muss ich (es).

F2. Elliptical change factors: In English as well as in German, the modal and the full verb may be omitted in answers to *yes-no* questions. Unlike English, however, German does not permit mention of the modal alone (unless there is inversion). For example,

(89) Can you play tennis? Yes, I can/No, I can't.
(90) Kannst du Tennis spielen? Ja/Nein. (*Ja, ich kann/*Nein, ich kann nicht. *But* Ja, kann ich/Nein, kann ich nicht.)

The final two options in (90) are due to the elliptical partial change factor of inversion. Other such factors include the following.

F3. The German verb TUN:
(91) You may do that.
(92) Das darfst du/Du darfst es (tun).

F4. Full verbs denoting certain skills:
(93) He can speak English.
(94) *He can English.
(95) Er kann Englisch sprechen.
(96) Er kann Englisch.

F5. Full verbs denoting various kinds of motion. A goal or direction indicator remains which can be
(a) a prepositional phrase:
(97) You can go home now.
(98) *You can home now.
(99) Du kannst jetzt nach Hause gehen.
(100) Du kannst jetzt nach Hause.

(b) a verbal prefix:
(101) We may pass there.
(102) Wir dürfen da durchgehen.
(103) Wir dürfen da durch.

Further factors may rearrange the syntactic structure. If, due to sentence type (see Section 2.6), the modal becomes the last element, the prefix originally modifying the full verb (as is the case with *durch-* in (102) and (105)) is directly linked to the modal:

(104) I wonder if we will be allowed to pass there.
(105) Ob wir da durchgehen dürfen?
(106) Ob wir da durchdürfen?

Prefixed modals such as *durchdürfen* might suggest that in German there are such things as 'modified modals' in addition to the six 'pure modals' listed in Section 1.2.2.2.; and due to the fairly large number of suitable space prefixes,[13] it might seem as though there were hosts of 'space modals.' But it should not be forgotten that it is, after all, the full verb that is modified in deep structure. This perspective is even obligatory for translation into English where the use of a full verb is inevitable. Sentences such as (101) and (102) clearly show that the local elements (*there*; *durch–*) refer to the full verb and not to the modal.

2.8 WORD CLASS

In most cases modals function as verbs, but there is also the possibility of using them as adjectives or nouns (Section 2.8.1), even in compounds (Section 2.8.2). Recognizing and taking into account their function in a given case is a vital factor of a formally adequate translation. Identification factors are all the more important in the case of homonyms, which share only their form with the modals (Section 2.8.3).

2.8.1 Nominal and Adjectival Use

MUST and MÜSSEN (in its singular indicative form *muss*) may be used as verbal nouns.

(107) This book is a must.
(108) Dieses Buch ist ein Muss.

The formal equivalence of both constructions presents itself as a bilingual invariance factor.

There is also an adjectival use of MUST:

(109) This is a must book.

Here, the impossibility of an equivalent construction in German acts as a transposition factor. The adjective in (109) would again have to be rendered as the verbal noun *ein Muss* (as in (108)).

Another change factor is the fact that *ein Muss* cannot be pluralized the way *a must* can; for example,

(110) Three important MUSTS in planning up-to-date wiring [heading in a manual on electrical wiring published by the American Sears group in 1969; capitalization as in the original].

If the nominal character of *musts* is to be an invariance factor, one would have to resort to a German noun that, unlike *Muss*, can be used in the plural; for example,[14]

(111) Drei wichtige Erfordernisse bei der Planung moderner Verkabelung.

If, however, the modal and its fixed idiomatic use *ein Muss* is decided to be the invariance factor, one would have to employ the compensation factor of shifting the numeral *three* onto another noun. Because no other noun exists in the sentence, a further aspect of compensation would consist in introducing such a noun (possibly being premodified by the demonstrative pronoun *diese* as a cataphoric element referring to the ensuing paragraph). The result could be

(112) Diese drei Dinge sind ein Muss bei der Planung moderner Verkabelung.

In addition to *Muss* (being capitalized in its nominal function), only *das Soll* exists as a nominalized free morpheme. It means "command," "target," or more commonly, "debit," and is used in the syntagma *Soll und Haben*— "debit and credit."

Besides the finite forms *muss* and *soll* being put to nominal service, the present infinitive of virtually all German modals can be nominalized; for example,

(113) Hat man ein hohes Ziel, ist schon das Wollen von Wert. [in Wildhagen and Héraucourt (1972: xvii, xix, Preface)]
(114) Sein Können beeindruckt mich.

The lack of the modal-verb infinitive in English again acts as an obligatory change factor; for instance,

(115) For a sublime goal the mere intention is a merit.
(116) I am impressed by his skill.

Wollen can also be rendered by *will(ingness), aspiration, inclination, purpose*; *können* may also be translated by *ability, faculty, power, efficiency*.

There is no adjectival construction such as *a must book* in German, but there do exist attributive uses of

(a) the present participle: *ein nicht enden wollendes Konzert* (see Section 2.5 (b)),
(b) the past participle: *(un)gewollte Komik, gekonnte Vorführung* (see (69)).

If the attributive use is to be an invariance factor, equivalences would be

• for *gewollt*, the adjectives *intended, desired, studied, intentional, deliberate*;
• for *gekonnt*, the adjective *skilled* or the participle construction *done well*.

2.8.2 Complex Words

The modals may occur as part of complex words or compounds, but not in their function as verbs. If they are the first element in a compound (Section

2.8.2.1), they are typically used attributively to premodify a noun. Appearing as final element of a compound (Section 2.8.2.2) is the privilege of the German modals, which are nominalized in this case and may themselves be premodified in various ways.

2.8.2.1 Modals as a First Element

The third person singular indicative forms of KÖNNEN, SOLLEN, and MÜSSEN may be used as determining elements in compounds:

(117) Dies ist weder eine Kann- noch eine Soll-Bestimmung, sondern eine Muss-Bestimmung.

For translating this sentence, the structure of *a must book* suggests itself. The result would be ungrammatical, however:

(118) *This is neither a can provision, nor a shall provision, but a must provision.

The blocking factor is that the attributive construction is restricted to MUST and that even the interpretation of *a must provision* as "a regulation which must be adhered to" would not be idiomatic. We suggest a rendition containing three adjectives used predicatively that collocate well with *provision.*

(119) This provision is neither permissive nor directory but mandatory.

Now let us ask the reverse question: Because compounds such as *Muss-Bestimmung* do exist in German, would it not be possible to translate (109) as (120)?

[109] This is a must book.

(120) *Dies ist ein Muss-Buch.

The blocking factor in this case is the fact that German compounds with finite forms of the modals as their first element must be conventionally established. Such compounds include (as can be verified by looking them up in dictionaries)

(121) Mussheirat   shotgun wedding
        Mussehe   involuntary marriage

Muss-Buch (or *Mussbuch*), however, is no such established compound and would therefore be considered to be completely unidiomatic.

Compounds beginning with *Soll–* include

(122) Sollarbeitsstunden   nominal work-hours
        Sollbestand   presumed assets
        Solleinnahmen   supposed/estimated receipts (due)
        Sollreichweite   rated coverage

Sollstärke
    (military):   required strength
    (technical):   paper strength

In addition, there are a number of compounds beginning with *Soll* in the sense of "debit" (see Section 2.8.1):

(123) Sollpostën   debit item
      Sollsaldo   debit balance
      Sollseite   debit/liabilities side
      Sollbeträge   debit amounts

There is also a compound element starting with *Möchte*, viz., *Möchtegern–*, itself modifying an indefinite number of nouns, such as *–Schriftsteller*. The equivalent of *Möchtegern-Schriftsteller* is *would-be writer*. Comparing this rendition with all the others listed previously as equivalents of German compounds starting with a finite form of a modal, we come to find that this is the first case of an English modal being part of a rendition.

Like *Möchtegern–*, *would-be* is a very productive building block for compounds. Many of its German equivalents do not contain the overt expression *Möchtegern*; for example,

(124) would-be painter   Farbenkleckser
      would-be poet   Dichterling
      would-be hunter,
      would-be sportsman   Sonntagsjäger

In these examples, the pejorative connotation of *Möchtegern–* has been incorporated into the meaning of the three German nouns. *Would-be* can also function as a nominal in its own right: A *would-be* is a *Gernegross* or *Möchtegern*. Note that also these German compounds are used nonattributively in this case.

In addition to the expression *would-be*, there are some other modal-first elements for compound nominalizations in English, see philosopher Strawson's (1979) paper 'May Bes and Might Have Beens.' In the first two lines of the actual text these syntagmas are hyphenated, thus conforming to the pattern of part of the dictionary entry s.v. *können*; viz., "(to remind people of) their might-have-beens" in Wildhagen and Héraucourt (1972: 778), where as German equivalent the relative clause *was sie hätten sein können* is given; see also the final remarks in the next subsection.

2.8.2.2 Modals as a Final Element

As a final element in 'standard' compounds, only WOLLEN can be found; viz., in WOHLWOLLEN ("goodwill")—unless one is willing to accept as compounds derivations of the form (DAS) DURCHDÜRFEN mentioned in Section 2.7, F5(b). Such prefixed (nominalized) infinitives or their finite forms are, of course, to be found with all modals, giving rise to many different combinations (see the list of prefixes in note 13).

But there are also compounds that are 'nonstandard' in the sense of being coined ad hoc. They consist of nominalizations of modals each premodified by a prepositional phrase (itself being premodified by one of the definite articles or a possessive pronoun), as in

(125) Das/Dein Nach-Hause(-gehen)-Können freut mich.

the ellipsis being traceable to the verbal basis of this construction (see Section 2.7, F5(a)):

[100] Du kannst jetzt nach Hause.

Again, the unavailability of English nonfinite forms of the modals acts as an obligatory transposition factor, the possessive pronoun *dein/your* being a factor calling for the use of the gerund:

(126) I am glad of your being able to go home.

Admittedly constructions such as (125) are not exactly the most common kind of wording chosen in German. This is why the English gerund construction (53) was translated as (54)

[53] His being able to sit the exam made him happy.
[54] Dass er an der Prüfung teilnehmen konnte, machte ihn glücklich.

and not as

(127) Sein An-der-Prüfung-teilnehmen-Können machte ihn glücklich.

Also sentence (125) would rather be expressed differently:

(128) Schön, dass du nach Hause kannst.

just as (126) would more usually be worded as

(129) I'm glad you can go home.

Nonetheless, nominalized modal compounds are so popular that equivalence pairs such as the following one may be found in dictionaries:

(130) Das Über-sich-hinauswachsen-Wollen →
     the urge to accomplish something beyond one's capabilities.

Here the lexicographer chose the nominal character of WOLLEN to be the invariance factor. In contrast to (125), in this case the full verb (WACHSEN) must be verbalized to convey the specific meaning intended.

All in all, such modal compound constructions are by no means unusual in German, even in the spoken language. This may be illustrated by the following authentic stretch of conversation, interlocutor B being one of the authors.

(131) **A:** Die Fähre dauert zwei Stunden.
  B: Was? So lang?
  A: Naja, das ist wegen des langen Durch-bestimmte-Kanäle-fahren-Müssens.

(132) **A:** The ferry takes two hours.
  B: Gee, that long?
  A: Well, this is due to the necessity of a long passage through certain canals.

Here, *the necessity* was chosen as the equivalent of *des Müssens*. The corresponding nominal rendition containing *the must* is ruled out because of a syntactic factor. The expression *wegen des . . . –Müssens* cannot be rendered by *due to the long-passing-through-certain-canals-must*, because MUST as a noun cannot be premodified except by adjectives or numerals or both (see the *Three important musts* discussed in Section 2.8.1).

Even though restricted to more elaborate codes, ad hoc constructions as in (131) suggest that the number of compounds with modals as their final element is indeed vast—indefinitely many combinations of words are conceivable, for example,

(133) das Tore-schliessen-Müssen
  Dein Immer-so-früh-ins-Bett-gehen-Wollen
  Peters Jedes-Jahr-in-den-Ferien-nach-England-Dürfen, etc.

One distinguishing feature of all these examples is suggested by the function of their pervasive hyphenation indicating syntactic unity. As a consequence, the semantic unity of the elements of a given situation is highlighted. This syntactico-semantic iconicity would seem to be the pertinent factor in favor of these otherwise clumsy constructions.

Yet some restrictions to their use must be kept in mind by the translator. These become obvious if one attempts to use these nominal compounds as renditions for English constructions that, by virtue of being hyphenated themselves, might seem to be proper equivalents. Consider, for example, the dictionary entry *was sie hätten sein können* with its rendition "(to remind people of) their might-have-beens" quoted in the last subsection. If this English pattern were applied to German, the following sentence pair would result:

(134) He reminded them of their might-have-beens.
(135) *Er erinnerte sie an ihr Hätte-sein-Können.

However versatile and varied the German construction under discussion may be in terms of possible meanings to be expressed, there are some formal

limits to it. The one relevant here is the impossibility of using it for counter-
factuals. The equivalent

(136) Er erinnerte sie daran, was sie hätten sein können.

suggested by the dictionary is a satisfactory solution.

2.8.3 Homonyms

In the previous two sections we saw that modals can function not only as
verbs but also as adjectives or (part of complex) nouns.

But not every instance of a seemingly modal verb form is in fact related
to the modals. This will be shown in the following sections.

2.8.3.1 Nouns

Some nouns look or sound like modals but are not. In certain cases, *will* will
be a first name, *can* can be a container, and *may* may denote a month of the
year. *May Week* has nothing to do with the modal MAY, nor is the spoken
word *wood* related to *would*.

So modals have to be distinguished from their homonyms; that is, homographs and homophones. This requirement may seem trivial, because human translators should have no difficulty in identifying factors such as the
syntactic function of the lexemes CAN, MAY, and MIGHT. Their position in
a sentence indicates to them whether these lexemes are to be classed as
modal verbs or as nouns (KANISTER, MAI, MACHT); such as in

(137) You may go now.
(138) In May, we hope to get started.

But the chances are that machine translation will fail to distinguish between
these heterogeneous forms because computer programs may lack the facili-
ties for differentiating between modal verbs and the formally correspondent
homographs (see Butler 1985: 146).

Consequently, in case lemmatized word lists are not available, it is not
always possible to differentiate between homographs in establishing the frequency of modals for various corpora: "*Can* therefore includes both the
modal and the lexical word *can*, *may* both the modal and *May* (month and
proper name), etc." (Johansson 1985: 125, n. 5).

But if the relevant clues are incorporated into the translation program,
they can be important factors for the correct identification of forms as members of a specific word class. Let us consider some examples.

(139) "Kum Kong has six cooler bag radio models with AM/FM wave
      bands, a built-in water-resistant speaker and a headphone jack. . . .

The K-240 ($8.30), with earphones, consists of a cylindrical ice-pack waistbag that *can* hold three soft drink *cans*. The K-186 ($7.90) is a *can*-sized 'cooler bag' radio that accomodates a single drink *can* . . ." (MBE Merchandising and Buying Electronics [Hong Kong], September 1990, p. 49, col. 3; *our italics*).

Because the first instance of CAN is directly followed by a full verb, it is easily identified as modal verb.

The second CAN shows an *−s* suffix that is impossible for the modal, so it must be a noun. (Of course, the first CAN could also be a noun if *hold* had an *−s*; but it does not.)

CAN in *can-sized* is identifiable by the computer if it is fed with some semantic information—the topic of our next chapter—specifying that only containers, but not the modals, can be sized. The simplest solution would, of course, be to store away as a unit the whole of *can-sized*.

The last instance of CAN can easily be identified because it is syntactically premodified by the indefinite article—*a single drink can*. But then what about

(140) Even a single drink can bring great relief to a thirsty man.
(141) It is amazing to see what one liter of water can do for a very thirsty man, and what even a single drink can.

Correctly identifying *can* in these examples takes some ingenuity, but it is not impossible even for computers.

- If *can* in (140) were a noun, then *bring* would have to have an *−s* suffix.
- If *can* were a noun in (141), then the last object clause would have to contain a full verb.

Formulating these facts in a more general way as rules and integrating them into the computer program as incompatibility factors would ensure correct identification of the function of a form in a particular instance.

There are also acronyms in the form of modals, for example *MUST* (as M[anned] U[nderwater] St[ation]). Other abbreviations include *Can.* for "Canada," "Canon," or "Canto." Capitalization, punctuation, and syntax should make clear which function is intended in a given case.

The same is true for proper names such as Karl May or Richard Will; for example,

(142) MAY macht mehr aus Milch. (blurb spotted on a German truck)

2.8.3.2 Verbs

In addition to the homonymous noun CAN, there is also a full verb CAN, whose formal identity with the modal is being played upon in the following remark by the Iowa farmer who was asked what he intended to do with all the fruit in his garden. He replied:

(143) We eat all we can, and what we can't we can. (Steiner 1991: 77)

Unless a machine-translation program gets to 'know' the impossibility of the logical inconsistency of an affirmative and a negative use of the same modal in the same clause, it is bound to fail here.

But there are cases of ambiguity where a sentence itself does not contain such a formal identification factor, such as

(144) They can milk.

Only co(n)textual factors will indicate whether this sentence is to be rendered by (145) or (146):

(145) Sie konservieren Milch.
(146) Sie können melken.

As for the past-tense form *canned*, there is, of course, no danger of confusing forms even for the computer; for example,

(147) They canned milk.
(148) They could milk.

2.9 SELECTION RESTRICTIONS

Some German full verbs, unlike their English equivalents, cannot take inanimate subjects; for example,

(149) Money can't buy everything.
(150) *Geld kann nicht alles kaufen.
(151) Mit Geld kann man nicht alles kaufen.

(152) This tent can sleep four people.
(153) *Dieses Zelt kann vier Leute schlafen.
(154) In diesem Zelt können vier Leute schlafen.

This change of a noun phrase into a prepositional phrase is necessary only if the invariance factors are both the modal verb (*can* → *kann*) and the full verb (*buy* → *kaufen*) with its restriction just mentioned.

If, however, the nominative status of the subject is to remain invariant, other verbs that do not impose the said restriction may (or have to) be chosen, such as in

(155) Geld ermöglicht nicht alles.
(156) Dieses Zelt kann vier Leute aufnehmen/beherbergen.

It is clear that in both types of rendition not just syntactic factors are involved: "(in)animate" is a semantic feature, and *instrumental* (*mit Geld*) and *locative* (*in diesem Zelt*) are looked upon as representing semantic rather than syntactic roles in Fillmore's (1968: 24 f.) case grammar. It could be argued that these restrictions are essentially semantic in nature, even though they are related to syntax via the word-order category of subject. But as long as semantic features directly enter into the description of syntactic regularities, they are taken to be syntactic features (Lewandowski 1975: 716). For this reason the last examples were included under the rubric of syntax.

In the next chapter we will go into more genuinely semantic matters, taking up, among other points, the phenomenon of semantic ambiguity already briefly touched upon in the discussion of sentence (144). This time we will focus on different meanings of the modals themselves (Section 3.1.1) causing ambiguity (Section 3.1.4.3).

3. SEMANTIC FACTORS

Newmark (1981: 44) holds that "the overriding factor in deciding how to translate is the intrinsic importance of every semantic unit in the text." SL information taken to be an invariance factor, this statement can certainly be said to be true.

In the polysemy section (3.1), the principle that different meanings can give rise to different renditions will be highlighted.[15] Then the modals will be characterized with respect to other expressions of the modal system, various aspects of which will be discussed in Section 3.2. After that our scope widens still further to encompass semantic aspects of language in general—types of meaning (Section 3.3).

In the final part of this chapter the three topics of voice, tense, and indirect speech and their relevance to translation of the modals will be illustrated (Sections 3.4–3.6).

3.1 POLYSEMY

Multiplicity of meanings or polysemy is of utmost importance to translation theory and practice since it can easily be shown that different meanings of a word have a different impact on the translation of that word. Let us probe into the truth of this statement with respect to the modals.

3.1.1 Multiple Meanings of the Modals

It may be tempting to establish interlingual pairs of modals, as did Raith (1963: 109, 112) in his grammar:

(157) I can (ich kann)
(158) I will (ich will)

(159) I shall (ich soll)
(160) I may (ich mag)
(161) I must (ich muss)

It is even easy to find examples confirming the adequacy of these modal pairs, such as

(162) I can do it.
(163) Ich kann es tun.

(164) I will not do it.
(165) Ich will es nicht tun.

(166) Shall I accompany you?
(167) Soll ich Dich begleiten?

(168) I may have left the keys in the car.
(169) Ich mag die Schlüssel im Wagen gelassen haben.

(170) I must go now.
(171) Ich muss jetzt gehen.

The formal principle underlying these juxtapositions of modals is captured by the simple translation formula *SL expression a* → *TL expression b*, representing a *one-to-one correspondence*[16] as shown in Figure 3.1.

This kind of translation schema might suggest that the SL form MAY itself is an invariance factor in the sense of always being rendered by *mag*. Now from our discussion of conjugation in the previous chapter we know that this seemingly absolute correspondence must be relativized. Because the German form of each modal is variable according to person and number, all one could say is that MAY is rendered by *one of the forms of* MÖGEN.

This means that the alleged one-to-one correspondence could be said to hold between the two lexemes MAY and MÖGEN only as such, not between MAY and only one specific form of MÖGEN, as might be inferred from Figure 3.1. So in addition to *SL expression or form* and *TL lexeme*, a third factor (F3), *TL person and number*, must be added to our translation chart. Considering only the indicative forms, we arrive at the equivalences listed in Figure 3.2.

$$\boxed{\text{SL expression } may \;\rightarrow\; \text{TL expression } mag}$$

FIGURE 3.1.
German Rendition of MAY (1)

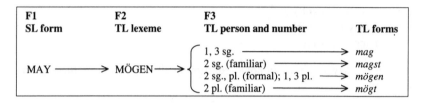

FIGURE 3.2.
German Renditions of MAY (2)

See how much simpler English is:

(172) I/you/he, she/we/they may be right.
(173) Ich/er, sie mag recht haben.
(174) Du magst recht haben.
(175) Ihr mögt recht haben.
(176) Sie/sie mögen recht haben.

But is the correlation of the lexemes MAY and MÖGEN really invariable? Consider the following sentence:

(177) No one may enter this territory.

MAY being used in the third person here, the corresponding German sentence might be thought to be

(178) ! Keiner mag dieses Gebiet betreten. (The exclamation mark denotes unacceptability in the relevant sense.)

Although perfectly acceptable in terms of syntax, (178) cannot be claimed to be an adequate rendition of (177), just because it means something different, which is

(179) No one likes to enter this territory.

This factor of meaning is the crucial point here. In

[168] I may have left the keys in the car.

MAY was used in the sense of possibility, which can be rendered by MÖGEN (see (169)). But to properly render the meaning of permission as expressed by MAY in (177), only DÜRFEN can be used:

(180) Keiner darf dieses Gebiet betreten.

So MAY in the sense of permission is rendered by one of the forms of DÜRFEN. This means that even the alleged one-to-one correspondence between two lexemes such as MAY and MÖGEN turns out to be an illusion. *SL meanings* must be added to the translation schema in Figure 3.2 as an-

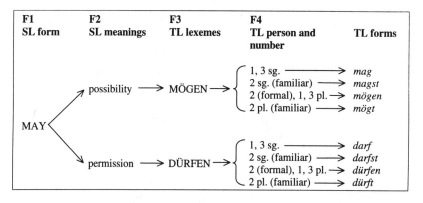

F1 SL form	F2 SL meanings	F3 TL lexemes	F4 TL person and number	TL forms

FIGURE 3.3.
German Renditions of MAY (3)

other factor (F2). Our findings so far can be summarized as in Figure 3.3, representing a *one-to-many correspondence* (Koller 1983: 158).

3.1.2 Root and Epistemic Meanings

If MAY in

[168] I may have left the keys in the car.

is said to denote a possibility, then what about CAN in

(181) This game can be played by young children. (Leech 1987: 74)

Is it not also used in the possibility sense? Indeed it is, but many will feel a difference between the possibility related to MAY in (168) and the one related to CAN in (181).

This difference can be captured by paraphrasing the two sentences. Leech (1987: 74) states that (181) means

(182) It is possible for this game [to be played by young children].

Sentence (168) can be glossed by

(183) It is possible that I left the keys in the car.

These two different constructions (*possible for* vs. *possible that*) justify speaking of two kinds of possibility:

• In (181) and (182), there is the possibility of doing something. This is why this possibility is referred to as *action oriented* by Nehls (1989: 283, n. 3).
• In (168) and (183), possibility is a degree of likelihood (of something

being the case), so this possibility is called *probability oriented* by Nehls
(1989: 283).

Because action-oriented possibility is felt to be more basic, it is often referred to as *root possibility*, while probability-oriented possibility is usually
called *epistemic possibility*.[17]

So we can say that CAN in (181) is used to express root possibility,
whereas MAY in (168) is used to express epistemic possibility. Root CAN as
in (181) is rendered by KÖNNEN:

(184) Dieses Spiel kann von kleinen Kindern gespielt werden.

Figure 3.3 can now be expanded, giving rise to the structure of Figure 3.4.

Now it might be argued that as long as epistemic possibility expressed
by MAY and root possibility expressed by CAN are both rendered by one
specific modal, why distinguish between the two kinds of possibility? After
all, Figure 3.4 conforms to the principle *one meaning of one modal: one
lexeme for a rendition.*

But again correspondences are not that absolute: KÖNNEN is not only
the proper rendition of root CAN, it is also much more common than MÖ-
GEN as a rendition of epistemic MAY. The reason is that in most cases of
epistemic possibility, MÖGEN sounds rather old-fashioned as compared to
KÖNNEN—for example,

[169] Ich mag die Schlüssel im Wagen gelassen haben.
(185) Ich kann die Schlüssel im Wagen gelassen haben.

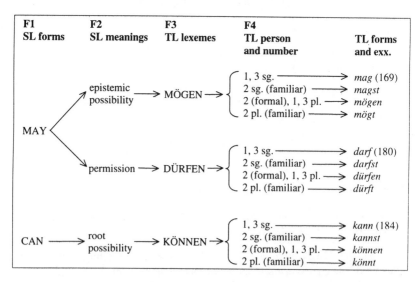

FIGURE 3.4.
German Renditions of MAY (4) and CAN (1)

This means that also our tenet *one SL meaning: one TL lexeme* is shaken.

But because KÖNNEN was found to be the usual rendition for *both* root and epistemic possibility, there seems to be even less reason to distinguish between the two kinds of possibility for the purpose of translation.

This perspective is further strengthened by another two facts. To prepare the ground for their presentation, let us first mention that MAY can also express root possibility and CAN may be used to express epistemic possibility:

(186) The doorbell is ringing. Can this be the postal carrier?

In this sentence, the speaker inquires about the likelihood of this being the postal carrier, so CAN is used in the epistemic sense here. As regards MAY in the sense of root possibility, Palmer (1979a: 158) observes that in

(187) Cader Idris, however, may be climbed from other points on this tour.

"MAY is to be paraphrased by 'possible for,'" which is Leech's criterion for root possibility (called *theoretical possibility* by him).

The salient point to be made is that these additional uses of CAN and MAY can *both* be rendered by KÖNNEN:

(188) Es klingelt. Kann das der Postbote sein?
(189) Cader Idris kann jedoch von anderen Punkten dieser Tour aus bestiegen werden.

There is also the possibility of expressing permission by using CAN. Even this use, as well as the permission use of MAY, can be rendered by KÖN-NEN:

(190) You can go now.
(191) You may go now.
(192) Ihr könnt jetzt gehen.

Also DÜRFEN could be used for rendering (190) and (191), but because it is the formally marked alternative to KÖNNEN, its use is restricted to such contexts:

(193) Ihr dürft jetzt gehen.

Last, just like epistemic MAY, epistemic CAN also can be rendered by MÖ-GEN, for which the same stylistic characterization holds as given previously:

(194) Where can he be?
(195) Wo kann er sein?
(196) Wo mag er sein?

Figures 3.5 and 3.6 summarize the equivalences established so far.[18]

So, KÖNNEN being a possible rendition for *both* CAN and MAY in *all* these root and epistemic meanings, there seems to be no reason for distin-

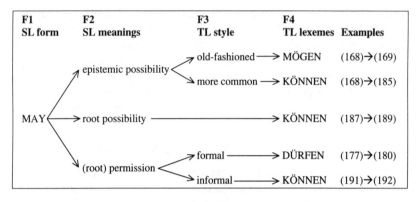

FIGURE 3.5.
German Renditions of MAY (5)

guishing the two "possibilities" (and, neglecting the style dimension, even for distinguishing permission and possibility).

There is a reason, however, if we change the translation direction. Look at Figures 3.5 and 3.6 and follow the items from right to left. Our translation situation this time is to translate epistemic KÖNNEN. What we find is two possible renditions: MAY (Figure 3.5) and CAN (Figure 3.6). Are they interchangeable? Compare:

(197) Kann das der Postbote sein?
(198) Can this be the postal carrier?
(199) *May this be the postal carrier?

(200) Das kann der Postbote sein.
(201) This may be the postal carrier.
(202) *This can be the postal carrier.

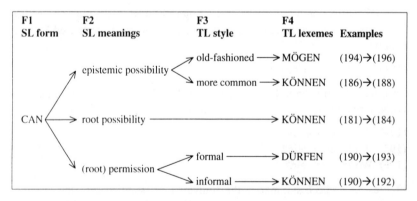

FIGURE 3.6.
German Renditions of CAN (2)

As the German sentences show, KÖNNEN can be used in both constructions. But the use of the English modals is subject to two important constraints. In questions about epistemic possibility (such as (198)), MAY cannot be used, and in affirmative statements about epistemic possibility (such as (201)), CAN cannot be used. These blocking factors of sentence mood and negation can be used for setting up a little chart for the translation of epistemic KÖNNEN; see Figure 3.7.

We are now in a position to give an answer to our question about why to differentiate between root and epistemic possibility: There are restrictions to CAN and MAY in their epistemic use. Translators may feel free to disregard these restrictions when translating instances of *root* possibility and to give English renditions such as

(203) May Cader Idris be climbed from other points on this tour?
[181] This game can be played by young children.

Another case in which these restrictions are irrelevant is the translation direction English-German (see earlier). So only when epistemic possibility is to be rendered in English do these constraints act as (obligatory) blocking factors.

As the last two sentences show, the formal restrictions mentioned are indeed of no relevance to root possibility. But does this mean that CAN and MAY are interchangeable here? As regards the noninterrogative counterpart of (203), that is,

[187] Cader Idris, however, may be climbed from other points on this tour.

which is contained in a written corpus, Palmer (1979a: 157 f.) observes that "it is possible to substitute CAN . . . with very little change of meaning, if any," and adds that "it would . . . be much more normal, especially in colloquial English, to use CAN." This said, the use of CAN in

[181] This game can be played by young children.

KÖNNEN$_{epistemic}$				
F1:	questions	(197)	→ CAN (198),	*MAY (199)
F2:	affirmative statements	(200)	→ MAY (201),	*CAN (202)
(As for the third category – F3: negative statements – refer to our section on negation (3.1.5).)				

FIGURE 3.7.
English Renditions of Epistemic KÖNNEN

could also be regarded as being 'more normal' than the use of MAY:

(204) This game may be played by young children.

So it would seem that for all their interchangeability, CAN and MAY in their root-possibility sense may be distinguished by a factor very much like the one that distinguishes epistemic KÖNNEN and MÖGEN—cf. (169) vs. (185) and (188) vs. (196)—namely, colloquial usage.

Along the same lines, Coates (1980a: 217) remarks that with root possibility, "where in terms of meaning both MAY and CAN are possible, they are distinct in terms of formality. CAN is the unmarked member of the pair, while MAY is marked for formality."

Next, what about the interchangeability of CAN and MAY in their permission sense as suggested by Figures 3.5 and 3.6? Parkes et al. (1989: 45) count among their "101 myths about the English language" the old-fashioned claim that "CAN cannot be used if you are talking about permission: you must use MAY" and add that the sentences

(205) Can I borrow your typewriter, please?
(206) Can I go out and play now?

"are nowadays far more common than the synonymous version containing MAY." Here again, (present) usage distinguishes the two modals.

Ascribing permissive MAY greater formality, Coates (1980a: 218) shows that "the same formal-informal distinction" operates in the case of permission as in the case of root possibility.

To complete the overall picture, the meaning most typically associated with CAN must be mentioned: "ability." In this meaning, it can never be replaced by MAY. It is translated by KÖNNEN:

(207) He can play the piano.
(208) Er kann Klavier spielen.

Summing up, it may be said that there are three kinds of relationships between CAN and MAY:

(a) exclusiveness of a semantic domain (CAN in its ability sense)
(b) overlap in meaning, but no free variation, due to
(ba) stylistic differences (both root possibility and permission: CAN is informal, MAY is formal)
(bb) differences in syntax and negation (epistemic possibility: CAN is impossible in affirmative statements, MAY is impossible in questions).

These are the theoretical possibilities of the two modals; their practical implementation is best illustrated with reference to their relative frequency. As a result of her analysis of instances of CAN and MAY found in the

	ability	root possibility	permission	epistemic possibility
MAY			7 | 32	147
CAN	41	129	10	

FIGURE 3.8.
Frequency of CAN and MAY

Survey of English Usage, Coates (1980a: 210; 1983: 103) set up a diagram for the different meanings of the two modals, Figure 3.8.

This diagram shows the little practical overlap of the two modals. Coates (1983: 102) mentions that there was only one example of epistemic *can't* in the two samples of written and spoken English. This illustrates the predominance of MAY in the epistemic domain.

But even with the sense of permission, there are three times as many instances of MAY as of CAN. This might suggest taking with a grain of salt the claim quoted previously that, in talking about permission, CAN sentences "are nowadays far more common than the synonymous version containing MAY." As Coates herself (1980b: 340) points out, however, the material in the Survey has been collected since the early 1950s. At that time, the onward march of CAN onto the "permission" terrain was much less pronounced, which probably accounts for the high percentage of instances of MAY in this category.

The same is recommendable, it seems, for Coates's findings about epistemic CAN: Palmer (1979a: 53), who also searched through the Survey, lists two more examples of *can't* used in this manner. About epistemic CAN in questions (which is not even mentioned by Coates (1980a, 1980b; 1983), Palmer (1979a: 56) writes: "With epistemic possibility . . . we should expect to find, and shall in fact find, that CAN is used," again quoting from the Survey. Figures 3.9 and 3.10 integrate the points made after Figures 3.5 and 3.6 were presented.

Faced with these charts, several questions come to mind immediately. How can MAY denoting "formal permission" be turned into "informal" KÖNNEN? And, vice versa, how can "informal permission" expressed by CAN become "formal" DÜRFEN?

For Nehls (1986: 106), the situation is very simple: "CAN used for the expression of 'permission' is to be rendered by KÖNNEN, whereas MAY, being more formal, corresponds to DÜRFEN (which is mostly formal, too)" (our translation). But if it is true that CAN has largely replaced the MAY of "permission," this will include instances pertaining to more formal situations. Precisely in such cases CAN could be rendered by DÜRFEN to preserve the factor of formality. As regards the first question just mentioned,

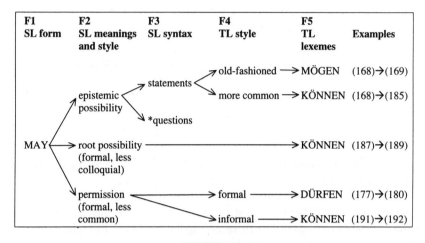

FIGURE 3.9.
German Renditions of MAY (6)

"permissive" MAY *must* even be rendered by KÖNNEN if the authoritative nature of a stipulation is to be understood (see Sections 3.3.2 on connotative meaning and 7.5 on deference to the TL hearer; see also Section 8.3.2).

Even without going into detail at this point, this situation suggests that apparent contradictions between factors (such as SL: *formal* → TL: *informal*) can be resolved by reference to some revision factor.

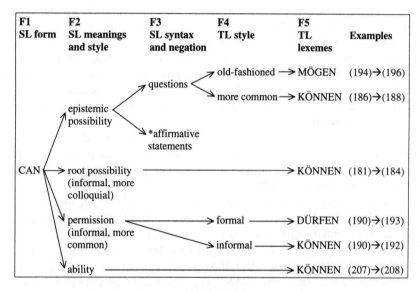

FIGURE 3.10.
German Renditions of CAN (3)

3.1.3 Identification Factors for Meanings

Another question coming up in view of Figures 3.9 and 3.10 is this: Why list all the 'impossibles' (marked by an asterisk), if they do not occur anyway? Even more so, as was said already, because the formal restrictions in the area of epistemic possibility become pertinent only if SL is German, and possible English renditions have to be considered.

These arguments are certainly valid, but the translator who is faced with a modal must first determine which meaning will have been intended by the speaker. If, for instance, one has to translate a question containing MAY, then one's knowledge that in this context the meaning of epistemic possibility is ruled out will immediately indicate that MAY can have been used here in the root sense only. This has the effect of luckily narrowing down the list of possible renditions; in this case MÖGEN is skipped.

But if this is so, some will ask, why not signify the translation path directly by connecting *MAY-in-questions* with *root meaning*? This is done in Figure 3.11. The same applies to CAN. Once I know that it occurs in an affirmative statement, it *must* be root; so this is the meaning I can start focusing on; see Figure 3.12.[19]

The justification for organizing factors this way is that syntax (sentence mood) and, in the case of CAN, affirmation, actually *determine* the root meaning of each modal. Factors being definable as elements determining other elements (see Section 1.1.2), the sequence of items under F2 and F3 in Figures 3.11 and 3.12 is quite appropriate. The advantage of this sequence is obvious. It renders the move from those factors to root meaning an unquestionable one.

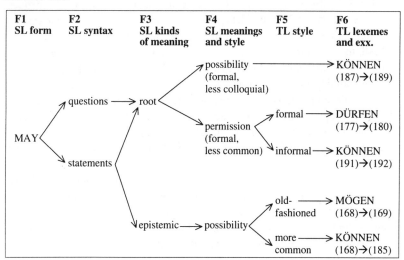

F1 SL form	F2 SL syntax	F3 SL kinds of meaning	F4 SL meanings and style	F5 TL style	F6 TL lexemes and exx.

FIGURE 3.11.
German Renditions of MAY (7)

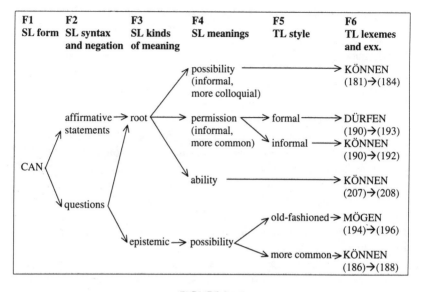

FIGURE 3.12.
German Renditions of CAN (4)

Other factor connections present themselves as bifurcations still lacking criteria of choice: Having arrived at root meaning in the two charts, how do I know which of the submeanings (i.e., possibility, permission and, in the case of CAN, ability) is intended; how to step from F3 to F4?

The identification situation for MAY in statements and CAN in questions (F2 in Figures 3.11 and 3.12) is still more basic. Here it is even open to question if these modals are used in the root or in the epistemic sense.

All these questions are, of course, unilingual in nature, because they pertain to identification factors that are not just relevant to translation, but to understanding the sentence in English. Yet, from all that has been said so far, it should be obvious that correct identification of meaning is a prerequisite for appropriate translation, because the word (form) is not transferred, but rather its meaning. Clearly, a translation theory of the modals must provide criteria for identifying the SL uses and their subcategories just referred to.

The identification factors for specific meanings of a modal are the respective typical co-occurrences with syntactic and semantic features. As a result of her in-depth corpus study of the semantics of the English modals, Coates (1983) lists such characteristics. We are going to present those given for CAN and MAY, preceded by examples that are clear enough to show the validity of these criteria.

CAN

(a) "Permission"

[190] You can go now.

Criteria: (i) The subject is animate. (ii) The verb is agentive. (iii) The utterance can be paraphrased with the words *permitted* or *allowed* (all on p. 87).

(b) "Ability"

[207] He can play the piano.

Criteria: (i) The subject is animate and has agentive function. (ii) The verb denotes action or activity. (iii) The possibility of the action is determined by inherent properties of the subject (all on p. 89).

(c) "Root possibility"

[181] This game can be played by young children.

Criteria: (i) No necessary association with an agentive subject function (p. 93). (ii) Unmarked with respect to human restriction (p. 93). (iii) The possibility is not determined by inherent properties of the subject (pp. 14, 92).

(d) "Epistemic possibility"[20]

(209) Where can the money be?

Criteria: (i) The main predication refers to a state or an activity in the present or past. (ii) The subject is frequently inanimate. (iii) The verb is usually stative. (iv) The speaker expresses confidence in the truth of the utterance (statements only) (all on p. 42).

These factors can now be integrated into Figure 3.12, giving rise to Figure 3.13.

As we can see, the occurrence of CAN in affirmative statements is in itself an obligatory identification factor, compelling the root reading. This alone, however, is insufficient for arriving at a definite German rendition. For this it must be determined which of the three root meanings—permission, possibility, or ability—is intended. For permission, also the German style dimension is essential.

MAY

(a) "Root"

As regards the identification factors of the root meanings of MAY, Coates (1983: 139) comments: "When the context identifies some form of authority, or involves the making of rules and regulations, then MAY is understood in terms of permission. When however the constraining factors are not identified with human authority but with external circumstances, then MAY is understood in terms of possibility."

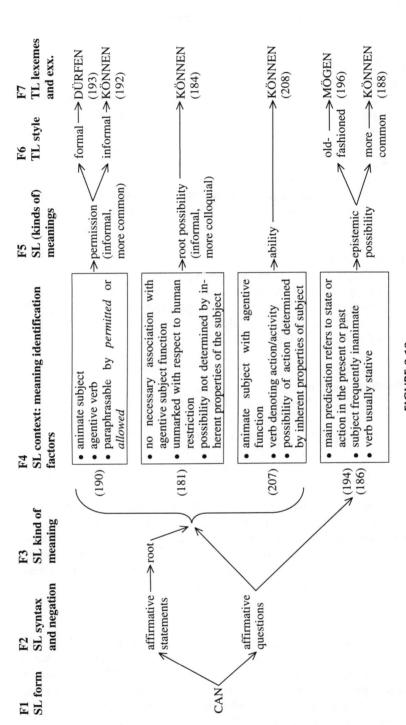

FIGURE 3.13.
German Renditions of CAN (5)

(b) "Epistemic"

For epistemic MAY, Coates (1983: 137) found the following invariable syntactic co-occurrence patterns:[21]

(i) Perfective aspect

(210) I may have put it there, out of the way.

(ii) Progressive aspect

(211) They may be reading something by Shakespeare.

(iii) Existential subject

(212) I suppose there may be an interview round about January.

(iv) Quasi-modal

(213) I may be able to leave here and still owe them my notice.

We are now in a position to augment Figure 3.11 by the identification factors for MAY, see Figure 3.14.

As was the case with CAN (see the final remarks pertaining to Figure 3.13), so too for MAY, the factor of syntactic mood does have the effect of narrowing down the number of possible interpretations, but this alone is insufficient for leading up to an unambiguous German rendition: MAY in questions does compel the root reading; but the co(n)textual identification factors under F4 are *further* necessary for pinpointing which of the two meanings (F5), permission or possibility, will have been intended.

Considering this stepwise approach to the German renditions, it seems that the factor sequence F1–F6 well deserves the term *translation flowchart*.

As regards the German modals, Brünner (1981) explicitly addresses herself to the question of how to ascertain if a modal is used with root or with epistemic meaning.

All the identification factors mentioned so far have the status of sufficient conditions; that is, once they exist for a sentence, they will determine the reading of the modal in that sentence.

Several caveats are in place, though. They are concerned with some phenomena that can be subsumed under the umbrella term *indeterminacy*.

3.1.4 Indeterminacy

3.1.4.1 Strength of Meaning Identification Factors

To begin with, not all the identification factors are *definite* determinants. It is true that some contexts of the modals were empirically found by Coates (1983) to correlate 100 percent with the presence or absence of a certain meaning. These include

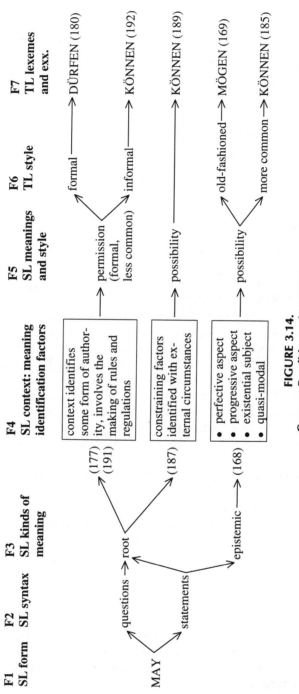

FIGURE 3.14.
German Renditions of MAY (8)

- for CAN: stative verb: 100 percent + root possibility (p. 97),
            100 percent − permission (p. 88);
   inanimate subject with active verb:
            100 percent − permission (p. 88);
- for MAY: progressive aspect, perfective aspect, existential subject,
   quasi-modal: each   100 percent + epistemic (p. 137).

Other features, however, were found to correlate to a smaller degree with a specific modal meaning:

- for CAN: inanimate subject: 88 percent + root possibility (Lancaster corpus),
            83 percent (Survey) (p. 97);

- for MAY: stative verb: 83 percent + epistemic (Lancaster corpus),
            95 percent (Survey) (p. 137).

Consequently, the strength of these features as meaning indicating factors is less. To increase the certainty of interpretation in these cases, it seems to be wisest to consider the interplay of several identification factors taken together; see the factor sets in Figures 3.13 and 3.14, under F4.

Determining the strength of an identification factor is one thing. Determining if it is present at all in a given instance is another, more basic, consideration. Indeterminacy relating to this question is dealt with next.

3.1.4.2 Gradience

The certainty about the presence of a factor hinges upon the possibility of reliably identifying it. Coates (1983: 14) observes that "the clearest cases are those where the enabling or disabling circumstances are actually specified," as in

(214) You can't see him because he's having lunch with a publisher. (1983: 15)

In other cases, she says, it is "not clear" (p. 142) which factor is intended. There are three kinds of such unclear cases: gradience, ambiguity, and merger. Often these unclear cases are intermediate points on a cline between two meanings of a modal. They conform 'more or less' to one category or the other. This is why Coates sets up gradients between two root meanings of a modal. Because her data showed that "it was only true to say that one extreme of any cline was 'clearly distinct'—the other extreme seemed often to be as fuzzy as any intermediate point" (p. 11), she opted for a fuzzy set with a central core, an intermediate skirt, and a periphery.

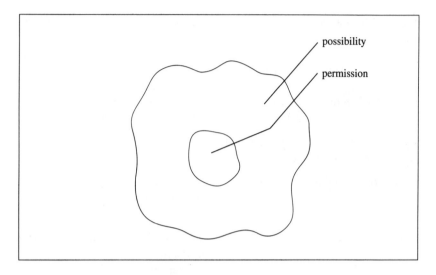

FIGURE 3.15.
Fuzzy Set Diagram of Root MAY

Permission being the predominant root meaning of MAY, it is allotted the core, with possibility at the periphery, giving rise to the fuzzy set diagram in Figure 3.15 (Coates 1983: 139).

The following sequence of sentences is meant to illustrate that "there seems to be no cut-off point between 'permission' and 'possibility'" (Coates 1983: 142 f.):

(215) If you want to recall the doctor you may do so.
(216) No student may postpone or withdraw registration or entry for any examination without the consent of the Dean.
(217) It is subject to the final prerogative of mercy of the Home Secretary who may recommend a reprieve.
(218) But assuming that the distinction is maintained one may ask which is to be analytically prior?
(219) To save money any scrap may be used, and if this is nailed and glued together strongly, it may be marked and cut to shape later.

Coates (1983: 143) comments:

The 'permitting factor' in (215) and (216) is clearly either personal authority or rules sanctioned by society, while the 'permitting factor' in (219) ('nailing and glueing') is external. (217) and (218), the intermediate cases, are indeterminate. Other factors, besides legal ones, may affect the Home Secretary's decision in (217); example (218) can be paraphrased either by 'it is permissible to ask . . .' or by 'it is possible to ask . . .' In other words, a line drawn from the core of the set to the periphery will distinguish between cases of root MAY on the basis of 'permitting factors.'[22]

If, as Coates mentioned, "other factors" also are involved, this may lead to a situation that is still more complex. Coates (1983: 15) presents the gradient of inherency of CAN with intermediate cases that "are common, where it is difficult to decide whether the property in question is inherent or not, and moreover whether the possibility of the action is determined by a *combination* of the inherent properties of the subject and external factors" (italics ours). Leech and Coates (1980: 84) even state: "In practice, an action may be possible by virtue of a *multiplicity* of factors, some of which may be inherent to the subject-referent, and some not" (italics ours).

It is evident that such complex factor situations are even more challenging for the translator, who is faced with the necessity of committing himself or herself to but one TL rendition. Considering all these identification factors marks one of his or her first steps toward an adequate translation (see F4 in Figure 3.14). How is the TL rendition itself affected by the results of this consideration? There are several possibilities:

(a) As regards the 'clear' cases, we can simply refer back to our earlier charts. Once it is known that an instance of CAN or MAY is used with a specific meaning (column F5 in Figures 3.13 and 3.14), then, after considering the style factor F6, the appropriate German rendition will just follow.

(b) In cases of gradience there are three possibilities:
(ba) The core and periphery of a cline are each rendered by the same German modal. This is the case with the gradient of CAN ranging from ability (core) to possibility (periphery) (Coates 1983: 92 f.: *gradient of inherency*). Because both meanings are rendered by KÖNNEN (see our Figure 3.13), each 'intermediate' meaning is, too.
(bb) There are different renditions for core and periphery. This is so with Coates's *gradients of restriction* for CAN (1983: 88 f.) and MAY (1983: 142 f.), each ranging from permission (core) to possibility (periphery). Again, both meanings can be rendered by KÖNNEN, but this time DÜRFEN is a formally marked alternative for permission. It must be chosen for those cases in which it is absolutely clear and vital that the formal permissive nature of the situation is to be emphasized. Permission being at the core of the two gradients, however, such clear cases are no instances of gradience at all. This means that neither gradience nor 'clear' cases present any problem for translation.
(bc) There is a combination of (multiple) core and periphery factors, and the different gradient areas require different renditions. Let us take an example from the *Brown Corpus of American English*:

(220) You can build this vacation cottage yourself.

Here, Leech and Coates (1980: 84) say that divers "enabling factors" may include

(a) the addressee's physical capacities,
(b) his technical know-how,
(c) his financial resources,
(d) the simplicity of the house's design,
(e) the availability of land,
(f) the availability of building materials, etc.

Complex as this situation may seem, the translator's task is simple: All these factors relate only to the gradient of inherency running from ability to possibility, and both these meanings can be rendered by KÖNNEN (see Figure 3.13):

(221) Sie können dieses Ferienhaus selber bauen.

Now it is imaginable that there is one more factor, (g), which is the permissibility in terms of the building bylaws, possibly in view of factor (d), the construction of (small) simple houses not being subject to specific government regulations. With this permitting factor added, the overall practical meaning situation of CAN in (220) now corresponds to the entire range of its root-meaning scope as depicted by Coates (1983: 86) and augmented in Figure 3.16 by the possible permitting factors for (220).

In analogy to case (bb), one could say that only if permission is clearly dominating could DÜRFEN be used as a rendition for CAN. But there is a blocking factor commonly ruling out rendition (222):

(222) !Sie dürfen dieses Ferienhaus selber bauen.

This factor is that, for reasons of tact, in German permission is not usually granted by DÜRFEN because it evokes associations of authority (see Section 3.3.2). So even if permission dominates as meaning and the subject-referent is identical to the hearer, KÖNNEN would be preferred. KÖNNEN can even be called the ideal rendition for CAN in (220), because its range of meaning covers exactly the same two gradients associated with CAN (see Figure 3.17).

Sentence (220) illustrates another point regarding a multiple factor situation. As was mentioned, factor (g) goes together well with factor (d), but it would not normally co-occur with factor (a) or (c)—building permits do not necessarily have anything to do with the physical strength or financial resources of the builder. Such aspects would rather be highlighted by considering the personal subjective situation of the builder. Yet another situation would be talking about the objective building conditions involving the availability of land and building materials. In each of these three situations we

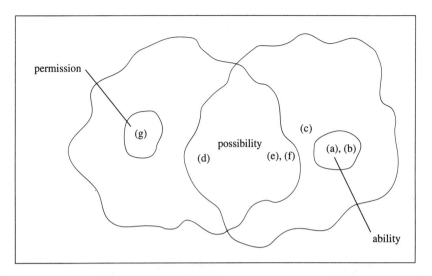

FIGURE 3.16.
Fuzzy Set Diagram of CAN

see that *factors come in sets*—an idea already familiar from a different perspective. In Section 3.1.4.1 the fact that different features have different strength as identification factors led to the conclusion that, to optimize certainty, it is most expedient to consider *sets* of factors. The overall translation situation with regard to sentence (220) is depicted in Figure 3.17.

With the phenomenon of gradience introduced, it becomes obvious that our discussion now takes a second turn. We initially started from the recognition of discrete meaning categories, but through the phenomenon of gradience we became aware of the interconnectedness of these meanings. Now that we see that different sets or clusters of meaning identification factors are mutually rather exclusive, the different gradient areas begin to separate again (as *gradient clusters*). This leads us on to another topic, where, as in the case of gradience, we can attempt to decide which of several meanings will (not) have been intended. In the case of ambiguity, however, these meanings are truly mutually exclusive.

3.1.4.3 Ambiguity

A third kind of indeterminacy regarding identification of meaning is ambiguity. Here the immediate cotext fails to disambiguate two mutually exclusive meanings. It is, for example, not obvious if sentence (223) is supposed to be taken in the epistemic (224) or in the root (225) sense (see Leech and Coates 1980: 81):

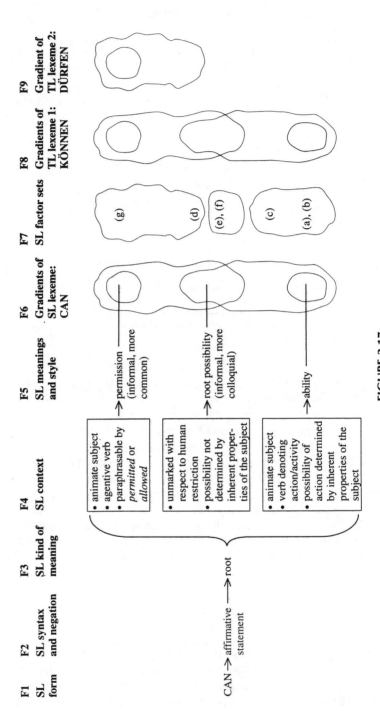

FIGURE 3.17.
The Translation Situation of Sentence (220)

(223) He must understand that we mean business.

(224) Surely he understands that we mean business.

(225) It is essential that he understand that we mean business.

The corresponding German sentence (226) is equally ambiguous between the two readings, which themselves are unambiguously stated in (227) and (228):

(226) Er muss verstehen, dass wir Ernst machen.

(227) Sicherlich versteht er, dass wir Ernst machen.

(228) Es ist nötig, dass er versteht, dass wir Ernst machen.

So if the ambiguity of (223) is to be an invariance factor, MÜSSEN is a fitting rendition.

This leads to a possibly surprising conclusion. Even if ambiguity usually necessitates disambiguation for the sake of identification of intended meaning, this need not be so in the case of translation. If the ambiguity has to be retained, no disambiguation is necessary!

Nevertheless in such cases it is necessary to find a TL equivalent that is as ambiguous as the SL modal, such as MÜSSEN in (226) for MUST in (223). But what about rendering MAY? Perkins (1983: 100 f.) presents as ambiguous sentence (229) and explicates two of its readings as (230) and (231):

(229) He may go.

(230) It is permissible for him to go.

(231) Perhaps he goes.

As is obvious, MAY in (229) is ambiguous between permission (230) and epistemic possibility (231). In a more formal style, (229) could also be taken to convey the idea of root possibility:

(232) It is possible for him to go.

In terms of the gradient of restriction, MAY in (229) may even refer to any intermediate point between permission and possibility.

Given this combined ambiguity-gradience situation, which German modal fits best? KÖNNEN and DÜRFEN come to mind:

(233) Er darf gehen.

(234) Er kann gehen.

The former sentence can, however, be paraphrased only by

(235) Er hat die Erlaubnis zu gehen.

This means that DÜRFEN can be used only in the permission sense; it is not ambiguous at all.

Now let us have a look at the possible meanings conveyed by KÖNNEN in (234). They include permission as in (235) (albeit of a more informal style), but also epistemic possibility (236), and even ability (237):

(236) Vielleicht geht er.
(237) Er ist fähig zu gehen.

It can, in fact, justifiably be argued that, regarding root meaning, KÖNNEN in (234) can convey the entire range of the two gradients connecting permission, possibility, and ability, as was already the case with regard to sentence (221).

Like MAY, so KÖNNEN represents a combined case of ambiguity and gradience, covering even one more gradient than MAY. Figure 3.18 summarizes the range of meanings possible for sentences (229), (233), and (234), respectively. Which German modal to choose, then? Because root-epistemic ambiguity is our concern, it is clear that DÜRFEN cannot be used. Choosing KÖNNEN, one might wish to employ a blocking factor, ruling out the ability reading of this modal, thus leaving a picture of ambiguity and gradience in German that corresponds to that of MAY.

Note that the ambiguity of sentences such as (223) or (229) exists only in isolation from context. As Leech and Coates (1980: 81) point out, "contextual clues generally make clear which meaning is appropriate."

Yet there are contexts in which it does not even matter which of two

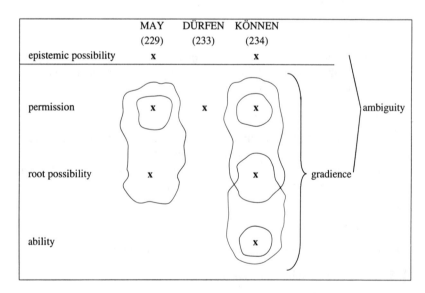

FIGURE 3.18.
Combined Ambiguity and Gradience

otherwise mutually exclusive interpretations of a sentence is chosen. This last kind of indeterminacy to be mentioned here is merger.

3.1.4.4 Merger

What gradience and ambiguity have in common is the need of weighing meanings with or against each other. For ambiguity, the reason is that only one of two possible, but inconsistent, interpretations of a sentence is intended by the speaker.

In some contexts, however, correct understanding does not necessitate distinguishing between two readings, because they are no longer mutually exclusive (Coates 1983: 17).

What this practically means is illustrated by Leech and Coates (1980: 86). They first refer to two clear cases of epistemic (238) and root (239) MAY taken from Lancaster corpus:

(238) I may not get back there today—it depends on the work here.
(239) There are many theories about the balance of these forces in a perfect society, and many reasons for believing that X's party, class or nation may be trusted with them where Y's cannot.

The criteria given for each meaning are these:

- Epistemic MAY may be followed by *well* or *possibly*, may be followed by *or may not*, may be substituted by *perhaps*. The construction *I may not . . .* may be replaced by *It may be that I will not*.
- Root MAY allows for none of these criteria but can be replaced by CAN (which is not possible for epistemic MAY).

If it is true that instances of merger are not subject to an either-or interpretation, they should satisfy all the tests for *both* meanings, while conveying approximately the same message. These conditions, the authors say, are indeed fulfilled by the following sentence taken from Brown corpus:

(240) With tone, individual differences may be greater than the linguistic contrasts which are superimposed on them.

The logic for the unity of the two meanings in this case is, we might add, that if something is theoretically *possible for* something to be, then it is also practically *possible that* it will be so: "The common semantic element of possibility (as shown in the paraphrase formulae) is indicative of the close connection between the two meanings" (Leech and Coates 1980: 86).

Finding an appropriate German modal for this phenomenon of semantic convergence is not difficult: KÖNNEN conveys both meanings associated with MAY in (240).

Let us again review the steps of our overall progress. We started our discussion with discrete meanings, then proceeded toward nondiscrete gradients. Having detected partially discrete gradient clusters, as well as fully discrete ambiguous interpretations, we have now arrived at merger, the unity of otherwise discrete meanings.

So our story has been one of (varying degrees of) unity and diversity. Incidentally, this topic also threads the literature on translation, because the (varying degrees of) unity of an SL and a TL text is the crucial factor in this field.

We will continue to ring the changes on this topic by dealing with the relationship of the modals and their cognates. First, however, it is necessary to round off the treatment of the modals themselves by taking a look at the factor of negation.

3.1.5 Negation

In Figures 3.12 and 3.13, we deliberately omitted the categories of negative statements and negative questions because they involve rendition patterns that are different from those of affirmative sentences.

Affirmative statements containing CAN were invariably rendered by KÖNNEN, DÜRFEN being a formal alternative. For affirmative questions also MÖGEN was used, see Figure 3.13.

Affirmative statements involving CAN invariably showed root meaning, but both negative statements and questions—these two categories being subsumed by Quirk et al. (1972: 54) under the term *nonassertion*; cf. Palmer (1979b)—can be either root or epistemic. Which are the meaning-indicating factors for these sentences? How are they rendered in German?

According to Coates (1983: 101), there is just one invariant epistemic form: *can't*. This would suggest that the form *cannot* is itself an identification factor for root meaning. Epistemic *cannot* is, however, mentioned by other authors; for instance, by Tottie (1985: 89), Nehls (1986: 79), and a number of grammarians. So both *can't* and *cannot* can be root as well as epistemic, after all. How to distinguish the two meanings?

Coates (1983: 44, 101) found that all of the following syntactic features are incompatible with root *can't/cannot* (see Section 3.1.3):

- progressive aspect (can't be running)
- perfective aspect (can't have been)
- existential subject (There can't have been)
- stative verb (can't be)
- inanimate subject (This can't be)

Turning to the German rendition situation, the first half of the story is already known. Just like root *can*, root *can't/cannot* can invariably be rendered by *kann nicht*, unless the prohibitive nature of the action is highlighted; in this case *darf nicht* can also be used, for example,

(241) I can't go swimming today.
(242) Ich kann heute nicht schwimmen gehen.
(243) Ich darf heute nicht schwimmen gehen.

When it comes to rendering epistemic possibility, however, *can't* differs from *can*; compare Figure 3.13 with these sentences:

(244) He can't have been there.
(245) *Er mag nicht dort gewesen sein.
(246) Er kann nicht dort gewesen sein.

(247) He can't be there.
(248) !Er mag nicht dort sein.
(249) Er kann nicht dort sein.

These examples show that *mag nicht* is impossible as a rendition for epistemic *can't* and that *kann nicht* appropriately translates *can't* in sentences with perfective aspect (such as (244)); in other co(n)texts (see (249)) it is ambiguous between a root and an epistemic reading. If *can't* in (247) is also taken to be ambiguous, *kann nicht* would be the appropriate reading. Otherwise it would be better to rule out the root reading by adding a negative adjective such as *unmöglich*; for example,

(250) Er kann unmöglich dort sein.

Figure 3.19 summarizes the points on *cannot* und *can't* in statements. For negative questions see note 19.

Just like CAN, so MAY shows different rendition patterns in the area of epistemic negation; compare Figure 3.14 with the following sentences:

(251) He may not be in Berlin.
(252) !Er mag nicht in Berlin sein.
(253) !Er kann nicht in Berlin sein.

Mag nicht and *kann nicht* are normally ruled out because they evoke meanings undesirable in this context: *mag nicht* would be taken to mean "doesn't like to," and *kann nicht* may be interpreted in the root sense. Both modals could be used, however, if some affirmative element is provided in addition; for example,

(254) Er mag in Berlin sein, er mag auch !nicht in Berlin sein.
(255) Er kann in Berlin sein, er kann auch !nicht in Berlin sein.
(256) Er kann/mag in Berlin sein oder auch nicht.

As it stands, *may not* in sentence (251) is better rendered by an unmistakable indicator for epistemic possibility, such as in

(257) Vielleicht ist er nicht in Berlin.

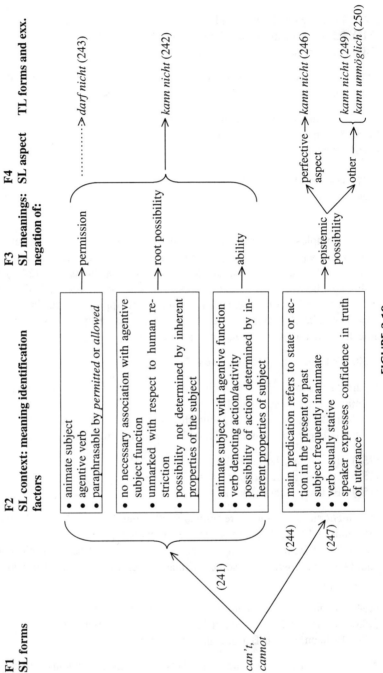

FIGURE 3.19.
German Renditions of *Cannot* and *Can't* in Statements

With the word VIELLEICHT in (257) we leave our discussion of the modals as a closed set of expressions and open our perspective to include other cognate expressions as well. We have, in fact, already mentioned such expressions occasionally

- as forms suppleting the missing nonfinite forms of the English modals (see Sections 1.2.2.1, 2.5, 2.8) or missing uses of the German ones (see Section 2.8);
- for disambiguating ambiguous sentences containing modals (see Section 3.1.4.3).

The first of these two points is an answer as to the formal necessity of using these forms; the second is a hint at their semantic relationship to the modals.

Two questions remain unanswered at this point, however: Which suppletive is to be chosen on semantic grounds? What is the exact semantic relationship of these expressions to the modals? To answer these questions takes an expanded frame of reference: the modal system.

3.2 THE MODAL SYSTEM

The modal system as a translation factor? Experience has shown that even though the modals are our object of focus, confining our attention to them alone will not do:

- Faced with epistemic MAY, the translator may need to use the adverb VIELLEICHT for an unmistakable rendition;
- if *konnte* is to be translated, it is sometimes even imperative to use a suppletive such as *was able to.*

In short, the translator can be expected to know the ins and outs of all sorts of expressions having to do with the modals in one way or the other. This alone can secure one's position as a versatile pivot meeting the demands of all kinds of translation situations concerning the modals.

3.2.1 The Modals and Their Cognates

We have repeatedly seen that the meanings of the modals may also be conveyed by means of expressions other than the modals themselves. VIELLEICHT is semantically akin to epistemic KÖNNEN (see Section 3.1.5), BE ABLE TO is a suppletive for CAN (see Section 1.2.2.1). As the term *suppletive* suggests, these 'near synonyms' or cognates are all too often regarded as a mere surrogate of the modals; "they are rarely considered in their own right, but are used almost incidentally as paraphrases which serve to illuminate the meanings of the modal auxiliaries that are the primary focus of interest" (Perkins 1983: 2). As will be shown in this section, this does not do justice to the semantic content of these expressions which *is* different from that of the modals, at least in certain respects (see Section 3.2.1.1). This recognition has consequences for making word class an invariance factor (see Section 3.2.1.2); the exception proves the rule (see Section 3.2.1.3).

3.2.1.1 Degrees of Semantic Identity

In Section 3.1.5 we encountered a syntactic variant for epistemic *mag (nicht)*: the adverb VIELLEICHT. The same phenomenon also exists in English; for instance,

[251] He may not be in Berlin.
(258) Perhaps he is not in Berlin.

How to go about dealing with such semantic equivalents? We can take a cue from Tottie (1980: 47), who opens a paper with the following remark: "The problem of the semantic equivalence of variants is an important one in the study of syntactic variation. . . . Before undertaking a study of the factors that govern the choice of syntactic variants, it is necessary to establish the degree of semantic identity of the forms under investigation."

This is precisely what Perkins (1983: 100–5) has done for MAY and its multifarious cognates, all reflecting some kind of possibility. In our section on ambiguity, we already quoted two of these cognates of MAY mentioned by Perkins:

[229] He may go.
[230] It is permissible for him to go.
[231] Perhaps he goes.

What is common to the expressions MAY, BE PERMISSIBLE TO, and PERHAPS is part of their meaning; that is, some kind of possibility. Moreover, MAY shares with BE PERMISSIBLE TO its root meaning and with PERHAPS its epistemic meaning.

So the factor distinguishing the last two expressions is the *kind* of possibility expressed. MAY is not thus fixed; the twofold nature of the modal accounts for the ambiguity of sentence (229). Sentences (230) and (231) are not ambiguous this way. This knowledge enables us to make a basic statement about the relationship of MAY and its two cognates: MAY shows a greater degree of semantic generality. The same is true of KÖNNEN and its paraphrases as discussed previously; for example,

[234] Er kann gehen.
[235] Er hat die Erlaubnis zu gehen.
[236] Vielleicht geht er.
[237] Er ist fähig zu gehen.

In fact, the greater specificity of these paraphrases makes them ideal renditions when it comes to resolve ambiguity—hence the choice of VIELLEICHT in (257) for MAY in (251):

[251] He may not be in Berlin.
[257] Vielleicht ist er nicht in Berlin.

Unambiguity is one of the values of this adverb. But knowledge of VIELLEICHT alone will not do for rendering epistemic possibility nor will PERHAPS be a general servant for expressing this meaning. This can be shown by taking up some more of Perkins's variants for MAY:

(259) I think he goes.
(260) There is a possibility that he goes.

Starting again with similarities, we can say that both sentences bear epistemic meaning. I THINK reflects an evaluation of the likelihood of something being the case, and *possibility that* (vs. *possibility for*) is an indicator of epistemic meaning, as will be remembered.

The factor distinguishing the two expressions is that I THINK qualifies the evaluation as subjective, whereas the existential subject *there is* indicates that the possibility referred to is an objective one (see Section 3.2.4.2).

Objective epistemic possibility can also be expressed by adjectives, such as

(261) It's possible that he will go.

Both nominal and adjectival variants may be premodified by an adjective or adverb, respectively:

(262) There's a remote possibility that he will go.
(263) It's quite possible that he will go.

Further variation can be found in the field of syntax. All the examples of objective epistemic possibility mentioned so far are unmarked with respect to their syntactic position in a sentence, in the sense that their position is fixed. But in other expressions in this category, syntactic behavior is more flexible; for example,

(264) Possibly he will go.
(265) He will possibly go.
(266) He will go, possibly.

Here, the adverb POSSIBLY is fronted (thematized), interpolated, and adjoined, respectively. The same syntactic markedness can be observed with PERHAPS:

(267) Perhaps he will go.
(268) He will perhaps go.
(269) He will go, perhaps.

MAY is unmarked for thematization, interpolation or adjunction. As shown, it is also unmarked for the subjective-objective distinction within epistemic possibility. And it is even unmarked with respect to the root-epistemic distinction in general. These facts are evidence for the reality of the statement that "the modals are unmarked in regard to their periphrastic counterparts" (Bouma 1975: 325). This claim was, in fact, amply confirmed by Westney (1995).

As can be expected, MAY is also unmarked for the subjective-objective distinction within root possibility. Again other expressions are marked in this respect: There are a number of variants for "permission" (i.e., for *deontic* possibility, see Section 3.2.4.3 f.), such as

(270) I permit/allow/authorize him to go.

The verbal alternatives in this sentence all indicate subjective root or deontic possibility. There are also variants marked objectively:

(271) It is permitted/permissible for him to go.
(272) (Prompt) Permission is/has been granted for him to go.

In addition, it is possible to modify objective deontic possibility by adjective or adverb; for example,

(273) There's a presidential authorization for him to go.
(274) It is fortunately permitted for him to go.

Perkins (1983: 103) sums up his system of variants for the expression of possibility in English by means of a tree diagram, which we reproduce in Figure 3.20 in terms of a numerical index. What emerges here is a layered picture of subtle distinctions within a single concept of "possibility"—another instance of our theme *unity in diversity*, mentioned earlier (see Section 3.1.4.4).

It is true that all the expressions listed in Figure 3.20 reflect this concept of possibility in one way or another, but their syntactic and semantic characteristics make them all unique representatives of their respective subcategories of possibility. The overall system could be referred to as *functional variety*. Please note again only the modal MAY is syntactically and semantically completely unmarked.

Of course, Perkins's scheme is by no means complete—cf. his index of modal expressions, more of which could have been incorporated. Other expressions appear only once, although, just like the modals, they serve several functions. Consider, for example, the adjective POSSIBLE, which is listed under "epistemic possibility" (1.2.2.1.1.1 in Figure 3.20) as part of the syntagma IT'S POSSIBLE THAT, but that, of course, is also used in the root construction IT'S POSSIBLE FOR.[23]

"Possibility"

1. epistemic			
1.1 unmarked for subjective/objective			
	1.1.1 unmarked for thematization/ interpolation/adjunction		MAY (229)
	1.1.2 marked for thematization/ interpolation/adjunction		PERHAPS (231), MAYBE (267)–(269)
1.2 marked for subjective/objective			
	1.2.1 subjective		I THINK (259), I BELIEVE
	1.2.2 objective		
		1.2.2.1 unmarked for thematization/ interpolation/adjunction	
		1.2.2.1.1 modified	
		1.2.2.1.1.1 by adv.	IT'S ... POSSIBLE THAT ... (263)
		1.2.2.1.1.2 by adj.	THERE'S A ... POSSIBILITY THAT ... (262)
		1.2.2.1.2 unmodified	IT'S POSSIBLE THAT ... (261), THERE'S A POSSIBILITY THAT ... (260)
		1.2.2.2 marked for thematization/ interpolation/adjunction	POSSIBLY (264)–(266), CONCEIVABLY
2. deontic			
2.1 unmarked for subjective/objective			MAY (229)
2.2 marked for subjective/objective			
	2.2.1 subjective		I PERMIT (270), I AUTHORIZE (270)
	2.2.2 objective		
		2.2.2.1 modified	
		2.2.2.1.1 by adverb	IT'S ... PERMITTED TO ... (274)
		2.2.2.1.2 by adjective	... PERMISSION HAS BEEN GRANTED TO ... (272)
		2.2.2.2 unmodified	IT'S PERMITTED TO ... (271), PERMISSION HAS BEEN GRANTED TO ... (272)

FIGURE 3.20.
"Possibility" and Some of Its Expressions in English

3.2.1.2 Correspondence of Word Class

The real value of Figure 3.20 for the translator becomes apparent when it is supplemented by a similarly layered German scheme. In this, the equivalent of both POSSIBLEs would be MÖGLICH; THERE'S A POSSIBILITY THAT would correspond to ES BESTEHT DIE MÖGLICHKEIT, DASS. As we have already seen, VIELLEICHT corresponds to PERHAPS (see (258)). More equivalences will easily come to the mind of any translator:

(275) I THINK   ICH DENKE
(276) I BELIEVE   ICH GLAUBE
(277) POSSIBLY   MÖGLICHERWEISE
(278) I PERMIT   ICH ERLAUBE

Admittedly, there is some room for variation within one category: I BE-LIEVE can sometimes render ICH DENKE, just as I THINK can translate ICH GLAUBE, because all four expressions reflect subjective epistemic possibility. We contend, however, that equivalences are confined to the same category; for instance, subjective epistemic possibility in SL can be expected to be rendered by the very same category in TL, if translation is to be authentic and precise. This is why we are reluctant to accept as 'possible' equivalences of one SL sentence hosts of TL 'variants.'

To take a case in point, Duff (D), Newmark (N), and Wilss (W) present "a wide specter of TL equivalents" (Wilss 1983a: 190) or "potential translations" (Duff 1989: 110, Newmark 1981: 101) of the same German sentence (279):[24]

(279) Es ist möglich, das Problem zu lösen.

(280) One can solve the problem. (D, N)
(281) The problem can be solved. (W)

(282) It is possible to solve the problem. (N, W)
(283) It is possible to resolve the problem. (D)

(284) The problem is possible to solve. (D, N, W)
(285) Solving the problem is possible. (D, N)
(286) To solve the problem is possible. (D, N)
(287) The solution of the problem is possible. (W)
(288) A solution to the problem is possible. (D, N)

(289) The problem is soluble. (D, N)
(290) The problem is solvable. (W)

(291) The solvable problem . . . (W)

(292) There is a solution to the problem. (D, N)
(293) The problem has a solution. (D, N)

(294) Solving the problem is a possibility. (D, N)

(295) In view of the solvability of the problem . . . (W)

Against this proliferation of renditions we would argue that only sentences (282) and (283) reflect the original fully in syntactico-semantic terms.

If one accepts as a translation principle the tenet that renditions should resemble their original as much as possible, then all other English sentences are in fact renditions of different German sentences, namely,[25]

(296) Man kann das Problem lösen. → (280)
(297) Das Problem kann gelöst werden. → (281)
(298) Das Problem zu lösen, ist möglich. → (284)–(286)
(299) Die Lösung des Problems ist möglich.→ (287)
(300) Eine Lösung des Problems ist möglich.→ (288)
(301) Das Problem ist lösbar. → (289), (290)
(302) Das lösbare Problem . . . → (291)
(303) Es gibt eine Lösung für das Problem. → (292)
(304) Das Problem hat eine Lösung. → (293)
(305) Es besteht die Möglichkeit, das Problem zu lösen. → (294)
(306) Angesichts der Lösbarkeit des Problems . . . → (295)

We would say that the alleged formula 'sixteen English sentences for a German one' is *not*, in effect, another example of unity in diversity. This is substantiated by the fact that several of the English sentences unnecessarily deviate from the syntax of the German original. We would like to emphasize the word *unnecessarily*; we are, of course, well aware that translational shifts in syntax are sometimes inevitable in cases such as (284) where no congruent TL construction is possible; hence,

[284] The problem is possible to solve ≠ (i.e., is not rendered as)
(307) *Das Problem ist möglich zu lösen.

But (291), for instance, and even more so (295)

[291] The solvable problem . . .
[295] In view of the solvability of the problem . . .

are flatly deviations from the German structure of (279), which are really unnecessary because for this sentence an analogous English structure does exist, namely, that of (282) and (283)!

As is evident from our suggested list of equivalences, however, we are no proponents of any unrealistic one-to-one correspondences either: Sentences (279) and (301) were given two equivalents, sentence (298) even three. Rendering such groups of SL sentences by just one TL sentence can be traced to the convergence factor of syntactic ungrammaticality such as that of (307). Here the possibility of forming (298) acts as a compensation factor.

We are, of course, aware that the correlations suggested by us are not rigidly fixed. For instance, *solving* in (285) is a nonfinite form with nominal function, so even (300) containing the noun LÖSUNG may be said to be a justifiable rendition of (285). All we would argue is that, in the absence of any other task description, the translator should try to stick to the SL construction at hand as much as possible.

These remarks pertain to sentences containing modal adjectives or nouns. More central to our present consideration is the relation between the modals and their cognates. We have to ask, Why should the adjective MÖGLICH not be rendered by the adjective POSSIBLE, but by the modal verb CAN as was suggested by Duff, Newmark, and Wilss in (280) and (281), respectively?

Again, it is true that both MÖGLICH and CAN reflect root possibility, but this should not be taken to be the only translation factor. If optimum fidelity to the SL construction is aimed at, one would surely have to count membership to a word class or part of speech as *another* criterial feature to be an invariance factor. This simple reflection would justify setting up our sentence pairs (296) → (280), (297) → (281), and (279) → (282), (283).[26]

Another justification for translating modals as modals, and other expressions not as modals, is the nonmarkedness of the modals referred to above. POSSIBLE and MÖGLICH are syntactically marked in terms of thematization/interpolation/adjunction (this feature of root POSSIBLE again to be integrated into Perkins's chart)—cf. (282)–(283) vs. (284) vs. (285)–(288).

The syntactic positioning of MÖGLICH in the German counterparts of these sentences as suggested by us is restricted to thematization and adjunction—cf. (279) and (298)–(300) vs. *(307)—but even so MÖGLICH is marked in this respect compared to KÖNNEN.

This syntactic nonmarkedness of the modals is reinforced by their semantic nonmarkedness; that is, their semantic generality as referred to in Section 3.2.1.1. To demonstrate that this is a characteristic of both the English and the German modals, let us compare them with expressions that, unlike POSSIBLE but like most of the other periphrastic expressions, are confined strictly to one kind of possibility (see (229) and so on):

(308) BE PERMITTED TO   root $\Big\}$ MAY

      MAYBE   epistemic

(309) ERLAUBT SEIN   root $\Big\}$ KÖNNEN

      VIELLEICHT   epistemic

This juxtaposition shows that the modals actually cover two otherwise distinct meanings. Because the English and German modals are alike in this respect, it is only natural to relate them to each other as translation equivalents; that is, to go by the formula *SL modal* → *TL modal*.

In the beginning of this section we quoted Tottie, who made a case for establishing "the degree of semantic identity of the forms under investigation." We are now in a position to say that the relation of the modals and their cognates is indeed a matter of degree: Due to its being usable in the root and epistemic senses,[27] POSSIBLE shows a greater semantic identity to the modals than, for instance, BE PERMITTED TO and MAYBE.

Tottie regarded the determination of the degree of semantic identity as a prerequisite for "undertaking a study of the factors that govern the choice of syntactic variants." From the point of view of translation, we have already suggested an answer to this quest: The English and German modals being alike in their nonmarkedness, there is actually *no* choice: SL and TL birds of a feather flock together—modals render modals.

But there are exceptions to this principle. They occur when obligatory change factors come into play and do "govern the choice of syntactic variants," our next topic.

3.2.1.3 Change of Word Class

From what has been argued in the last section (see (308), (309)), the following sentence pairs would be considered natural equivalents:

(310) Er darf nach Hause gehen.
(311) He may go home.

(312) Ihm ist erlaubt, nach Hause zu gehen.
(313) He is permitted to go home.

But as soon as we shift to past tense, rendition patterns change:

(314) Er durfte nach Hause gehen.
(315) ! He might go home.
(316) He was permitted to go home.

Sentence (315) is grammatically well-formed, but it is inappropriate as a rendition of (314) because it is epistemic in meaning. We *have to* resort to a suppletive such as BE PERMITTED TO to convey the correct meaning. This means that tense here acts as an obligatory revision factor amending the otherwise standard translation formula *SL modal* → *TL modal*.

What is especially interesting about the last example is that there is a two-step sequence of factors:

- F1 is tense—*durfte* calls for the past form of MAY.
- F2 is the nonavailability of the meaning "permission" associated with MIGHT, the past form of MAY (see Section 3.5).

Of course, this sequence is evident only if MAY is chosen as a starting point corresponding to DÜRFEN; a lexical entry of DÜRFEN with examples of *durfte* would list an English suppletive form right away.

The need to render root DÜRFEN by means of a suppletive form arises only in non-present-tense constructions. In other cases, the possibility of using an English modal for a German one does not even exist in the present tense. Consider the following sentences:

(317) Ich will dorthin (gehen).
(318) I want to go there.

It is true that WOLLEN can be rendered by English WILL in emphatic contexts denoting insistence (see also Friederich 1964: 55 f.):

(319) Er ‖will es nicht tun# (The double bar ‖ indicates stronger stress.)
(320) He ‖will not do it#

But if WOLLEN in (317) is taken to be nonemphatic, it can be rendered only by full verbs such as WANT TO or INTEND.

There are even cases in which a German modal cannot be rendered by an English one under any circumstances whatsoever:

(321) Er soll in London gewesen sein.
(322) He is said to have been in London.

This is not to say that SOLLEN can never be rendered by an English modal; for example,

[166] Shall I accompany you?
[167] Soll ich dich begleiten?

All we can say is that SOLLEN *in the meaning of BE SAID TO*, unlike WOLLEN in the meaning of WANT TO, can never be rendered by an English modal.

In this section we have dealt with three kinds of phenomena where no English modal can be used:

• suppletion for past tense forms (*durfte* → *was allowed to*);
• special present tense context (*will* → *want*);
• specific meaning (*soll* → *is said to*).

Different as these cases may be, they are all indicative of one phenomenon: the different structure or anisomorphism of the English and German systems of modals. Note that the three conditions just mentioned are all *obligatory* change factors—no modal could be used. Things are different in this respect with the following sentence

[251] He may not be in Berlin.

which we recommended to be translated as

[257] Vielleicht ist er nicht in Berlin.

Here, the selection of VIELLEICHT as "an unmistakable indicator of epistemic possibility" was a *choice* made in favor of avoiding ambiguity.

So we find that obligatory change factors of three kinds as well as an optional change factor reveal the noncongruence of the systems of modals in the two languages.

For different reasons, in each of these four cases we had or preferred to step into a terrain that lay outside that of the modals themselves. What shall we call this extended area? Because it belongs to expressions that are renditions of SL modals it could be given the interlingual name *modal system*. Its *modal expressions* would, of course, include the modals themselves. But it will be wise to reflect for a moment on the relevance of these terms for the purpose of translation.

3.2.2 Definition of Modality

Taking the modals to be exponents of modality suggests defining the terms *modal* and *modality* in terms of them. A definition in formal terms would not do, however, because the formal criteria of the modals pertain just to this small set of expressions excluding all other modal expressions. The insufficiency of mere reference to the modals is shown in Palmer's (1987) paper 'What is Modality?' Having started dealing with this question in terms of the modals, he observes: "So far, this discussion of modality has proceeded without any indication of what might be meant by the term, though it has been illustrated by reference to the modal verbs" (1987: 392).

Switching to the *meanings* of the modals as a criterion of modality would entail that all the 'near synonyms' of the modals (such as those dealt with in Section 3.2.1) would be given access to the field of modality. However, by virtue of WILL being a modal, we would have to include also "futurity, which seems to belong more to the system of tense, and volition, which has little in common with the more obvious modal concepts of possibility and necessity" (Palmer 1979a: 2). As regards German, Palmer (1990: 12) observes that "SOLLEN can often be translated as 'It is said that . . . ,' and WOLLEN as 'He/she/they claim that he/she/they . . .'" Extending the criterion of the modals' meanings to their TL equivalents, this would mean that BE SAID TO as well as CLAIM would also have to be called *modal*.

At this point it should be clear that the definition of modality cannot be a necessary condition for the purpose of translating the modals. If some meaning of SOLLEN is translated by BE SAID TO, or some meaning of WOLLEN is rendered by CLAIM, then what does it matter if BE SAID TO or CLAIM are referred to as being modal or not? For the practical purposes of translation it suffices to find out the identification factors for the two meanings of WOLLEN and SOLLEN and, once these meanings are identified, to use the two English equivalents.

For theoretical unilingual purposes it may be interesting to discuss different notions of modality as does Kiefer (1987) in 'On Defining Modality':

1. modality as an expression of possibility or necessity,
2. modality as the meaning of propositional attitudes,
3. modality as expressions of speaker's attitudes.

But, from the translational point of view, *possibility, necessity, propositional attitudes* and *speaker's attitudes* are all just factors that, if appearing in SL, have to be taken into account for producing TL renditions, irrespective of the label *modal*.

If we nevertheless deal with meanings of the modals such as "possibility" and "necessity" in terms of modality in the following sections, this is mainly for the sake of going by established terminology; it is customary among linguists to use the terms *degrees of modality* (Section 3.2.3) and *kinds of modality* (Section 3.2.4). And we will also follow the convention of referring to other expressions reflecting one or both of these dimensions as *modal expressions*.

3.2.3 Degrees of Modality

There are two extreme degrees of modality, namely, *possibility* and *necessity* (Section 3.2.3.1). 'In between' we find *probability* and *advisability* (Section 3.2.3.2). There are also tentative forms of each of these notions. Thus emerges the picture of a 'scale of modality' with various degrees.

3.2.3.1 Possibility and Necessity

In classical modal logic (see Section 3.2.4.8), two notions feature prominently: *possibility* and *necessity*. In modern linguistic literature on modality these two concepts have come to be referred to as two *degrees of modality*. As regards the modals, their degree of modality is usually fixed: CAN and KÖNNEN express possibility, MUST and MÜSSEN express necessity.[28] Therefore, the degree of modality associated with a modal is a factor that should present no difficulty in translation.

Usually the degree of modality is an invariance factor when moving from SL to TL. So MÜSSEN is rendered by MUST, and not by CAN, and KÖNNEN or DÜRFEN are rendered by CAN or MAY, and not by MUST.

Yet distinctions are not so clear-cut as might seem. It must not be overlooked that the modal degree of possibility is itself a matter of degree: Compared to CAN, COULD expresses "tentative possibility," which corresponds to KÖNNTE. And it is in this area of relativization that possibility sometimes does meet with necessity as expressed by MÜSSEN and SOLLEN. Consider the following equivalence pair:

(323) Could the old man have been Peter's grandfather?
(324) Sollte der alte Mann Peters Grossvater gewesen sein?

Nehls (1986: 86), who set up this sentence pair, comments that *könnte* could also be used here, but that commonly *sollte* sounds more idiomatic in everyday language. *Sollte*, like *müsste* and SHOULD, can be characterized as signaling tentative necessity.

On the other hand, the difference between the present tense and past tense forms (CAN/COULD) of the English modals should not be overrated. Quirk et al. (1985: 233 f.) were able to verify that some native speakers perceive little or no difference between the epistemic use of MAY and MIGHT. The authors take this to be symptomatic of a gradual assimilation of the two forms of the modals.

We would like to illustrate the observation that MAY is also interpretable in a more tentative sense by referring to the following German rendition:

(325) We may, perhaps, assume that all societies . . . (Palmer 1976: 87)
(326) Wir könnten vielleicht annehmen, dass alle Kulturkreise . . . (Palmer 1977: 90)

In certain other classes of modal expressions in English and German, the degree of modality is even less specific. Høyem (1981: 4 f.) illustrates this with reference to the construction *SEIN + ZU + infinitive*, the so-called modal infinitive:

(327) Sein Wunsch ist zu erfüllen. = (i.e., is synonymous with)
(328) Sein Wunsch kann/muss erfüllt werden.

and points out that the traditional dichotomy consisting of a KÖNNEN variant and a MÜSSEN/SOLLEN variant is by no means sufficient to capture the divers modal variations of this construction.

Other linguistic phenomena with similarly unspecified degrees of modality include

1. the gerund (Kjellmer 1980: 47 f.):
(329) Fly, fly, my lord, there is no tarrying here. (from *Julius Caesar*) =
(330) . . . no one can/should/ought to tarry here.

It should, however, be noted that not all gerund constructions are modal in the sense of expressing possibility or necessity:

(331) There is no stir or walking in the streets. (from *Julius Caesar*)

can only be understood in the sense of "No one stirs . . ."

Kjellmer (1980: 50–59) examines the various factors that suggest either one or the other reading. A detailed knowledge of these factors is, of course, essential for the translator.

2. the relative infinitives (i.e., nouns postmodified by an infinitive, examined by the same author in another publication):
(332) Here is a book to settle your dispute. =
(333) . . . that can/may/will settle . . .

Here again, Kjellmer (1975: 323 ff.) analyzes the factors determining the different readings.

In a target-language rendition, one may aim at maintaining the same degree of ambiguity as in the source language. Possible equivalents for (327), (329), and (332) are

(334) His wish is to be fulfilled.
(335) Eilt, eilt, o Herr, hier gibt es kein Verweilen.
(336) Hier ist ein Buch zur Lösung deines Problems.

As will be obvious, there are also formal correspondences between the English and German constructions: SEIN ZU → BE TO; THERE IS → ES GIBT; nominal postmodification. Minor changes are inevitable: active → passive; gerund → verbal noun; postmodification by infinitive vs. prepositional phrase—each language has its different structure acting as an obligatory change factor.

3.2.3.2 Probability and Advisability

Sollte in (324)

[324] Sollte der alte Mann Peters Grossvater gewesen sein?

was described as signaling tentative necessity. This meaning being located in between possibility and necessity, it could be identified with a degree of modality of its own—*probability*. Unlike possibility and necessity, however, probability is an exclusively epistemic concept.

It is expressed by the modals WILL and SHOULD, as well as by other modal expressions, such as PROBABLE, LIKELY, and THINK.

As sentence (333) shows, this degree of modality may be among several interpretations of ambiguous sentences containing relative infinitives. But also "probability" modals such as *sollte* and SHOULD can produce ambiguous sentences; for instance,

(337) He should be there tomorrow.
(338) Er sollte morgen dort sein.

In addition to probability, these sentences can also express tentative necessity in the root sense, which could be termed *advisability*. This term can be taken to be the root counterpart to (epistemic) probability. Tentative possibility added to the list, we end up with altogether four degrees of modality:

(1) tentative possibility (both root and epistemic)
(2) possibility (both root and epistemic)
(3) tentative necessity (root: advisability; epistemic: probability),
(4) necessity (root and epistemic).

These four categories can at best be orientation markers on a continuum or scale of degrees of modality. Remember that Høyem (1981: 4 f.) spoke of the divers modal variations as regards the modal infinitives (see Section 3.2.3.1). Note also that we put epistemic WILL as well as SHOULD into the "probability" class. The need for differentiation between the two modals becomes obvious if one follows Matthews's (1993b: 61) characterization of two possible answers to the question, "Where's Tom?"

(339) He should be at home.
(340) He will be at home.

In (339), the speaker "can't say with certainty but says what seems a reasonable prediction"; in (340), the speaker "can't say with certainty but predicts on basis of general evidence."

As well as such relatively subtle distinctions of expressions within one degree of modality, the translator must be prepared for changes between categories. As the shift from tentative possibility to tentative necessity (probability) in moving from (323) to (324) showed, revision factors such as idiomaticity can intervene and modify otherwise standard linguistic factors of equivalence. So if an interlingual scheme for the expression of degrees of modality in English and German were to be set up, it would have to integrate all relevant factors.[29]

3.2.4 Kinds of Modality

Palmer (1979a: 21) refers to different "kinds of possibility and necessity" under the general heading of "kinds of modality." This perspective suggests taking possibility and necessity as representing modality. Because these are two notions, a unitary definition of modality would have to capture the element common to them. Being dual in nature, however, they are rightly referred to as *degrees of* modality. What then are the kinds of these degrees of modality, as we could formulate more precisely?

3.2.4.1 Root and Epistemic Modality

We are already familiar with the basic kinds of modality. All along we have been speaking of "root and epistemic possibility" (see Section 3.1.2). There is an analogous distinction for "necessity." The sentence

[223] He must understand that we mean business.

was ambiguous between root and epistemic necessity.

Possibility and necessity have been considered to represent modality. We can now refer to root and epistemic possibility and necessity as *root and epistemic modality*. These two concepts are generally regarded to be the two basic kinds of modality in ordinary language.[30]

Extending our remarks made in Section 3.1.2, we can say that root modality is always action oriented, which includes inaction and nonchange as in (341).

(341) You must remain where you are.

Epistemic modality, on the other hand, represents degrees of likelihood or probability; hence, Nehls's (1986: 9; 1989: 283) terms *action oriented* and *probability oriented* for root and epistemic modality.

The various degrees of likelihood can be arranged along an epistemic scale in terms of the four degrees of modality mentioned in the previous section. With root modality, the notion of degree may be understood in terms of greater or lesser degrees of the necessity (not) to act.

Degrees and kinds of modality can be depicted as two dimensions in a modality matrix. Table 3.1 lists the English modals arranged accordingly. Of course, root and epistemic modality can also be conveyed by all kinds of other expressions (see Figure 3.20).[31] Whereas nearly all modals can be used for both kinds of modality (see Table 3.1), other expressions are confined mostly to one of them (again see Figure 3.20). This is why in their case no special identification factors are necessary for pinpointing the intended kind of modality. For the modals, such factors are necessary (see Section 3.1.3). Identifying the pertinent kind of modality in a given case is important: Instances of root and epistemic modality can in themselves be translation factors in that they may lead to different renditions. Remember our lengthy

Kinds Degrees	Root	Epistemic
Tentative possibility	COULD MIGHT	COULD MIGHT
Possibility	CAN MAY	CAN MAY
Tentative necessity	SHOULD (advisability)	SHOULD, WILL (probability)
Necessity	MUST	MUST

TABLE 3.1.
The English Modals in Terms of Kinds and Degrees of Modality

discussion in Sections 3.1.1 and 3.1.2 about the various possibilities and restrictions of rendering CAN and MAY in German, according to which meaning they represent; and about the syntactic restrictions involved when rendering epistemic modality in English (see Figure 3.7).

But the knowledge of the intended kind of modality does not always suffice for coming up with *optimum* renditions. Edmondson et al. (1977: 256) found out that in English, epistemic modality is preferably expressed by modals, whereas German prefers modal adverbs.

This is *another* good reason for rendering (251) as (257) (see Sections 3.1.5, 3.2.1.1, and 3.2.1.3):

[251] He may not be in Berlin.
[257] Vielleicht ist er nicht in Berlin.

Palmer (1979a: 35) observes that epistemic modality is "rather different from the other kinds" of modality in that it refers to the likelihood of the truth of whole sentences. Therefore a change from epistemic to any other kind of modality seems highly unlikely. Yet it does occur now and then. One of the rare cases in which epistemic modality in SL is realized as root modality in TL can be found in the bilingual *Lufthansa Bordbuch/Logbook* (4/83: 54 f.) at the end of an article on the topography of Frankfurt Airport:

(342) . . . und eine der vielen Autoverleihfirmen hat bestimmt noch einen Mietwagen für Sie.
(343) . . . and you can get a car from any of the many car rental firms.

The modal adverb BESTIMMT conveys strong probability, yet not 100 percent epistemic necessity (certainty). CAN, on the other hand, stands for 100 percent root possibility. Due to its epistemic qualification, the German version appears to be 'weaker' than the English one. This means that a radical change in kinds of modality such as that from epistemic to root cannot establish full translation equivalence (which may not have been intended in this publication anyway, as is evident from other parts of it).

There are, however, *sub*kinds of epistemic modality that are much closer to each other. Here the question of shifting from one to the other via the unmarked modals appears to be more feasible.

3.2.4.2 Epistemic Modality: Subjective and Objective

Palmer (1979a: 3) remarks that "epistemic modality in language is usually, perhaps always, what Lyons (1977: 792) calls 'subjective' in that it relates to an inference by the speaker, and is not simply concerned with 'objective' verifiability in the light of knowledge. Epistemic necessity, indicated by MUST, is thus not to be paraphrased as 'In the light of what is known it is necessarily the case that . . . ,' but by something like 'From what I know the only conclusion I can draw is . . .'"

A later remark by Palmer reveals, however, that epistemic modality in natural language is by no means 'always' subjective: He mentions cases "where the epistemic judgment is not specifically that of the speaker," and adds that "it is even possible for the speaker to disclaim his own responsibility for the judgment" (1979a: 42), giving as examples,

(344) I know this may be true.
(345) Apparently he must have done it.

These two sentences suggest the existence of objective evidence, and could thus well be said to represent objective epistemic modality.

Members of the system of objective epistemic possibility in English were mentioned in Figure 3.20: IT'S (. . .) POSSIBLE THAT . . . , THERE'S A (. . .) POSSIBILITY THAT . . . , POSSIBLY, and CONCEIVABLY.

Now remember that epistemic modality in English is preferably expressed by the modals (see the previous subsection). Unlike the expressions just referred to, the modals are not marked objectively for epistemic modality but, according to Perkins (1983: 100), are unmarked for the subjective-objective distinction (see our Figure 3.20). How does this match with Palmer's (1979a: 42) claim that "epistemic modals are normally subjective"?

We would suggest that the apparent contradiction may be resolved as follows. The English modals are *theoretically* unmarked in the sense of *being able to* convey both subjective and objective modality. But, because they are usually used by speakers expressing their own judgments through them, for all *practical* purposes they often express subjective epistemic modality.

So the decisive factors to be distinguished here are *language system* and *language use*. Do they also become relevant as translation factors?

We would say no because even if, according to language use, a German epistemic adverb is preferably rendered by an English modal, it could be one that is equally unmarked for its subjective-objective status within the epistemic system and that could yet be used subjectively in practical terms. Thus, for the sentence

[251] He may not be in Berlin.

context will make it clear if the judgment is based on subjective or objective evidence, even though MAY 'as such' is theoretically 'open' to both. Likewise, if (251) is rendered by (257)

[257] Vielleicht ist er nicht in Berlin.

this sentence can be taken to reflect epistemic modality in the same way, because the givenness of subjectivity or objectivity will similarly be(come) evident, even though VIELLEICHT 'as such' (just like PERHAPS and MAYBE, see Figure 3.20) is theoretically as unmarked as is MAY. This means that, regarding unmarked expressions, the situationally conditioned subjectification or objectification of modality is no barrier to an adequate translation, even if this involves a change of word class.

As regards expressions that are theoretically *marked* for either subjective or objective epistemic modality, it would seem that adherence to their respective status is a translational must. According to Figure 3.20, I THINK is subjective, whereas IT'S POSSIBLE THAT is objective; likewise, ICH GLAUBE is subjective, while ES IST MÖGLICH, DASS is objective; finally, IT'S LIKELY THAT is objective, and I FANCY is subjective—hence the following acceptability patterns:

(346) Ich glaube, er ist da.
(347) I think he's there.
(348) ! It's likely that he's there.

(349) Es ist möglich, dass er da ist.
(350) It's possible that he's there.
(351) !I fancy that he's there.

As the markers for nonacceptability show, expressions of the two subkinds of epistemic modality cannot be exchanged freely.

But what about rendering these subjectively and objectively marked expressions by means of modals? Sentence (346) could be translated as (352), and (349) as (353):

(352) He will be there.
(353) He may be there.

If one takes the modals to be subjective, as Palmer does, there is a clash between the objectivity of (349) and the subjectivity of (353), whereas (346) and (352) are in conformity with each other.

If, on the other hand, as Perkins suggests, the modals are unmarked for the subjective-objective distinction, (352) will be less subjective, and (353) will be less objective than their respective German source sentences.

Will the hearer take the modals-in-use or the modals-in-context to be versatile enough to adapt to the subjectivity of (346) and the objectivity of (349) in a way similar to that suggested previously for (251)?

We are well aware that when talking about 'natural equivalents' in Section 3.2.1.2, we accepted variation of renditions within each subcategory of possibility where necessary, but decidedly argued for remaining within the scope of that subcategory itself. It is true that expressions marked for subjective or objective epistemic modality all belong to a subcategory different from one containing expressions that are unmarked in this respect. So, strictly speaking, (352) and (353) are ruled out as renditions for (346) and (349). But, as will have become obvious at several points in this book, whenever there was good reason for differentiating a translation rule, we would not hesitate to incorporate it as a revision factor modifying that general rule.

This applies here, too. The modals being more idiomatic for expressing epistemic modality in English, their usability for both subjective and objective modality makes them universal exponents of epistemic modality.

3.2.4.3 Root Modality: Deontic and Dynamic

Having so far dealt with variants of epistemic modality, we will now turn to several subkinds of root modality. Palmer (1979a: 35) points out that "epistemic modality is rather different from the other kinds. It is the modality of propositions as opposed to the modality of events . . . " In other words, whereas epistemic modality is concerned with a whole proposition or sentence being possibly, probably, or necessarily true, other kinds of modality— that is, the root ones—have to do with actions being possible, advisable, or necessary (for someone to perform).

This is what the root kinds have in common. But there are also factors distinguishing them. They have to do with what makes an event possible, advisable, or necessary. If this is a person, root modality manifests as permission, advisability, obligation, and prohibition. Such agent-instigated modality is called *deontic modality*. For all other cases, Palmer (1979a: 3) uses the term *dynamic modality*. Both these subkinds of root modality will now be discussed with respect to variants of their own.

3.2.4.4 Deontic Modality: Subjective and Objective

Deontic modality, we just said, includes the meanings of permission, advisability, and obligation. It is modality conditioned by the will of people.

Palmer (1979a: 58) further specifies this subkind of root modality by saying, "the kind of modality that we call deontic is basically performative. By uttering a modal a speaker may actually *give* permission (MAY, CAN), and *make* a promise or threat (SHALL) or *lay* an obligation (MUST)" (italics ours). Examples are the use of

(354) You may/can go now. (permission)
(355) You shall have it. (promise)
(356) You must be more careful. (obligation)
(357) You should take this one. (suggestion)
(358) I will come by tomorrow. (promise)

So the special feature about these sentences is that a speaker using them does not merely state the objective existence of a permission, obligation, and so forth, but subjectively creates it for the hearer (see Section 4.1). MAY, however, may also be used for *asking* permission:

(359) May I come in?

Palmer (1979a: 35) comments, "The permission then relates to the hearer and not the speaker." This is why, he says, he uses the term *discourse oriented* rather than *speaker oriented*.

It seems, however, that Palmer's (1979a: 39) categorical statement that "with deontic modality the speaker performatively creates the possibility or necessity for the coming into reality of the conceptual state of affairs" needs some relativization: Permission, obligation, and so on, cannot only be verbally created, but—just like possibility and necessity—also stated; for example,

(360) Aunt Mildred just said that Peter may leave now.

This means that deontic modality need not be discourse oriented, subjectively created, but can also be objectively stated or reported (as can objective epistemic modality, see Section 3.2.4.2).

Palmer (1979a: 106) himself mentions the possibility of a distinction being drawn "between 'subjective' and 'objective' deontic modality. . . . While MUST might sometimes be subjective, HAVE (GOT) TO would always be objective, but both would be deontic in that some kind of deontic necessity was involved."

This means that deontic necessity, that is, obligation, can be either stated or created by the speaker. It must be emphasized that both these acts are actually different uses of deontic modality. This is why we distinguish deontic modality as the semantic concept of permission, obligation, and so on, as such, from pragmatically using it in the speech acts of stating and creating it. The latter aspect will be further dealt with in our pragmatics chapter (Section 4.1).

3.2.4.5 Dynamic Modality: Subject Oriented and Circumstantial

Palmer (1979a: 3) uses the term *dynamic modality* to refer to those events that are not conditioned deontically. He gives examples such as

(361) He's one of the senior referees in the league, fairly strict disciplinarian, can handle games of this nature. (p. 73)
(362) The only way you can learn it is to think logically. (p. 72)

Palmer uses the terms *subject oriented* and *circumstantial* for these examples, respectively. With subject-oriented modality, the enabling or necessitat-

ing circumstances are "characteristics of the subject," whereas with circumstantial modality they are "circumstances in general" (p. 39).

Because "no very clear distinction can be made between what one is
able to do and what it is possible for one to do" (p. 3), dynamic modality
will cover exactly what was referred to by Leech and Coates (1980: 83 f.)
and, in a modified way, by Coates (1983: 92 f.), as the *gradient of inherency*
(see Section 3.1.4.2).

Coates (1983: 14) defines this gradient as "the continuum of meaning
extended from the core of 'ability' to the periphery of 'possibility,' as found
in CAN."

Now, even though it is fairly uncontroversial that CAN indeed covers
these meaning areas, there seems to be some disagreement among linguists
as to whether the CAN of "ability" actually deserves to be called *modal*.
Perkins (1983: 30 f.) gives a brief survey of the different views, which we
would like to comment upon.

Steele (1975: 38) does not grant CAN in

(363) She can swim a mile in two minutes.

the status of modality because it does not "indicate the possibility of the
situation which the sentence describes, but rather the potential . . . of the
subject of the sentence." Perkins's (1983: 30) immediate conclusion that "for
Steele, then, CAN is a root modal only when it conveys permission" is
surprising, because Steele contrasts "the potential . . . of the subject of the
sentence" (which can be equated with "ability") with "the possibility of the
situation which the sentence describes." Thus also "possibility," not just
"permission," may be taken to be looked upon as modal by Steele.

This view is, however, apt to lead to difficulties. If "possibility" is defined as modal, whereas "ability" is not, then what about the gradient connecting these two notions? If this gradient is a *continuum* (Coates 1983: 14),
where do we mark the 'end' of modality?

An alternative view would regard the entire gradient of inherency as
nonmodal. This is congruent with Boyd and Thorne's (1969: 71) decision to
consider CAN to be modal "only when it is an alternative form for MAY"
conveying permission. But then the same 'demarcation' problem arises
within the gradient of restriction; that is, between "possibility" and "permission."

Collins (1974: 154) also includes ability among the exponents of root
modality. But it would be wrong to assume that ability, *if* considered to be
modal at all, is unanimously looked upon as representing *root* modality:

Antinucci and Parisi (1971: 38) refer to the use of CAN in

(364) John can swim.

as "the so-called 'ability' sense," for which, along with another one, they
"tentatively suggest that these are instances of epistemic CAN . . . ," because

intrinsic properties of the subject "cause . . . the speaker not be bound not to believe that . . ."

Perkins sums up this bewildering picture of opinions. For him, his survey "reveals a rather puzzling situation: CAN in its 'ability' sense has been regarded by various linguists within the space of a few years exclusively as a root modal, exclusively as an epistemic modal, and as not a modal at all!" (1983: 30 f.).

Now let us pause for a moment and consider the implications of this controversy for the translator. As we know from our discussion of Figures 3.10, 3.12, and 3.13, the knowledge that CAN is used in the ability sense is enough for immediately coming up with KÖNNEN as a rendition.

As Figure 3.17 shows, also the gradient extending from ability to possibility does not present any problem, because both these meanings and all intermediate points are covered by KÖNNEN. Moreover, negation of ability and possibility (*cannot, can't*) has a straightforward rendition; namely, *kann nicht*. Finally, even epistemic *can't* may be rendered by *kann nicht* (see Figure 3.19).

What all this suggests is that, as far as the translator is concerned, the whole topic of whether a given use of a modal is to be classified as "modal" or not is of no relevance for one's job. As long as—or better, as soon as—one knows which meaning is intended, one can translate.

3.2.4.6 Volitive Modality

For Palmer (1979a: 35), "the subject-oriented modals refer to the ability or willingness of the subject of the sentence . . . " Accordingly, the notion of ability was dealt with in the previous section on subject orientation.

It is true that willingness also originates in the subject of the sentence;

(365) Ian needed somewhere to stay and I said, 'Why don't you go and see if Martin will let you stay?'

Palmer (1979a: 24) comments that "WILL here indicates the agreement, willingness or 'volition' of the subject . . . "

At the same time, the meaning of "volition" or "will" is an integral part of another kind of modality. In Section 3.2.4.4 we introduced deontic modality as conditioned by the will of people. Permission or obligation express the will of the 'permittor' or 'obligator' who is characteristically *not* identical with the subject of the sentence, such as in

(366) You may/must go to London tomorrow.

The concept of will thus has its share in subject-oriented as well as in deontic modality and is not necessarily identified with the subject of a sentence. Therefore it seems to be justified not to confine "the WILL of willingness"

(Palmer 1979a: 11) to either of these two kinds of modality, but to allow it a category of its own—*volitive modality.*

As with ability, however, so with will(ingness) there arises the question of whether it is to be considered modal at all. In the case of "will" expressed by WILL, one will be more inclined to grant it that status, because WILL is a modal. If will is expressed by the lexical verb WANT TO, one may be hesitant to call it modal, unless

- will is equally considered to be a modal category along with possibility, necessity, and so forth;
- WANT TO, being the rendition of WOLLEN, preserves its modal quality through English (see Section 3.2.2).

But as our discussion near the end of the last subsection suggests, for the translator it does not really matter if expressions are called *modal,* as long as their meaning is clear. In the case of WILL this means that as long as it is evident whether this expression is used in, say, the epistemic or the volitive sense, this knowledge will suffice for coming up with the appropriate renditions:

(367) Your purse will be in the cupboard.
(368) Dein Portemonnaie wird im Schrank sein.

(369) He will absolutely not do it.
(370) Er will es partout nicht machen.

Of course, in linguistic publications on WILL, the traditional distinction is made between "pure" and "modal future," the former indicating courses of future action that are independent of human will (as in (371)), the latter indicating those that are not (as in (372)).

(371) My babe-in-arms will be fifty-nine on my eighty-ninth birthday . . .
(372) Well, I'll ring you tonight sometime. (Palmer 1979a: 112, 109)

Again, realizing that either "pure future" or "volition" is involved, the translator can translate—without any reference to the term *modal*:

(373) Mein Baby hier in meinen Armen wird an meinem 89. Geburtstag 59 sein.
(374) Also, ich ruf dich heut' abend mal an.

On the other hand, the advantage of still continuing to describe volition as modal is that in this way "pure future" can be juxtaposed to "modal future." For such purposes of easy reference by means of established terms, the expression *modal* is useful. This applies also to the other kinds of modality (to be) presented in the preceding and the following sections.

3.2.4.7 Existential and Sporadic Modality

CAN can be used in a sense that has to do with quantification, as in

(375) She can be very charming.
(376) Frenchmen can be tall.

Sentence (375) means that she *sometimes* is very charming, (376) means that *some* Frenchmen are tall.

The term *existential modality*, chosen by Palmer (1979a: 152), seems to fit especially the second example, and the more common term *sporadic modality* seems to be more appropriate for the first.

As with many other instances of CAN, this use also presents no problem to translation, because KÖNNEN may be used in just the same way:

(377) Sie kann sehr charmant sein.
(378) Franzosen können gross sein.

Palmer (1979a: 153 ff.) also quotes examples containing MAY and MUST. These may be rendered by KÖNNEN and MÜSSEN.

Before finishing our survey of the more common kinds of modality in Section 3.2.4.9, we will briefly touch upon one kind that is equally popular, although not so much in natural language as in logic: *alethic modality*.

3.2.4.8 Alethic Modality

When we started Section 3.2.3.1 with the remark that *possibility* and *necessity* feature prominently in classical modal logic, what was alluded to is *alethic modality*, which is expressed in sentences like the following:[32]

(379) Alfred is a bachelor, so he must be unmarried.

Because "unmarried" is one of the semantic features of the noun *bachelor*, the strength of MUST in (379) is that of absolute logical inclusion.

It is often pointed out by linguists that the alethic use of the modals is not very typical of everyday language. Therefore, it will suffice to say that, for translation, this kind of modality is easy to handle by simply taking MÜSSEN as an equivalent for MUST.

(380) Alfred ist Junggeselle, also muss er unverheiratet sein.

There is also alethic modality of possibility, which is as unproblematic as that of necessity: MAY → KÖNNEN.

3.2.4.9 Other Kinds of Modality

Palmer (1979a: 151) interprets examples of the present tense negative form of CAN such as

(381) We cannot go on fining and levying our people for the benefit of farmers, whether rich or poor, inefficient farmers in the Market.

as describing situations that are unreasonable and unacceptable for the speaker, even though they are not strictly impossible. He is inclined to "treat the CAN forms as essentially dynamic but with the meaning of reasonable rather than actual possibility" (1979a: 152). He seems to consider this use special enough to deserve a name of its own: *rational modality*.

Because, semantically speaking, CAN is here essentially used in the root-possibility sense, all that was said about the translation of this sense into German is also applicable to rational modality. To convey the rational character of corresponding KÖNNEN sentences, it is possible to use in addition different modal particles (see Section 6.3.9), according to the respective flavor of emphasis:

(382) Wir können doch nicht . . .
(383) Wir können eigentlich nicht . . .
(384) Wir können wirklich nicht . . .

- DOCH signals rejection, indicating that the action would run counter to accepted standards of rationality, and is a strong appeal to the hearer not to act in the said manner.
- EIGENTLICH is a more modest marker hinting at the inadvisability of the action.
- WIRKLICH gives the action under evaluation a touch of virtual impossibility that is attempted to be impressed upon the hearer.

The three *modal particles* DOCH, EIGENTLICH, and WIRKLICH all add to rational modality (itself being an aspect of circumstantial or subject-oriented dynamic modality) a different flavor of what Bublitz (1978) calls *emotive modality*. This kind of modality is used by the speaker for expressing "his assumptions and attitudes relating to the mutually presupposed knowledge of the communication partners, their expectations, emotions, and social relationships to each other" (1978: 7 f., our translation).

It is commonly held that English lacks modal particles for the expression of emotive modality. But, because SHOULD is sometimes "found after adjectives indicating some kind of emotion . . ." (Standwell 1979: 259) it is a good candidate for expressing this kind of modality:

(385) I'm surprised that he should resign.
(386) I'm surprised that he has resigned.

The utterance of each of these sentences indicates factuality of resignation. But Quirk et al. (1972: 784) note that "there is still a difference of feeling" between them: "in the first, it is the 'very idea' of resignation that surprises; in the second, it is the resignation itself, as an assumed fact." The two sentences differ only in the presence of 'putative' SHOULD evoking a different feeling, so this use of the modal may well be said to express emotive modality.

Furthermore, the notion of 'very idea' of a fact mentioned by Quirk et al. correlates with what Nehls (1989: 287) considers to be "a pensive mood on the part of the speaker or writer" as expressed by putative SHOULD. Since he proposes this characteristic to be shared by the German modal particle EIGENTLICH, both expressions seem to be fitting translation equivalents of each other. Thus, sentence (385) could be rendered by (387):

(387) Ich bin eigentlich erstaunt darüber, dass er zurückgetreten ist.

EIGENTLICH may be seen as a suitable rendition for putative SHOULD following constructions involving adjectives (APPROPRIATE, FITTING, FORTUNATE, PROPER), deverbal adjectives (ADMIRABLE, COMMENDABLE, REMARKABLE), and participles (PLEASING, SURPRISING) listed by Quirk et al. (1972: 825 f.); for example,

(388) It is appropriate that he should get the post.
(389) Es ist eigentlich angemessen, dass er den Posten bekommt.

Having added rational and emotive modality to our modality list let us ask what more can there be to it. There are definitely further possibilities if one attempts to subdivide kinds of modality.

Not surprisingly, the further one enters into the subkinds of modalities, the more subtle the distinctions between them become. Consider, for instance, Matthews's (1993b: 56) term *pithanotic*, chosen "for the probability of the truth of p[roposition] holding." He characterizes

(390) He'll be at home.

as "'epistemically' uncertain and 'pithanotically' probable" (1993b: 64, 66) and adds: "One is tempted to infer that modals permit as many interpretations as we can think of parameters of modality" (1993b: 56). This would mean that each (sub)kind of modality has at least one modal representing it. But there is proof to the contrary. Bailey (1980) distinguishes *modalities made with modals* (p. 138) from *timeless stative/narrative modality* (p. 114), *passive modality* (p. 118), *progressive modality, DO modality, past modalities* (p. 128), *past-posterior modalities* (p. 130), and *futuritive modalities* (p. 131). Here, dimensions of tense, aspect, and voice are regarded as modal, taking the notion of modality far beyond the concepts of possibility, necessity, and volition discussed so far. The impression is created that in linguistics, the term *modality* could be freely used to denote just about any variation of *any*thing, in much the same way as in colloquial German, *Modalität* is commonly understood as "Art und Weise."

If modality is understood in such broad terms it is legitimate to ask what is the value of reference to modality.

3.2.4.10 Reference to Modality and Its Kinds

In the previous nine sections we introduced various kinds of modality. This introductory survey was neither intended to be exhaustive nor was it our ambition to compare different conceptions of the modal system, let alone different names for the various kinds of modality proposed by different linguists.

What remains is a critical reevaluation of the term *modal(ity)* itself, as to its usefulness for the translator.

In Section 3.2.4.5, we saw that CAN in its meaning of "ability" was not unanimously granted the status of modality. We ignored this controversy with the remark that the question about meanings being modal or not is of no relevance for the translator because all one need know to translate is the specific meaning intended in a given case.

Such specific meanings include "ability," "probability," "objective epistemic necessity," "subjective deontic possibility," "circumstantial dynamic necessity," and "subject-oriented dynamic possibility," to mention just a few.

As we said in Section 3.2.3.1, possibility and necessity are degrees of modality. We added that, for the modals, the degree is usually fixed: MUST denotes necessity; CAN, possibility, and so forth. Therefore, replacing "necessity" and "possibility" in these meanings by "modality" will lead to unmistakable semantic characterizations such as these: In certain contexts, MUST expresses "objective epistemic modality," in others "circumstantial dynamic modality"; sometimes CAN denotes "subjective deontic modality," sometimes "subject-oriented dynamic modality."

Here, the individual modals make it clear which degree of modality is meant in each case. So, provided a pertinent modal is also mentioned, there is no harm in using the term *modality*.

If no modal is mentioned, reference to modality can still make sense, such as in statements that are applicable to *all* degrees of a specific kind of modality; see the following quotations from several linguists (italics ours):

- "gradience . . . is an essential feature of *root modality*" (Coates 1983: 21);
- "*epistemic modality* is rather different from the other kinds. It is the modality of propositions as opposed to the modality of events . . ." (Palmer 1979a: 35);
- "Lyons's distinction between *subjective* and *objective epistemic modality* is roughly that in the former case an uncertainty exists in the speaker's own mind about a given state of affairs, whereas in the latter case the unverifiability is due to the nature of the state of affairs itself" (Perkins 1983: 24, n. 14).

So, for general statements such as these, *modality* is a welcome cover term for an economic metalanguage, obviating the enumeration of all degrees of modality in each case.

We can sum up our findings as follows:

- For determining the meaning of a modal in a given case, use of the term *modality* is not a necessary identification factor.
- For stating general characteristics shared by various meanings, *modality* can be a useful abstract term.
- For "purposes of easy reference by means of established terms" (Section 3.2.4.6), the expression *modality* is useful (see also Section 3.2.2).

3.2.5 Modes of Appearance of Modality

Following the discussion of so many kinds of modality, the headings of the following subsections might suggest the continuation of this topic. But the terms *covert* and *implicit modality* together with their counterparts *overt* and *explicit modality* refer to modes of appearance of modality rather than to kinds of modality. The common element of covert and implicit modality is the phenomenon of one modal meaning being contained in another (modal) meaning.

3.2.5.1 Overt and Covert Modality

When we dealt with degrees of semantic identity of the modals and their cognates in Section 3.2.1.1, we found that the modals are the most general modal expressions. They are unmarked for various dimensions, where other expressions are more or less marked:

- MAY is completely unmarked, usable for any kind of possibility;
- MAYBE is marked for epistemic possibility;
- THERE'S A POSSIBILITY THAT is further marked for expressing objective epistemic possibility, and so on.

This relative progressive markedness gives rise to a gradient ranging from the most unspecific to the most specific modal expressions.

There is also a gradient in terms of formal similarity of form and meaning that works just the other way round: POSSIBILITY reflects the meaning of "possibility" most directly, next come POSSIBLE and POSSIBLY, whose forms still show some resemblance to their meaning, and only then come CAN and MAY.

On a third level of consideration it could be said that CAN and MAY express "possibility" most directly or obviously, whereas more specific or marked modal expressions such as TONNAGE express this meaning in a more indirect or covert way. If you look up TONNAGE in a dictionary you may find as its German equivalent "Ladungsfähigkeit" or "Tragfähigkeit (eines Schiffes)." Because "Fähigkeit" is expressed by KÖNNEN, TONNAGE could be defined as "die Ladung, die ein Schiff aufnehmen kann." TONNAGE thus turns out to be a highly special form of KÖNNEN or "possibility/ability/capacity," which meanings could be said to be 'included' in that of TONNAGE. This semantic inclusion of the more unspecific modal meaning in the specific one, a hyponymy relation, may be referred to as *covert unspecific modality*. The unspecific meaning "possibility" is covert in TONNAGE, but overt in POSSIBILITY.

Covertness of unspecific meanings can be an important translation factor. Let us take the example of an expression similarly specific as TONNAGE, this time reflecting the modal meaning "obligation": the German legal expression BRINGSCHULD. The nonexistence of a corresponding English term acts as an obligatory change factor. Sykes (1989: 36) suggests the following periphrasis: "a debt that must be discharged on the creditor's premises." This translation contains the modal MUST typically associated with the more unspecific meaning "obligation," thus rendering modality more overt. Vice versa, if Sykes's English expression were to be translated into German, skipping the modal and using BRINGSCHULD would amount to making modality more covert. The expert reader of German legal texts can be expected to know the modal character ("necessity," "obligation") of the compact expression BRINGSCHULD. This knowledge would act as a compensation factor for the lessened obviousness and increased covertness of modality.

3.2.5.2 Explicit and Implicit Modality

There is a second kind of meaning inclusion, which differs from covert modality in that the expressions in question seem to have no association with modality. A case in point is the noun ACTION. This word definitely does not refer to modality in the sense of "possibility," "necessity," or "volition." Yet any action, it could be argued, presupposes its possibility. We thus come to find that modality can also be traced within expressions that, taken at face value, seem to be completely devoid of modality. We would like to refer to this phenomenon as *implicit modality*, in contrast to *explicit modality* covering the gradient between overt and covert modality, see the schema in Figure 3.21.

Another example of implicit modality is the sign

(391) English spoken.

in shop windows. You may enter such a shop without hearing a single English word. The reason is that (391) is the elliptical version not of (392), but of (393):

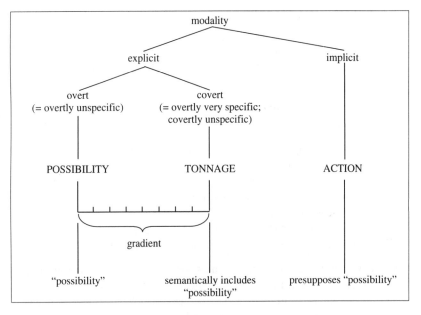

FIGURE 3.21.
Modes of Appearance of Modality

(392) Here English is (being) spoken.
(393) Here English can be spoken.

The German equivalents of (391) are (394) and (395):

(394) Hier wird Deutsch gesprochen.
(395) Hier spricht man Deutsch.

Sentence (394) formally corresponds to (392), and in this respect deviates from (391), but it shares with the latter sentence the factor of modality being implicit.

Note that both the word ACTION and sentence (391) are translated without reference to modality. But there is an important difference: In ACTION and its rendition HANDLUNG, modality (i.e., possibility) is only presupposed and does not surface as a criterial feature of meaning. In (391), (394), and (395), however, the implicit assertion of modality (i.e., ability in the explicit sense of (393)) can be said to be the essential purpose of statement. So here modality is, strictly speaking, not a translation factor, but one that is crucial for correctly understanding the implicit import of the SL and TL sentences (see sentence (625) in Section 4.3.1).

3.2.5.3 Interrelation of Modalities

All cases of explicit and implicit modality discussed so far were related to individual words the meaning of which contained some (more abstract) modal meaning. There are also cases of pairs of words the modal meanings of which are interrelated. Consider the following example:

(396) You must go immediately.
(397) You can go immediately.

MUST in (396) expresses necessity, yet it assumes possibility as expressed by CAN in (397). So the overall semantic modal structure of (396) is that of two modalities being interrelated.

The notion of modal interrelation is especially helpful in analyzing otherwise perplexing cases of translation equivalence. Take, for example, the bilingual information sheet found distributed in a guest room of Frankfurt Intercontinental Hotel in 1983. It contains the following sentences:

(398) Erwarten Sie einen Anruf? Dann sagen Sie bitte in der Telefonzentrale Bescheid, wohin Ihr Anruf weitergeleitet werden soll.
(399) Expecting a phone call? Please advise the telephone operator where your call can be transferred to.

Usually one would say that SOLLEN represents necessity or obligation, whereas CAN has the meaning of possibility. Moreover, no tentativity is involved connecting necessity and possibility, as was the case with (323) and (324) discussed in Section 3.2.3.1. How then can the two preceding sentences be said to be translation equivalents?

What appears to be a semantic discrepancy between the two versions may be resolved by considering the dependence of one modality upon the other. The possibility of a transfer is a necessary condition for requesting or ordering the transfer. If something *is to* (SOLLEN) be transferred, it is necessary that it *can* be transferred. Thus the English version is semantically contained in the German one. The overall unity of the two modalities as depicted in Figure 3.22 explains the equivalence of the two sentences (see further Section 4.1.2). The examples discussed so far represented one or two modals expressing different interrelated degrees of modality. There is also the possibility of kinds of modality being interrelated.

As we know, a modal may be used to express root as well as epistemic modality. When we say

[234] Er kann gehen.

we can mean (400) as well as (231):

(400) He has permission—possibility—ability to go. (root)
[231] Perhaps he goes. (epistemic)

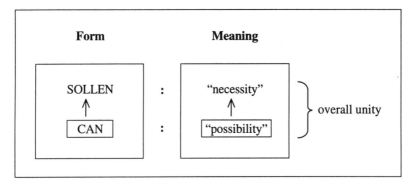

FIGURE 3.22.
Interlingual Interrelation of Two Modalities

Just as MUST in (396) was based on CAN in (397), we can say that the 50 percent probability of 'his' coming expressed by PERHAPS in (231) is based upon (the assumption of) 'his' being able to come expressed in (400).

How do we reword in English this interrelation of root and epistemic modality represented by the single modal KÖNNEN in (234)? There seems to be a choice between CAN and MAY:

(401) He can go.
[229] He may go.

But CAN in (401), being confined to root modality, does not offer the possibility of extending the interpretation to epistemic possibility.

MAY in (229), on the other hand, excludes the meaning "ability," thus narrowing down the whole range of the two gradients of meaning encompassed by KÖNNEN (see Figure 3.18 and sentence (400)). Also, MAY is confined to more formal use within the remaining area of root modality (see Section 3.1.2).

Yet MAY, like KÖNNEN, permits the meaning extension from (400) to (231), which is our point of focus here. So we can say that (234) is best rendered by (229) in this respect.

Note that, like CAN, so DÜRFEN is confined to expressing root modality:

[233] Er darf gehen.

This gives rise to the translation picture in Figure 3.23, the two pairs of modals just mentioned being linked by arrows.

The reason why KÖNNEN and CAN are listed in one column is their usual correspondence; that is, their distinction from DÜRFEN and MAY in terms of formality (see Section 3.1.2). As we have just seen, the requirement

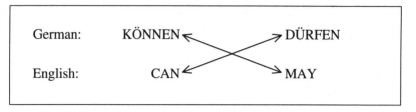

FIGURE 3.23.
Modals Linked by Root-epistemic Extension

of root-epistemic extension acts as a revision factor for the usual pattern of correspondences, correlating KÖNNEN and MAY.

As indicated by the bidirectional arrows, this special correspondence of KÖNNEN and MAY is valid for both translation directions. For the translation of MAY preserving both root and epistemic modality in German, we refer back to our discussion of sentences (229)–(237) in Section 3.1.4.3.

3.2.5.4 Interrelation of Modality and Nonmodality

In the first part of the previous subsection we dealt with the meaning of one modal being contained within the meaning of another modal in terms of interrelation of modalities. Interlingual interrelation of modalities was then accepted as a sufficient condition of (partial) translation equivalence.

But how do we go about interrelations of meaning in which only one of two expressions shows modality? Let us approach this question by having another look at two sentences we are already familiar with:

[342] . . . und eine der vielen Autoverleihfirmen hat bestimmt noch einen Mietwagen für Sie.
[343] . . . and you can get a car from any of the many car rental firms.

In Section 3.2.4.1 we pointed out the nonequivalence of these sentences in terms of kinds of modality.

To answer our initial question, let us now delete epistemic BESTIMMT in (342); the result is

(402) . . . und eine der vielen Autoverleihfirmen hat noch einen Mietwagen für Sie.

Sentence (343) contains root CAN, but (402) shows no modality. Yet both sentences are felt to be connected somehow. How can this be explained?

Neglecting the difference in quantifiers—*eine* being just one, *any* meaning whichever one—we can simply say that only if a car rental firm *has* a car *can* the hearer get a car. So the German version (402) is a necessary condition for the proposition expressed by the English one, that is, (343). In other words, both sentences are interrelated even though (402) is not modal at all. But (343) being modal, this kind of interrelation also deserves our attention. It represents nonmodality (HAVE) as the basis of modality (CAN). In this sense (402) could be said to be the *modal source* of (343). This factor takes us one step further in our interlingual exploration of modality. It becomes our next point of consideration.

3.2.6 Modal Source and Modal Goal

Modality manifests in different degrees, kinds, and modes of appearance. Having dealt with these aspects in the previous three sections, we just came across another facet of modality—*modal source*. It centers around a cluster of topics that themselves are important translation factors. Let us first systematically approach the concept of modal source in its explicit and implicit modes of existence.

3.2.6.1 Explicit and Implicit Modal Source

In Section 3.2.1.2 we set up the standard translation formula *SL modal → TL modal*. In the section following we considered past tense as an obligatory revision factor overruling this standard formula. We thus have (310) → (311), but (314) → (316):

[310] Er darf nach Hause gehen.
[311] He may go home.

[314] Er durfte nach Hause gehen.
[315] !He might go home.
[316] He was permitted to go home.

Even though no modal, the suppletive BE PERMITTED TO conforms to the syntactic pattern of MAY; so does BE ALLOWED TO; for example,

$$(403) \text{ He } \left\{ \begin{array}{l} \text{may} \\ \text{was permitted to} \\ \text{was allowed to} \end{array} \right\} \text{ go home.}$$

Other expressions of deontic possibility show different syntactic patterns, such as in the following sentences:

(404) It was permitted/permissible for him to go home.
(405) Permission was/had been granted for him to go home.

Even so, these sentences contain the same semantic elements as the group of sentences in (403): *he*, (reference to) *permission*, and *go home*. Still other modal expressions are different in this respect; for instance,

(406) I permitted/allowed/authorized him to go home.

Here the 'permittor' *I* is also expressed. Now consider the following series of renditions for (314):

[314] Er durfte nach Hause gehen.
[316] He was permitted to go home.
[404] It was permitted/permissible for him to go home.
[406] I permitted/allowed/authorized him to go home.

Again we can see a gradient of deviance from the original in terms of the characteristics of each expression just given.

As in (406), so too in (316) and (404), there must have been someone who in fact granted permission. It may even have been the same person; but the *mention* of this permittor makes (406) so decidedly different from the other two English renditions that we would not grant the expression *I permitted . . .* the status of a normal suppletive for the past tense of MAY. Therefore (406) cannot be looked upon as a standard rendition of (314).

Yet even dictionaries list pairs of equivalents showing the structures of (406) and (314). Consider the following one taken from Wildhagen and Héraucourt (1972: 429) where the permittor appears in the German version:

(407) Meine Mittel/Verhältnisse erlauben das nicht.
(408) I cannot afford it.

The reason why these two sentences may legitimately be regarded as equivalents is that the permittor explicitly expressed in (407) is implicitly contained in the semantics of AFFORD, which acts as a compensation factor.

This ultimate presence of the permittor in both sentences is not paralleled in the relationship of (314) and (406). It is true that (314) presupposes that someone granted permission, but this does not warrant the inference that it was the speaker. Therefore, (406) contains more information and implies (314) but not vice versa. This is why the two sentences cannot be said to be on a par with each other or to be translation equivalents.

As will have been noticed, the concept of 'permittor' is already a familiar one:

• As regards sentences (215)–(219) containing MAY, Coates (1983: 143) comments on their "permitting factors." In fact, the very existence of gradience discussed in connection with these sentences is a matter of different

kinds of permitting factors, ranging from those actually granting permission to those creating a possibility (see Section 3.1.4.2).
• As regards sentence (220), Leech and Coates (1980: 84) mentioned divers "enabling factors." Different interpretations of this one sentence along the gradient of inherency hinge upon different enabling factors.

Similarly, for sentences containing MUST, *obliging factors* could be postulated. These factors constitute the grounds of obligation. For both kinds of factors, Calbert (1975: 22) uses the term *source of obligation or possibility*. In a wider sense, enabling, obliging, or necessitating factors existing for all kinds of possibilities and necessities may be referred to as *modal sources*.

3.2.6.2 Source and Goal Orientation

The term *modal source* seems to be particularly appropriate, as the following sentence illustrates:

(409) Von mir aus kannst du gehen.

The preposition *von . . . aus*, taken literally, indeed denotes movement originating in a source. At the same time, (409) shows that the modal source (or source of modality) need not be realized as sentence subject, as was the case in

[406] I permitted/allowed/authorized him to go home.

It must be emphasized, though, that sentences containing modals do not necessarily show an explicit modal source—see (310), (311), (314), and the majority of the other sentences with modals discussed so far in this book.

In contrast, modal lexical verbs such as PERMIT, AUTHORIZE, and ERLAUBEN, when used in active sentences, *require* the modal source as their subject; see (406) and (407).

Following Calbert (1975: 24 ff.), we will refer to the latter group as expressing *source-oriented modality* and to the former one as expressing *goal-oriented modality*. The term *modal goal* denotes the person who is (not) permitted or obliged to perform the action referred to, like *he* in

[311] He may go home.

Note that pairs of source- and goal-oriented sentences partially correspond to each other, see (311) and

(410) I permit him to go home.

As was explained already, an implicative relation strictly holds only between the source-oriented sentence and the goal-oriented sentence, not vice versa.

Hence, translations from SL source-oriented sentences to TL goal-oriented sentences are legitimate only if the loss of explicit modal source is somehow compensated for, as was the case in the move from (407) to (408). The important point to remember is that modals are typically goal oriented, whereas modal full verbs, used actively, are source oriented. Exceptions are WOLLEN and root MÖGEN, whose subjects represent modal sources, as in

(411) Ich will dorthin gehen.
(412) Ich möchte jetzt baden.

The schema in Figure 3.24 illustrates this point. On the left-hand side you find source-oriented expressions with x representing the modal source, and y the modal goal, on the right-hand side are listed the goal-oriented modals. English has similar correlations, as can be seen in Figure 3.25.

Some of the English modals can be both source and goal oriented; for example,

(413) I will go there. (source oriented)
(414) You will apologize immediately. (goal oriented)

The latter sentence is based on the source-oriented sentence

(415) I want you to apologize immediately.

Similar relations hold for SHALL:

(416) I shall go there tomorrow. (source oriented)
(417) You shall do as I want. (goal oriented)

The most extreme case of modal 'double orientation' is CAN. As listed in Figure 3.25, y *can* is usually goal oriented, its corresponding source orientation being provided by expressions such as x *enables* or x *allows*. Usually modal source and modal goal, that is, x and y, are distinct entities, as in

Source orientation	Goal orientation
x verpflichtet y zu ...	y muß ...
x fordert y auf zu ...	y soll ...
x ermöglicht y zu ...	y kann ...
x erlaubt y zu ...	y darf ...
x will ...	
x mag ...	

FIGURE 3.24.
Source- and Goal-oriented Modality in German

Source orientation	**Goal orientation**
x obliges y to...	y must...
x enables y to...	y can...
x permits y to...	y may...

FIGURE 3.25.
Source- and Goal-oriented Modality in English

(418) *He* can go home.
[410] *I* permit him to go home.

But now consider the following sentence:

[149] Money can't buy everything.

If this sentence were to be traced back to its modal source, we would not reach beyond *money*:

(419) Money does not allow (you) to buy everything.

True, *money* could be said to be the modal source in (419), assuming the role of modal goal in (149). But, because it essentially denotes the same 'permittor' in both cases, it may be said that CAN in (149) is both source and goal oriented.

So (419) and (149) differ from those preceding sentence pairs containing WILL and SHALL ((413) and (414), (416) and 417)), which, even though equally differing in modal orientation, do not each show one identical sentence subject.

Also the German schema is more flexible than Figure 3.24 suggests; for instance,

(420) Sie wollen die Unterlagen unverzüglich einreichen.

Such use, even though restricted to administrative language, seems to be source oriented but is not; the real source-oriented basis of (420) is

(421) Wir wollen, dass Sie die Unterlagen unverzüglich einreichen.

For this reason, the purely source-oriented WANT, which can be used only in the sense of (421), is ruled out as a rendition for WOLLEN in (420):

(422) !You want to hand in the documents immediately.
(423) You are hereby urged to hand in the documents immediately.

This shows that what really counts in translation is not overt source or goal orientation, but the true covert semantic relationships.

3.2.6.3 Modal Perspectives

In the previous subsection we said that source-oriented sentences such as (410) imply goal-oriented ones such as (311):

[410] I permit him to go home.
[311] He may go home.

Let us have a closer look at the relationship of these two sentences. Sentence (410) could be paraphrased by

(424) He is permitted by me to go home.

Sentences (410) and (424), being active and passive variants, can be said to be synonymous. Deleting the prepositional phrase *by me* in (424) yields

(425) He is permitted to go home.

This sentence is synonymous with (311) given a root interpretation. Therefore (311) could well be referred to as the passive variant of (410), lacking only the overt realization of the agent (see also Calbert 1975: 24).

Active and passive sentences are often characterized as two different perspectives of the same situation. Taking the sentence subject to open up the specific perspective of a sentence, we can say that source-oriented sentences show the perspective of the modal source being active (in granting permission, laying an obligation, etc.), whereas goal-oriented sentences have the perspective of the modal goal being passively granted permission or laid an obligation.

This factor of *modal perspective* must be taken into account when considering source and goal equivalents such as

[407] Meine Mittel/Verhältnisse erlauben das nicht.
[408] I cannot afford it.

However synonymous these sentences may be in terms of overall identity of semantic features (see the previous two subsections), they open up different perspectives. In (407), the instrument is modal source, subject, theme (see Section 3.3.6), primary referent, and thus 'perspective giver'; in (408), the modal goal is subject, theme, primary referent, and 'perspective giver.' Moreover, in (407), the modal goal is only implied by the possessive pronoun *meine*, whereas in (408) the modal source is implicit.

If all these differences cannot stop lexicographers from entering (407) and (408) as bilingual equivalents, then the (active-passive) relationship of such pairs of source- and goal-oriented sentences must be considered to be strong indeed.

3.2.6.4 Syntactic Variation of Modal Source

The observation made in Section 3.2.6.2 that modals are typically goal-oriented needs some supplementation. Consider the following sentence from *Lufthansa Bordbuch/Logbook* (4/83: 50):

(426) Mit nebenstehender Entfernungstabelle können Sie die Gesamtlänge Ihrer Flugroute berechnen.

Here, the modal source is realized as a(n instrumental) prepositional phrase, even though KÖNNEN is used.

It is true that syntax and semantics of KÖNNEN do not require expression of the modal source; for example,

(427) Sie können die Gesamtlänge Ihrer Flugroute berechnen.

So the mention of modal source in (426) is optional (even though in this case it is necessary for the message to be fully intelligible).

This means that the description of modals as goal oriented is accurate, but it must not be taken to the sentence level. Otherwise sentences such as (426) would have to be described as 'goal oriented, but source oriented.' To avoid this misleading characterization, we will speak of *goal-oriented modals*, but *source(-oriented) sentences* (containing them) when describing sentences such as (426).

Interestingly, for an English equivalent of (426), Lufthansa chose a different structure:

(428) The opposite table of distances enables you to find out the total length of your own route.

As we can see, the modal source, which was realized as a prepositional phrase in German, appears as subject in English.

The requirements for source and goal sentences such as

[407] Meine Mittel/Verhältnisse erlauben das nicht.
[408] I cannot afford it.

to be translation equivalents was compensation for the loss of modal source in the goal sentence (see Section 3.2.6.1 and so forth).

But sentence (426), even though containing the goal-oriented KÖNNEN, explicitly contains the modal source (as an instrumental phrase). This is why *both* (426) and (428) are in fact source sentences and can be considered equivalent as far as mention of the modal source is concerned.

Why should a syntactic relocation of the modal source, accompanied by a shift from the goal-oriented KÖNNEN to the source-oriented ENABLE have been deemed necessary or advisable? After all, the goal-oriented CAN (which is analogous to the goal-oriented KÖNNEN) could have been used equally well:

(429) You can find out the total length of your own route by means of the opposite table of distances.

A syntactically even more congruent version would have been

(430) By means of the opposite table of distances you can find out the total length of your own route.

Alternatively, to match the structure of the printed English sentence (428), (431) could have been chosen as the German version:

(431) Die nebenstehende Entfernungstabelle ermöglicht (es) Ihnen, die Gesamtlänge Ihrer Flugroute zu berechnen.

The source-oriented ERMÖGLICHEN would thus have paralleled the source-oriented ENABLE in (428).

The reason for suggesting these different correlations is the assumption that it would be natural to have source-source ((431) → (428)) or goal-goal ((426) → (430)) pairs of equivalents, this being another example of the principle of having maximum equivalence by having as many invariance factors as possible.

Because the translator of the *Lufthansa Logbook* did not follow this principle, he or she must have had in mind something supposedly better than maximum equivalence—maybe optimum equivalence in terms of doing justice to important revision factors causing a deviation from standard equivalence patterns. Which factors can these be?

To find an answer to this question, let us first reconsider several sentences dealt with in Section 2.9 and (partly) in Section 3.2.6.2:

[149] Money can't buy everything.
[150] *Geld kann nicht alles kaufen.
[151] Mit Geld kann man nicht alles kaufen.
[155] Geld ermöglicht nicht alles.

Sentence (149) resembles (430) in that CAN is followed by an action verb (BUY, FIND OUT). But this resemblance is only superficial: *You* in (430) indeed performs the semantic role of an agent, but *money* in (149) is an instrument. In German, agents can be subjects, but instruments such as *money* cannot. This is why (430) can be rendered by (426), but (149) cannot be translated as *(150). The suppletive rendition (155) corresponds to (431) in syntactic and semantic terms:

- Both sentences contain the source-oriented verb ERMÖGLICHEN.
- In both sentences, the instrumental modal source appears in subject position. So ERMÖGLICHEN is not restricted the way KÖNNEN is.

This means that (431) would be the justified German version of an English sentence that is structurally analogous to (149); namely, (432):

(432) The opposite table of distances can show you the total length of your own route.

Now the German original (426) does not have the structure of (155), but that of (151). This does not really matter, however, because (151) and (155) can both be rendered by (149). Given the structural equivalence of (149) and (432), this means that, just as (151) can be rendered by (149), so (426) could have been rendered by (432). Why then was (428) chosen as an English version and not (432) or (430)?

Let us consider the factor of modal perspective. All of (426), (428), (430), and (432) have the instrument as modal source first; but it is mentioned in different ways. In (428) and (432) it appears as sentence subject, in (426) and (430) it is part of a prepositional phrase, the prepositions *mit/by means of* emphasizing the instrumental character of *Entfernungstabelle/table of distances*.

This difference might be taken as a clue to answering our question. The construction in (426) focuses on introducing an instrument to the reader, whereas (428) presents an 'enabling circumstance' in the sense of Palmer's circumstantial modality (see Section 3.2.4.5).

We would, however, reject this idea as quibbling and propose a much simpler solution. Supposing the translator desired to follow the structure of the German sentence (426) as closely as possible, he or she would immediately have met with a first blocking factor to the congruent rendition (430). In English, prepositional phrases are rarely fronted (König 1974: 251). This fact being a revision factor, the translator was next faced with the possibility of having as invariance factors

- either the modal (as in (429) and (432));
- or the same sequence of nominal elements and hence of theme and rheme (see Sections 3.3.6 and 4.2) (as in (428)).

Note, though, that (432) requires SHOW as a full verb (* . . . *can find you out* . . .); and sentence (429) may have seemed to unnecessarily deviate in terms of syntax. So the choice fell on (428).

3.3 TYPES OF MEANING

Kinds of modality as presented in Section 3.2.4 are semantic categories pertaining not just to the modals but to modal expressions in general. Types of meaning to be dealt with in this section are an even more general phenomenon: They are characteristics of the whole of language. In discussing them, we will of course focus on the modals and other modal expressions. There are different taxonomies of types of meaning. We will go by Leech (1981: Chap. 2) and augment his categories by a few.

3.3.1 Denotative or Conceptual Meaning

The lexical meaning of a word denoting a physical object can be defined by a combination of the criterial properties of that object in terms of semantic features (see Leech 1981: 12), for instance:

(433) BOY = +human, +male, −adult

Modals do not denote physical things, but refer to abstract concepts such as ability, possibility, necessity, obligation, willingness, as well as root, dynamic, deontic, epistemic, objective, subjective, and so forth. If these concepts are properly combined, they yield feature sets describing modal meanings in much the same way as those of other lexemes such as BOY; for example,

(434) MUST = +necessity, +epistemic, +subjective

Of course this characterization of MUST represents only one meaning of that modal; polysemous lexemes like the modals (see note 15) require one feature set for each of their meanings. But the juxtaposition of (433) and (434) shows that even though modals are often granted the status of bearing (a) grammatical meaning(s) only, techniques of componential analysis typical of lexical semantics can be applied to them as well. Leech (1987: 71) speaks of the logical element of their meaning and elsewhere (1981: 9) refers to "logical meaning or (as I shall prefer to call it) *conceptual meaning* . . . " Ever since we introduced the notion of "multiple meanings of the modals" (Section 3.1.1), we were in fact speaking of their conceptual or denotative meanings; that is, their meanings by virtue of the concepts they denote ("possibility," "ability," etc.).

Showing eclectically how these meanings act as translation factors, we have, however, never given a full account of all the conceptual meanings of each modal. To provide at least some graphical overview, we reproduce in Figure 3.26 the "interrelationships of modals and meanings" provided by Coates (1983: 26). She differentiates between *primary, secondary,* and *infrequent uses.* She also observes that "groups of modals share certain meanings. For example, MUST, SHOULD and OUGHT share 'obligation' and 'inference' meanings, WILL and SHALL share 'prediction' and 'volition' meanings. . . . four clusters are clearly distinct, and can be associated with semantic concepts such as obligation/necessity, intention/prediction/futurity, possibility/ability/permission and epistemic possibility" (p. 27). By running two informant tests, she further confirmed that paraphrases of the modals

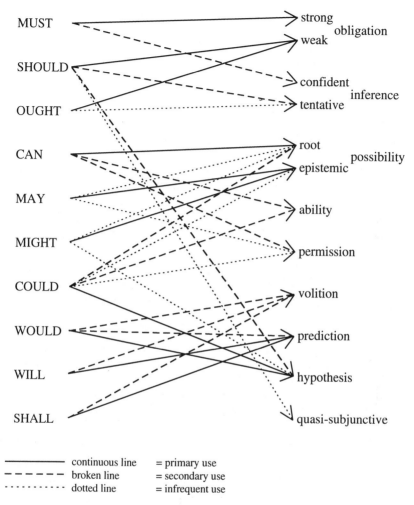

FIGURE 3.26.
The English Modals and Their Conceptual Meanings

(such as ALLOWED, POSSIBLE FOR, PERHAPS, POSSIBLE THAT)
were "strongly associated with their respective modal forms" (p. 27; see also
pp. 28, 105, 249).

To present one of the meaning clusters in greater detail was Perkins's
(1983: 103) concern, see our Figure 3.20. If this were extended to encompass the modal system as a whole, a complete picture of the conceptual
meanings of English modal expressions would emerge. If supplemented by
the corresponding German system, groundbreaking work for a comparison of

the two conceptual systems would be achieved. The fundamentals of such a system were laid out by Nehls (1986: 27) in his chart of the English and German modals and their suppletives.

3.3.2 Connotative Meaning

Connotative meaning represents "noncriterial properties" of what a word denotes, including psychological and social ones (Leech 1981: 12). Consider the following examples.

A leaflet published by Deutsche Bundesbahn (German Railways) in 1986, advertising advance reservation of seats for Christmas time contains the following sentence:

(435) Wenn der gewünschte Platz ausverkauft ist, können Sie nach Belieben umdisponieren.

A necessary condition for this sentence is

(436) Wenn der gewünschte Platz ausverkauft ist, müssen Sie umdisponieren.

According to Panther (1981b: 246), the use of (root) KÖNNEN, as opposed to that of MÜSSEN, often has a connotation of pleasantness and agreeableness. It is not surprising, therefore, that German Railways should make a virtue of necessity and rather emphasize the pleasant aspect of the situation (see Section 4.4.1), which is that the reader can choose among remaining possibilities.

The factor of connotation also accounts for the publisher's decision not to use DÜRFEN. The deontic use of this modal evokes associations of authority of the speaker over the hearer, such as in

(437) !Wenn der gewünschte Platz ausverkauft ist, dürfen Sie nach Belieben umdisponieren.

True, German Railways is creating rules and regulations of its own, and granting the reader the right to freely choose among remaining possibilities is in itself something positive; yet (437) would still be no serious candidate for inclusion into their brochures, simply for its said connotation.

By contrast, MAY, which otherwise is the English modal closest to root DÜRFEN, does not share the word's associations. The corresponding sentence (438) would be perfectly possible:

(438) If the seat requested is booked already you may freely choose among remaining possibilities.

This use of MAY parallels the one in the following sentence, which, according to Leech (1987: 97, 108), could be found in a brochure:

(439) Visitors may ascend the tower for 50p this summer.

Again, MAY could not be rendered by DÜRFEN,

(440) !Besucher dürfen den Turm diesen Sommer für 50p besteigen.

except in internal communication (for instance by members of the tourist office). For public purposes, KÖNNEN has to be used instead.

(441) Besucher können den Turm diesen Summer für 50p besteigen.

This narrowing down of expressive possibilities by the factor of connotation has the effect of blurring the distinction between deontic DÜRFEN and KÖNNEN in such cases; see further Section 7.5.

3.3.3 Stylistic Meaning

In Section 3.2.1 we dealt with the relationship between the modals and their cognates in terms of conceptual meaning. There is also a difference between these two groups of modal expressions in terms of style. Due to their more frequent use and greater centrality within the modal system, the modals are more common as a means of expressing modality. But there seems to be an important difference between their use in English and German. Snell-Hornby (1984: 209) found that, in English public directives, "everyday modal verbs" were used where German preferred modal adjectives—*must not* vs. *verboten* instead of *darf nicht*.

This tendency to evade the common modals is also found in other contexts. Consider, for instance, the following sentence that occurs in the printed translation of Palmer's *Grammar*:

(442) . . . they are features of languages with both sound and meaning and ought therefore to have a place in the grammar. (Palmer 1971: 120)
(443) . . . handelt es sich um Sprachmerkmale lautlicher und bedeutungs-mässiger Art, denen darum ihr Platz in der Grammatik gebührt. (Palmer 1974b: 111)

Gebührt expresses a much more elevated style than *sollte* or *müsste*; for example,

(444) . . . sind sie Sprachmerkmale mit Laut und Bedeutung und müssten/ sollten deshalb einen Platz in der Grammatik haben.

The following translation from Lyons's *Language and Linguistics* shows a related stylistic facet:

(445) The same point can be made about borrowing as was made about analogy . . . (Lyons 1981: 206)

(446) Über Entlehnung lässt sich dasselbe sagen wie über Analogie . . . (Lyons 1992: 189)

Instead of using KÖNNEN as in

(447) Über Entlehnung kann dasselbe gesagt werden wie über Analogie . . .

the translator used the reflexive LASSEN, which sounds a bit more elaborate. But the contrast between these two alternatives is much less than that between OUGHT TO and GEBÜHREN in the previous example. It might be said that the natural tendency for variation of expression accounts for the use of LASSEN instead of KÖNNEN in (446).

But not all aspects of meaning referred to as stylistic necessarily are. Perkins (1983: 19), for instance, reports Kempson's (1977: 73 f.) claim that "the following two sentences:

(448) The reports you send in must be as simple as possible.

(449) It is obligatory that the reports to be sent in by you be maximally simple.

are semantically equivalent but differ in terms of their stylistic characterization." This amounts to saying that MUST and IT IS OBLIGATORY THAT share the same conceptual meaning, but differ as regards their stylistic meanings (the latter ones being a matter of pragmatics). It must not be ignored, however, that MUST, being a modal, is unmarked for the root-epistemic distinction, whereas IT IS OBLIGATORY THAT is clearly root in meaning. This suggests that the difference between the two expressions is one of conceptual meaning potential rather than (or, at least, in addition to) stylistic meaning. As Figure 3.20 shows, the same kind of relation holds for the modals and many other modal expressions. This suggests that "expressions such as MAY and BE POSSIBLE THAT are not merely synonymous 'stylistic' variants" (Perkins 1983: 4). So the "relative 'appropriateness' of different modal expressions" (1983: 20) is not so much a matter of style, but one of subtleties in conceptual meaning. This should be borne in mind by translators when an apparently 'long list of stylistic variants' seems to be at their disposal (see our discussion of an allegedly "wide specter of TL equivalents" in Section 3.2.1.2).

In a similar fashion, Leech (1981: 14) uses the term *stylistic meaning* to refer to "the range of style differentiation possible within a single language" or "socio-stylistic variations," along the following dimensions set up by Crystal and Davy (1969):

- *Dialect* (the language of a geographical region or of a social class)
- *Time* (the language of the eighteenth century, etc.)

- *Province* (language of law, science, advertising, etc.)
- *Status* (polite, colloquial, slang, etc., language)
- *Modality* (language of memoranda, lectures, jokes, etc.)
- *Singularity* (the style of Dickens, Hemingway, etc.)

Leech deals with these, however, in his section on *social meaning*. Because they, as well as what Leech calls *affective meaning*, "have to do with the situation in which an utterance takes place" (1981: 14), we prefer to deal with them in our pragmatics chapter (Section 4.4.2), and, as far as *province* is concerned, in the sections on text (6.8.1 and 6.8.2).

3.3.4 Reflected Meaning

Leech (1981: 16) defines *reflected meaning* as "the meaning which arises in cases of multiple conceptual meaning, when one sense of a word forms part of our response to another sense."

Given this definition, reflected meaning should be easily detected in different meanings of polysemous words such as the modals. Consider the following simple sentence:

(450) Peter must be in his office now.

This sentence is ambiguous between a root and an epistemic reading. The root meaning of MUST gives a strong impression as far as the degree of modality is concerned. Necessity or obligation is much stronger a concept than 'mere' possibility (CAN) or advisability (tentative necessity) (SHOULD). Likewise the epistemic meaning of MUST conveys an impressively strong degree of probability, much stronger than that of MAY or SHOULD. Sometimes the epistemic use of the modals is referred to as an extension of the root one. This relation is also found in the diachronic development of the modals (see Sweetser 1990: Chap. 3). It could thus be said that the strong epistemic force of MUST is *based upon* the strong root force of this modal. "One sense of a word seems to 'rub off' on another sense in this way . . . ," as Leech (1981: 16) puts it (without reference to the modals).

What was said about MUST is equally valid for MÜSSEN, as in

(451) Peter muss jetzt in seinem Büro sein.

Note that only the modals can show reflected meaning; other modal expressions such as MAYBE, HAVE PERMISSION TO, ERLAUBT SEIN, or VIELLEICHT cannot because they are not polysemous the way the modals are, polysemy being a prerequisite for reflected meaning. This means that if speakers intend to play upon root modality in the sense of extending its "suggestive power" (Leech 1981: 16) onto a possible epistemic interpretation of the sentence used by them, they can do this only by means of the modals. Likewise translators, to be able to achieve the semantic 'rubbing-off' effect, must render (450) by (451)—they cannot translate it by

(452) Peter ist verpflichtet, jetzt in seinem Büro zu sein.

even if they definitely know that the speaker is referring to Peter's obligation to be in the office.

There is also the possibility for the root use of a modal 'rubbing off' on the epistemic one in yet another sense. When someone must (root) be in the office it is reasonable to infer that person must (epistemic) be in the office— from the knowledge of someone's obligation or necessity of being some- where there arises the speaker's necessity of inferring that the person is in fact there. To avoid missing this possibility of extended-reflected modal meaning, the translator had best use a TL modal allowing for the same effect as is possible in SL.

3.3.5 Collocative Meaning

This kind of meaning consists of the associations acquired by a word on account of the meanings of a word tending to occur in its environment (Leech 1981: 17). By virtue of this association, collocative meaning is akin to reflected meaning, only the sense 'rubbing off' on another one in this case pertains to a word to be found in the cotext of the other word.

As collocations of modals we will here present other modals appearing in their immediate cotext (Section 3.3.5.1) or conjoined by *and* (Section 3.3.5.2), as well as modal adverbs, nouns, and adjectives (Section 3.3.5.3).

3.3.5.1 Double Modals

A modal precedes the infinitive of another verb (e.g., *must go, can swim*; *muss gehen, kann schwimmen*). Because the German modals have infinitives, these may be preceded by other modals (e.g., *kann müssen, muss können, möchte dürfen*). The English modals lacking infinitives (see Section 1.2.2.1), German double modals have to be rendered by means of suppletives; com- pare:

[48] Er muss kommen können.
[46] *He must can come.
[47] He must be able to come.

So in Standard English this formal difference is a change factor in transla- tion. But some varieties of English permit double modals (see Section 4.5.1). Pampell (1975: 117, n.1) observes: "They enjoy an East-West provenance from the Carolinas to eastern New Mexico, and are even said to occur in some Scottish dialects." Informant tests performed by him yielded the following modal combinations: *might oughta, might could, might should, might should oughta, might could oughta, might would, might will, should oughta, may can,* and *might can* (p. 111). With the availability of these forms, certain German double modals cease to be change factors; for example,

(453) Er könnte hier sein sollen.
(454) He might should be here.

3.3.5.2 Modal Conjunction

In addition to being directly conjoined as double modals, modals may be linked by conjunctions such as *and, but,* and *or.* Luelsdorff (1979) examines modal *and*-coordination and postulates three semantic principles for predicting the proper sequencing of *and*-conjoined modals (p. 136):

1. Principle of Implication. If $M(odal)_2$ implies $M(odal)_1$, then M_1 will occur before M_2; for instance,

    (455) I can and may go to Munich tomorrow.
    (456) *I may and can go to Munich tomorrow.

Because "CAN is always a part of the meaning of MAY" (p. 133), (456) is ungrammatical.

2. Principle of Identity Exclusion. If two modals have the same meaning, they cannot be conjoined; therefore,

    (457) *I can and could . . .
    (458) *I could and can . . .

Luelsdorff maintains: "The meaning of COULD is the same as the meaning of CAN" (p. 132), which is correct only if the factor of tentativity or tense is neglected.

3. Principle of Obligation Precedence. If M_1 implies obligation and M_2 expresses the speaker's assessment of the probability of the occurrence of the predication, then M_1 must precede M_2:

    (459) He must and will . . .
    (460) *He will and must . . .

Because the English and German systems of modals are not isomorphic, complete correspondence of modal *and*-coordination cannot be expected. The three principles postulated seem to be transferable onto German, though. Thus, (459) could be translated as

(461) Er muss und wird . . .
(462) *Er wird und muss . . .

As regards principle 2, constructions such as

(463) *Ich kann und könnte . . .
(464) *Ich könnte und kann . . .

are ruled out due to the two modals being near synonyms.

Principle 1 must be scrutinized as to the nature of modal interrelation. As for (455) and (456), the tenet that "CAN is always a part of the meaning of MAY" makes most sense if MAY is taken to have epistemic meaning. But does *root* MAY always imply root CAN? It does in the sense that someone granting permission presupposes the physical possibility and the ability of the actor. This is why (456) would be redundant. If (455) is not considered to be so, the reason is that CAN here denotes physical possibility and ability and MAY denotes only the cognitive possibility created by permission. MAY in (456) representing all three aspects taken together, the additional use of CAN amounts to an undue repetition, which makes this combination of modals inadmissible. The same modal sequencing applies in German:

(465) Ich kann und darf morgen nach München fahren.
(466) *Ich darf und kann morgen nach München fahren.

But we are reluctant to ascribe downright ungrammaticality to (466). Someone might well say

(467) Ich darf morgen nach München fahren, aber ich kann nicht, weil ich kein Geld habe.

A speaker who has enough money could say:

(468) Ich darf morgen nach München fahren, und ich kann auch, denn ich habe genug Geld dafür.

From (468) it is only a small step to (466), which could thus become grammatical by arguing that *darf* does not necessarily include all kinds of possibilities, for instance financial ones.

Luelsdorff takes it for granted that the order of *and*-conjoined modals is rigidly fixed and therefore refers to them as *modal and-conjoined freezes* (p. 131). With examples such as (467) and (468) 'warming up' the possibility of allegedly impossible combinations such as (466), however, we would tend to conceive of modal conjunctions with more flexible temperatures.

3.3.5.3 Harmonic Combinations

Another example of collocation is the modification of epistemically used modals by epistemic adverbs as in (469):

(469) You may possibly prefer that one.

The resulting pleonasm observed by Palmer (1979a: 57) is particularly obvious in the *harmonic combinations* as found in (469) (cf. Nehls 1986: 171 f.), where both kinds of modal expressions share one degree of modality. The same type of combinations is possible in a German rendition. But when rendering (469), we would tend to use the past subjunctive form of KÖNNEN:

(470) ?Sie können vielleicht den da mögen.
(471) Sie könnten vielleicht den da mögen.

The argument for using *könnten* runs as follows:

1. If (469) contained no modal adverb, remaining epistemic MAY would not be rendered by indicative *können*:

   (472) You may prefer that one.
   (473) ?Sie können den da mögen.

The reason is that second person present tense indicative use of KÖNNEN is not typical of epistemic modality if MÖGEN is main verb; with present perfect, things are different:

(474) Sie können den da gemocht haben.

So (472) would rather be rendered by expressions that are typically epistemic, like the modal adverb VIELLEICHT or the subjunctive form *könnte* (which latter expression would also do justice to the SL part of speech):

(475) Sie mögen vielleicht den da.
(476) Sie könnten den da mögen.

2. If there is pleonastic use of epistemic modality, that is, if this kind of modality is expressed by more than one linguistic means, as in (469), then the epistemic forms in (475) and (476) are simply combined, *könnte* plus VIELLEICHT, resulting in (471).

Exactly this principle is found applied in the translation of Palmer's *Semantics*:

[325] We may, perhaps, assume that all societies . . . (Palmer 1976: 87)
[326] Wir könnten vielleicht annehmen, dass alle Kulturkreise . . . (Palmer 1977: 90)

Harmonic combinations also occur with root modality in constructions such as *must necessarily, must of necessity,* and *muss notwendigerweise/ notgedrungen.* Hence in both English and German the root combination of *modal verb plus modal adverb* is possible, but the construction *modal verb plus prepositional phrase* is restricted to English. It would also have to be rendered by the adverbial construction:

(477) He must necessarily come.
(478) He must of necessity come.
(479) Er muss notwendigerweise/notgedrungen kommen.

This greater flexibility of English must, however, not be assumed to pertain to all constructions involving modal nouns. If the sequence of modal expressions is reversed, German offers more possibilities. Consider the syntagma

(480) ?Die Erlaubnis/Möglichkeit, euch besuchen zu können . . .

Dückert and Kempcke (1984: 203) refer to this construction as pleonastic and mention as the correct version

(481) Die Erlaubnis/Möglichkeit, euch zu besuchen . . .

In spite of their alleged ungrammaticality, constructions such as (480) involving modal noun plus modal verb are common coin in spoken as well as written, even printed German.[33] English, however, does not allow for such constructions at all:

(482) *The permission/possibility of being able to visit you . . .
(483) The permission/possibility of visiting you . . .

Also certain German epistemic constructions are criticized as being pleonastic, like the following one by the Duden (1985: 475):

(484) Es kann möglich sein.

Again, also such combinations of modal verb plus modal adjective are common in German. As in the *modal noun plus modal verb* construction (480), the point of criticism will be that each modal expression is in itself sufficient to convey the kind of modality intended; for instance,

(485) Es kann sein.
(486) Es ist möglich.

The same point could be made as regards the English harmonic combinations in (469), (325), (477), and (478), as well as the German ones in (471), (326), and (479). The argument ultimately leads to the question of why have harmonic combinations at all.

There seems to be something special about the latter group of seven modal collocations as compared to the other ones. Here the pleonasm underlines the degree of modality expressed (see Nehls 1986: 171 on the degree of epistemic modality). In the other kinds of combinations—modal noun plus modal verb (480) or modal verb plus modal adjective (484)—the redundancy resulting from the combination of two (near) synonyms is foregrounded to an extent of appearing to be unnecessary, undesirable, or even ungrammatical.

But not all cases of redundancy are as obvious as in

[480] ?Die Erlaubnis/Möglichkeit, euch besuchen zu können . . .

Consider the following text of a newspaper ad:

(487) Die Freiheit sich heute für das eine, morgen für das andere zu ent-
scheiden (ad by Landhaus Mode, *Fränkischer Anzeiger* 8-19-1993, p.
4; punctuation as in the original).

In everyday language use, (487) could well be expressed as

(488) Die Freiheit, sich heute für das eine, morgen für das andere ent-
scheiden zu können.

Even to grammarians, (488) may be more acceptable than (480). The reason
is that the word *Freiheit* expresses the meaning of "Erlaubnis/permission"
more covertly than does *Erlaubnis* (see Section 3.2.5.1). The effect is that
the presence of two tokens of modality is less obvious in (488) than in (480).

Remember the gradient with overt modality on one end and covert modality on the other (Figure 3.21, Section 3.2.5.2). At the latter end modal
meanings may be so covertly contained in expressions that a second, overt
mention of modality by means of a modal will not be felt to create redundancy at all:

(489) Er hat genug Platz, um zehn Leute unterbringen zu können.

English would still do with one instance of modality:

(490) ?He has enough space to be able to lodge ten people.
(491) He has enough space to lodge ten people.

Let us now consider yet another factor of harmonic combinations. These are
defined by two modal expressions having the same *degree* of modality. But
what about *kinds* of modality? In all the examples discussed so far we seem
to have found correspondence in this dimension as well. Combinations were
epistemic plus epistemic and *root plus root*. But now have another look at

[484] Es kann möglich sein.

In our earlier discussion of this sentence we tacitly assumed that both modal
expressions contained in it are epistemic. But are they necessarily? They are
not, because MÖGLICH can very well be given a root interpretation, as the
second of the following continuations of (484) shows:

(492) Es kann möglich sein, dass er da ist. (epistemic plus epistemic)
(493) Es kann möglich sein, diesen Berg zu besteigen. (epistemic plus root)

If the criterion of harmonic combinations is identity of kind of modality,
then (493) must be declined membership to this category, even though both

modal expressions in this sentence belong to the same modal degree of "possibility."

English parallels German in all respects:

(494) It may be possible.
(495) It may be possible that he is there.
(496) It may be possible to climb that mountain.

Rendering harmonic combinations with adverbs as well as other constructions of the type *modal auxiliary* + *modal adverb* in English requires knowledge about the positioning of both elements. Jacobson (1980a: 31) presents "a survey of factors influencing the placement of PROBABLY" in

(497) The delegation probably will return tomorrow.
(498) The delegation will probably return tomorrow.

See also Jacobson's book *Factors Influencing the Placement of English Adverbs in Relation to Auxiliaries* (1975).

3.3.6 Thematic Meaning

Thematic meaning represents "what is communicated by the way in which a speaker or writer organizes his message, in terms of ordering, focus, and emphasis" (Leech 1981: 19). Consider the different syntax of an active-passive pair of sentences:

(499) Mrs. Bessie Smith donated the first prize.
(500) The first prize was donated by Mrs. Bessie Smith.

Leech explains: "It is often felt . . . that an active sentence such as (499) has a different meaning from its passive equivalent (500), although in conceptual content they seem to be the same . . ." (p.19). For Leech, the "different communicative values" of the two constructions "suggest different contexts." The noun phrase appearing first in each sentence, the *theme* or *topic*, is presupposed as known information, while the noun phrase at the end of each sentence, the *rheme* or *comment*, represents the piece of new information called for in the specific context of that sentence.

This analysis seems to be sufficient for nonmodal sentences. As regards sentences containing modals, however, also conceptual meaning (which was said to be identical for (499) and (500)) may change as voice changes. Leech (1987: 74) provides a good example of this possibility. Because it does not involve thematic meaning as a relevant category, we will include it in our section on voice (Section 3.4).

We would like to continue here with modal examples of thematic meaning involving no change of voice. To prepare the ground for their discussion, let us start with Leech's (1981: 20) observation that "the kind of contrast by ordering and emphasis illustrated by (499) and (500) can also be contrived by lexical means: by substituting (for example) *belongs to* for *owns"* in the following pair of sentences:

(501) Peter owns this supermarket.
(502) This supermarket belongs to Peter.

For all their different means of achieving difference in thematic meaning—syntactic vs. lexical ones—both pairs of sentences mentioned so far have one thing in common: exchange of their noun phrases. But a difference in thematic meaning need not necessarily be accompanied by this permutation of what may be called *theme and rheme, topic and comment,* or *presupposition and focus.* This can be demonstrated with reference to a sentence pair already discussed in several sections (3.2.6.1 through 3.2.6.4):

[407] Meine Mittel/Verhältnisse erlauben das nicht.
[408] I cannot afford it.

Like *belongs to* and *owns* in the previous pair of sentences, *erlauben* and *cannot afford* have opened up different perspectives, hence the term *modal perspectives* applied to (407) and (408) in Section 3.2.6.3.

Whereas the former two sentences clearly differ in terms of thematic meaning (*Peter* vs. *this supermarket*), this cannot be categorically asserted in case of the latter ones: *Meine Mittel/Verhältnisse* and *I* at least refer to the same 'topic realm,' even though it is true that they are not (fully) coreferential. Let us analyze the two sentences in terms of Leech's (1981: 19 f.) distinction between presupposition and focus on new information. To arrive at the new information focused on in each sentence, we would have to ask two different questions. Sentence (407) is an answer to the question:

(503) Erlauben das deine Mittel/Verhältnisse?

In contrast, (408) would answer the question:

(504) Can you afford it?

So, in (407), knowledge of the existence of *meine Mittel/Verhältnisse* and *das* is presupposed, *erlauben nicht* is the new information focused on. In (408), *I* and *it* are familiar, *cannot afford* is new. (Note that CAN and ERLAUBEN appear in both questions and answers, but in the questions their assertion is, of course, not presupposed.)

Now, whatever is expressed in the English and German versions, the overall contents is ultimately the same: When I say (408) *I cannot afford it,* I imply that my means do not permit it; and when I say (407) *Meine Mittel/ Verhältnisse erlauben das nicht,* this in turn implies that I cannot afford it—means and their owner can be seen as a unit, even though only one or the other is expressed in each case.

So when we say that the two sentences are translation equivalents in terms of conceptual meaning, we refer to the *overall* conceptual meaning. Because not all concepts are expressed in both languages or, put somewhat differently, those that are expressed partly differ, the *surface* conceptual meaning of the two sentences is only partially equivalent.

The same is true of thematic meaning. Both sentences presuppose familiarity with the overall theme of the speaker and the existence (even though not the largeness) of his or her means seen as a unit, as well as the proposed financial object(ive). Both sentences also focus on the overall new information of the insufficiency of the speaker's means in view of the objective.

Again, the surface structure theme is partially different. *Meine Mittel/ Verhältnisse* is, strictly speaking, not coreferential with *I*; *it* is a personal pronoun, whereas *das* is a demonstrative one. Last, modality is seen from two different perspectives, the source-oriented one and the goal-oriented one (see Section 3.2.6.3). But, because the subjects of the two sentences are not completely different the way they are in (499)–(500) and (501)–(502), the source- and goal-oriented modal perspectives are not correlated with a difference in thematic meaning that is as distinct as in the two sentence pairs just referred to. In fact, because modal source and modal goal (the speaker and his means) are closely related, for all practical purposes their difference is negligible. All the different modal perspectives of *erlauben* and *cannot afford* do is demand different subjects: *Erlauben* must have an inanimate one (in this case); *cannot afford*, a human one.

So our finding about (407) and (408) in terms of thematic meaning is a moderate one. All we can say is that the two modal expressions correlate with different aspects of one and the same theme.

3.3.7 Metaphorical Meaning

"Metaphor . . . cannot be legitimately separated from the formal account of the conceptual . . . structure of meaning." This statement, made by Leech (1981: 230), seems to be particularly appropriate with reference to the modals. Their conceptual meanings are notions such as ability, possibility, necessity, obligation, or willingness (see Section 3.3.1). Yet these abstract notions often appear in terms of down-to-earth metaphors reminding us of their concrete origin. Referring to possibility, for instance, we can say:

(505) Diese Möglichkeit steht ihm offen.
(506) Diese Möglichkeit müssen wir uns offenhalten.

Here possibility appears to be a door that can be opened and closed. Modality can also be equated to the key for opening a door, see (507) meaning (508) or (509):

(507) This book is the key to your success.
(508) This book enables you to become successful.
(509) You can become successful by means of this book.

There also exist German structures corresponding to the latter two sentences; namely,

(510) Dieses Buch ermöglicht (es) Ihnen, erfolgreich zu sein.
(511) Mit Hilfe dieses Buches können Sie erfolgreich werden.

But all the lengthy discussions about ENABLE/ERMÖGLICHEN (or ERLAUBEN) and CAN/KÖNNEN and their difference in terms of modal perspective (see Sections 3.2.6.3 and 3.2.6.4) and thematic meaning (see the previous subsection) are practically irrelevant in the present connection: BE A KEY TO being a metaphor, this factor may be said to overrule all other considerations; that is, to call for a metaphor in TL also.

Even though paraphrases of (507) such as (509) or its German equivalent (511) demonstrate the semantic closeness of the modals to metaphors, the latter are so striking a phenomenon that it seems natural to make it an invariance factor.

Therefore the 'key' metaphor in (507) is most likely to reappear in a German rendition of this sentence, for instance as

(512) Dieses Buch ist der Schlüssel zu Ihrem Erfolg.

Likewise translations of (505) and (506) would tend to retain the idea of something being/remaining open:

(513) This option is open to him.
(514) We must keep this option open to us.

Note that in (505) there is overt modality ("Möglichkeit") *in addition to* the 'openness' metaphor, but in (507) modality is completely covert, appearing only as *the key*. Interestingly, both kinds of modal variants can correspond to each other in an English-German sentence pair:

(515) Dies lässt die Möglichkeit offen für weitere Fragen.
(516) This leaves an opening for additional questions.

Here overt modality appears only in the German version.

Even though the modals may be used for paraphrasing modal metaphors they do not themselves contain such metaphors (see (509)). Nevertheless they are analyzed in terms of them by some cognitive linguists. Sweetser, for instance, describes the English modals in terms of forces and barriers. MAY is understood in terms of a potential but absent barrier, and MUST is understood as a compelling force directing the subject towards an act (1990: 52). This characterization is immediately plausible, particularly if forces and barriers are taken to represent the modal source. One potential barrier for the affirmative use of MAY is the—metaphorical—lack of a way to do something. If someone *may not* go swimming then there is *no way* to do so. No surprise, therefore, that there are various phrases for speaking about a possibility in terms of a way; for example, (Wildhagen and Héraucourt 1963: 992),

(517) He had no way of doing it.
(518) Er hatte keine Möglichkeit, es zu tun.

(519) I don't see my way clear yet to say okay.
(520) Ich sehe zunächst keine Möglichkeit zuzustimmen.

As in (515) and (516), in these pairs of sentences, only the English ones contain a metaphor. In other cases, the concepts of "possibility" and "way" are both seen as possible renditions:

(521) I see my way to achieve my goal.
(522) Ich sehe den Weg/eine Möglichkeit, mein Ziel zu erreichen.

In still other cases modals, too, are part of possible renditions:

(523) I do not see my way to solve this problem.
(524) Ich sehe mich/bin nicht in der Lage, dieses Problem zu lösen.
(525) Ich kann mich nicht dazu verstehen, dieses Problem zu lösen.

Finally, some phrases require the 'way' metaphor to appear in TL also, such as

(526) This paves the way for even greater achievements.
(527) Dies ebnet den Weg für noch grössere Erfolge.

Regarding the 'way' metaphor, there are several possibilities of potential barriers for the affirmative use of modal expressions:

1. the nonexistence of a way (see (517)–(520), (523)–(525);
2. the inappropriate state of the way (see (526) and (527));
3. obstacles in the way, closed gates, and so on.

The last category may be illustrated with reference to phrases such as *die letzten Hindernisse aus dem Weg räumen für . . .* ; *der Weg ist jetzt frei für . . .*

Again English translations tend to preserve the metaphor or at least to use modal expressions other than the modals themselves, such as (Wildhagen and Héraucourt 1972: 1338)

(528) Nichts steht dem im Wege, dass sie . . .
(529) Nothing prevents them from . . .

rather than

(530) They can . . .

The reason for not choosing a TL modal in this case is that the latter would be goal oriented, whereas the SL sentence calls for preservation of source orientation (see Sections 3.2.6.2 and 3.2.6.3). If, however, the SL metaphor is goal oriented, then a TL modal may be used:

(531) She has a way with children.
(532) Sie kann gut mit Kindern umgehen.

As this and all the other examples given suggest, the field of metaphor is to a large extent characterized by idiomaticity.[34] So metaphorical meaning and use in one's nonnative language(s) as well as their correlation with corresponding TL expressions is something to be learned by heart (or to be looked up individually in the dictionary). Metaphor is often an invariance factor. (The exception proves the rule, see the previous example.) Knowing *that* a metaphor will have to be used also in TL must be supplemented by the knowledge of *which* TL metaphor to use and *how* to use it.

3.3.8 Typical Meaning

There are different kinds of 'typical' meaning:
1. What people would respond with if stopped at random and asked, "give me an example of MUST/MAY/CAN . . . " is referred to by Coates (1983) as *cultural stereotype* (p. 13) or *psychological stereotype* (p. 33); in her terminology it corresponds to 'core' examples (see our Section 3.1.4.2). She hastens to add, "and yet, statistically, core examples occur infrequently" (p. 13).
2. This suggests that in addition to the psychological stereotype there is also a *quantitative stereotype* (1983: 38), the meaning of a modal occurring most frequently, depicted as *primary use* in Figure 3.26 (our Section 3.3.1).
3. In addition to typical meanings in terms of psychological and quantitative predominance there are meanings typical for specific cotexts and contexts. As regards cotexts, it must be repeated that not all the meanings of the modals, whether representing primary, secondary, or infrequent use, can occur in any syntactic construction. In Section 3.1.2. we pointed out that epistemic MAY is impossible in questions and that epistemic CAN cannot be used in affirmative statements (see Figure 3.7).

Other uses are not impossible in specific cotexts but rather unlikely or untypical, and here the third kind of typical meaning comes in. Consider the following example:

(533) You must have passed an exam before you can work as a doctor.

Here we find the root use of MUST in a syntactic construction that is much more typical of epistemic modality, such as

(534) Peter must have passed his exam—he looks so happy.

The construction *modal + perfective aspect of full verb* in the root use is restricted to rules and regulations as in (533); otherwise it is typically epistemic.[35] We would like to refer to epistemic modality as the *prototypical meaning* of a modal used in that cotext. In a way, this kind of meaning can be said to emerge from a special form of collocation of a modal—co-occurrence not with specific lexemes, but with a specific syntactic environment. Given this prototypical correlation of meaning and cotext, the latter can be considered an identification factor for the former. This is precisely what we had in mind when we said in Section 3.1.3: "The identification factors for specific meanings of a modal are the respective typical co-occurrences with syntactic and semantic features." This statement served as an introductory remark to the listing of a number of such characteristics suitable for identifying different meanings of CAN and MAY. If you check there under *MAY:* (b) "*Epistemic,*" you will find "the following invariable syntactic co-occurrence patterns: (i) Perfective aspect . . ."

If Coates (1983: 137), on whom this characterization is based, refers to perfective aspect as an *invariable* co-occurrence pattern, it is because her study is corpus based and she did not detect any counterexamples. This shows that, in her corpus, the said association of syntactic pattern and a specific meaning of a modal is indeed very strong. But corpus studies, even though offering all the advantages of empirical research, are limited and may thus exclude rare but nevertheless existing uses. Coates (1983: 48) herself is aware of "the danger of generalizing from a particular corpus." Hence the strength of meaning identification factors as discussed in Section 3.1.4.1 is relative in nature even for those contexts marked by 100 percent correlation with a certain meaning (like the perfective aspect for epistemic MAY). For this reason, we recommend using the term *prototypical* also for those cotext-meaning correlations empirically found to be invariable and speaking of *prototypical identification factors* in this respect.

In the course of our factor study, prototypical meaning has played a role at several points, especially in renditions preceded by the exclamation mark (signaling unacceptability in the relevant sense). The reason is that, if a possible rendition carries a meaning that is different from that prototypically correlated with the kind of its cotext, then correct understanding is at stake. Remember the correspondence of

[172] I/you/he/she/we/they may be right.
[173] Ich/er, sie mag recht haben.
[174] Du magst recht haben.

[175] Ihr mögt recht haben.
[176] Sie/sie mögen recht haben.

where epistemic MAY may be translated as MÖGEN. This German rendition is not always advisable; for example,

[251] He may not be in Berlin.
[252] !Er mag nicht in Berlin sein.

The reason is that negated MÖGEN, especially in a present-tense construction, is so prototypically "volitive" in meaning that we suggested a rendition as unmistakably epistemic as is the SL sentence, even though it involves a change in part of speech:

[257] Vielleicht ist er nicht in Berlin.

So prototypical meaning can act as a revision factor—not necessarily an absolutely obligatory one, but one that is recommended for the sake of avoiding misunderstanding on the part of the TL hearer.

3.3.9 Metalinguistic Meaning

All the kinds of meaning dealt with so far share the characteristic of being used within *object language*. This is the language used to talk about objects in the world. There is also a second 'layer' of language: talk about language itself, usually referred to as *metalanguage*.

The difference between the two kinds of language can be illustrated with reference to the following sentences:

[401] He can go.
(535) In (401) CAN is used.

In (401) CAN is employed to modify the main verb GO, both being used to make an assertion about HE, which pronoun can be used to refer to a person in the real world. In (535), by contrast, CAN itself is the object of reference being talked about.

Because CAN and all the other modals are our object of consideration, all our statements about them contained in this book are metalinguistic in nature. But all the modals contained in our numbered examples are object-linguistic—with the exception of those in (535), (536), and a few others.

Also formal features of the modals themselves are correlated with these two modes of presentation. In this book, metalanguage modals are printed in capitals or italics, whereas object-language ones are not. Other authors also employ bold-face type for metalinguistic use of expressions. Some few do not mark this use at all, but the text type of their publications—that is, linguistic investigations—generally makes it clear which use is intended in each case. Such clarity about the kind of language used in every single case is important not just for the general reader but especially for the translator. Compare the following renditions of (401) and (535), respectively:

[234] Er kann gehen.
(536) In (401) wird CAN verwendet.

The different use of CAN in the two English sentences is made even more obvious by way of these translations. Object-linguistic (234) contains a German modal—the kind of rendition we are familiar with. Metalinguistic (536), however, retains the English modal. There is good reason for this. A statement about the modal in (401) can be about CAN only, because only CAN is used there (and not, for instance, KÖNNEN). Metalinguistic use of expressions thus is an invariance factor.

Note that only the modal remains unchanged—the rest of (536) is in German, even though this sentence is an instance of metalanguage. This shows that metalanguage is not wholly different from object language; it is, in fact, the same language differing only as far as the nature of its object of reference is concerned. And in those cases where the object of metalanguage is a modal, the translator's job is just to incorporate this SL modal as a citation word in the TL rendition.

But there are exceptions to this principle. Consider the metalinguistic use of MÜSSEN in the following small stretch of conversation.

(537) A. 22 Uhr. Schade, jetzt muss ich schon wieder schlafengehen.
    B. *Müssen*, sagst Du? Freu dich doch, dass du schlafen lkannst!
(538) A. It's 10 o'clock. What a pity, I have to go to bed.
    B. *Have to*, you say? Be happy that you lcan sleep!

Because A's remark is fully translated into English, *muss* becomes *have to*. When *muss* is taken up by B as *müssen* in (537), the translator can repeat A's *have to* in (538), even though *müssen* is used metalinguistically, as indicated by the nonfinite verb form.

So metalinguistic use alone is no sufficient condition for simply quoting SL expressions in TL. An additional factor to be taken into account is possible reference to preceding object language use in which the expression in question is already translated in the TL version.

To complete the picture it must be added that some intermediate cases are metalinguistic in nature but allow for translation of the modals for specific purposes. Suppose you sit at a breakfast table in Germany reading the following authentic text printed on your vacuum-packed cheese:

(539) Du darfst
    Aufschnitt Naturkäse

On the reverse side of the package you read

(540) Du darfst Beratungsdienst
Feldbrunnenstrasse 52
20148 Hamburg

A bit further down it says

(541) Du darfst Lebensmittel im Rahmen einer kalorienbewussten Ernährungsweise.

It must be emphasized that none of these short texts contains italics. Trying to make sense of (539) and (541), you may try to draw upon your knowledge of ellipsis in German and come up with:

(542) Du darfst Aufschnitt, Naturkäse essen.
(543) Du darfst Lebensmittel . . . essen.

But (540), analyzed this way, remains inaccessible. What is to be done? The solution comes when you finally read at the bottom

(544) Du darfst GmbH
Postfach 305588
20317 Hamburg

So *Du darfst* is a company name, as is *Soll & Haben Warenvertriebs-GmbH* located in the same city. And just as the latter is not to be confused with *debit and credit* mentioned in Section 2.8.1, it would not be correct to render (544) by

(545) You may Ltd. . . .

Accordingly, (539)–(541) would have to be rendered by

(546) Du darfst
Slices of natural cheese
(547) Du darfst Consultation Service . . .
(548) Du darfst food . . .

An additional remark seems to be in place, though. The translator cannot change a company name, but it would make sense for a German host to translate for his English-speaking guest *Du darfst* in (539) as

(549) You may

thus revealing that the product name is motivated by object language: The company specializing in low-calorie food (see (541)), the calorie-conscious consumer *may* indeed buy and eat this cheese. So the product name represents what was called *reflected meaning* in Section 3.3.4. It builds upon the object-language meaning of *Du darfst*. This link between the object language and metalanguage use of *Du darfst* may well be referred to as another kind of interrelation of modalities (see Section 3.2.5.3)—*object-language and metalanguage modalities*. By virtue of their link, they oscillate between a mere product name and the actual meaning of *Du darfst*. If this is also felt by the translator he or she may choose to translate the product name for heuristic purposes.

So far we have indicated different procedures for dealing with modals used metalinguistically: one of simply incorporating or 'importing' them into TL, and two ways of referring to their object-language source and translating them as modals. But how does this get along with Austin's (1956)

(550) 'Ifs and Cans'

(already briefly touched upon in note 14)? Obviously there are no modal *cans* in English, so we are faced with a philosopher taking the liberty of breaking morphological boundaries. But (550) is at least modeled along the archaic phrase

(551) (If) ifs and an[d]s (were pots and pans) . . .

Ifs existing, modal *cans* are imaginable. In a way, then, Austin plays upon the modal CAN and its homonym.

A morphologically adequate translation would be

(552) *Wenns und Könnens/*Wenne und Könnene

All this sounds decidedly odd, however, because there is neither a plural form to WENN and KÖNNEN nor a German structural analogue to (551).

Another strategy would be to take *ifs* as denoting conditions and *cans* as denoting possibilities, giving rise to

(553) Bedingungen und Möglichkeiten

This proposal is not completely far-fetched if we remember that *musts* was rendered as *Erfordernisse*:

[110] Three important MUSTS in planning . . .
[111] Drei wichtige Erfordernisse bei der Planung . . .

But as his paper shows, Austin did not have in mind various conditions and possibilities, but different uses of the *words* IF and CAN. His use of *Ifs* and *Cans* in (550) was thus metalinguistic, which is why (553) cannot be accepted as a rendition.

We propose the following strategy. Given the preceding morphological restrictions in German, the plural element must be shifted onto another noun, which at the same time serves as a marker for the metalinguistic use of the two expressions, these being italicized in addition, yielding

(554) Verschiedene Verwendungen der Ausdrücke *wenn* und *können*.

Note that the translator of the published German version of 'Ifs and Cans' (Austin 1975a) indicated the metalinguistic use of the expressions by specially marking and capitalizing them '*Falls* und *Können*.' As this title shows the translator did not, however, deem it necessary to convey the plural elements as contained in (554).

Summing up, we can list the following types of translational strategies for handling metalinguistic use of the modals:

1. Generally, incorporate SL modal in TL ((535) → (536)).
2. (a). In case of preceding object-language use, translate as TL modal (expression) ((537) → (538)).
   (b). In case of object-language use as an obvious basis for metalinguistic use, as in 1 ((539) → (546));
   if appropriate, explain link by translating ((539) → (549)).
3. Nonstandard metalinguistic use requires individual solutions ((550) → (554)).

3.4 VOICE

As mentioned in Section 3.3.6, active and passive sentences are usually considered to represent the same conceptual content or proposition; for example,

(555) Young children play this game.
(556) This game is played by young children.

The semantic contents of both sentences may be captured by the same logical formula: $Play_{(children, \; this \; game)}$. Differences exist, of course, for syntactic functions, as well as for topic and comment (see Section 3.3.6). All in all, it seems to be mainly a matter of putting the two nouns and the process of playing into different perspectives. But now compare the two sentences again after the modal CAN is inserted.

(557) Young children can play this game.
[181] This game can be played by young children.

Both these sentences express root modality, but there is a difference as far as its subdivisions are concerned. Leech (1987: 74) points out that the first, active sentence "could be interpreted in the 'ability' sense," but the second, passive one carries "the 'possibility' meaning." Of course one could say that both sentences make a statement about the modal nature of some entity, namely, that of young children in (557) and that of the game in (181). But the two entities being different in nature, animate vs. inanimate, the two sentences cannot be said to be modally synonymous beyond their common characterization of representing root modality—hence Leech's distinction between "ability" and "possibility." On a practical level, however, we would say that their difference is negligible or even nonexistent because the nature of the game and the nature of young children correspond to each other in this case: Young children are such that they can play this game because the game is such that it can be played by young children—and vice versa.

How can the two sentences be translated?

(558) Kleine Kinder können dieses Spiel spielen.
[184] Dieses Spiel kann von kleinen Kindern gespielt werden.

Paralleling English, the active sentence expresses the meaning of ability, and the passive one expresses that of possibility. We thus find two invariance factors correlated: voice and subkinds of root modality.

3.5 TENSE

Translating from German into English, certain gaps relating to past tense must be filled on the basis of compensation factors. Leech (1987: 95 ff.) distinguishes between nonavailability of past-tense forms and past-tense meanings.

MUST lacking a past-tense form, *had to* has to take over:

(559) Ich musste es tun.
(560) I had to do it.

But note, *had to* is necessary only in case of deontic or circumstantial dynamic modality; with subject-oriented dynamic modality, MUST can be used also in the past (see also its use in indirect speech, Section 3.6):

(561) Nachdem ich ihr meinen Rat gegeben habe, muss sie natürlich genau das Gegenteil tun!
(562) Naturally, after I gave her my advice, she must go and do the opposite! (*Longman Dictionary of English Language and Culture* 1992: 877)

As regards nonavailability of meanings, MIGHT is not used for epistemic possibility, COULD to be used instead; for example,

(563) It may rain today.
(564) Yesterday's view was that it could rain.

Leech (1987: 97) adds,

Even in the 'permission' sense, MIGHT in direct speech is sufficiently rare to be discounted. We may therefore present a simplified picture of past modal meaning as follows: for all intents and purposes, neither MAY nor MUST have past tense equivalents, and their special nuances of meaning can therefore not be expressed in the past. Instead, COULD and *had to* are the natural past tense translations of MAY and MUST:

[439] Visitors may ascend the tower for 50p this summer →
(565) Visitors could ascend the tower for 50p last summer.

Because COULD is to be used for MIGHT, not only do the special meaning nuances of MAY itself become inexpressible but also the distinction between MAY and CAN in the permission sense gets blurred! This suggests an easy job for the translator: All uses of the German modals in the following sentences can be rendered by COULD:

(566) Besucher durften den Turm diesen Sommer für 50p besteigen. ("permission," internal communication, see Section 3.3.2) → (565)
(567) Besucher konnten den Turm diesen Sommer für 50p besteigen. ("permission," "possibility") → (565)

Of course, there are in addition past-tense suppletive forms such as *had the opportunity to*. These suggest factuality of the event referred to by the full verb, so we prefer to deal with them in the appropriate pragmatics section (4.3.3).

3.6 INDIRECT SPEECH

Even though MIGHT as a past-tense form cannot be used in direct speech for epistemic modality and is rare for deontic modality (see the previous section), in indirect speech it can be used without exception (see Leech 1987: 108):

[439] Visitors may ascend the tower for 50p this summer. →
(568) The brochure declared that visitors might ascend the tower for 50p that summer.

[563] It may rain today. →
(569) Yesterday he said that it could/might rain.

In German, indirect speech requires the *present* subjunctive in the reported clause, irrespective of whether the reporting clause is in present or past tense:

(570) Gestern sagte er, es könne regnen.

However, if the present subjunctive form is identical to the present indicative one, the past subjunctive ought to be used:

(571) Die Broschüre besagte, dass Besucher den Turm im Sommer für 50p besteigen könnten.

More usual is use of the past indicative, though:

(572) Die Broschüre besagte, dass Besucher den Turm im Sommer für 50p besteigen konnten.

In contrast to its use in direct speech, deontic MUST is retained in reported clauses of indirect speech (Leech 1987: 109):

(573) You must reach camp by ten. →
(574) They were told that they must reach camp by ten.

(575) Ihr müsst das Lager bis 10 Uhr erreichen. →
(576) Ihnen wurde gesagt, sie müssten das Lager bis 10 Uhr erreichen.

In contrast to (572), the past indicative form cannot be used in (576) because no *dass* clause is involved here.

4. PRAGMATIC FACTORS

The inspiration to integrate pragmatic studies and contrastive studies dates back at least two decades (see Kühlwein in Barrera-Vidal and Kühlwein 1975: 122). It was taken up by Snell-Hornby (1984: 210), deploring the largely unilingual approach of pragmatics, on the one hand, and the abstractness of contrastive studies, lacking reference to communicative function, on the other. She made a case for contrastive studies working pragmatically and pragmatic linguists working contrastively and expected from this integration "quite a breakthrough in the study of language" (p. 210).

Instead of looking for "some abstract equivalent" the translator is advised by her to have recourse to empirical contrastive research. In a later publication she actually ascribes to translation studies the qualities postulated before: "While the classic approach to the study of language and translation has been to isolate phenomena (mainly words) and study them in depth, translation studies is essentially concerned with a web of relationships, the importance of individual items being decided by their relevance in the larger context of text, situation and culture" (1988: 36).

Here we see the pragmatic dimension of translation factors including linguistic as well as nonlinguistic elements. Linguistic factors are those relating to the illocutionary force of utterances (Section 4.1); nonlinguistic factors relate to concepts such as situation (Section 4.4) and culture (Section 4.6). In between, that is, sharing characteristics of both, are the notions of perlocution (Section 4.2) and factuality (Section 4.3). Permanent language varieties (Section 4.5) are included in the pragmatics chapter because they are the product of language use. The factor of text will be dealt with in Chapter 6 because it is also relevant as a translation unit.

4.1 ILLOCUTIONARY FORCE

The concept of illocutionary force or illocution denotes one aspect of the verbal action or speech act performed by uttering a sentence. The following sentences containing modals may be used to perform the acts stated in parentheses (Kussmaul 1977: 202 ff.):

(577) You may go to the pictures. (permitting)
(578) May I go to the pictures? (asking for permission)
(579) No, you may not. (prohibiting)
(580) You must pay your debts. (ordering)
(581) Can you shut the window? (demanding, requesting)
(582) He may come tomorrow. (assuming)
(583) May you be happy! (wishing)

As will have been noticed, pragmatics in terms of illocutionary force slightly modifies the characteristics of the modals given so far, that is, in terms of semantics; cf. (577)–(583) vs. (354)–(358) in Section 3.2.4.4. Whereas in semantics MAY in (577) would be described as conveying "permission," its pragmatic description is "permitting"; and whereas MUST in (580) would mean "obligation" in terms of semantics, we find "ordering" in pragmatics. The illocutionary act of ordering may even be performed by means of using CAN. Leech (1987: 71) explains this by pointing out that the meaning of the modals

> has both a logical [or semantic; see Section 3.3.1] and a practical (or pragmatic) element. We can talk about them in terms of such logical notions as "permission" and "necessity," but this done, we still have to consider ways in which these notions become remoulded by the psychological pressures of everyday communication between human beings: factors such as condescension, politeness, tact, and irony. Condescension, for example, intervenes to make the *can* of *You can go now* (which in logical terms means no more than "permission") into something approaching a command . . .

Having already mentioned the illocutions for (577) and so on, we would like to add that most of these sentences can also be used as 'mere' statements or questions—hence the phenomenon of illocutionary ambiguity (see Section 4.1.4.3). Other aspects of illocutionary indeterminacy include gradience (Section 4.1.4.2) and merger (Section 4.1.4.4). Before dealing with these we will have to say a word about the special position of the modals in permitting such pragmatic versatility in the first place. This requires a comparison with other, partially synonymous modal expressions.

4.1.1 Pragmatic Generality

The greater semantic generality of the modals in contrast to the much greater specificity of other modal expressions (see Section 3.2.1.1) is paralleled in the field of pragmatics. As regards their illocutionary force, the two sentences

(584) Do you have enough will power to finish your thesis?
(585) Can you finish your thesis?

can both be interpreted as direct questions. However, due to the greater length, semantic specificity, and prosodic prominence of HAVE ENOUGH WILL POWER TO, (584) is less likely to be interpreted as an indirect request, Panther (1981a: 298 f.) points out.[36] The semantic generality and shortness of CAN, on the other hand, has the pragmatic effect of shifting it from a lexical status to that of a quasi-grammatical marker for illocutionary indirectness.

In German, a similar situation holds:

(586) Hast Du genügend Willenskraft, Deine Examensarbeit zu beenden?
(587) Kannst Du Deine Examensarbeit beenden?

Modal particles such as DENN can underline the question character of (586), whereas *nicht endlich* would strengthen the directive reading of (587). All in all, English and German modals correspond to each other in terms of greater illocutionary versatility. Because illocutionary acts are performed by way of using a present-tense verb form, there is no question of other modal expressions serving as suppletives for the English modals in indirect speech acts. This means that here modals can be rendered as modals. For direct speech acts other kinds of modal expressions used in SL can also be used in TL.

Special attention must, however, be paid to the differences in usage norms with regard to a subclass of indirect speech acts.[37] Gutknecht and Panther (1973: 166, n. 7) point out that, in German, verbs used by a speaker to express his or her mental attitude toward a certain state of affairs are followed by an embedded performative predicate that *must* contain a modal. In English, this is not required:

(588) Ich freue mich, Sie hier begrüssen zu können/dürfen.
(589) I am happy to welcome you here.

4.1.2 Interrelation of Illocutions

In our semantics chapter (Section 3.2.5.3), we discussed the following two sentences:

[398] Erwarten Sie einen Anruf? Dann sagen Sie bitte in der Telefonzentrale Bescheid, wohin Ihr Anruf weitergeleitet werden soll.
[399] Expecting a phone call? Please advise the telephone operator where your call can be transferred to.

It was shown that the interrelatedness of the two modalities represented by CAN and SOLLEN accounts for translation equivalence of these sentences: CAN (KÖNNEN) is included in SOLLEN (BE TO). This semantic inclusion being unilateral, however, equivalence can be said to be partial at best. Let us see how pragmatics can contribute to a greater degree of equivalence.

The utterance of (399) is a request not just for a statement about a possibility of transfer, but for a directive for action. Even though the speaker seems to be interested in only getting to know where calls *can* be transferred to, he or she will definitely take such information as an injunction about where they *are to* be transferred. Therefore (399) is closely related to a corresponding speech act containing BE TO:

(590) Expecting a phone call? Please advise the telephone operator where your call is to be transferred.

This illocutionary relatedness is paralleled by the possible reply

(591) My call can be transferred to Conference Room B.

which equally contains not just descriptive (representative) but also directive elements. This can be delineated as follows. One of the factors determining the pragmatic interpretation of CAN statements is identified by Panther (1981a: 296) as being the degree of familiarity with the information conveyed by such utterances (see Section 4.1.4.1). If the information is new to the hearer as is the case with (591), the utterance may be taken to be a direct speech act of informing. The specific context of (591) as a reaction to (399), however, permits and even necessitates the *additional*, indirect reading of a directive illocution. Uttering (591), the speaker would certainly not only wish the hearer to know that he or she is being informed properly; the speaker would want to *direct* the hearer toward action by informing that person where he or she *is to* actually transfer calls appropriately. Because this is exactly what is expressed by SOLLEN in (398), pragmatic analysis reveals an even greater degree of equivalence of (398) and (399) than the semantic one. Not only does SOLLEN imply CAN, but CAN implicates SOLLEN in this special context.

Moreover, the directive character of (591) is paralleled by the corresponding German version

(592) Mein Anruf kann nach Konferenzraum B weitergeleitet werden.

as well as by the more personal variant

(593) Sie können meinen Anruf nach Konferenzraum B weiterleiten.

In a way analogous to that indicated for (591), utterance of these sentences will also be interpreted as giving indirect directives. Due to the positive connotation of KÖNNEN (see Section 3.3.2), the hotel guest will give the impression of being particularly polite.

4.1.3 Subtleties in Illocutionary Force

Figure 3.20 in Section 3.2.1.1 presented "a layered picture of subtle distinctions within a single concept of 'possibility'." A similar system could be set up for the modal degree of "necessity." We will deal here with one facet of such a system, including certain subtle differences in illocutionary force corresponding to nuances of necessity.

Table 3.1 in Section 3.2.4.1 presented two different degrees of modality within the field of necessity. SHOULD was related to tentative necessity (advisability); MUST, to necessity. Corresponding speech acts show the stronger illocutionary force of MUST:

(594) You should go there tomorrow.
(595) You must go there tomorrow.

Now, other modal expressions allow for still finer differentiation. In 'Getting the Subtle Distinctions: SHOULD versus HAD BETTER,' Altman (1986) researched into the relative strength of these expressions as reported by native and nonnative speakers of English. He proved by experiment that nonnative speakers tend to understand HAD BETTER in the literal sense of "it would be better," whereas native speakers of English take this expression as denoting a definitely binding instruction, the force of which lies between that of MUST and HAVE TO, on the one hand, and that of SHOULD, on the other hand, thus exceeding the force of SHOULD!

Taking *it would be better if* to correspond to *es wäre besser, wenn*, the latter clause is ruled out as a German rendition of HAD BETTER. Also *sollte* as equivalent to SHOULD seems to denote too low a degree of modality. Dictionary entries can be found to equate HAD BETTER, itself being no modal in the strict sense, but a quasi-modal[38] or modal idiom (Quirk et. al. 1985: 137), to *sollte lieber*, an expression containing a modal: *Langenscheidts Enzyklopädisches Wörterbuch*, Vol. 2, Part 2, p. 1415, lists it as variant 6 of SOLLEN, together with the following example:

(596) Du solltest lieber jetzt gehen, sonst kommst Du in die Dunkelheit.
(597) You had better go now, otherwise it'll be getting too dark.

In both sentences the strong advisability of an action for avoiding a disadvantage is expressed clearly. Altman (1986: 83) found this factor to be the unanimous characterization of the meaning of HAD BETTER by native speakers of English.

Because nonnative speakers were found not to be aware of the strong directive character of HAD BETTER and its intermediate position between

SHOULD and MUST, their training as translators had better include treatment of such subtleties in degrees and kinds of modality and in related illocutionary force.

4.1.4 Illocutionary Indeterminacy

In Section 3.1.4 we presented semantic indeterminacy relating to the interpretation of modals as part of the proposition of sentences. We dealt with the strength of meaning indicating factors and also with gradience, ambiguity, and merger. It is interesting to find that the same aspects of indeterminacy exist in the pragmatic domain of illocutionary force.

4.1.4.1 Strength of Illocutionary Force Indicators

Panther (1981a: 295) refers to the English and German modals as "*indirect illocutionary force indicators* (or more shortly, *indirect force markers* or *indicators*)." It is true that in sentences such as

[585] Can you finish your thesis?
[587] Kannst du deine Examensarbeit beenden?

the modals indicate the possibility of indirect illocutions, and in

[584] Do you have enough will power to finish your thesis?
[586] Hast du genügend Willenskraft, deine Examensarbeit zu beenden?

other modal expressions exclude this possibility (see Section 4.1.1).

But this does not mean that (585) and (587) are invariably used as indirect speech acts; they may well be intended to be literal questions. So the strength of modals as illocutionary force indicators is indeterminate. The decisive force indicator for these two sentences as well as for

(598) Can you fix that plug for me?
(599) You can fix that plug for me.

is not merely the presence of the modals. Panther (1981a: 296) argues,

> It seems to me that one of the factors influencing the pragmatic reading of (598) and (599) is related to what the speaker and the hearer regard as given information. If it is known to both the speaker and the hearer that the latter can fix the plug then the utterance of (598) and (599) would violate the felicity conditions that one should only ask questions if one doesn't know the answer (598) or only inform people about things they don't know (599). Therefore, if it is assumed that the violation of the felicity conditions was done on purpose, a non-literal interpretation follows almost automatically.

This means that (a) the choice of a modal in contrast to that of another kind of modal expression, in combination with (b) the givenness of the information stated or asked about are the two pragmatic identification factors that can be looked upon as unmistakable indicators of indirect illocutions of (585), (587), (598) and (599).

This principle applies to both CAN and KÖNNEN in statements and questions, so that both can freely be rendered by each other, see (585) ↔ (587), (598) ↔ (600), and (599) ↔ (601).

(600) Kannst du mir den Stecker reparieren?
(601) Du kannst mir den Stecker reparieren.

Admittedly, communication situations appropriate for (599) or (601) to be uttered as direct speech acts of informing someone about his or her abilities may be less usual than those for the corresponding interrogative sentences (598) and (600) asked as direct questions. This does not, however, invalidate the principle of given information involving modals as an identification factor for indirect illocutionary force.

4.1.4.2 Gradience of Indirectness and Politeness

Commenting further on the interpretive possibilities of sentences such as those just dealt with, Panther (1981a: 296) writes that

> there are many communication situations where the speaker is not so sure about the ability . . . of the hearer to perform certain actions. In other words, information may be *more or less given*, there are degrees of certainty of what is the case in a given communicative situation. I assume that the degree of given information has an influence on what I would like to call 'pragmatic prominence.' A high degree of given information concerning the hearer's abilities in (598) and (599) will result in a high degree of prominence of the indirect request interpretation with a corresponding low degree of prominence of the literal interpretation. (italics as in the original)

This approach gives rise to a gradient of illocutionary interpretation. Panther (1981a: 296 f.) depicts "the relationship between contextually given information and pragmatic prominence" as the three gradients shown in Figure 4.1.

In the context of translation, the utterance situation becomes more complex: The translator's state of knowledge is also involved. Because both CAN and KÖNNEN can be used in case of both full knowledge about the givenness of information in statements and questions or no knowledge at all (see the previous subsection), they can certainly also be used for any intermediate point of interpretation lying between full and zero certainty about

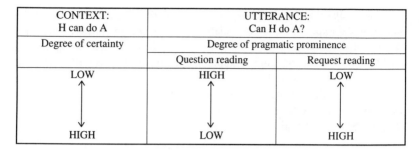

FIGURE 4.1.
Gradience of Illocutionary Interpretation

givenness. This means that gradience in illocutionary interpretation is no translational change factor for the two modals.

In the example just discussed, illocutionary gradience was conceived of in terms of the speaker's (and the translator's) degree of certainty about the hearer's ability to perform certain actions.

There is yet another aspect of gradience. When Leech (1981: 336) says that "illocutionary force is very often a matter of degree rather than kind," he refers to a scale of politeness according to the following sequence of sentences:

(602) Shut the door!
(603) Will you shut the door?
(604) Can you shut the door?
(605) Could you shut the door?
(606) I wonder if you'd mind shutting the door?

The increasing degrees of politeness here correlate with decreasing degrees of modality (DO–WILL–CAN–COULD–WOULD). Each modal can therefore serve as an identification factor for a particular degree of politeness chosen by the speaker. If this degree is to be kept in TL as an invariance factor, the translator has to choose from a corresponding TL scale the form that is nearest equivalent to the SL form. Neglecting the distinction between the formal and the familiar pronouns of address in German (*Sie* vs. *du*), the following TL scale could be proposed:

(607) Schliess die Tür!
(608) Schliesst du die Tür?
(609) Kannst du die Tür schliessen?
(610) Könntest du die Tür schliessen?
(611) Ob es dir etwas ausmacht, die Tür zu schliessen?

Rendition (608) presupposes that the direct speech act performed by uttering (603) is that of asking a question about a possible future action of the hearer. This can be expressed in German by using the present tense.

It is interesting in this connection that Leech (1981: 337) describes the direct speech act performed by uttering

(612) Will you open the window?

as "a question about the hearer's willingness to do something." Because (603) is equivalent in structure to (612), Leech would probably give the same description for (603). This entails, however, that WILL in this sentence would have to be rendered by WOLLEN:

(613) Willst du die Tür schliessen?

A third possibility would be to expressly indicate future time reference by using WERDEN:

(614) Wirst du die Tür schliessen?

This shows that the polysemy of the English modals and the possibility of having several German variants for individual meanings account for the incongruity of the two illocutionary scales. So the task of weighing the English-German pair of scales toward a point of balance is indeed a delicate one.

This delicacy is even increased by the possibility of adding in the preceding German sentences modal particles such as MAL or WOHL (see Sections 6.3.9.5 and 6.3.9.6). Their effect might be said to be akin to that of other 'speech act modifiers' such as the epistemic "possibility" marker POSSIBLY, researched into by Blum-Kulka (1985). She argues that their presence in utterances such as

(615) Could I possibly get a lift home with you?

is not essential for the utterance to be understood as a request (1985: 214) but that they act as pragmatic force indicators raising the level of illocutionary transparency (1985: 215). This claim was, in fact, empirically verified by her. Native speakers of English were presented with a questionnaire containing sentences such as the following:

(616) Could you possibly give your presentation next week

It was shown that the presence of POSSIBLY had a tangible effect on the results of interpretation, as depicted in Table 4.1 (on the basis of Blum-Kulka 1985: 224). This means that the notion of increased illocutionary transparency amounts to a shift in the degree of probability of a specific reading having been intended. A notion like this qualifies speech act modifiers such as POSSIBLY as another factor influencing the gradience of il-

	Without POSSIBLY	With POSSIBLY
Question only	25 %	50 %
Request only	17 %	25 %
Both interpretations	58 %	25 %

TABLE 4.1.
The Effect of POSSIBLY on Illocutionary Interpretation

locutionary interpretation shown in Figure 4.1. Note that *could possibly* is another instance of harmonic combinations (see Section 3.3.5.3).

4.1.4.3 Illocutionary Ambiguity

Speech acts containing modals can show ambiguity between a direct and one or more indirect readings. Both of the following sentences

[190] You can go now.
[192] Ihr könnt jetzt gehen.

are ambiguous in three ways: between the direct illocution of a statement and the indirect illocutions of granting permission and laying an obligation. Utterance context will tell which interpretation is (likely to be) intended in a given case (see Sections 4.1.4.1 and 4.1.4.2) because "context acts obviously as a disambiguation factor" (Blum-Kulka 1985: 218, n. 6).

In addition to illocutionary ambiguity being 'merely' a matter of interpretation of readings, Leech (1981: 337) presents the interesting possibility of illocutions being "often deliberately ambivalent" by virtue of their syntactic form. The tag question

(617) You will come, won't you?

shows the characteristics of two illocutionary acts, because it carries the force of an assertion that is "softened by the following question . . . , so the whole utterance can play the role of a pressing invitation" (p. 337).

German lacks modal tags, so the softening must be achieved in a different way, and the assertion itself is best augmented by emotive ODER suitable for expressing its presumptive character (see Section 6.6.3):

(618) Du kommst doch, oder?

4.1.4.4 Illocutionary Merger

In our semantics chapter (Section 3.1.4.4), merger was said to occur in contexts in which correct understanding does not necessitate distinguishing between two readings because they are no longer mutually exclusive (Coates 1983: 17). So we said that instances of merger are not subject to an either-or interpretation.

A comparable pragmatic phenomenon exists in connection with indirect speech acts. Leech explains that sentences such as

[612] Will you open the window?

"are not ambiguous in the sense of being . . . *either* a directive *or* a question. . . . Rather . . . it is *by virtue* of being a question of a certain kind (a question about the hearer's willingness to do something) that (612) succeeds in being a more polite variant of a command" (1981: 337, italics as in the original). Utterances such as that of (612) "keep their question-like character, even while they are interpreted as having a . . . directive force" (1981: 337).

Merger in the strict sense of the word means, however, that no matter which of two readings of a sentence or utterance you choose, you end up with the same interpretation. What the quotes from Leech suggest is that in the interpretation of indirect speech acts, the indirect reading is based upon and coexists with the direct one. But it does not mean the same thing as the direct one. So indirect illocutions in this sense do not meet the strict requirements of merger, but are instances of illocutionary interrelation.

Illocutionary merger had better be based not merely on the notion of coexistence of different illocutions (as conceived of in the interpretation of (612)), but on the notion of identical perlocutionary effect. We will deal with this possibility in the next section on an interlingual basis.

As regards rendering indirect speech acts of the form (612) in German, we refer back to the different ways of rendering (603), which is equivalent in structure (see Section 4.1.4.2).

4.2 PERLOCUTION

Translation equivalence on the level of perlocution would mean that the TL rendition produces the same effect in the hearer as does the SL original. This identical effect could be expected if identical means are employed, that is, if the same acts of reference, predication, and illocution are performed; for instance, by saying

[207] He can play the piano.
[208] Er kann Klavier spielen.

The effect of uttering either of these two sentences will be that the hearer is informed that the person referred to can play the piano.

The principle of identity of effect correlated with identity of linguistic means employed also holds for indirect speech acts, such as

[190] You can go now.
[192] Ihr könnt jetzt gehen.

Hearing either of these two sentences the hearer will know that he or she is being informed or permitted or ordered to go. Certainly both sentences are ambiguous among the three readings, but because they are equally ambiguous the same potential effect can be produced by each of them.

At several points in the course of our survey we have come across cases of divergence of reference, predication, or illocution. We have to ask whether an identical perlocution can be achieved nonetheless. Let us start with the following sentence pair (see Sections 3.2.4.1 and 3.2.5.4):

[342] . . . und eine der vielen Autoverleihfirmen hat bestimmt noch einen Mietwagen für Sie.
[343] . . . and you can get a car from any of the many car rental firms.

With all their difference in kinds of modality both sentences can be used to give the hearer confidence in the possibility of getting a car. BESTIMMT is epistemic in character and presents a state of affairs as less than 100 precent certain; yet it approaches this 100 percent and therefore sounds very encouraging. The English version states unlimited root possibility and in terms of illocution almost assumes the character of a promise. The use of ANY instead of ONE makes (343) especially promising.

This means that both utterances, even though different in terms of modality, predication, and illocution, can produce the common effect of instilling confidence in the hearer. Why heterogeneous means were used to achieve this common goal is a different question. But faced with (342)–(343) we can at least explain their ultimate equivalence on the level of perlocution. This would justify the choice of rendition. The translator could say that the ultimate factor guiding his or her activities was identity of perlocution, and this was achieved.

A similar argumentation is possible where there is no actual difference in SL and TL propositions but just one in syntax, as in

[149] Money can't buy everything.
[151] Mit Geld kann man nicht alles kaufen.

König (1974: 251) points out that these sentences are the expression of different syntactic possibilities in English and German (see Section 2.9). At the same time both sentences share the same communicative structure. Their subjects, MONEY and GELD, referentially corresponding to each other, both appear as theme. This shows, he argues, that in different languages different grammatical phenomena interact to produce the same *overall effect*, namely, maximum expressiveness.

The same is true of the following sentence pair, which also shows that different syntactic habits were taken into account (see the end of Section 3.2.6.4), and yet the overall communicative effect is the same:

[426] Mit nebenstehender Entfernungstabelle können Sie die Gesamtlänge Ihrer Flugroute berechnen.

[428] The opposite table of distances enables you to find out the total length of your own route.

4.3 FACTUALITY

Modality is sometimes understood as part of a predication that denotes an *unrealized* event. When we say

(619) John kann schwimmen.

[364] John can swim.

we do not usually imply that the person referred to as John actually swims; we 'only' mean that he has the ability/possibility/permission to swim. This is what distinguishes modality from *(f)actuality* as expressed by

(620) John schwimmt.

(621) John swims/is swimming.

Of course, the latter two sentences do not by themselves imply that someone called John is actually swimming, but their object-language use by a speaker does. This is the double tie of our current topic to pragmatics: its relation to speaker use and its reference to real world facts.

But if factuality is distinct from modality, why then deal with it here? Those who have worked their way through this book up to the present point may have an idea that a link exists between the two concepts. In Section 3.2.5.2 we scrutinized the word ACTION and found 'in' it the notion of "possibility"—no action without its possibility. We referred to this phenomenon as *implicit modality*.

This observation can be extended to (the utterance of) whole sentences implying modality. Everyone would agree that someone who utters (620) or (621) implies that the person swimming has the possibility/ability to do so. Accordingly, we would like to extend application of the term *implicit modality* to such utterances that report mere facts but imply the presence of some modality.

As was the case with the noun ACTION, however, translation of 'factual' sentences does not involve any reference to modality—(620) and (621) can be translated into each other without any thought about possibility or ability implied by them. But this is not so with all interlingual pairs of 'factual' sentences, as will be shown in Subsections 4.3.1 and 4.3.3 pertaining to present and past reference, respectively.

4.3.1 Present-Tense Forms

When a sentence such as

(622) Ich sehe zwei Schiffe.

is to be translated into English, its 'factual' equivalent would be

(623) !I see two ships.

However, as every native speaker of English will agree, this sentence would be unidiomatic, (624) being used instead:

(624) I can see two ships.

Even though what is stated in (624) is modality, the point of uttering this sentence is stating the actual (process of) seeing, not making a statement about one's visual power or the possibility of seeing two ships.

Many pages have been written hypothesizing about the possible reason why English uses CAN in connection with the factuality of full verbs of inert perception such as SEE or SMELL. For our present purposes it will suffice to say that English here has a modal where it means a fact.[39]

We would rather deal with the interlingual relation of sentences (622) and (624). If we take them at their face value, then certainly (622) implies (624): My seeing two ships implies the possibility of my doing so. Factuality implies modality. Yet remarkably, this sentence pair can illustrate not just the semantic relationship of implication but also that of translational equivalence.

Now a sentence implying another one would not normally be said to be equivalent to it; for example, (621) implying (364):

[621] John swims/is swimming.
[364] John can swim.

How then can (622) and (624) be said to be equivalent? The reason is that in this special case, utterance of *both* sentences means more than what their words suggest:

- (622) (semantically) implies the meaning of (624).
- (624) (pragmatically) implicates the meaning of (622).

For this kind of interrelation of modality and nonmodality (see Section 3.2.5.4) we would like to introduce a special term. Having in Section 4.3 extended the use of *implicit modality* to sentences such as (622), we now suggest speaking of *implicit factuality* as regards sentences of the type (624). To supplement the description, it would be natural to add the term *explicit factuality* for characterizing (622), whereas (624) could be said to represent *explicit modality* (which amounts to extending the use of the latter term from simple nouns as conceived of in Section 3.2.5.2 to (the utterance of) whole sentences. This gives rise to the matrix depicted in Table 4.2.

The term *explicit factuality* must be further subdivided because it subsumes two phenomena that are quite distinct. Usually when factuality is explicitly stated (as in (621) or (622)), this is what is meant—a fact stated is a fact meant. But this is not always so—see Wertheimer's (1972: 90) quote from the Harvard University *Supplement to the General Announcement on Higher Degrees in Philosophy* (p. 5):

(625) The completed thesis is read and appraised by a committee of two, usually identical with the candidate's Thesis Advisory Committee.

Like (621) and (622), (625) presents a proposition as a fact and thus qualifies as a sentence of explicit factuality. But this is not the real point of utterance. Sentence (625) is part of injunctions that *must* be adhered to for the sake of a proper procedure of examination. So (625) is another instance of implicit modality. Yet is differs from (621) and (622), which also belong to this category. In the latter two sentences modality is 'merely' implied, but in (625) it is the essential message conveyed. This sentence thus resembles

[394] Hier wird Deutsch gesprochen.
[395] Hier spricht man Deutsch.

where the implicit assertion of modality was said to be the essential purpose of statement (see Section 3.2.5.2).

With *explicit modality*, possibilities are structured differently; for example,

[364] John can swim.
[624] I can see two ships.

The whole point of uttering (624) is to focus on its implicit factuality. But (364), equally containing CAN, does not even contain implicit factuality. This suggests two differences between explicit modality and explicit factuality:

- Whereas *all* explicitly factual sentences contain some kind of implicit modality—remember, no action without its possibility—not all explicitly modal sentences have implicit factuality (see (364) and Section 4.3).

	Modality	Factuality
(622) Ich sehe ...	implicit	explicit
(624) I can see ...	explicit	implicit

TABLE 4.2.
Explicit and Implicit Modality and Factuality

- With explicit factuality implicit modality may exist but not be the point of utterance, see (622); but when explicitly modal sentences contain implicit factuality, that automatically becomes the point of utterance, as in (624). Implicit factuality merely existing but not becoming point of utterance is highly improbable.
- A more fundamental difference is that, with explicit modality, the modality stated really exists (see (364)), but with explicit factuality, the factuality stated need not exist (see (625)).

Table 4.3 sums up the points made so far.

Let us focus once more on interlingual correspondence. With all their differences, sentences (622) and (624) have the same point of utterance: stating factuality (see Table 4.3). This is not surprising—after all, there must be some basic likeness qualifying both sentences as interlingual equivalents.

Other pairs of sentences would have identical entries in Table 4.3, which makes their status as equivalents even more plausible:

- In both of the following sentences, modality is stated and is also the point of utterance:

[364] John can swim.
(626) John kann schwimmen.

- Stated factuality as in

[625] The completed thesis is read and appraised by a committee of two
. . .

has a German equivalent that equally shows simple present and whose point of utterance is also implicit modality:

(627) Die abgeschlossene Dissertation wird von einem Zweier-Gremium gelesen und beurteilt, das i.a. mit dem Beratungsgremium des Doktoranden identisch ist.

Accordingly, different degrees of equivalence can be detected in the first vs. the other two of the sentence pairs (622)–(624), (364)–(626), and (625)–(627).

Factuality as point of utterance is explicit for (622) but implicit for (624), whereas (364) and (626) *both* focus on explicit modality; and (625) and (627) *both* focus on implicit modality. This less than full equivalence of the first two sentences is due to idiomaticity, which at the same time becomes a compensating factor for the divergence regarding explicitness of factuality.

It should not be thought that divergences along the columns of Table 4.3 are rare for English-German 'equivalents.' Let us consider the next example, found in the leaflet *Fahrplan und Anschlüsse InterCity-Express 596 Lessing*

	Modality stated (explicit modality)				Factuality stated (explicit factuality)			
	Modality		Implicit factuality		Factuality		Implicit modality	
	Really exists	Is point of utterance	Exists	Is point of utterance	Really exists	Is point of utterance	Exists	Is point of utterance
	1	2	3	4	5	6	7	8
(622) Ich sehe …					X	X	X	
(624) I can see …	X		X	X				
(625) The … thesis is read …					– !		X	X
(364) John can swim.	X	X						

TABLE 4.3.
Stated Modality and Factuality and Their Points of Utterance

issued by Deutsche Bundesbahn (German Railways) in 1992. It contains the following trilingual text (italics ours):

(628) Dieses Faltblatt *möchte* Sie über den Fahrplan und die wichtigen An-schlüsse des Zuges informieren.
(629) This leaflet *gives* you information on the timetable and the most important connections with other services.
(630) Cet imprimé vous *tiendra* au courant de l'itinéraire et des correspondances importantes de ce train.

The German version is like (364) in terms of explicit modality that is the point of utterance. It differs from (364) in that the use of the modal is an-thropomorphic—a leaflet cannot really be said to *like* giving information. In (628), the speaker projects his or her own intentions into an inanimate entity. The real basis of this sentence is

(631) Wir möchten Sie mit diesem Faltblatt . . . informieren.

The English version is like (625) in that it purports to present a proposition as a fact that in reality does not exist (the leaflet does not 'give' the reader information unless one starts informing oneself by reading it). Its 'real meaning' or point of utterance could be formulated as follows:

(632) This leaflet is to/is designed to/is meant to give you information . . .

BE TO would be the equivalent of SOLLEN, which itself could also have been used for the German version:

(633) Dieses Faltblatt soll Sie . . . informieren.

This would have had the advantage of being loyal to the modal source as stated in (631), at the same time retaining the subject of (628), which is coreferential to that of (629) and (630).

BE TO being referred to by Quirk et al. (1985: 137) as *modal idiom,* (629) equals (625) also in terms of implicit modality as its point of utterance.

Note that the French *tiendra* in (630) is a simple future form that almost carries the illocutionary force of a promise, thus presenting a third kind of structure for the allegedly identical interlingual speech act. Such diversity among 'equivalents' suggests that there are even more types of SL-TL divergence in the area of factuality and modality.

4.3.2 Implicative and Factive Predicates

In the previous section, a distinction was drawn between implicit modality and implicit factuality. Usually when factuality is implied, this is by virtue of an expression that is either *implicative* or *factive*:

(634) John managed to solve the problem.
(635) John solved the problem.

Implicative verbs/predicates such as MANAGE, REMEMBER, and SEE FIT imply the truth or factuality of the sentence embedded under (dependent upon) them: (634) implies (635). *Factive verbs* such as IGNORE, MIND, and FORGET behave in the same manner:

(636) He ignored the fact that it was raining.
(637) It was raining.

What distinguishes the two groups of predicates is their behavior under negation:

(638) John didn't manage to solve the problem.
(639) He didn't ignore the fact that it was raining.

Sentence (638) no longer implies (635) but its negation, whereas (639) still implies (637), which sentence can thus be referred to as the presupposition of both (636) and (639).

Equipped with this background knowledge, let us now test the expression *can see* in (624).

[624] I can see two ships.
[623] ! I see two ships.
(640) I cannot see two ships.
(641) I do not see two ships.

Sentence (624) implicates (623), and (640) implies (641), so it may be said that CAN in (624) functions as an implicative verb.

In the previous section the latter sentence was characterized as expressing explicit modality and implicit factuality. In the light of the terms just introduced, it might be claimed that an expression implicitly signaling factuality or signaling implicit factuality is an implicative (or even factive) expression, so the word *factuality* in *implicit factuality* is redundant. But remember that there are also expressions with opposite modality/factuality values. The German counterpart of (624), sentence (622), was said to express explicit factuality and implicit modality ("ability," "possibility"):

[622] Ich sehe zwei Schiffe.

This shows that not only can factuality be implied but also modality. For this reason we recommend differentiating between *implied* or *implicit factuality* and *implied* or *implicit modality*. Furthermore it would only be logical to extend this distinction onto the use of the term *implication* itself and to speak of *implication of factuality* and *implication of modality*. In the former sense, Palmer (1979a: 75) uses the term *implication of actuality*. Alternatively, for the convenience of sticking to established terminology, *implication* (and *implicative (verb/predicate)*) could continue to be used for *implication of (f)actuality*; but the term *implication of modality* seems to be necessary as well because its addition does more justice to the dual nature of implication.

As explained at the beginning of this section, implication of factuality is achieved not only by implicative predicates but also by factive ones. Here we see no problem because the term *factive* is indicative of the object of factuality: facts.

Let us now return to our CAN examples. We ended saying that CAN in (624) functions as an implicative verb. In the majority of cases, however, CAN is nonimplicative (see the beginning of Section 4.3), as in

[364] John can swim.

The behavior of CAN is largely paralleled by that of KÖNNEN: Even though this German modal is not used to render CAN in (624), it is also typically nonimplicative when used in the present tense; but it can be implicative as well:

[619] John kann schwimmen. (nonimplicative)
(642) John kann aber schwimmen! (implicative)

As regards the implicativeness of (642), CAN corresponds to KÖNNEN (see also Section 5.2.2.2):

(643) John can swim!

Finally, also CAN and KÖNNEN in hedged performatives are implicative:

(644) I can assure you that I saw him.
(645) Ich kann dir versichern, dass ich ihn gesehen habe.

Table 4.4 summarizes the points made about the implicative status of CAN and KÖNNEN in some of their present-tense uses.

Even though CAN and KÖNNEN are not completely identical in behavior as regards the factor of implicativeness, they share the general potential of being both implicative and nonimplicative. Other modal expressions belong to the same category. König and Legenhausen (1972: 36) list the following modal predicates: BE ABLE, BE IN THE POSITION, HAVE THE TIME/OPPORTUNITY/CHANCE.

Just like CAN and KÖNNEN, these expressions are generally nonimplicative when used in the present tense. This is illustrated by the following examples, supplemented by their German counterparts, which are equally nonimplicative:

(646) She has the opportunity to make an inexpensive journey.
(647) Sie hat die Gelegenheit, eine preiswerte Reise zu machen.

Explicit factuality	Explicit modality	
	Implicative (implicit factuality)	Nonimplicative
	(642) John kann aber schwimmen! = (643) John can swim!	(619) John kann schwimmen. = (364) John can swim.
(622) Ich sehe zwei Schiffe. =	(624) I can see two ships.	
	(645) Ich kann dir versichern, dass ich ihn gesehen habe. = (644) I can assure you that I saw him.	

TABLE 4.4.
Implicativeness of CAN and KÖNNEN in Present Tense

(648) He is able to lift 50 lbs.
(649) Er ist fähig/in der Lage, 50 Pfund zu heben.

Moreover, English root modals are generally nonimplicative, as are the corresponding German ones (but cf. (624) and (642)–(645)):

[170] I must go now.
[171] Ich muss jetzt gehen.

(650) You may go swimming.
(651) Du darfst schwimmen gehen.

In their epistemic use, both the English and German modals are nonfactive and nonimplicative:

[168] I may have left the keys in the car.
[185] Ich kann die Schlüssel im Wagen gelassen haben.

Other epistemic expressions such as modal adverbs (POSSIBLY, CERTAINLY; MÖGLICHERWEISE, SICHERLICH), and modal adjectives (POSSIBLE, CERTAIN; MÖGLICH, SICHER) are also nonfactive and nonimplicative:

(652) Possibly he is in New York.
(653) Möglicherweise ist er in New York.

(654) It is possible that he will go to London.
(655) Es ist möglich, dass er nach London geht/gehen wird.

The same applies to source-oriented epistemic full verbs (SUPPOSE, ASSUME; VERMUTEN, ANNEHMEN):

(656) I suppose he is there.
(657) Ich vermute, dass er dort ist.

So in the present tense, all these expressions are nonfactive and nonimplicative. The group of modal expressions illustrated by (646)–(649) was said to have the potential of being either implicative or nonimplicative. Their implicativeness shows up in the past tense, which is dealt with in the next section.

4.3.3 Past-Tense Forms

For the epistemic adverbs, adjectives, and source-oriented full verbs just mentioned ((652) and so forth), a change from present tense to past tense involves no change in status of nonfactivity or nonimplicativeness:

(658) Possibly he was in New York.
(659) Möglicherweise war er in New York.

(660) I supposed he was there.
(661) Ich vermutete, dass er dort war.

As regards the modals, let us reconsider some examples already touched upon in our section on tense (3.5). It will be clear that both modals in the following pair of sentences expressing subject-oriented dynamic modality are implicative:

[561] Nachdem ich ihr meinen Rat gegeben habe, muss sie natürlich genau das Gegenteil tun!
[562] Naturally, after I gave her my advice, she must go and do the opposite! (*Longman Dictionary of English Language and Culture* 1992: 877)

But what about (559) and (560) taken in the deontic sense?

[559] Ich musste es tun.
[560] I had to do it.

Sentence (559) may well imply that the speaker actually did it, but this need not be so; co(n)text will tell. As regards *had to*, the following example by Leech (1987: 96)

(662) Children had to behave themselves when I was a boy.

if merely taken to be a rule, does not necessarily suggest factuality (even though practically it does because the rule will have been adhered to). Compare with this Palmer's (1979a: 97) interesting comment on the following example (using *actuality* for *factuality*):

(663) Oh no! We had to go one better.

With *had to* there is undoubtedly an implication of actuality, the event took place. This is particularly noticeable in the last example, which can almost be paraphrased 'We went one better, as we naturally would.' By contrast if *had got to* had been used there would be simply the meaning 'It was necessary . . .' without the implication that the event took place, e.g.:

(664) We'd got to make a special trip down to Epsom anyway, so it did not matter very much.

Leech (1987: 96) again says *"had got to* [British English] is rare and limited to indirect speech . . ."

For our purposes it will suffice to say that *had to* must invariably be used as a past form suppleting deontic MUST, irrespective of factuality. So the defectiveness of MUST, not the possible existence of factuality, acts as a transposition factor when *musste* is to be rendered in English.

Factuality correlated with past tense use is, however, a transposition factor for CAN. We are going to show this now with reference to its German equivalent KÖNNEN. Used in the past tense, this modal tends to be implicative. Panther (1981b: 242) points out that (665) often implicates (666):

(665) Hans konnte seine Dissertation rechtzeitig einreichen.
(666) Hans reichte seine Dissertation rechtzeitig ein.

Because, in addition, the negation of (665) implies the negation of (666), KÖNNEN in (665) is implicative.

For an English equivalent of *konnte* in this sentence, COULD is ruled out because it is nonimplicative. To convey the factuality of *einreichen* in English, an implicative predicate such as *was able to* must be used:

(667) Hans was able to submit his dissertation in time.

According to Leech and Svartvik (1975: 129) *was able to* means "could and did"; COULD cannot be used to refer in this way to a single past action because it merely means "knew how to" in the sense of constant capability, as in

(668) When he was young he could play the piano.

This pragmatic difference between the two modal expressions can be clearly seen in the following example taken from Nehls (1986: 93):

(669) The students who could speak English were able to make themselves understood.

Because *konnte* can be both implicative and nonimplicative, it can be used to render both COULD and *was able to* in this sentence:

(670) Die Studenten, die Englisch (sprechen) konnten, konnten sich verständlich machen.

Likewise, nonimplicative COULD in (668) can also be rendered by KÖN-
NEN:

(671) Als er jung war, konnte er Klavier spielen.

As regards the translation direction German-English, however, factuality acts
as a transposition factor dictating the nonuse of a modal: (670) → (669) and
(665) → (667).

In terms of the distinctions introduced in Section 4.3.1, all four sentences just referred to express explicit modality (even though in most of the
English sentences it is not expressed by means of the modals) and—except
for the relative clauses in (669) and (670)—implicit factuality (due to the
modal expressions used being implicative, that is, implying factuality). Now
remember the following sentences (and see Table 4.2 in Section 4.3.1 for
their status of modality and factuality):

[622] Ich sehe zwei Schiffe.
[624] I can see two ships.

CAN in (624) being implicative, it might be assumed that the corresponding
English sentence in past tense would have to contain *was able to*. But this is
not so; for instance,

(672) Ich sah zwei Schiffe.
(673) I could see two ships.

COULD may be retained in such collocations with verbs of inert perception.
Nehls (1986: 97 f.) explains that here the animate subject is not an agent but
an experiencer and adds the following pair of examples:

(674) Als ich sie endlich ganz deutlich sah . . .
(675) When at last I could see her before me . . .

Table 4.5 summarizes the possibilities of *was able to*, COULD, and their
German counterparts as regards the factor of implicativeness.

The last examples have shown that COULD can not only be nonimplicative but also implicative. As already mentioned, also BE ABLE, BE
IN THE POSITION, HAVE THE TIME/OPPORTUNITY/CHANCE can be
both implicative and nonimplicative. The examples just given show that the
reason for the dual status of BE ABLE TO is the factor of tense. *Is able to*
can be nonimplicative (as in (648)), but *was able to*, indicating a single
event, is implicative (as in (667) and (669)). Palmer (1979a: 77) states: "The
use of BE ABLE TO to indicate (simultaneous) actuality is closely related to
its use in the past . . ." Likewise, the other modal expressions just referred to
are nonimplicative when used in the present tense (as in (646)). But their

Explicit factuality	Explicit modality	
	Implicative (implicit factuality)	Nonimplicative
	(665) Hans konnte seine Dissertation rechtzeitig einreichen. = (667) Hans was able to submit his dissertation in time.	(671) Als er jung war, konnte er Klavier spielen. = (668) When he was young he could play the piano.
(672) Ich sah zwei Schiffe. = (673) I could see two ships.		

TABLE 4.5.
Implicativeness of *Was Able To*, COULD, and *Konnte*

past-tense use is no sufficient condition for their being implicative. To demonstrate this, let us have a look at comparable German expressions that are also nonimplicative in the present tense (as in (647)) and can be implicative in past tense.

Gutknecht and Panther (1973: 155 ff.) observe that the constructions DIE GELEGENHEIT HABEN and DIE ZEIT HABEN (which obviously translate HAVE (THE) OPPORTUNITY TO and HAVE (THE) TIME TO) suggest factuality when used affirmatively in the past tense; for example,

(676) Er hatte die Gelegenheit, eine preiswerte Reise zu machen.

(677) He had the opportunity to make an inexpensive journey.

But the alleged validity of the implication of factuality may be canceled by adding an appropriate supplementary clause:

(678) Er hatte die Gelegenheit, eine preiswerte Reise zu machen, aber er nahm sie nicht wahr.

(679) He had the opportunity to make an inexpensive journey, but he didn't make use of it.

This leads the authors to conclude that such constructions do not count among implicative predicates in the strict, logical sense, where no cancellation of implication is possible. Rather, they are instances of what was coined by Geis and Zwicky (1971) *invited inference* characteristic of everyday conversational logic.

The versatility of KÖNNEN as exemplified by its implicative and nonimplicative uses in one complex sentence (670) can also be found in the case of invited inference and its possible cancellation, such as

(680) Er konnte an der Klausur teilnehmen.

(681) Er konnte an der Klausur teilnehmen, hatte aber einfach keine Lust.

Sentence (680) invites the assumption of factuality (i.e., that he did in fact take part in the exam), whereas in (681) this invited inference is canceled by the adversative clause.

Can COULD be used to render *konnte*? In (681) it could: "COULD may be used if there is no implication of actuality, but only a statement of possibility" (Palmer 1979a: 80). Because after cancellation of the invited inference *konnte* can no longer be seen to be implicative but merely indicative of possibility, it may be rendered by COULD:

(682) He could take part in the written exam but he just didn't care.

In (680), there being at least a potential implication of actuality, COULD could be used only if the context made it clear that he did in fact not take part in the exam. *Was able to*, on the other hand, would move the pendulum to the other extreme—it could be used only if the context definitely indicated factuality. If, however, the pragmatic ambiguity is to be an invariance factor, that is, if the interpretive possibilities of the English rendition are to be left as unspecific as those for (680) itself, then a TL expression is required that, like *konnte*, can be implicative as well as nonimplicative. HAVE THE OPPORTUNITY is such an expression (as exemplified in (677) and (679)):

(683) He had the opportunity to take part in the written exam.

This shows that not only factuality of single actions (as in (667)) but also potential invited inference acts as a transposition factor replacing COULD by other modal expressions.

4.3.4 Counterfactuality

Sentences (678)–(679) and (681)–(682) have opened up another facet of factuality: counterfactuality, the contrary-to-fact status of propositions. If someone had the opportunity of making a journey but did not make use of it (as stated in (679)), then the person obviously did *not* make that journey. But counterfactuality cannot, as in the example just referred to, be only the logical result of the interaction of two clauses making up one complex sentence; it can also be implied by negatively implicative and factive predicates, as in

(684) He could have taken part in the written exam but he just didn't care.
(685) He took part in the written exam.

In (684), which is an alternative for (682), *COULD + perfective aspect* is sufficient to imply the counterfactuality of (685). In contrast to (679), the adversative clause (*but . . .*) here merely gives a reason for the action not having taken place; it is no necessary indicator of counterfactuality. Correspondingly, *hätte* . . . *können* could have been used instead of *konnte* in (681):

(686) Er hätte an der Klausur teilnehmen können, hatte aber einfach keine Lust.

Many readers will feel (686) to be more 'correct' than (681) because it puts the hearer on the right—counterfactual—track right away, whereas (681) achieves this goal only after a 'detour,' namely, the cancellation of an invited inference questionably (or at least unnecessarily) presented first. There is, however, some justification for still using (681) due to a tendency in modern colloquial German to do just this: use the nonimplicative *konnte* for *hätte* . . . *können* in case the ensuing clause clearly indicates cancellation or non-validity of invited inference.

If no such adversative clause follows, *konnte* will invite the inference of factuality; see (665) and (680). Given this situation it must seem surprising that German football reporters are more and more often heard saying,

(687) Das musste ein Tor sein.

when they 'merely' mean

(688) Das hätte ein Tor sein müssen.

Just like *konnte*, so *musste* in simple sentences is normally subject to invited inference: (689) will in all probability imply (690).

(689) Gestern musste ich eine Stunde früher als sonst aufstehen.
(690) Gestern bin ich eine Stunde früher als sonst aufgestanden.

This is why the phenomenon of counterfactual *musste* in a simple sentence such as (687) is remarkable.

As an English equivalent for *musste/hätte* . . . *müssen* in (687) and (688), only *should have been* is possible. Commenting on such constructions, Leech (1987: 100) ascribes "a stronger negative connotation 'contrary to fact'" to *ought to have* and *should have* and explains that

(691) She should have seen my car coming.

"has the presupposition ' . . . but in fact she didn't.'"
One final point on counterfactuality. Unlike English, in German perfective modal constructions, the modal does not come as first verbal element; rather the indicator of counterfactuality comes first, as in the rendition of (691):

(692) Sie hätte sehen sollen, wie mein Wagen kam/Sie hätte meinen Wagen kommen sehen sollen.

Hätte . . . sollen thus parallels *hätte . . . können* in (686) and *hätte . . . müssen* in (688).

4.4 SITUATION

Leech (1981: 329 f.) views the meanings of sentences (as part of the language system) to be the object of semantics, and the meanings of sentences in particular situations, that is, the meanings of utterances, to be the object of pragmatics. Taking reference to *situation* as being criterial for pragmatics, we would have to say that ever since we started dealing with pragmatic factors we have in fact dealt with situation. In a way this is true because all the sentences mentioned since Section 4.1.1 are indeed dependent for their interpretation as utterances upon aspects of situation. But it will be expedient to have an extra section for focusing on several specific *kinds* of situation: situation of reference (Section 4.4.1) and situation of utterance (Section 4.4.2). Regarding the latter we will show how illocutions are influenced by the relationship of speaker and hearer (Section 4.4.2.1) and the time of utterance (Section 4.4.2.2). As regards the former it will be shown how also the elements of a modal proposition can vary with different aspects of the situation of reference being highlighted (Section 4.4.1).

A common trait of these two kinds of situation is expression of modality by means of verbalization. Yet modality can also be expressed by nonverbal means. Such nonverbal communication will be dealt with in Section 4.4.3.

4.4.1 Situation of Reference

Sometimes translation equivalents do not show exactly the same proposition, see Section 4.2 and the following conventional specifications printed on food packages:

(693) Best before end (of)
(694) Mindestens haltbar bis Ende

The common element of these sentences is (implicit) reference to a product and a predication about its condition up to a specific date. *Best* and *mindestens haltbar* are not exactly the same thing, however, as can be demonstrated by translating them into the other language, respectively:

(695) Am besten/in bestem Zustand vor Ende
(696) Durable at least up until end (of)

But these are minor differences compared to those becoming evident by considering some more interlingual 'variants' of (693) and (694):

(697) Use best before end
(698) To be consumed by end of
(699) (A) Consommer (de préférence) avant le/fin (de)
(700) Date limite de vente jusqu'à fin
(701) Da consumarsi preferibilmente entro (fine/il)
(702) (A) Consumir preferentemente/preferiblemente antes de (fin de)
(703) Tenminste houdbaar tot (einde)
(704) Mindst holdbar til

All these formulations were found printed on various food packages (hazelnuts, almonds, etc.) produced or imported by German companies. Because (694) was on each of them, (693) and (697) through (704) can all be said to be translation equivalents. But with all their practical equivalence, there are obvious differences. Not counting minor ones, we can set up the following three groups of formulations:

1. statements about the *condition* (of the product): (693), (694), (703), and (704);
2. statements or directives about (the necessity of) *consuming* (the product): (697)–(699), (701), and (702).
3. statement about *selling* (the product): (700).

Within a group, further variation exists, such as the difference between *best* and *haltbar* referred to previously, as well as the alternatives given for some of the sentences, not to mention the different sentences themselves. How then can we say these heterogeneous elliptical statements or directives are equivalents of each other? We would suggest that they all represent aspects of *one* overall situation of reference that can be described as follows.

There are food products the condition of which can be said to be 'good' or 'best' only up to a certain point in time (group 1). Presupposing that the consumer wants to or should eat only food that is in good or the best condition, it follows that it is best to consume the products/that the products should (preferably) be/are to be/are best consumed/used by that time (group 2). Since these products must be bought before they can be eaten, the time limit correlates with the selling date (group 3).

Such a concept of one overall situation with its different aspects or perspectives is akin to Fillmore's (1977) "discussion of meaning in its relation to what he calls 'scenes'—psychological schemes of which a reference to one part will conjure up the remaining parts. Thus the concept of 'buying' and 'selling,' 'paying' and 'spending,' each focus on different aspects of a basic commercial 'scene' in which buyer and seller exchange goods and money" (Leech 1981: 358).

In our basic 'durability scene,' modality is evident in all the three groups of perspectives:

(a) in the suffix *–bar*: *haltbar, holdbar, houdbaar*;
(b) in the stated necessity of consuming by a specific date: *to be, à, da*;
(c) in the concept of 'selling deadline,' that is, a point in time up to which the product *must* (have) be(en) sold: *limite . . . jusqu'à*.

The entire situation thus being pervaded by modality, it could be referred to as a *modal situation* or *modal scene*. What is more, the three aspects of modality just enumerated are interrelated.

"Possibility" can be regarded as the modal source of "necessity": The product *can* be kept (see *haltbar*) up until a certain point in time, so it *is to* be sold and consumed by that time. This shows that the two degrees of modality are interrelated. Because each statement belongs to only one group, none contains both modalities explicitly. Some, (693), (697), (699) lacking *A*, (700), contain neither of them; here modality is only implicit.

Note that the three groups are not specific to individual languages: English appears in groups (1) and (2), French in (2) and (3). German, however, appears only in one group, group (1), and moreover, only by way of one expression, (694). It is even difficult to imagine a different formulation printed. (It is true that consumer advice such as

(705) Geöffnete Packung im Kühlschrank zwei Tage haltbar.
(706) Nach dem Öffnen bald(möglichst) verbrauchen.

is sometimes given, but it describes different situations—see later.) So (694) must definitely be accepted as *the* idiomatic German expression for the kind of situation at hand.

In some of the other languages there is more room for variation. But there are degrees of idiomaticity: (693) is definitely the standard English expression for the given purpose, whereas (697) (belonging to a different group of expressions) is not. Statement (696) is completely untypical, as is (695) in German.

This is the principle to be kept in mind when faced with a situation that can be seen from different angles. Widely different propositions are possible, but this does not mean that anything could be said in any language. Sometimes only specific angles are conventionally verbalized, and formulations corresponding to these angles are more or less fixed.

Now it is interesting to see how a slight change in situational structure can lead to partially different formulations. In Germany, the Italian company *Pan* sells "prebaked deepfrozen pizza" produced in Austria. Pizza is one of those products that are 'best before end' of a certain date. Accordingly, the same Italian version (701) is printed on the pizza package, albeit without *da*. But pizza is different from hazelnuts or almonds (package texts of which were considered in the first part of this section) in that its 'being best' more crucially depends upon the way it is stored. Accordingly, (701) appears un-

der the topic of *conservazione*, and different time spans are given according
to the temperatures chosen for storage:

(707) Conservazione:
Consumarsi preferibilmente entro:
A − 18°C (***) vedere punzonatura sul lato destro dell'astuccio.
A − 12°C (**) 1 mese, o comunque entro la data di scadenza, indicata
sul lato destro dell'astuccio.
A − 6°C (*) 1 settimana.

Also the English version is structured according to storage times, but the
information given is much less detailed. No *best before* can be found, instead
it says:

(708) Storage instructions:
* up to 1 week
** up to 1 month
*** up to several months

Also the allegedly invariable German version (694) is replaced by an expression that seems to be more fitting for the changed situation of informing the
consumer about different storage times:

(709) Mindesthaltbarkeit:
im Kühlschrank: 1 Tag, im Eiswürfelfach: 2–3 Tage,
bei − 18°C: mehr als 18 Monate . . .

Interestingly, *Mindesthaltbarkeit* represents the otherwise standard expression (694) in a compact compound version.

Having become familiar with the company's approach to informing the
customer, let us have a look at the French, Spanish, Portuguese, Dutch, and
Danish versions, without going into the details of storage times:

(710) Conservation:
(711) Conservación minima: . . .
(712) Conservação: . . .
(713) Bewaren: . . .
(714) Holdbarhed: . . .

As we can see, the Danish version (714) corresponds to the German one, but
it lacks the aspect of *minimum*. The same is true of the French (710) and
Portuguese (712) versions vs. the Spanish (711) one.

The Dutch (713) *Bewaren* is most noteworthy, because the angle the
situation is seen from here is completely different from that taken in the
versions surrounding it: Like the English one, (708), it focuses on the consumer's action of storing the product. So this angle could be called *consumer
oriented. Mindesthaltbarkeit* and *Holdbarhed*, on the other hand, refer to the

nature of the product. This angle is therefore *product oriented*. *Conservation, conservazione*, and so on oscillate between these two groups: They indicate the *state* of conservation, the time of which depends upon the nature of the product, and they refer to the *action* of conservation by the consumer.

As with our first situation, the possibility of equivalence in spite of different kinds of renditions hinges upon reference to the same situation. So here the factor of situation represents the aspect of unity in diversity, our topic found recurring again and again.

4.4.2 Aspects of Situation of Utterance

As mentioned in Section 3.3.3, Leech relates his category *social meaning* to the situation in which an utterance takes place. Here "features of language tell us something about the social relationship between the speaker and hearer" (1981: 14). Modal features of this kind will be dealt with in the first subsection.

Leech (1981: 326) states that a situation of utterance includes (a) the utterance itself, (b) the speaker, (c) the hearer, and (d) the speech act. He adds: "One might wish to extend the specification of a situation of utterance to include two further factors: (e) the place of utterance; (f) the time of utterance." The latter aspect as determining the choice of a modal will be dealt with in the second subsection.

4.4.2.1 Relationship of Speaker and Hearer

As an example of his category of *affective meaning*, Leech (1981: 15) points out that "personal feelings of the speaker, including his attitude to the listener" can be disclosed by "scaling our remarks according to politeness"— cf. the scale of politeness available for getting someone to close the door by saying . . . *Will/can/could you shut the door?* . . . (see Section 4.1.4.2).

Certain linguistic politeness formulas, however, are appropriate for specific relationships between the speaker and the hearer only. The utterance of

(715) You might want to close the door.

presupposes a speaker-hearer relationship that is not symmetrical. Along this dimension of what Leech (1981: 14) calls *status*, idiomaticity is an eminent translation factor. It is, for instance, not enough to render epistemic MIGHT in (715) by *könnte*, a rendition that in other contexts (i.e., that of 'mere' epistemic possibility) would be sufficient:

(716) !Sie könnten die Tür schliessen wollen.

Rather, an idiomatic rendition, more suited to the social situation, is required, something like

(717) Vielleicht möchten Sie mal die Tür schliessen.

Pragmatic idiomaticity here is a transposition factor suggesting the choice of the modal adverb VIELLEICHT over the modal verb KÖNNEN.

Social relationships may even become identification factors of illocutionary force. Behre (1962: 132 ff.) counts the relationship between speaker and hearer among the social factors determining the interpretation of utterances starting with *you will*. A senior officer uttering

(718) You will place a guard over this fellow.

in a military context will be understood as having given an order. In other social contexts this sentence can have the weaker illocution of a request. If different such contexts require different TL renditions, then correct understanding of the speaker-hearer relationship is a decisive translation factor. Thus, for (718), the military context would require a rendition such as (719), but talk between equals would allow for (720):

(719) Sie nehmen diesen Burschen in Gewahrsam!
(720) Du hältst jetzt mal diesen Knaben fest!

Coates makes similar observations with reference to speech acts starting with *will you*: "As Downes says: 'The command potential of an utterance varies with content and speaker's and hearer's belief of its truth from specific situation to specific situation.' Thus the utterance *will you sign it* . . . will be interpreted as a question or as a command depending on factors like the authority of the speaker, and the nature of the event referred to, which clearly lie outside linguistic theory." (1983: 172)

As our preceding remarks suggest, we would agree with what Coates says, but we would rather make a case for conceiving of linguistics as not excluding pragmatics. Just as Snell-Hornby has repeatedly argued for pragmatics to be included in translation studies (see the introduction to this chapter), pragmatics as the *speaker*-related aspect of language ought to be granted a place in linguistics.

4.4.2.2 Time of Utterance

Leech (1981: 341) refers to "situational factors in the analysis of pragmatic force" and includes among them *the time of utterance* (p. 326). The relevance of this aspect for English renditions of the modal MÜSSEN was researched into by Doherty (1979). Choice of MUST vs. HAVE TO as renditions of root MÜSSEN depends on the situation of utterance:

(721) Wir müssen die letzten drei Übungen wiederholen.
(722) We must repeat the last three exercises.
(723) We have to repeat the last three exercises.

The relevant factor distinguishing MUST and HAVE TO is that MUST may be used only if a demand is made by the speaker by means of the sentence uttered. Because demands can be made only in the present, the use of MUST is inevitably linked to the time of utterance. Of course, demands made prior to this time may also be stated in the present but in this case they require use of HAVE TO (as in (723); see Doherty 1979: 133 f., 142 f.; for further discussion, see Perkins 1983: 60). German does not make this difference.

4.4.3 Nonverbal Acts of Communication

When we refer to an *act* or *action* we typically think of it as being performed by means of the limbs of the body. Yet ever since it was found that one can also do things with words, speech acts came to be recognized as a valid category of action as well. Our object of inquiry, the modals, being linguistic in nature, it comes as no surprise that in this book we are concerned mainly with acts performed by means of language (in the written and spoken modes). Yet it seems worthwhile to pause for a moment to consider whether or not the acts performed by means of the modals cannot also be performed by nonverbal or nonlinguistic means. Two possibilities come to mind: other, that is, physical kinds of actions, and inaction. What could sensibly be meant by these will be explored in the following subsections.

4.4.3.1 Physical Actions, Gestures, and Mimicry

Root modality is concerned with notions such as "possibility" and "permission." To grant permission and thus create a possibility for the hearer the modals MAY and CAN may be used in indirect speech acts (*You may/can . . .*). But it is also possible to perform some physical action to this effect. Leech (1980: 96) gives as examples "non-linguistic actions such as standing up to *allow* someone else to sit down, or opening a door to *allow* someone to pass through a doorway" (our italics). ALLOW being the source-oriented counterpart of goal-oriented MAY, Leech's examples illustrate the closeness of linguistic and nonlinguistic *modal actions*. In fact, having stood up or opened the door, the speaker would be in a position to say:

(724) Now you may/can sit down.
(725) Now you may/can pass through the doorway.

The fact obviating this additional linguistic activity is the obviousness of the meaning or function of the physical act, which may, however, be accompanied by some instance of body language—an inviting movement of the hand, the nodding of the head or a smile—or by some verbal acts such as

(726) Please.
(727) Bitte (sehr).

Leech describes the two physical actions just referred to as instances of politeness, thus being on a par with indirect speech acts, which serve the same purpose (see Section 4.1.4.2). Obviously taking speech acts as a sub-kind of acts in general, he sees the pragmatics of indirect illocutionary force to be "a sub-theory of a more general theory of the principles underlying human interactive behavior" (1980: 96). Accordingly, modalized speech acts would have to be seen as one kind of modal action; that is, action involving the creation of possibilities, the granting of permission, and so forth.

Now the question arises, What does all this have to do with translation? Standing up or opening a door are, after all, actions the modal nature of which is so obvious in certain interactive situations as not to require any verbal comment, let alone its translation.

This is certainly true. Still it might happen that, if a host performs such an act, its meaning may not be immediately obvious to a foreign guest. Being familiar with the phenomenon of illocutionary indeterminacy (Section 4.1.4), we may expect indeterminacy also to exist in the interpretation of physical actions. And this is exactly where the attentive interpreter accompanying the guest comes in. We hold that the interpreter's task is not just to render verbal acts but also to 'translate' relevant physical action into verbal action should need arise. And in doing so he or she may well use a modal to 'interpret' the situation for a hesitant client, by saying:

(728) Sie können sich gerne setzen.
(729) Oh, you can take a seat.

4.4.3.2 Silence

When we produce words we expect the reader or hearer to take them in a direct, literal or indirect, metaphorical way. When we do not say or write anything, we may be understood as not conveying anything. In most cases this will be correct. But there are special situations where silence does mean something, something specific, sometimes even something modal.[40]

When we ask someone for something we usually expect a reaction, verbal or otherwise. If that person does not react and can be assumed to have understood our request, we will give this nonreaction some interpretation; for instance, that of indifference or negligence. If we do not talk with the individual about this nonreaction, we may be uncertain about the correct interpretation of it.

But there are cases of silence bearing a specific meaning, even a conventional or institutionalized one. So if you ask the German finance department for permission to regularly hand in your quarterly VAT reports one month later than is customary, you may get no reply. Indifference, negligence on the part of the government? Not necessarily so. Your tax adviser will tell you that this is one way of the authorities expressing their consent. Their nonreply, their silence, is equivalent to the modal statement

(730) Yes sir, you may go ahead the way you want to.

to be 'translated from silence' by the tax advisor.

But the time factor must not be overlooked. You may get no reply for two weeks, but then they may explicitly express their refusal. Now, no specific 'official' time span is fixed, after lapse of which you are entitled to take it that the silence 'means' "permission." So in case of doubt or urgency of getting to know the decision you had better call up and verify. Otherwise, if there is no reaction for one or two months, the permission may be assumed.

4.5 PERMANENT LANGUAGE VARIETIES

Illocutionary force, perlocution, factuality, situation—these factors dealt with so far in this chapter are all related to individual speech acts and are therefore short-lived. Other pragmatic aspects also change but are of a more permanent nature. They relate to the state of language in general. Two of these aspects will be glimpsed here:

* synchronic variants of standard language in terms of dialects and regionalisms;
* diachronic variation of standard language, i.e., earlier states of the language.

4.5.1 Dialects and Regionalisms

In addition to Standard British and American English as well as High German there are dialectal and regional varieties. If translation into one of these is required, the ideal translator will be a native speaker of it. Understanding printed dialectal variants of modals does not necessarily require special knowledge. Presumably everyone familiar with High German would be able to make sense of

(731) Mer söllets net meen.

which sentence was printed in a TV journal as subtitle of a broadcast about (Bavarian) Franconia. It means

(732) Man sollte es nicht meinen (glauben).

Swiss German may be more difficult to access, especially for North Germans and native speakers of English only familiar with High German. Just to give a glimpse of its modal specialities, here are some divergences between Swiss and High German as found by Werlen (1985: 97):

Differences are not limited to phonology and morphology, but also comprise syntax, semantics, and frequency of use. As regards 'small-scale' characteristics, in some Swiss dialects *wollte* is used instead of *möchte*. The semantics of MÖGEN in Wallis German differs considerably from that in High German. The low frequency of epistemic uses of the modals was found to be a 'large-scale' feature.

As regards varieties of Standard English there are several cases of 'divided usage' that are of importance for the translator. On the basis of elicitation tests, Tottie (1985: 109) arrives at the conclusion that British and American English have two different systems of negation for epistemic modality. In both varieties CAN prevails, but in British English this is set off only against the rarely used COULD, which in turn is more commonly used in American English. Here, however, MUST is added to the list of possible expressions. "Epistemic *must not* is indeed an almost exclusively American phenomenon" (Tottie 1985: 99). Consequently, the translator must be prepared to encounter epistemic modality in a sentence such as the following one:

(733) John mustn't be there.

He must be alert to render (733) not as (734), but as (735):

(734) !John darf nicht da sein.
(735) John kann nicht/kann unmöglich da sein.

The clues to a correct interpretation of negative sentences such as (733) are diverse. As Tottie is able to prove, "the choice of negative form is influenced by a number of syntactic, semantic, and pragmatic factors" (1985: 87; see also 95, 99 ff.).

Quirk et al. (1985: 136) point out another difference between British and American English. The less frequently occurring modals SHOULD, SHALL, and OUGHT TO are even less common in American English than in British English.

As regards regionalisms, *The Columbia Guide to Standard American English* (1993: 154) states that most of the double modals mentioned there "have some regional limitations . . . : *might can* and *might could* have usually been limited to Southern and South Midland dialects, and *hadn't ought* is probably mainly Northern" (see Section 3.3.5.1).

Finally a note on pronunciation. As already stated, reference to geographical variants is not just a matter of differences in syntax and semantics only but also one of phonological differences. Remember the Iowa farmer saying:

[143] We eat all we can, and what we can't we can.

Jennings et al. (1957: 67) allude to the articulatory dimension of CAN when they say: "It seems that an old lady in North Carolina once said of a crop of tomatoes,

(736) 'Oh, we'll eat what we *kin*, and what we *cain't* we'll *can.*' "

This sentence is formally less ambiguous than (143) because it contains three graphologically different forms of CAN. It would therefore present less of a problem to machine translation—were it not that such dialectally colored utterances seldom appear in print (except for metalinguistic purposes as in the present case). Furthermore special dialect programs would have to be set up.

4.5.2 Historical Variation

The possibility of using *must not* for the negation of epistemic MUST in American English is relatively new and, as Jacobsson (1979: 311) observes, has so far been largely ignored in linguistic publications (but see Section 4.5.1). Root MUST, on the other hand, is today no longer used as a past tense form. These are examples of meanings extended and restricted in the course of time. In view of the dynamism of the language system thus exemplified, it stands to reason that the translator should consider the time factor not just in cases where texts from bygone periods are to be translated into modern English or German, but also keep up-to-date with recent and latest developments. In this connection, interesting material is provided by the journal *English Studies* in its reader service *Points of Modern English Syntax* continued as *Points of Modern English Usage* in 1995.

In vol. 68 (1987: 458 ff.), for instance, a use of MAY is discussed that is formally typical of epistemic modality but semantically corresponds to counterfactual MIGHT, as in

(737) They may have seen us, if they had been looking.

As Wekker observes, very few grammarians have so far commented on this usage, which has been referred to as "a striking development of recent years" (1987: 458).

German renditions that might come to mind to someone not familiar with the construction in (737) include

(738) !Sie hätten uns gesehen, wenn sie geschaut hätten.
(739) !Es hätte sein können, dass sie uns gesehen hätten, wenn sie geschaut hätten.
(740) Es könnte sein, dass sie uns gesehen hätten, wenn sie geschaut hätten.
(741) Sie hätten uns vielleicht gesehen, wenn sie geschaut hätten.
(742) Sie hätten uns sehen können, wenn sie geschaut hätten.

Sentence (738) is ruled out on account of the fact that *hätten* does not express "possibility" as conveyed by MIGHT; the English equivalent for *hätten . . . gesehen* in (738) would be *would have seen*.

If counterfactuality in (737) is considered to be within the scope of *epistemic* modality, the point of inference must not be past as in (739) but present as in (740) or (741), the latter two sentences mainly differing in terms of the means employed for expressing epistemic modality (i.e., modal verb vs. modal adverb).

Alternatively, (737) may be understood in terms of counterfactual *root* modality as expressed by (742) and paraphrased by (743):

(743) They would have been able to see us if they had been looking.

Note, however, that (743) is confined to the root reading, whereas (737) may also be epistemic (cf. Leech 1987: 128, § 176).

Confirmation of the appropriateness of rendering *may have seen* in (737) in the root sense along the lines of (743) as *hätten sehen können* in (742) comes from the following sentence pair found in a dictionary entry, showing the parallel constructions *must have met* and *hättest treffen müssen* (Wildhagen and Héraucourt 1963: 542):

(744) You must have met him if . . .
(745) Du hättest ihn treffen müssen, wenn . . .

4.6 CULTURE

Culture can be defined as consisting of explicit and implicit patterns of and for behavior (C. Kluckhohn 1962: 73). Verbal interaction is certainly one form of behavior, grammatical phenomena such as the imperative being an example of its means. Silverstein (1973: 203) states that the function of an imperative is culturally defined as a certain kind of linguistic behavior symbolizing inter alia the duties and obligations of the hearer. Certain constructions similar to the imperative are regarded to be 'polite,' to be requests. Consider the following one:

(746) Passengers are kindly requested not to travel on the roof.

The claim that requests are 'similar' to the imperative seems to be especially justified with regard to this sentence. Snell-Hornby (1984: 207), who spotted (746) as a public sign at the railway station of Old Delhi, says about it: "This same message could well have been expressed as a command . . .:

(747) Passengers must travel *inside* the train. [emphasis as in original]

or as a prohibition . . . :

(748) Passengers must not travel on the roof . . ."

These 'paraphrases' reveal that (746) is not only implicitly imperative but also implicitly modal.

It is interesting to note that formulations (747) and (748) would be characteristic of public signs in English, as opposed to German. Snell-Hornby (1984: 209) sums up her research into public sign posts in several English and German speaking countries as follows: "the word *verboten* (or a stylistic variant) is omnipresent on German prohibition signs, while in English prohibition can be expressed by everyday modal verbs or in the harmless negative determiner *no*, and is hence less overt."

In other words, German parallels Indian English in that no modals are preferred to express public prohibitions. But whereas the latter language uses (746) as an overtly mild request, the German word *verboten* is a strong directive expression marked for administrative language, thus sounding much more impressive than a 'mere' *darf nicht* would—an example of perlocutionary strategy.

So cultural norms determining the ways of expressing (public) illocutionary acts are among the factors to be taken into account when translators are faced with different SL and TL cultures.

At the same time one should be aware that *culture* is not only a relative concept. As to its reflection in literature, Dasenbrock (1987: 10 ff.) points out that there is both

- multicultural literature, which follows 'universal laws' and which therefore poses no difficulties in understanding to its 'universal readership' coming from different cultures, and
- regional literature, which may be understood by 'outsiders' only with the help of literary critics.

Facilitating understanding of literature of the latter type can, however, be achieved even at an earlier stage. Mediation between cultural worlds (as conceived of by Vermeer 1986: 32 ff.) can be practiced by the translator. Translating, one can take into account the linguistic factors mirroring cultural differences mentioned previously. One can thus render the Indian mild directive (746) by the German strong prohibition:

(**749**) (Das) Reisen auf dem Dach (ist) streng verboten!

This would ensure adhering to TL cultural-linguistic norms. Care must be taken, though, not to neglect those very characteristics that are SL culture specific. Rendering (746) by (749) amounts to ignoring the way public directives are given in India. The optimal way of steering one's course between these two opposing factors may be to produce literal translations with annotations regarding SL and TL cultural differences. This would practically mean that (746) could be translated as

(**750**) Die Fahrgäste werden höflich gebeten, nicht auf dem Dach zu reisen.

together with a footnote reading

(751) Anmerkung: In Indien werden selbst strenge Verbote oftmals als höfliche Bitten formuliert.

Such annotations may be superfluous in case the intended illocution is self-evident. Would (746) or (750) straightforwardly be taken by the German reader to indicate a strong prohibition? Because there is probably no immediate cotext to the English sign text itself, the following remark by Behre (1962: 132) about *you will* requests is applicable also to (746): "the verbal environment does not provide any indication as to whether the 'request' should be taken as 'command,' 'order,' 'direction,' 'instruction,' 'injunction,' 'entreaty' or a 'mild request.'" Snell-Hornby does not hesitate to produce the 'strong' paraphrases (747) and (748); but will the German reader spontaneously react in the same way and interpret (750) along the lines of (749)? We would say it depends upon the translator's cultural competence when it comes to decide if any commentary is needed as a compensation factor for cultural differences. In case he or she thinks it is, the translator assumes the role of a *traducteur-rédacteur* (Juhel 1982: 109; see Section 6.8.2).

Such additional activity extending beyond merely 'replacing SL items by TL items' (as translating is sometimes mechanistically referred to) is also necessary in the following cases.

Suppose in a TL culture there exists no concept usually expressed by a modal, and hence no modal expressing this concept. In such situations componential analysis of modal concepts can prove useful. As an example, Wierzbicka (1987: 26) analyzes *I can* . . . as *if I want* . . . *I will* . . . Provided the TL culture is familiar with the concepts of *want* and *will*, this is a viable way of circumscribing the meaning of CAN and making it intelligible.

Now it might be argued that variants of English and German all have modals, so the preceding periphrasis is necessary for more or less 'exotic' languages only.

But even within major variants such as British and American English the translator may have to act as a cultural mediator circumscribing modal concepts. Remember the legal expression BRINGSCHULD and the need to paraphrase it in English by means of a modal verb construction such as *a debt that must be discharged on the creditor's premises* (see Section 3.2.5.1).

Such circumscription is one way of rendering the so-called *realia*; that is, "affairs of a political, institutional, social, or geographical nature specific to certain countries (which is why they are also referred to as elements regarding the *conventions of a country*" (Koller 1983: 162; our translation, his italics).

Another way would be to simply 'import' a term such as BRING-

SCHULD as an *emprunt,* which is a term denoting a TL carryover un-changed in form and meaning (as conceived of by *stylistique comparée*). This, however, is possible only if the average—here, the learned—English reader can be expected to know what the German expression means. This point is again up to the translator's evaluation. He or she could even use the German expression and make a note explaining it in English. But in case the translator decides not to use the SL expression at all, the task is to find appropriate TL means for bridging the genuine gap in the TL lexical system corresponding to the SL expression.

It should, however, not be thought that it takes special language (LSP) vocabulary (such as BRINGSCHULD) to detect cultural gaps or incongruen-cies. An American lady having lived and worked in Germany as an opera musician for twenty years was heard to have spoken the following bilingual message onto her answering machine:

(752)   Here is the answering service for 47 . . . I can't speak with you at the moment, but if you leave your name and telephone number I'll be happy to call you back as soon as I can.
Ich bin im Moment leider nicht zu erreichen. Wenn Sie mir aber eine Nachricht auf dem Band hinterlassen, rufe ich Sie gern so bald wie möglich zurück.

When asked why she had translated the English sentence *I can't speak with you at the moment* by *Ich bin im Moment leider nicht zu erreichen,* she replied, "Das war für mich eigentlich keine Übersetzung; das kannst du nicht wörtlich übersetzen—es sind zu viele Faktoren." Compared to American English, German was "eine andere Welt" for her, and she explained, "Ameri-kaner denken ganz anders—sie sind lockerer, schneller, ganz klar, kommen schneller zur Sache. Die Deutschen sind andere Menschen, sprechen sehr ernsthaft und sind sehr korrekt. Ich bin anders!"

Beyond translation, toward spontaneous formulation in another lan-guage, the translator acting as a paranative speaker *and* biculturalist—this seems to be the way to cope with the factor of culture in translation.

5. FACTORS RELATING TO SPOKEN AND WRITTEN LANGUAGE

In the conclusion to her corpus study on the English modals, Coates (1983: 248) writes: "In this study, using spoken as well as written material, I have been able to establish what prosodic patterns are associated with modal meaning, and have been able to show that in certain areas (e.g. frequency of certain forms, frequency of certain meanings) written and spoken language differ considerably."

These findings are clearly relevant to the translator. Because "prosodic features serve to disambiguate utterances" (Coates 1983: 246), an interpreter who is in a situation where different modal meanings would lead to different renditions will be grateful to have intonation and stress come to his or her aid as identification factors for arriving at the correct meaning. And the translator who silently sits pondering over a written text will be better prepared for understanding the use of a modal correctly by knowing which meanings of that modal occur more typically in the written language and are therefore more likely to have been intended by the author.

But the attested frequency of certain meanings differing considerably in spoken and written language is also an important production factor. For instance, a particular English modal known to occur very infrequently in spoken language had better not be 'overused' by the interpreter translating from German; in contrast, a modal being favored in written language should be actively used to make the text sound 'more English.'

We will first briefly report on the relative frequency of some forms in written and spoken language (Section 5.1) and then focus on each medium individually, presenting prosody (Section 5.2) and punctuation (Section 5.3) as identification factors of semantic and pragmatic phenomena related to the modals. Finally, it will be shown how anticipation of syntactico-semantic phenomena can be achieved for the sake of speedy simultaneous interpreting (Section 5.4).

5.1 RELATIVE FREQUENCY OF FORMS

Here are some of Coates's findings about the relative frequency of the various modals: "The spoken and written corpuses differ considerably. The most common written form (WOULD) is only the third most common spoken form, while the modals in general appear to occur more frequently in spoken language (with the notable exception of MAY). WILL and CAN, the two most frequently occurring spoken forms, seem to be far more common in spoken than in written language . . . SHALL and OUGHT, though still relatively infrequent, seem to occur considerably more often in spoken language" (1983: 23 f.).

5.2 PROSODY

It is the merit of Coates (1983) to have taken prosody into account to a greater extent, an area of research that had been largely neglected before.

5.2.1 Identification of Semantic Phenomena

"It is often asserted that the polysemy of the modals leads to ambiguity. Corpus study reveals, however, that, in context, sentences containing modal auxiliaries are very rarely ambiguous; in particular, prosodic features serve to disambiguate utterances" (Coates 1983: 246). To illustrate this point, Coates contrasts the following two utterances:[41]

(753) I /mày come tomórrow #
(754) I may /come tomòrrow #

Because in (753), "the modal is stressed (receives onset and nuclear stress) and the utterance has fall-plus-rise intonation," it "is unambiguously epistemic." (754), where "the modal is unstressed and the utterance has falling intonation . . . is root" (1983: 246).

The prosodic features of (753) are characteristic of epistemic modality in general. It is "regularly associated with fall-rise and fall-plus-rise intonation," and "the epistemic modals all have a high proportion of examples with stress of some kind" (1983: 243 f.; for percentages see her p. 244). Not surprisingly then, all modals with a quantitatively significant epistemic usage—MUST, OUGHT, MAY, and MIGHT—normally receive stress of some kind. The other modals—SHOULD, CAN, COULD, WILL, SHALL, and WOULD—are normally unstressed (1983: 243).

Exceptions again show prosody to be an identification factor for modal meanings: "To underline the sense of 'intention,' SHALL is sometimes stressed (i.e., receives onset) in certain formal contexts. Since SHALL (like WILL) is normally unstressed, this seems to be a definite disambiguation strategy" (1983: 187); for example,

(755) I /shall of course take account of all relevant factors in seeking
    to make what I hope will be the correct decisions #

WILL ("willingness") can have the special meaning "insistence" as in (756), which is paraphrasable by (757):

(756) look # . . . if you /will play it this way then this immediately brings
    in the funds of another division #
(757) . . . if you insist on playing it this way . . .

Coates (1983: 173) comments: "The stress found with WILL in such cases is a crucial signal of its meaning."

5.2.2 Identification of Pragmatic Phenomena

Prosodic information is an identification factor not just for meanings of the modals but also for illocutions of utterances containing them (Section 5.2.2.1) and for factuality of propositions (Section 5.2.2.2).

5.2.2.1 Illocutionary Force

Concerning intonation as an illocutionary force indicator consider the following examples adapted from Coates (1983: 171 f.):

(758) I /gìve it to you # [legislation to protect wild animals]—/will you
    sígn it #
(759) /Gordon /will you ˈcome out of the bùshes#

The rising tone on *sign* indicates that (758) is a genuine question, whereas the falling tone on *bushes* reveals that (759) is not a question, despite the inversion of subject and auxiliary; the hearer is not asked about his willingness to act, but is given a directive to act.

The same phenomenon of falling intonation near the end of a sentence for directive purposes exists also in German. In the following authentic example,

(760) tja—wollen wir schlàfengehen#

the speaker is not asking whether the hearer shares his wish of going to bed but urges the hearer to prepare for bed by way of using an intonation pattern typical of making a statement—as if the intention of going to bed were a mutual decision.

In a German equivalent of (759), falling intonation can be placed at two points, one corresponding to that in (759); but for a stronger directive illocution, falling intonation can also come on the modal:

(761) /Gordon /wirst du wohl aus dem ᴵBùsch rauskommen#
(762) /Gordon /wìrst du wohl aus dem Busch rauskommen#

Instead of WERDEN, WOLLEN can be used as an equivalent of WILL ("willingness"):

(763) /Gordon /wìllst du wohl aus dem Busch rauskommen#

Despite inversion, falling intonation is also an indicator for the following sentence not being a question (Coates 1983: 99):

(764) /Can we examine this then more càrefully#

In addition to intonation, stress is an important illocutionary identification factor for questions starting with a modal such as (758) and so on. Coates (1983: 243) points out: "All the modals receive stress (onset) in interrogative utterances . . ."; but this principle does not seem to apply to indirect speech acts. After setting up a gradient of indirectness according to the degree of givenness of the proposition in point (see Section 4.1.4.2), Panther (1981a: 297) continues his observations: "The degree of prominence of an indirect reading is also connected with some prosodic features of the indirect force marker. In particular, heavy stress on that marker will result in a cancellation or at least low pragmatic prominence of the indirect illocutionary force. It directs the listener's attention towards what is literally expressed in the sentence. The indirect meanings of the following utterances seem practically canceled if the modal carries heavy stress." Panther gives these examples:

(765) ‖can you close the door#
(766) ‖could you lend me your car#
(767) ‖must you continue hammering that way#

Panther adds that destressing the modal is no sufficient, but a necessary condition for the utterance of (765)–(767) to receive an indirect reading.

Heavy stress on the modals in corresponding German sentences would likewise result in foregrounding the direct reading:

(768) ‖kannst du die Tür schliessen#
(769) ‖könntest du mir dein Auto leihen#
(770) ‖musst du immerzu so hämmern#

But again it would be wrong to generalize and assume that these stress patterns and their pragmatic interpretation are interlingually invariable and hold for all speech acts that can be direct or indirect. First, if *musst* in (770) is stressed, this utterance could still be taken to be directive in nature, the strategy being that, if the speaker knows that the hearer knows that his hammering is unnecessary, there would be no reason to continue. Weak or no stress on *musst* would, in fact, be highly unusual. Note also the booster before WILL and *wirst* in the following sentences:

[759] /Gordon !will you ˈcome out of the bùshes#
[762] /Gordon !wìrst du wohl aus dem Busch rauskommen#

It may be said to give additional emphasis to the indirect directive reading of this utterance, which was said previously to be due to the falling intonation on *bushes.* Would it not be true to say that, in all of (759)–(770), ultimately the falling intonation near the end of the utterances identifies them as directives rather than questions?

Second, MUST in one subgroup of indirect speech acts, namely, hedged performatives, regularly does receive strong stress. Coates (1983: 49) reports: "An important subcategory of root MUST (examples involving *I must say/admit/warn*) is almost always associated with strong stress . . ." She provides the following example:

(771) /well# I /mùst ˈsay# /this is !àwfully kínd#

Here again differences between English and German show up. The most eminent one is probably the impossibility of rising intonation at the end of the tone unit. As regards the modal, this could be stressed, but it would hardly receive primary stress:

(772) /also# ich /muss (schon) ˈˈságen# /das ist ˈfurchtbar ˈˈnètt#

In other indirect speech acts, though, MÜSSEN conforms to MUST and its stress pattern; see the rendition of Coates's (1983: 7) example (773):

(773) you ˈˈmust come toˈnight#
(774) Sie ˈˈmüssen heute abend ˈkommen#

Unity of emphasis can also be found in the utterances of particularly well-meaning hosts saying:

(775) you ˈˈmust have some more of this ˈcake#
(776) Sie ˈˈmüssen noch ein Stück von diesem ˈKuchen nehmen#

In examples (758) and so on we showed how illocutionary indeterminacy can successfully be dissolved by prosodic features serving as identification factors. In all these cases, utterances carrying the potential of different illocutionary acts were disambiguated, with one illocution remaining as the one probably intended by the speaker.

We will now approach the question of how one kind of illocutionary force—directives—can be varied by means of varied intonation patterns. Overt questions containing modals can be ranked on a gradient of politeness according to which modal is used; remember the scale . . . /will/can/could you . . .? set up by Leech (1981: 336), see Section 4.1.4.2. At a different point in his book, Leech gives another example of the possibility of "scaling our remarks according to politeness" (1981: 15). This time he presents just the two extremes of a scale of politeness:

(777) I'm terribly sorry to interrupt, but I wonder if you would be so kind as to lower your voices a little.
(778) Will you belt up.

Utterance of (778) can of course be analyzed in terms of one characteristic mentioned earlier: Falling intonation indicates its indirect directive reading. The idea of rising intonation for a genuine question reading seems to be rather improbable in this case, though.

What is remarkable about both (777) and (778) is the possibility of radically deviating from their 'standard' indirect reading and arriving at a second, completely different indirect reading. This can be achieved by means of prosody. Leech (1981: 16) explains: "Factors such as intonation and voice-timbre—what we often refer to as 'tone of voice'—are also important here. The impression of politeness in (777) can be reversed by a tone of biting sarcasm; sentence (778) can be turned into a playful remark between intimates if delivered with the intonation of a mild request." As German equivalents of (777) and (778) we propose:

(779) Es tut mir ja schrecklich leid, dass ich störe; ob Sie wohl so freundlich wären, etwas leiser zu sprechen.
(780) Wirst du wohl ruhig sein!

The falling intonation giving (759) and (762) their directive character would also be appropriate for (778) and (780). The latter two sentences have two directive illocutions, however, which have to be distinguished. The 'mild request' reading may be achieved by less loudness and a more friendly and relaxed way of articulating.

Finally, a word on other modal expressions. As mentioned in Section 4.1.1, expressions such as HAVE ENOUGH WILL POWER are less likely to give rise to indirect illocutions because they are pragmatically much more specific than the modals. This greater pragmatic specificity is paralleled in terms of prosody. Panther (1981a: 297) argues that, whereas the modals are typically weakly stressed, other modal expressions such as BE ABLE TO or

HAVE THE ABILITY TO are prosodically more prominent. This is why the hearer will focus on the literal meaning of utterances containing them.

True as this principle will be for such modal expressions as the two or three just mentioned, there are other expressions, idiomatic phrases, that permit only an indirect reading. Think of *I wonder if you would be so kind as to* contained in (777). The possibility of a speaker being genuinely interested in getting to know if the hearer 'would be so kind as to . . .' is highly unlikely.

5.2.2.2 Factuality

In our factuality section (4.3.2) we presented as implicative sentences (642) and (643):

[642] John kann aber schwimmen!
[643] John can swim!

In the spoken language, the factuality of John's swimming can be indicated by stress and intonation:

(781) ‖Jòhn kann aber ǀschwimmen#
(782) ‖Jòhn can ǀswím#

Exclamatory statements such as these signal what Leech (1981: 14 ff.) would call *affective meaning*, and what others have referred to as *emotive modality* (see Sections 3.2.4.9 and 6.3.9).

In this particular case, the speaker expresses enthusiasm/admiration/surprise about John's ability to swim as evidenced by his actual swimming. As (781) and (782) show, primary and secondary stress patterns correspond to each other in English and German. Intonation may differ: the rise in (782) is not necessarily paralleled in (781). This is, however, due to the modal particle ABER used here to express admiration. If it were omitted, the same intonation as in (781) would be possible, but also the one in (782):

(783) ‖Jòhn kann ǀschwimmen#
(784) ‖Jòhn kann ǀschwímmen#

The difference is that the latter utterance expresses an even greater degree of surprise or admiration than the former one.

5.3 PUNCTUATION

Quite obviously, punctuation can serve as an identification factor for syntactic mood and the corresponding direct illocutionary act. The period is correlated with statements; the exclamation mark, with imperatives (or exclamations, see (642) and (643)); the question mark, with questions. In indirect speech acts punctuation correlated with the primary illocution (i.e., the one that is the point of utterance) can overrule the one correlated with the secondary illocution. Accordingly, Coates (1983: 172) remarks that in

(785) Will you listen to me and stop interrupting!

the exclamation mark reveals that, despite inversion, this utterance is not a question about the hearer's willingness to do something but is imperative in character. So the exclamation mark parallels falling intonation in spoken language employed for the same purpose (see (759) in Section 5.2.2.1).

But, in English, the exclamation mark is not necessarily used even in such strong *will you* directives as Leech's example (778):

[778] Will you belt up.

For the corresponding German sentence

[780] Wirst du wohl ruhig sein!

the exclamation mark is a must—unless, maybe, it is "turned into a playful remark between intimates" (Leech 1981: 16) the way (778) can be. But generally speaking, at least regarding the exclamation mark, punctuation in German will more often be a definite identification factor for illocutionary force than in English.

5.4 SYNTACTIC ANTICIPATION

In simultaneous interpreting (SI) the time factor is typically more crucial than in consecutive interpreting or in translation performed in the written mode. "The decisive factor in SI is the moment when the simultaneous interpreter actually sets his reproduction process going," Wilss (1978: 346) says, quoting Mattern (1974: 28) for a specification of that moment: "In practice . . . , the optimal moment of interpretation will differ depending on the subjective and objective factors involved; the objective or speech-language-linked factors being those which originate from the SL text and from relations of equivalence existing between SL and TL, and the subjective factors being those which depend on the interpreter himself."

In view of the time pressure under which the simultaneous interpreter has to work, one crucial subjective factor is the interpreter's memory. How long one is able to wait before one starts interpreting each sentence will depend upon the capacity to keep in mind what was said by the SL speaker. To be relieved from information overload one should be in a position to start as soon as possible.

But there are cases in which the simultaneous interpreter seems to be forced to await the coming to an *end* of a long SL sentence before he or she can even *start* interpreting it. To evaluate this claim let us take a sentence from Wilss (1978: 348):

(786) Namens meiner Fraktion darf ich den beiden Herren Berichterstattern für die Arbeit, die sie geleistet haben, sehr herzlich danken.

It is true that, upon hearing the first three words, the German-English simultaneous interpreter might immediately start saying: "On behalf of my political party." Hearing the next two words he might add: "I may." But English requiring the full verb to follow the modal, the interpreter would *then* have to wait until the very last German word is uttered, because this is the full verb DANKEN. Such a late takeoff or late continuation is "an extremely heavy stress on the short-term memory of the interpreter" (Wilss 1978: 347). Could no compensation factor provide a shortcut in this situation?

Mattern (1974: 3) suggests one such strategy, as reported by Wilss. If (786) is uttered in an E(E)C debate the experienced interpreter will know that "the German segment 'Namens meiner Fraktion darf ich (danken)' is a standard phrase which is frequently used as an opening gambit in a follow-up speech statement of one or several EEC rapporteurs. Once the simultaneous interpreter has heard 'Namens meiner Fraktion darf ich . . .' he can legitimately infer from previous experience that some form of saying 'thank you' can be expected" (Wilss 1978: 348). This is why, having heard only the first five words the translator can start or continue his TL rendition.

This form of "intelligent textual prediction," referred to by Wilss (1978: 348 f.) as *syntactic anticipation*, has yet another advantage. It saves the interpreter from mistakenly rendering DÜRFEN by MAY, as suggested previously. Instead WOULD LIKE TO/SHOULD LIKE TO has to be employed, as the following complete rendition of (786) shows:

(787) On behalf of my political group I should like to thank the two rapporteurs very cordially for their work.

Even though MAY has repeatedly been shown to be the adequate rendition of DÜRFEN, in the present case this principle seems to be annulled by a revision factor, namely, the modal's being embedded in a syntactic construction that has to be considered as a whole. This recognition takes us to the topic of our next chapter. As we have just seen, it is by no means invariably sufficient to go by a modal alone for the sake of rendering it; rather, different *translation units* may be relevant to different renditions.

6. FACTORS RELATING TO TRANSLATION UNITS AND TYPES OF EQUIVALENTS

The almost 800 numbered examples discussed up to this point were mainly sentences, in many cases English-German sentence pairs. It seemed to be natural to present the modals and their equivalents within sentences, because we speak and write in sentences, and it is sentence by sentence that the translator translates.

In some cases a more cogent reason was that certain renditions were found to be bound to specific clause or sentence types. This means that, even though the modals are words, sometimes the unit to be considered for translating them is sentences. But are sentences, once found to be relevant to translating the modals occurring in them, the only modal translation unit?

Remember, for instance, modal collocations such as those with verbs of inert perception (*can see*, etc.). Here the full verb is the decisive factor for the nonuse of a modal in the corresponding German rendition (see Section 4.3.1). Therefore, in this case, the relevant translation unit consists of the modal and its immediate verbal cotext.

Dealing with the factor of translation units in this chapter, we will show that even much smaller and much bigger stretches of speech can be translation units relevant to the modals.[42]

As suggested by the chapter heading, translation units will be discussed with reference to types of equivalents. Let us take the example just touched upon to illustrate this point. The expression *can see* representing the translation unit *verb group* is rendered in German by *sehe* (or another finite form of the verb SEHEN). Here translation unit and type of equivalent coincide in scope. For rendering

[197] Kann das der Postbote sein?

it is relevant to identify the modal as being epistemic in meaning. But this alone will not do. The whole sentence and its syntactic mood must be considered. Interrogative sentences containing an epistemic modal of the "possibility" degree of modality do not allow for MAY but only for CAN (see Figure 3.7). Here translation unit and type of modal equivalent differ in scope: The translation unit is the whole sentence, but the translation equivalent of the modal is only one word—CAN—again a modal.

In discussing various translation units in this chapter, our focus will again be on the modals. This is why we will not generally include into our consideration equivalence pairs with none of the equivalents being or containing a modal (such as SURELY → SICHERLICH; OBLIGATORY → OBLIGATORISCH; THERE IS THE POSSIBILITY → ES BESTEHT DIE MÖGLICHKEIT).

Section 6.3.1 will be devoted to the equivalence type *SL modal → TL modal*. In all other parts of this chapter we will consider 'nonmodals' as well as expressions containing modals as equivalents of modals. Section 3.2.1 shed light on the relationship between modals and their cognates, leading to the insight that modals are 'naturally' rendered by modals. This means that in all parts of this chapter except for Section 6.3.1 those revision factors will be reviewed that give rise to equivalents that are not (only) modals.

Many examples in this chapter are familiar ones. The purpose of briefly taking them up again is to present them in a new context. Whereas in the preceding chapters they were organized according to their identities as formal, semantic, and pragmatic factors, here they will be grouped according to kinds of equivalents. This will amount to far from mere repetition, because the factors giving rise to a specific kind of equivalent can be quite divers, and consequently the corresponding examples are originally found scattered in Chapters 2–6. Vice versa, because equivalents of the modals can also be SL items, the special benefit of grouping examples as indicated is in demonstrating which translation factors are relevant to rendering a certain kind of SL item.

6.1 ZERO EQUIVALENCE

To really start from 'zero,' we must begin with the most extreme of all signs signaling modality: deliberate conventional silence. A tax adviser interpreting the nonreaction on the part of the German finance department (see Section 4.4.3.2) may well 'translate' that silence for an English-speaking client by using a modal, saying:

(788) Two months have passed since we asked them for their consent, and they haven't replied as yet, so now

—you may take it that they don't object;
—you may go ahead the way you want to.

Other cases of zero-to-one or one-to-zero correspondence are linguistic in nature. Remember the following pair of sentences:

[89] Can you play tennis? Yes, I can/No, I can't.
[90] Kannst du Tennis spielen? Ja/Nein.

As the result of elliptical partial change factors, the second part of (90) is an extreme case of zero equivalence to a whole clause (albeit a short one). In other renditions at least the subject is retained:

(789) Can anyone of you play tennis? Yes, I can.
(790) Kann einer von euch Tennis spielen? Ja, ich.

Note that *Yes, I can* occurs in both (89) and (789). In the latter sentence *I* is main element of the answer. The corresponding pronoun *ich* in (790) serving the same purpose cannot be omitted. As regards the verbal aspect, the answers in (90) and (790) share a 'zero for verb group.' In other examples at least the full verb is retained:

[624] I can see two ships.
[622] Ich sehe zwei Schiffe.

As in the previous two renditions there is a 'zero for modal,' however. But the relevant translation unit, the verb group *can see*, has an equivalent: the finite full-verb form *sehe*. This is why we refer to (622) not as an instance of *zero equivalence*, but of *nonmodal equivalence*. This type of equivalence will be further dealt with in Section 6.3.10.

6.2 MORPHEME

Modals are free morphemes. A common way of using a bound morpheme for paraphrasing the root meaning of CAN in a passive main-verb construction is choosing an expression that contains a modal suffix such as *–able,* *–ible,* or *–uble,* thus

(791) (CAN + be redeemed) = is redeemable

As the basic compositional meaning of lexemes of the form *Xable,* Aronoff (1976: 127) states "liable to be Yed" or "capable of being Yed." Mettinger (1986: 22) remarks that this description applies only to verbal adjectives with a suffix expressing modality ("possibility," "necessity") and illustrates such cases by means of modal paraphrases (p. 24):

(792) These coupons are redeemable for cash.
(793) These coupons can be redeemed for cash.
(794) One can redeem these coupons for cash.

His equivalents

(795) eatable	"(sth) can be eaten"
(796) fixable	"(sth) can be fixed"
(797) lovable	"(sb/?sth) can/may be loved"

show that the base verb must be able to take the passive and that the deriva-
tion must be formed according to the preceding definition; *considerable*, for
instance, would be ruled out because it does not express possibility and
hence cannot be paraphrased by "(sth) can be considered."

But this does not necessarily mean that such adjectives do not express
modality at all. For *acceptable, lik(e)able,* and *readable*, Hansen et al. (1985:
112) also mention paraphrases including OUGHT TO: "that is worthy of
being V–ed/ought to be V–ed." These paraphrases also appear to be applicable to (797) *lovable*. This openness to degrees of modality other than "possibility" also does more justice to the term chosen by Mettinger (1986: 24) for
equations such as (795)–(797)—'*can/may/must be Xed*' *analysis*.

There are even more possibilities for derivations in *–able*, both in terms
of meaning paraphrases, and in terms of base expressions. The following list
of meanings taken from Kastovsky (1989: 207) gives an idea of their wide
range:

1. *eatable, understandable*: "that can/is fit to be V–ed";
2. *acceptable, lik(e)able*: "that is worthy of being V–ed";
3. *changeable, suitable*: "that is likely to V, that V–s";
4. *knowledgeable, sensible*: "having N";
5. *fissionable, marriageable*: "that is able, fit to be subjected to N";
6. *fashionable, reasonable*: "that is in accordance with N";
7. *comfortable, profitable*: "capable of giving N."

The reader is invited to determine which of these expressions denote the
meanings of possibility, ability, other modal meanings, or no modality at all.

Turning now to interlingual considerations, it may be said that the same
kind of equations initially set up for modals in passive constructions is valid
for German; (791) corresponds to (798):

(798) kann eingelöst werden = ist einlösbar

The suffix *–bar* being a standard German equivalent of *–able, redeemable*
can be rendered by *einlösbar, drinkable* by *trinkbar,* and so forth. This
means that in principle, the *–able/–bar* pair is interlingually self-sufficient.
The preceding equations involving modals theoretically come into play only
if TL lacks a corresponding expression in *–able/–bar*. But when is this the
case? Consider, for instance, sentences with modals in passive constructions,
such as the following one mentioned by Leech (1987: 74):

[181] This game can be played by young children.

Even for explicating its meaning, Leech does not prefer a version with an adjective in –*able*, such as

(799) This game is playable by young children.

but one with *possible*:

[182] It is possible for this game [to be played by young children].

It seems that for all its productivity, the suffix –*able* gives rise to expressions that sometimes sound too unusual to be used,[43] and this is exactly where modal passive constructions come in.

Another change factor for rendering SL modal bound morphemes by TL modals is what Leech (1981: 14) calls *province*, by which term he means "language of law, of science, of advertising, etc." As an English equivalent for *nicht übertragbar* used in the commercial field, Wildhagen and Héraucourt (1972: 1222) give *nonnegotiable (receipt)*, but they also mention a modal-verb construction:

(800) (the license) shall not be transferred (by the licensee).

The same translation principle can be applied to the expression of physical law, see Beilhardt and Sutton (1954: 22):

(801) Papier ist brennbar.
(802) Paper will burn.

Here the "possibility" meaning of –*bar* is turned into "timeless truth" expressed by WILL. A different use of WILL is found in the following rendition of –*bar* (see Wildhagen and Héraucourt 1972: 1236):

(803) Er ist unbelehrbar.
(804) He will take advice from no one/listen to no one.

Here, "impossibility" or "inability" is turned into "insistence." Of course, the WILL constructions in (802) and (804) can be replaced by adjectives ending in –*able (is inflammable, is unteachable)* paralleling the German –*bar* constructions in (801) and (803).

Equally remarkable are variations and ambiguities in degrees of modality. Mettinger (1986: 26) mentions two meanings of the adjective *payable*, "(sth) can be paid" and "(sth) must be paid." The *Longman Dictionary of Contemporary English* (hereafter *LDCE;* 1987: 756) adds another meaning facet s.v. *payable*: "that must or may be paid." By "may," the permissive character of *payable* is expressed. Accordingly, the first edition of the *LDCE* (1978: 798) gives as an example for "may be paid":

(805) This bill is payable at any time up to next Tuesday.

All three meanings mentioned so far are contained in *Webster's New Collegiate Dictionary* (1993: 854) s.v. *payable*: "that may, can or must be paid."

Kjellmer (1980: 50, n. 15) explains that *payable* generally means "that can be paid," but that it means "that should be paid" in a sentence such as

(806) All invoices are payable within 30 days.

This sentence is semantically similar to the sentence:

(807) This bill is payable next Tuesday.

which is given by the *LDCE* (1978: 798) as an example for "must be paid." So both "must" and "should" appear to be among the potential meanings of payable. This is obvious from *Longman Modern English Dictionary* (1976: 821), which offers all four modals as meanings s.v. *payable*: "that must, can, should or may be paid . . ." Therefore the lexeme *payable* again shows that polysemy must be considered as a factor not just of the modals but also of other modal expressions (see the gerund and the relative infinitives dealt with in Section 3.2.3.1 ((329) and so on)).

The German adjective corresponding to *payable, zahlbar*, is equally polysemous. This is why it is natural for it to be used as a rendition. Having ambiguity or the unspecific degree of modality as an invariance factor is a reason for choosing an equally polysemous TL modal adjective. Choice of a TL *modal* would require presence of a revision factor; for instance, the necessity of focusing on a specific meaning (as reflected by the modal paraphrases given previously).

For other, nonpolysemous SL-TL pairs of adjectives, the relevant factor is idiomaticity of expression. Compare the following piece of information printed on a blister package containing buttons produced by *Jill fashion— world of buttons* (Germany, 1992).

(808) farbecht—reinigungsbeständig
        washable—dry cleanable
        lavable—nettoyable à sec

Here, *waschbar* could have been used as a literal equivalent of *washable*; but *farbecht*, conveying a touch of textile LSP, expresses more elevated style. The factor accounting for the use of the similarly sophisticated adjective *reinigungsbeständig* is different: **reinigungsbar* would not be grammatical. In both cases a modal-verb construction—*kann gewaschen/(chemisch) gereinigt werden*—appears to be too wordy, in addition to being unidiomatic in the present context of brief user information. This then is a case in which adjectives in *–able* are not paralleled by adjectives in *–bar*. The French version, however, is congruent with the English one, at least as far as the suffix *–able* is concerned.

The German adjectives used in (808) are just two examples of a variety of renditions corresponding to *–able,* including *–lich (understandable—verständlich), –fähig (marriageable—heiratsfähig), –wert (endorsable—empfehlenswert),* and so forth. This variety results from the following factors: (a) idiomaticity, (b) different parts of speech as a base, and (c) the wide semantic range of adjectives in *–able* hinted at already.

So much for modal suffixes. For prefixes we refer back to our mention of German modals and their nonmodal prefixes such as *hin–, her–, fort–,* or *weg–* (see Section 2.7 and the list in note 13). For German modals as bound morphemes (*Kann-, Soll-Bestimmung, Sollsaldo,* and so on) see Section 2.8.2.

6.3 WORD

In this section we will deal with words corresponding to words—modals corresponding to modals (Section 6.3.1), to other modal expressions (Sections 6.3.2–6.3.9), and to nonmodal expressions (Section 6.3.10). The common element of these three major types of equivalents on the word level is that here a TL part of speech or simple lexematic unit translates an SL modal—and vice versa.

Modal adjectives (Section 6.3.3), participles (Section 6.3.4), and nouns (Section 6.3.6) can also be used within corresponding modal constructions such as *IT IS* LEGITIMATE *TO, IT IS* PERMITTED *TO, THERE'S A* POSSIBILITY *THAT.* These will be discussed in Section 6.4.2 based on the translation unit *phrase.*

6.3.1 Modals

Rendering modals as modals seems to be just natural. There are good reasons for it:

- sameness of syntactic and morphological factors: The English and German modals share three of their formal defining criteria (see Section 1.2.2);
- sameness of semantic factors: Both English and German modals are unmarked as to the expression of various (sub)kinds of modality (see Sections 3.2.1.1 and 3.2.1.2);
- sameness of pragmatic factors: Both English and German modals are unmarked in terms of illocutionary force, thus being suited for direct as well as indirect speech acts (see Section 4.1.1).

Given these striking formal, semantic, and pragmatic correspondences between the English and German modals, it must be legitimate to establish interlingual pairs of modals corresponding to each other whenever possible. The word class *modal auxiliary* can therefore be regarded as a normal invariance factor that does not require for its justification any further factors beyond the *birds of a feather principle*.

Of course, due to (obligatory) change factors a modal sometimes is not, and in certain cases cannot be, rendered by a modal. But this is a different matter. Whenever a modal appears in an SL text, the translator should first probe the possibility of rendering it by a modal, provided the largest possible preservation of word class is demanded.

6.3.2 Modal Adverbs

Modal adverbs often convey epistemic modality, as is the case in the following German renditions:

[251] He may not be in Berlin.
[257] Vielleicht ist er nicht in Berlin.

[247] He can't be there.
[250] Er kann unmöglich dort sein.

[715] You might want to close the door.
[717] Vielleicht möchten Sie mal die Tür schliessen.

VIELLEICHT in (257) was chosen for the sake of avoiding ambiguity, a rendition with MÖGEN being less desirable due to its prototypical "volitive" meaning in that cotext (see Section 3.3.8). The same factor of possible but undesirable ambiguity accounts for the addition of UNMÖGLICH in (250). It must be emphasized that (247) as such is ambiguous, and if the corresponding German rendition is also requested to be so, this would require skipping UNMÖGLICH. Only if co(n)text or prosodic features weigh the interpretation of (247) toward the epistemic side should a marker such as UNMÖGLICH be added, signaling this kind of modality.

The factor responsible for adding VIELLEICHT in (717) is different from that operating in (257). Here pragmatic idiomaticity suggests not saying *Sie könnten* . . .

Viewed from yet another angle, idiomaticity can also be said to be a transposition factor for (257). In addition to avoiding ambiguity, VIEL-LEICHT could also be chosen in accordance with the German tendency to use modal adverbs where English prefers epistemic modals (see Section 3.2.4.1). This language-specific characteristic thus comes to be an optimizing factor for a more adequate rendition.

6.3.3 Modal Adjectives

Whereas modal adverbs often have epistemic meanings, modal adjectives tend to express root modality.

First, remember that even root MUST can be used attributively like an adjective:

[109] This is a must book.

German lacks such constructions with modals, so a nominal solution is appropriate:

[108] Dieses Buch ist ein Muss.

Second, genuine English modal adjectives used predicatively can have as equivalents German modals that are constituents of compounds:

[119] This provision is neither permissive, nor directory, but mandatory.
[117] Dies ist weder eine Kann- noch eine Soll-Bestimmung, sondern eine Muss-Bestimmung.

Participles of German modals rendered by English adjectives will be dealt with in the following section.

6.3.4 Modal Participles

As verified by empirical research, modal past participles such as *verboten* appear in German public directives where English prefers modals (see Section 4.6). This means that the syntagma *must not* on an English prohibition sign ought to be rendered by a participle:

(809) Cars must not be parked here.
(810) Parken verboten.

Here, the past participle has almost assumed an adjectival character (as in *nicht statthaft*). This tendency can also be found in past participles of modals used attributively, as in *(un)gewollte Komik, gekonnte Vorführung* (see Section 2.8.1). English lacks participles of modals, and the factor decisive for choosing an appropriate rendition is *part of speech*, so participles of full verbs and genuine adjectives take over the grammatical function: *(un)desired/(un)intentional humor; skilled performance*.

Present and past participles of modals must likewise be formed by suppletives:

[56] He liked being able to demonstrate his strength.
[65] He has/had had to work.

For the various functions of present and past participles of modal suppletives, see Section 2.5 (b) and (c), (49) and so forth. The German equivalents of these participles are modals, but not necessarily used in participle constructions. Renditions (51), (57), and (66) show modal infinitives, and (54), (60), and (63) contain modal past forms in subject, object, and adverbial clauses. These will be dealt with in Sections 6.5.4, 6.5.3, and 6.5.6, respectively. Sentence (69), however, contains the past participle *gekonnt*:

[69] Das wurde von ihm gekonnt.

The English version

[68] This was done well by him.

again shows the invariance of a part of speech, but the participle construction *done well* no longer shows explicit modality the way (69) does; cf. *gekonnte Vorführung* rendered by *skilled performance* as mentioned previously.

6.3.5 Modal Lexical Verbs

In Section 3.2.6.2 some modal lexical verbs were presented as being source oriented; unlike the modals they require expression of the modal source:

[311] He may go home.
[410] I permit him to go home.

We therefore argued against granting TL source-oriented sentences the status of standard renditions of SL goal-oriented sentences (see Section 3.2.6.1).

Acceptable exceptions are renditions that largely preserve the elements of the respective modal situation in one form or another, as in

[408] I cannot afford it.
[407] Meine Mittel/Verhältnisse erlauben das nicht.

But this shift in modal perspective is not cogent, because the following German sentence is perfectly acceptable:

(811) Ich kann es mir nicht leisten.

Only explicit focus on the modal source would justify preferring (407) over (811).

The following example is structured in a slightly different way:

[149] Money can't buy everything.
[150] Mit Geld kann man nicht alles kaufen.
[155] Geld ermöglicht nicht alles.

Because *money* in (149) is both modal source and modal goal (see Section 3.2.6.2), shifting to source orientation in (155) is not that much of a contrast as that of rendering (408) by (407), even though both renditions involve a transposition from a modal auxiliary to a modal lexical verb. If the identity of modal source and modal goal is not considered to be sufficient as a revision factor, additional justification for preferring (155) over (150) would be keeping the nominative case of the sentence subject invariable. Otherwise, if the modal is considered to be the most salient factor, (150) will be the translator's choice.

In the following example the modal lexical verb is not found in the German but in the English version:

[426] Mit nebenstehender Entfernungstabelle können Sie die Gesamtlänge Ihrer Flugroute berechnen.

[428] The opposite table of distances enables you to find out the total length of your own route.

Here the shift to a source-oriented modal lexical verb cannot be justified by keeping the grammatical case of the modal source invariable; on the contrary, the (instrumental) dative is changed to the nominative. The relevant change factor is the untypicality of beginning an English sentence with a prepositional phrase. The modal source instead being presented in the nominative case, it requires continuation with a modal lexical verb.

Another transposition factor is the incongruity of the English and German modal systems:

[317] Ich will dorthin (gehen).

[318] I want to go there.

(812) Er will dort gewesen sein.

(813) He claims to have been there.

In (813) use of a lexical verb is obligatory, but for (318), in certain contexts WILL ("insistence") could be used. WANT, however, is a modal lexical verb (see Perkins 1983: 98).

There are also optional transposition factors:

• The more elevated style chosen for TL accounts for rendering OUGHT TO by the lexical verb GEBÜHREN:

[442] . . . they are features of languages with both sound and meaning and ought therefore to have a place in the grammar. (Palmer 1971: 120)

[443] . . . handelt es sich um Sprachmerkmale lautlicher und bedeutungs-mässiger Art, denen darum ihr Platz in der Grammatik gebührt. (Palmer 1974b: 111)

• The natural tendency for variation can prompt a translator to prefer SICH LASSEN to KÖNNEN when rendering CAN in

[445] The same point can be made about borrowing as was made about analogy . . . (Lyons 1981: 206)

[446] Über Entlehnung lässt sich dasselbe sagen wie über Analogie . . . (Lyons 1992: 189)

Reflexive LASSEN is one of those modal expressions that are versatile in meaning. (For other such expressions, see Section 3.2.3.1). This factor accounts for finding this lexical verb as the equivalent of a range of English modals—of CAN as in (445), but also of WILL, SHOULD, and MUST (Wildhagen and Héraucourt 1972: 821 f.):

(814) Das lässt sich machen.
(815) That can be done.

(816) Es lässt sich biegen.
(817) It will stand bending.

(818) Das lässt sich denken.
(819) I should (just) think so.

(820) Lass dir das nicht einfallen.
(821) You must not think of such a thing.

Polysemy is, however, not the sole factor giving rise to these equations. The idiomaticity of the expressions also is decisive.

6.3.6 Modal Nouns

Infinitives of some German modals used as verbal nouns have no direct equivalent in English (*das Können* → **the can(ning)*). The relevant translation factor taken to be invariance of word class entails using an English modal noun:

[114] Sein Können beeindruckt mich.
[116] I am impressed by his skill.

[113] Hat man ein hohes Ziel, ist schon das Wollen von Wert.
[115] For a sublime goal the mere intention is a merit.

The same principle works also in the opposite translation direction, when a German modal noun has to be selected for rendering *musts*:

[110] Three important MUSTS in planning up-to-date wiring.
[111] Drei wichtige Erfordernisse bei der Planung moderner Verkabelung.

Here the plural form *musts* acts as a revision factor, because there is no plural to the infinitive MÜSSEN. The corresponding singular use of MUST as a verbal noun is paralleled by *das/ein Muss*:

[107] This book is a must.
[108] Dieses Buch ist ein Muss.

In contrast to (110) and (111), for rendering a modal plural form used meta-linguistically as in

[550] Ifs and cans

nominal and plural elements are carried over onto two nonmodal nouns, leaving the German modal in its infinitival form:

[554] Verschiedene Verwendungen der Ausdrücke *wenn* und *können.*

The principle of the invariance of word class operates also in translating German compounds (see Sections 2.8.2.1 and 2.8.2.2):

[130] Das Über-sich-hinauswachsen-Wollen = the urge to accomplish something beyond one's capabilities.

Different syntactic possibilities in English act as change factors turning nominal premodification into postmodification. A similar shift occurs when the morphological principles of forming compounds differ in the two languages, and the modal element has to be realized predicatively:

[117] Dies ist weder eine Kann- noch eine Soll-Bestimmung, sondern eine Muss-Bestimmung.
[118] *This is neither a can provision, nor a shall provision, but a must provision.
[119] This provision is neither permissive, nor directory, but mandatory.

A major deviation from a noun-noun rendition can occur when a shift to a more informal style is preferred:

[125] Das/Dein Nach-Hause(-gehen)-Können freut mich.
[126] I am glad of your being able to go home.
[129] I'm glad you can go home.

A rendition such as (129), however, fails to preserve a major characteristic of German modal complex words including the infinitive of a modal verb. This characteristic is their focus on the modal situation as a unit. Syntactically, this unity is overtly indicated by hyphenation. Semantically, what is commented upon by the verb phrase *freut mich* in (125) is the wholeness of a structured possibility. As the possessive pronoun *Dein* indicates, the hyphenated unit is somehow looked upon as one object. Sentence (126) partially retains the object-like nature of the possibility by use of the corresponding pronoun *your.*

'Compactness' of expression is also a feature of modal compounds not based upon the modals; for instance, of MINDESTHALTBARKEIT (see (709) in Section 4.4.1) and of UMSTEIGEMÖGLICHKEIT. The latter noun was heard in an announcement of the upcoming bus stop:

(822) Hauptpost—Umsteigemöglichkeit.

It denotes in a condensed form a whole modal situation that could be explicated as follows:

(823) Hier können Sie in einen anderen Bus/in andere Busse umsteigen.

Due to the factor of ellipsis, in (822) the modal noun is but the remnant of a modal verbal construction—UMSTEIGEMÖGLICHKEIT HABEN—and other elements of the overall modal situation. Therefore a closer paraphrase of (822) would be

(824) (Die nächste Haltestelle ist) 'Hauptpost'; hier haben Sie (die) Umsteigemöglichkeit in einen anderen Bus/in andere Busse.

Note that the special characteristic of UMSTEIGEMÖGLICHKEIT in (822) is the nonmention of the hearer. Use of this noun presents the possibility of changing buses as an objective fact existing as if irrespective of individual hearers. It might just as well be expanded to

(825) Hier besteht Umsteigemöglichkeit.

This impersonal reference of the modal noun corroborates Perkins's (1983: 87) statement: "Modal nominal expressions represent the ultimate stage in the objectification of modality; namely, its nominalization."

This does not mean, however, that modal nouns cannot be explicitly 'embedded' in personal constructions—see the following service information for customers printed on a small sheet of paper in four languages and mailed by Deutsche Bank AG in Hamburg:

(826) Ab 8. September 1990: Neue Telefon-Nummer (040) 37011.
Bitte nutzen Sie die Durchwahlmöglichkeit: 3701– . . .

(827) Our telephone number changes as from September 8, 1990, to: (040) 37011.
You can take advantage of our direct dialing facility under: 3701– . . .

(828) A partir du 8 Septembre 1990: nouveau numéro de téléphone (040) 37011.
Utilisez, s.v.p., les possibilités d'appel direct en composant le: 3701– . . . suivi du numéro du poste de votre interlocuteur.

(829) A partir del 8 de septiembre de 1990: nuevo número de teléfono (040) 37011.
Por favor, utilicen la posibilidad del discado directo: 3701– . . .

The second sentence of all four versions contains a modal noun supplemented in language-specific ways (as a compound, pre- or postmodified): DURCHWAHL*MÖGLICHKEIT*, DIRECT DIALLING *FACILITY*, LES

POSSIBILITES D'APPEL DIRECT; LA *POSIBILIDAD* DEL DISCADO DIRECTO.

'Genuine' compounds, it might be said, show premodification. Hence only the English and the German versions could be said to contain compounds. They come as handy building blocks used by the writers. Their compactness allowing for economic expression surpasses any verbal alternative also in terms of style:

(830) Sie können auch durchwählen: 3701– . . . Bitte nutzen Sie es!
(831) You can dial direct to your advantage under 3701– . . .

For certain compounds the syntactic 'savings' are especially large—remember BRINGSCHULD defined as "a debt that must be discharged on the creditor's premises." English lacking a corresponding compound, the definition just given also serves as a rendition. Vice versa, if this long English expression consisting of a modal noun postmodified by a relative clause is to be translated into German, BRINGSCHULD is all that is needed.

As well as the equivalences of SL modal noun and TL modal noun *or* TL modal verb discussed so far there is also the possibility of rendering an English modal noun by means of a German modal noun *plus* a modal verb—remember the expression *possibility of visiting* . . . rendered by *Möglichkeit,* . . . *besuchen zu können* (Section 3.3.5.3). Even though pleonastic and hence redundant, such constructions are very popular in German; see also the syntagma *the right to be known as* . . . translated as *das Recht, sich* . . . *nennen zu dürfen* in Gutknecht (1996: 91).

6.3.7 Modal Infinitives

Modal infinitives are not to be confused with the infinitive of (German) modals, as in

[45] Er wünschte sich, Gitarre spielen zu können.

In contrast, modal infinitives are instances of the infinitive of a full verb preceded by a form of HABEN ZU or SEIN ZU, both of which are modal (in the sense of "possibility" or "necessity"); for example,

(832) Das ist jetzt zu tun.
(833) Das hast du jetzt zu tun.

In Section 3.2.3.1 we said that the construction *SEIN + ZU + infinitive* is polysemous in terms of degrees of modality:

[327] Sein Wunsch ist zu erfüllen. =
[328] Sein Wunsch kann/muss erfüllt werden.

As indicated by periphrastic WERDEN in (328), the SEIN ZU construction is covertly passive. German modal infinitives often being rendered by English modals, the English passive is therefore required:

(834) Die Aufstellung in einem Raum, der eine Temperatur unter 10°C erreichen kann, ist zu vermeiden. (BBC Kühlschränke. Bedienungsanleitung.)

(835) Installation in a room which may reach a temperature below 10°C should be avoided. (BBC Refrigerators. Operating instructions.)

An example of SEIN ZU with (negated) "possibility" meaning is the following:)

[752] . . . I can't speak with you at the moment . . .
Ich bin im Moment leider nicht zu erreichen . . .

In spite of the equivalence of the subject—*I*/*ich*—the two sentences covertly differ in voice. This may not be immediately obvious because the SEIN ZU construction lacks an overt indicator of passive voice. Nevertheless the sentence subjects differ in their semantic function: *I* is agent, while *ich* is patient, which are the characteristics of active and passive sentences, respectively (cf. *Ich kann . . . nicht erreicht werden*). Why did the 'speaker-translator' choose two constructions involving such a covert change of voice? *Ich bin nicht zu erreichen* must be regarded as a standard formal way of informing the hearer about one's absence in situations as the one in which (752) was uttered. The English wording can be taken to be an informal counterpart. The difference between the formal and informal style of the two versions could therefore be explained by the factor of idiomaticity rooted in different cultural values (see Section 4.6).

As regards English 'nonmodals' rendering German modal infinitives, there is an interesting surface similarity between HABEN ZU and HAVE TO, as well as SEIN ZU and IS TO. But someone considering these as equivalence pairs would often trust false friends. Not that they cannot be equivalents at all; but more often than not they will not be:

(836) Sie haben morgen um 5 hier zu erscheinen.
(837) !You have to turn up at 5 here tomorrow.
(838) You must turn up at 5 here tomorrow.

Sentence (836) can be 'performative' in that, in speaking, the speaker lays an obligation. This is exactly what (837) cannot be used for; MUST as in (838) is required. HAVE TO would be possible only if (836) were uttered as a report.

In the past tense, HAVE TO renders MÜSSEN:

[559] Ich musste es tun.
[560] I had to do it.

Similar to the HABEN ZU/HAVE TO equivalence there are cases in which SEIN ZU translates IS TO:

(839) Such an outcome is to be expected. (Perkins 1983: 69)
(840) Ein solches Ergebnis ist zu erwarten.

(841) These tablets are to be taken four times a day.
(842) Diese Tabletten sind viermal täglich einzunehmen.

The equivalence of such sentence pairs hinges upon the English sentences being passive constructions, however. An active construction could never be rendered by means of SEIN ZU:

(843) You are to take these four times daily. (Perkins 1983: 69)
(844) *Du bist diese hier viermal täglich einzunehmen.

HABEN ZU, not being subject to the passive constraint, would be an alternative:

(845) Du hast diese hier viermal täglich zu nehmen.

But then HABEN ZU sounds pretty authoritarian (see also (836)), which factor suggests refraining from using it unless such an effect is explicitly intended. A more common rendition would be one containing the modal SOLLEN:

(846) Du sollst diese hier viermal täglich einnehmen.

Similarly, in Section 4.1.2 we pointed out the relationship between the following two speech acts:

[398] Erwarten Sie einen Anruf? Dann sagen Sie bitte in der Telefonzentrale Bescheid, wohin Ihr Anruf weitergeleitet werden soll.
[590] Expecting a phone call? Please advise the telephone operator where your call is to be transferred.

The equivalence of IS TO and SOLLEN also holds in the past tense:

[86] The house she was to sell . . .
[85] Das Haus, das sie verkaufen sollte, . . .

Sometimes SOLLEN is replaced by an anthropomorphic use of MÖGEN, both of which may be rendered by IS TO:

[633] Dieses Faltblatt soll Sie . . . informieren.
[628] Dieses Faltblatt möchte Sie . . . informieren.
[632] This leaflet is to give you information . . .

Conversely, SEIN ZU is sometimes rendered by an English modal. Consider the following construction found in an article containing tips for holiday trips:

(847) Sachsen. Einmaliges, reizvolles Elbsandsteingebirge, in Jahrmillionen durch Wind und Wetter geformt . . . Tip: Gut mit einem Dresden-Besuch zu kombinieren (nur 30 bis 50 km entfernt). [*Hörzu extra* no. 2/94: 13]

The terse style of the article accounts for ellipsis of *ist* in *ist (gut) zu (kombinieren)*. The full version of (847) could be

(848) Als nächstes wenden wir uns Sachsen zu. . . . Diesbezüglich möchten wir Ihnen folgenden Tip geben: Der Aufenthalt im Elbsandstein-gebirge ist gut mit einem Dresden-Besuch zu kombinieren, da Dresden nur 30 bis 50 km von dort entfernt ist.

SEIN ZU here does not denote necessity (as in (834) or (840)) but possibility. Yet it can equally be rendered by IS TO because "IS TO is also used to refer to what can be, or what can reasonably be, in both present and past . . ." (Palmer 1979a: 147):

(849) Saxony . . . Tip: To be combined well with a visit to Dresden (only 30 to 50 km away).

Using the adverb WELL in a rendition with a modal sounds more idiomatic, however:

(850) Saxony . . . Tip: May well be combined with a visit to Dresden . . .

As already mentioned, sentences with SEIN ZU can be ambiguous between possibility and necessity, and even more variants of meaning (see Section 3.2.3.1). However, co(n)text is a disambiguation factor that is likely to narrow down the range of interpretive possibilities. In this way *Die Aufstellung . . . ist zu vermeiden* in (834), being part of instructions for the installation of a refrigerator, can denote only necessity. *Ich bin im Moment . . . nicht zu erreichen* in (752) unambiguously carries the idiomatic meaning of (negated) possibility. The modal meaning in sentence (842) *Diese Tabletten sind viermal täglich einzunehmen* is equally clear, due to the typical context of this sentence. In virtually all cases it will be uttered to inform the hearer about prescribed use, not about optional use. And *gut . . . zu kombinieren* in (848) is easily identified as carrying the meaning of possibility because it is part of an article presenting possibilities for holiday trips.

Other sentences, devoid of co(n)text, remain ambiguous:

[327] Sein Wunsch ist zu erfüllen.
[840] Ein solches Ergebnis ist zu erwarten.

But this is no blocking factor to a straightforward rendition because SEIN
ZU is as ambiguous as IS TO:

[334] His wish is to be fulfilled.
[839] Such an outcome is to be expected.

6.3.8 Relative Infinitives

Modal infinitives are not the only modal expressions that are ambiguous
between different degrees of modality, so are the relative infinitives (nouns
postmodified by the infinitive of a full verb; see Section 3.2.3.1):

[332] Here is as book to settle your dispute. =
[333] . . . that can/may/will settle . . .

Even though relative infinitives are not explicitly referred to as modal, the
paraphrase in (333) clearly shows that they are. Yet it is not possible to
render them in German in a way that is syntactically completely congruent:

(851) *Hier ist ein Buch, dein Problem zu lösen.

Rendering modal infinitives by way of modals à la (333) is a possibility,
albeit one involving a transposition *and* committal to one specific degree of
modality; for example,

(852) ?Hier ist ein Buch, das dein Problem lösen kann.

As indicated by the question mark, something is uncomfortable about (852):
the active voice in the relative clause. Dynamic KÖNNEN as in this sentence typically calls for an agentive subject, which a book is not. A passive
variant would, however, deviate greatly from the original:

(853) Hier ist ein Buch, mit dem dein Problem gelöst werden kann.

But why have two disadvantages if two advantages are possible? What we
mean is this—German has in stock a construction that is just as ambiguous
as the English relative infinitives:

[336] Hier ist ein Buch zur Lösung deines Problems.

Admittedly, postmodification by means of a prepositional phrase (itself being postmodified by a noun phrase) again differs from verbal postmodification. But the factors of unspecificity of modal degree, as well as 'nonfinite'
postmodification are good reasons for looking upon this construction as an
acceptable equivalent of English relative infinitives.

6.3.9 Modal Particles

In Section 3.2.4.9 several German modal particles were said to express *emotive modality*. They "express different kinds of emotional attitudes in interpersonal communication such as 'astonishment,' 'doubt,' 'emphasis,' 'encouragement,' 'impatience,' 'reassurance,' 'reproach,' 'surprise,' etc." (Nehls 1989: 282). Because the modals typically represent root and epistemic modality with their degrees of "possibility," "advisability," and "necessity," as well as "volition," it may be wondered how modal particles can intersect with the semantics or pragmatics of the modals.

Yet at several points in this book we have in fact come across connections of the two kinds of modal expressions; and an article by Nehls (1989) is even titled: 'German Modal Particles Rendered by English Auxiliary Verbs.' We will here deal with a handful of particles and see how they can be added to German renditions of English modals, or even translate the modals themselves.

6.3.9.1 ABER

In Section 5.2.2.2 we presented the following sentences for the expression of enthusiasm/admiration/surprise:

[781] ‖Jòhn kann aber ‖schwimmen#
[783] ‖Jòhn kann ‖schwimmen#

The modal particle ABER in (781) is typically used to express this kind of emotive modality. But, as (783) shows, the same attitude can be conveyed without use of this particle. Does this corroborate Esser's (1984: 189 ff.) tenet that the modal particles may be omitted because their respective meanings can be expressed by intonation alone (cf. Nehls 1989: 284 f., n. 8)?

In Section 4.1.4.2, modal particles were suggested to increase illocutionary transparency. MAL and WOHL, for instance, support indirect illocutions (see Sections 6.3.9.5 and 6.3.9.6). This idea of increased transparency created by means of the modal particles may be extended to other functions of them. Thus ABER in (781) could be said to reinforce emotive modality.

On the other hand, ABER does not invariably indicate this kind of modality:

(854) ‖reiten kann John ‖nicht# ‖fechten ‖auch nicht# ‖John kann aber ‖schwîmmen#

The primary stress and rise-fall intonation on *schwimmen* shows that ABER is here used in a different function, that of indicating a semantic contrast (of *reiten* and *fechten* vs. *schwimmen*). As can be demonstrated by fronting it, ABER here serves as an adversative conjunction:

(855) ˡreiten kann John ‖nicht# ˡfechten ‖auch nicht# aber ˡJohn kann ‖schwîmmen#

In (855), syntax indicates that ABER is not used as a modal particle; in (854), the indicators are stress and intonation alone. Even without ABER these indicate that what is emphasized is not John's special skill as expressed by (781) and (783) but his general ability to swim:

(856) ˡJohn kann ‖schwîmmen#

For the adversative function to be expressed, however, ABER is indispensable. As against this, ABER used as a modal particle was shown not to be an absolute must. Even so, Esser's tenet can be accepted only on the theoretical level; practically speaking, ABER as well as all the other modal particles cannot be fancied away; as Hammer (1978: 145) observes: "Colloquial German stands or falls by an ample scattering of *denn, doch, ja, mal, schon, so* etc., without which it sounds bleak and impersonal . . ."

For the translator it is important to recognize the intended kind of emotional attitude or emotive modality—be it expressed with or without a modal particle—and to employ those means of the English language suited for conveying that attitude.[44] Translating from English, one should make use of the rich repertoire of German modal particles and properly add them whenever explication of a specific attitude seems appropriate.

6.3.9.2 ETWA

In our discussion of ABER we found that the presence of a modal particle can bring about a change of focus on modal information contained in an utterance. In addition to such a change in thematic meaning, connotative meaning can be affected through use or omission of a modal particle. This is evident from the following example involving ETWA:

(857) Ist das etwa die ganze Wahrheit?
(858) Is that supposed to be the whole truth?

According to Nehls (1989: 287 f.) sentence (857) can be paraphrased by

(859) Soll das etwa die ganze Wahrheit sein?

the English rendition of which, he says, is also (858). Now if the modal particle ETWA in (859) is omitted, "the connotation of ironical indignation is not so prominent in such epistemic *yes-no* questions:

(860) Soll das die ganze Wahrheit sein?" (Nehls 1989: 288)

If one accepts Esser's thesis of the invariance of meaning in the omission of modal particles one would, however, have to say that (859) and (860) are synonymous. Which tenet should we follow? We would say that in this case it makes no difference whether ETWA is added or not because (860) is ambiguous: Just like (859) it may be a question expressing suspicion, but it may also be a genuine question. For the latter reading, Nehls proposes a rendition with BE MEANT TO (p. 288):

(861) Is that meant to be the whole truth?

All these sentences taken together once again show that modal particles cannot be dismissed so lightly; their presence may rule out renditions otherwise possible. Whereas (860), being ambiguous, can be rendered by both (858) and (861), sentence (857) and (859) can be rendered only by (858). From the perspective of the modals, this presents no problem for (859). But (860) must be disambiguated first before an 'innocent' (861) or a skeptical (858) English version can be chosen.

The expressions *ist . . . etwa* and *soll . . . etwa . . . sein* in (857) and (859) are rendered as *is . . . supposed to* in (858). The function of the modal particle is thus incorporated into an English construction containing the past participle of a modal full verb. There are also cases in which a German modal particle is rendered by an English modal auxiliary, our next topic.

6.3.9.3 EIGENTLICH

Remember the following sentence pair (see Section 3.2.4.9):

[388] It is appropriate that he should get the post.
[389] Es ist eigentlich angemessen, dass er den Posten bekommt.

It is striking to observe that the German and English modal expressions manifest at unusually distinct places in these two sentences. Nevertheless Nehls (1989: 286) maintains: "The German modal particle EIGENTLICH in the introductory clause of evaluative statements can best be rendered by 'putative' SHOULD (Quirk and Greenbaum 1973: 340 f.) in the English *that* clause . . ."

The factor of syntactic discrepancy seems to be overruled by the fact that *both* modal expressions "convey a pensive mood on the part of the speaker or writer . . ." (Nehls 1989: 287). EIGENTLICH used in this way expresses emotive modality. If the equivalence of EIGENTLICH and SHOULD is accepted, this would mean that this kind of modality is also conveyed by SHOULD.

6.3.9.4 JA

In Section 4.1.3 we found that the expression *sollte lieber* may be rendered by the quasi-auxiliary HAD BETTER. Nehls (1989: 289) points out that also the German modal particles NUR, BLOSS, and JA used in "warnings expressing apprehension on the part of the speaker" can be rendered by HAD BETTER:

(862) Sei nur/bloss/ja pünktlich!
(863) You'd better be on time.

It must be borne in mind, though, that each of the three modal particles conveys its own shade of illocutionary force. So interlingual discussion of HAD BETTER in connection with illocutionary subtleties as initiated in Section 4.1.3 should be extended to consideration of modal particles.

Besides its illocutionary function, JA is also used in concessive sentences such as

(864) Die Gebäude mögen ja alt sein, aber es ist eine ausgezeichnete Schule.

Note that only MÖGEN, not KÖNNEN, can be used in such sentences. As regards the English counterpart of (864), Leech (1987: 75) refers to the "colloquial concessive use of MAY ('possibility') in remarks like:

(865) The buildings may be old, but it's an excellent school.

(i.e.: 'I admit that the buildings are old, but . . .')." As indicated by the *that* clause, the speaker admits a fact; hence MAY in (865) might be assumed to be implicative. This would be surprising because MAY evidently signals epistemic modality in which use it denotes no more than the *possibility* of a fact. As just mentioned, Leech himself referred to *MAY ('possibility')*. But this very situation may be strategically used by the speaker. Overtly playing down the degree of factuality of the first clause (containing nonconducive information for his argument) by means of MAY, the stated or claimed—unmodalized—factuality of the second clause will impress the hearer all the more. German JA supports exactly this function of concessive MÖGEN paralleling MAY.

Plainly stating that MAY and MÖGEN are always implicative in sentences such as (864) and (865) raises doubts, however. There may be cases where the two modals merely denote epistemic possibility. If the age of the school buildings referred to in (865) is definitely unknown to the speaker he or she may still utter this sentence. Interestingly, JA would not be used in this case:

(866) Die Gebäude mögen alt sein, aber es ist eine ausgezeichnete Schule.

This leads to the following conclusion: Factuality is not necessarily signaled by the epistemic use of the modal auxiliary MÖGEN in the first clause of a complex sentence, the second one of which is an adversative clause; rather, factuality is conveyed by the modal particle JA following MÖGEN. It is therefore not MÖGEN that is implicative but only JA. This modal particle could thus be labeled a *factuality marker*, a role it also plays in utterances such as

(867) Zum Glück ist er ja da.

English lacking a corresponding modal particle, implicative clauses containing MAY cannot offhand be told from clauses in which this modal 'merely' denotes epistemic possibility—at least in written language lacking clear cotext. Such ambiguity between 'mere' epistemic possibility and another interpretation also exists in the field of illocutionary force. Again a modal particle supports disambiguation: MAL.

6.3.9.5 MAL

In connection with the politeness phenomena we discussed the following two sentences (see Section 4.4.2.1):

[715] You might want to close the door.
[717] Vielleicht möchten Sie mal die Tür schliessen.

Even though theoretically ambiguous between a statement of epistemic possibility and an indirect request, (715) will in certain situations unquestionably be understood as conveying the latter kind of speech act. In this case it should be legitimate to give the German equivalent an indicator of the indirect request reading by means of the modal particle MAL in (717).

The following sentences contained in the two illocutionary scales dealt with in Section 4.1.4.2 are also ambiguous between a direct and an indirect interpretation (question and request):

[603] Will you shut the door?
[604] Can you shut the door?
[605] Could you shut the door?

[613] Willst du die Tür schliessen?
[609] Kannst du die Tür schliessen?
[610] Könntest du die Tür schliessen?

Even though modals are used here (in contrast to other modal expressions such as BE ABLE TO; see Section 4.1.1), these sentences (at least the first two in each triplet) are not so idiomatically disposed toward an indirect illocution as (715). However, if co(n)text strongly suggests that this kind of illocution is intended, in the three German sentences the modal particle MAL also may be added as an unmistakable identification factor of illocutionary force:

(868) Willst du mal die Tür schliessen?
(869) Kannst du mal die Tür schliessen?
(870) Könntest du mal die Tür schliessen?

If WILL in (603) is rendered by WERDEN, the insertion of MAL conveys a very impatient directive:

[614] Wirst du die Tür schliessen?
(871) Wirst du mal die Tür schliessen?/!

WERDEN is also compatible with the modal particle WOHL, the final particle to be considered here.

6.3.9.6 WOHL

As in the case of MAL, also WOHL conveys a very strong directive[45] when used in conjunction with WERDEN; for example,

(872) Wirst du wohl die Tür schliessen!

As indicated by the exclamation mark, (872) is no request but an injunction.
   Sentence (872) and its English equivalent (873) are syntactically based upon questions (614) and (603), respectively:

[614] Wirst du die Tür schliessen?
(873) Will you shut the door!
[603] Will you shut the door?

The same is true of the following sentence pair:

[785] Will you listen to me and stop interrupting!
(874) Wirst du wohl zuhören und mich nicht immer unterbrechen!

Use of the exclamation mark is, however, no must in English (see Section 5.3):

[778] Will you belt up.

But in German it is:

[780] Wirst du wohl ruhig sein!

So in the latter two sentences the identification factors for illocutionary force differ in the two languages:

- In English, the absurdity of a direct reading forces an indirect one;
- in German, punctuation and a modal particle typically associated with injunctions are additional factors.

In the spoken language, prosody is the factor indicating an indirect illocution, as in the following *Will you* directive. In its German rendition the modal particle WOHL again acts as another identification factor:

[759] /Gordon ⌐will you ⌐come out of the bùshes#
[761] /Gordon ⌐wirst du wohl aus dem ⌐Bùsch rauskommen#

6.3.9.7 Further Possibilities

In addition to those modal particles dealt with previously are others, such as DENN, DOCH, SCHON, GERADE, and EBEN. Each makes a unique contribution to the semantics and pragmatics of an utterance in terms of emotive modality. To provide just one example, if DENN were added in

[587] Kannst du deine Examensarbeit beenden?

the direct question reading would be underlined:

(875) Kannst du denn deine Examensarbeit beenden?
(876) Kannst du deine Examensarbeit denn beenden?

Different syntactic positioning of the modal particle highlights different aspects of the modal situation the speaker is concerned with: In (876) the focus on *finishing* the thesis is much greater than in (875).

Further nuances can be created by combining modal particles with each other. For instance, if you take the sentence frame

(877) Könntest du . . . die Tür schliessen?

the following combinations are just a few of many possible ones to be inserted:

vielleicht mal   vielleicht eben mal
gerade mal   vielleicht gerade mal
eben mal   wohl vielleicht mal
wohl mal   wohl eben mal
vielleicht eben gerade mal
wohl vielleicht mal gerade eben
wohl vielleicht mal eben gerade
wohl vielleicht gerade eben mal
wohl vielleicht gerade mal eben
wohl vielleicht eben gerade mal
wohl vielleicht eben mal gerade

There seems to be no limit to grading and shading politeness by such particle strings.[46] They show that the modal particles are a vast field of study and suggest that "their correct use is a considerable test for the foreigner" (Hammer 1978: 282). Because correctly correlating them with features of another language is an even more sophisticated task, they present an even greater challenge to the translator.

6.3.10 Overtly Nonmodal Equivalents

It would be very difficult trying to find for the modals any equivalents that are completely devoid of modality. Even if there is no overt or explicit expression of modality, in most cases there will be at least covert or implicit reference to it. Take the following sentence pair:

[624] I can see two ships.
[622] Ich sehe zwei Schiffe.

The activity of seeing stated as a fact in (622) implies its possibility, which is explicitly expressed in (624) (see Section 4.3.1). But taken at face value, (622) does not show modality. This is what we mean when we speak of overtly nonmodal equivalents of the modals. The specific equivalence type of a nonmodal full verb as in (622) will be dealt with in the first subsection, followed by the equivalence types of imperative and adverb, representing a small choice of a variety of nonmodal types of equivalents.

6.3.10.1 Full-Verb Constructions

TL full verbs are often the result of an SL modal being deleted from a verb group consisting of that modal and a full verb. This can easily be verified by comparing the full verbs in the following SL-TL versions:

[624] I can see two ships.
[622] Ich sehe zwei Schiffe.

[588] Ich freue mich, Sie hier begrüssen zu können/dürfen.
[589] I am happy to welcome you here.

[372] Well, I'll ring you tonight sometime.
[374] Also, ich ruf dich heut' abend mal an.

[603] Will you shut the door?
[608] Schliesst du die Tür?
[878) Schliesst du mal die Tür?

[718] You will place a guard over this fellow.
[719] Sie nehmen diesen Burschen in Gewahrsam!

[720] Du hältst jetzt mal diesen Knaben fest!

[628] Dieses Faltblatt möchte Sie über . . . informieren.
[629] This leaflet gives you information on . . .

The pairs of full-verb constructions are *see—sehen, begrüssen—welcome, ring—anrufen, shut—schliessen, place a guard over—in Gewahrsam nehmen/festhalten, informieren—give information on*. That none of these TL renditions contains a modal or any other modal expression is due to different factors:

- (622) follows the TL tendency not to use modals before verbs of perception;
- (589) illustrates that in English, expressions for mental attitudes may hedge performatives but not statements about their possibility.
- (374), (608), (719), (720), and (878), the modal particle MAL in the latter sentence again underlining the indirect speech act, express future time in the more common way of German present tense. English also offers this possibility as shown by (629). This sentence does not parallel the anthropomorphic use of *möchte* in (628). The reason why WILL was not used is probably the intention of the speaker (as judged by the translator) to emphasize the immediate availability of the information referred to.

6.3.10.2 Imperative

The following two sentences are excerpts from a small information sheet enclosed with audio cassettes manufactured by BASF, Germany, in the 1970s (italics ours):

(879) Lagerung und Versand *sollten* nur mit eingelegter roter Kern-Arretierung bzw. in der "snap-pack"-Klappdeckel-Schachtel *erfolgen*, wodurch ein Abspulen des Bandes vom Wickel verhindert wird.

(880) To prevent the tape from unwinding during transportation or storage *insert* the red locking clip into the drive holes or put the cassette into the "snap-pack" box.

Here the English imperative (*insert*) renders a modal verb construction (*sollten . . . erfolgen*). This is not the only difference between the two versions:

- sentence type: German, complex sentence consisting of main clause plus consecutive clause; English, final *to*-construction plus imperative clause.
- topic: German, (activity of) transportation or storage; English, goal regarding transportation or storage.
- case: German nominative where English has prepositional phrase (*Lagerung und Versand* vs. *during transportation or storage*); German prepo-

sitional phrase where English has accusative (*mit eingelegter roter Kern-Arretierung* vs. *the red locking clip*).

• argumentative structure: German, advice followed by justification; English, goal or benefit (corresponding to justification in German) followed by instruction.

Without going into further differences we can say that the overtly nonmodal equivalent of SOLLEN is just one of many changes that occurred during the translation process. The translator will have had in mind the conviction that the results of these changes are more typical of English usage (e.g., opening a sentence by stating the goal or benefit of a proposed activity to increase the reader's motivation for reading). If this idea includes the change from a piece of advice as expressed by means of a German modal to an English imperative relative to a goal, then the factor accounting for transposition is idiomaticity.

This assumption is, however, shaken by the fact that there exist cases where features are just the other way around:

[826] . . . Bitte nutzen Sie die Durchwahlmöglichkeit: . . .
[827] . . . You can take advantage of our direct dialing facility under: . . .

Here, German has the imperative form where English shows an indirect request containing a modal. Incidentally, as well as the German version, the French and Spanish ones (see Section 6.3.6) also are direct requests performed by means of the imperative plus a request particle: *Bitte nutzen Sie*; *utilisez, s.v.p.*; *por favor, utilicen*.

For the English rendition, the translator favored an indirect speech act overtly looking like a mere piece of information. Along the lines of Panther (see Section 4.1.4.2), (827) is in fact merely a piece of information, because both writers and readers are well aware that the information provided is new to the readers. If identity of perlocutionary effect is assumed for all four versions, the English one will, however, also have to be taken to be directive—unless the translator intended to grant the English-speaking community in Hamburg an extra status; or should saying 'less' than actually intended be taken to be a special form of understatement in this particular case? The latter interpretation does not seem to be too far-fetched when considered in the light of the following example:

(881) . . . Sir Harold seemed to have finished. "I mustn't keep you," he said and rose to his feet.
Doosie, wichtige Wendung: "I mustn't keep you," ich darf Sie nicht aufhalten. Auf deutsch: "Machen Sie, dass Sie rauskommen."
Ich machte.
(W. Lansburgh 1978: *Dear Doosie*. Munich; here p. 135)

Quoting this excerpt, Schreiber (1993: 203) explains that here, in a slightly caricaturing way, the author attempts to make his fictive reader Doosie familiar with British understatement.

Admittedly the German imperative in (881) . . . *Machen Sie,* . . . is no request as is (826) . . . *Bitte nutzen Sie* . . . But in both directives (827) . . . *You can* . . . and (881) . . . *I mustn't* . . . , the English versions, each containing a modal, are indeed less imposing than the German ones.

Yet another factor is to be considered in this connection, namely, that of pragmatic adequacy. Lansburgh produced two German versions as part of (881):

(882) Ich darf Sie nicht aufhalten.

(883) Machen Sie, dass Sie rauskommen!

Sentence (883) represents the wording of a speech act hardly ever to be uttered by any tactful person, least of all by a 'Sir Harold.' Had the English speaker really wished to give such a harsh order he would have used plain language in English, too.

Sentence (882), even though containing *darf nicht* as the literal translation of *mustn't,* lacks the idiomaticity of *I mustn't keep you* in (881). But German has a similar way of decently bowing out a guest:

(884) Jetzt will ich Sie aber nicht länger aufhalten.

The difference between the English and the German versions would thus be merely one of modal subkind—deontic or circumstantial dynamic vs. volitive, the latter (i.e., *will nicht* instead of *darf nicht*) seeming to us to be more idiomatic in German. This means that neither of the two versions given by Lansburgh is situationally adequate.

6.3.10.3 Adverbs

Because Section 6.3.10 is devoted to overtly nonmodal equivalents of modals, we do not have in mind here modal adverbs such as POSSIBLY, PERHAPS, or SURELY, but nonmodal ones such as NUR:

(885) Nachdruck auch auszugsweise nur mit ausdrücklicher Genehmigung des Verlages.

(886) No part of this magazine may be reprinted without the express permission of the publisher.

This bilingual copyright information printed in the *Lufthansa Bordbuch/Logbook* (4/83: 96) is an interesting example of the phenomenon of unilingual ellipsis. The German version can effortlessly be expanded into a full sentence containing a modal corresponding to the English one:

(887) Nachdruck auch auszugsweise darf nur mit ausdrücklicher Genehmigung des Verlages erfolgen.

An expansion by means of other modal expressions is also possible:

(888) Nachdruck auch auszugsweise nur mit ausdrücklicher Genehmigung
des Verlages gestattet.

The obvious reason why neither of these two full versions was chosen is that
(885) is a standard way of providing information on copyright in German.
But why should the adverb NUR be regarded as an equivalent of MAY? It
could be maintained that this adverb plus the preposition MIT in (885) semantically correspond to *no . . . without*, not to the modal MAY whose
counterpart, DÜRFEN, is, after all, missing in (885). This is true, but we
would say that, in addition, NUR comes closest to overtly fulfilling the function of MAY (namely, that of referring to a right), because NUR is the only
surface-structure indicator of *some* right to reprint being granted (*gestattet* in
the sense of MAY) at all.

6.4 PHRASE

The translation unit *phrase* relates to several expressions linked syntactically
and semantically, thus being bigger than a word but smaller than a clause.
Here first modals and their cotext will be dealt with, followed by constructions involving modal adjectives, participles, and nouns.

6.4.1 Modals and the Immediate Cotext

In Section 3.3.5 we discussed collocative meaning as the meaning resulting
from the modals being part of a syntagma. We found that modals conjoined
by *and*-coordination are restricted in sequence. This means that the relevant
translation unit here is not the individual modals but the structure of their
coordination (see Section 3.3.5.2). Double modals are largely restricted to
German, which is why generally they also have to be considered as a whole
(see Section 3.3.5.1). The same is true of certain harmonic combinations of
modals and modal adverbs, which unit can require different TL renditions
(see Section 3.3.5.3).

   In the present section we will deal with modals in two kinds of environment: idiomatic phrases (Section 6.4.1.1) and other syntagmas containing
important cotextual elements acting as translation factors (Section 6.4.1.2).

6.4.1.1 Modals in Idiomatic Phrases

Modals are classified as auxiliaries because usually they cannot occur by
themselves but require a full verb in addition: *He can go, must be, might*

stay, and so forth. If they do occur alone, this is due to ellipsis of the full verb:

[89] Can you play tennis? Yes, I can/No, I can't.

In Chapter 4 we saw that certain kinds of full verbs require the translator's special attention, such as verbs of perception:

[624] I can see two ships.
[622] Ich sehe zwei Schiffe.

Such cotextual specialities also include phraseological expressions. These are characteristically made up of several lexemes giving rise to an overall meaning that is not necessarily predictable from the individual meanings of the lexemes. A phraseological unit containing a modal may be called a *modal phrase.* A case in point is MAY/MIGHT (JUST) AS WELL, which Palmer (1979a: 159) paraphrases as "it would be (just) as good if . . ." Because this meaning requires the presence of cotextual (JUST) AS WELL, he argues that it should be treated as idiomatic. Now let us see whether this English unit thus postulated is turned into a relevant translation unit. Here is a first example:

(889) Having come so far, we might just as well walk the extra couple of miles and complete the journey today. (Ball 1983: 15)

Several renditions suggest themselves:

(890) Wo wir jetzt schon so weit gekommen sind, könnten wir (ja) genausogut/ebensogut/auch gleich noch die paar Kilometer weitergehen, dann kämen wir heute noch ans Ziel.

In other co(n)texts, different renditions seem to be more appropriate, however. Let us start with an example taken from *Alice in Wonderland:*

(891) "Then you should say what you mean," the March Hare went on. "I do," Alice hastily replied. "At least—at least, I mean what I say— that's the same thing, you know."
        "Not the same thing a bit!" said the Hatter. "Why you might just as well say that 'I see what I eat' is the same thing as 'I eat what I see'!"

Of course, the last sentence can be translated as

(892) Da könntest du/könnte man ja genausogut/ebensogut sagen: 'Ich sehe, was ich esse' ist dasselbe wie 'Ich esse, was ich sehe.'

A rhetorically more adequate rendition would be, however:

(893) Das ist/wäre ja genauso/gerade so, wie wenn man sagen würde . . .

The reason is that the latter version is more suitable for expressing what the speaker of (891) aims at: critical ridicule. In contrast, (889) serves as a rational argument in favor of a proposed action. The fact that the rendition *könnte genausogut/ebensogut* offered for that sentence may equally well be used for rendering (891) by (892) suggests that the formula MAY/MIGHT (JUST) AS WELL has a unified basic meaning of "equivalent alternative (of action)." If the 'marked' nature of a critical context is to be highlighted, a marked rendition as in (893) is possible. In the absence of this context no such rendition is possible:

(894) *Wo wir jetzt schon so weit gekommen sind, ist/wäre es ja genauso/ gerade so, wie wenn wir die paar Kilometer weitergehen würden . . .

Conversely, in the context of (891) the last of the three renditions proposed for (889) is not possible:

(895) !Da könntest du/könnte man (ja) auch gleich sagen: 'Ich sehe, was ich esse' ist dasselbe wie 'Ich esse, was ich sehe.'

The reason is that *(ja) auch gleich* is marked for the 'argument in favor of' reading. As we have seen, the other two renditions used for this reading in (889)—*könnte . . . genausogut/ebensogut*—can also be used for the 'critical' one, which shows that they are more flexible in semantic scope.

Up to now we have considered only root examples involving MAY/ MIGHT (JUST) AS WELL, but there are also epistemic ones, such as the following object-language sentence used by Seiler (1971: 80):

(896) Of course, we might say with E. Schwyzer in his Greek grammar . . . that volition was historically first and prospectivity developed later; or it might just as well have been the other way round.

The two marked renditions mentioned previously being confined to root readings, only the unmarked equivalents *könnte genausogut/ebensogut* may be used here:

(897) . . . oder es könnte genausogut/ebensogut umgekehrt gewesen sein.

But epistemic MAY/MIGHT (JUST) AS WELL also has a marked rendition of its own: *Es kann/könnte genausogut/ebensogut sein, dass*:

(898) . . . oder es könnte genausogut/ebensogut sein, dass es umgekehrt war.

Table 6.1 summarizes the various renditions of the modal phrase under consideration.

In addition to the rhetorical *kann auch gleich* there is also *kann gleich*, rendering impersonal root constructions involving MAY . . . JUST AS WELL:

	Kinds of modality		
	Root		Epistemic
Context	Rational argument in favor of sth	Critical ridicule	(General)
Renditions			
Marked	*kann/könnte (ja) auch gleich* (890)	*ist/wäre ja genauso/ gerade so, wie wenn + past subjunctive* (893)	*es kann/könnte genausogut/ ebensogut sein, dass* (898)
Unmarked	*kann/könnte genausogut/ebensogut*		
	(890)	(892)	(897)

TABLE 6.1.
Some German Renditions of MAY/MIGHT (JUST) AS WELL

(899) Before beginning this story it may be just as well to tell you that it is perfectly true . . . (*The Beacon. The English Student's Own Magazine* 5, no. 6 [March 1954]: 5)

In a footnote to this first sentence of a short story published for German students of English, the editors provide the following equation: *it may be just as well to tell you: ich kann euch gleich sagen.*

Wildhagen and Héraucourt (1963: 997) give another equivalent for *it may be (just) as well*: *es mag ebenso günstig sein (to do).* This German syntagma, however, cannot be used for rendering (899), because it is marked for a different context—it is used for making conjectures about how favorable something is.

Remember that also several renditions for MAY/MIGHT (JUST) AS WELL were marked for different contexts (see Table 6.1). Also in this case the English expression itself is invariable. This means that only by virtue of the different, mutually exclusive German marked renditions do the different contexts of the English phrases become apparent. This may be taken as evidence for the truth of Goethe's general dictum: "Wer fremde Sprachen nicht kennt, weiss nichts von seiner eigenen."

In this connection it is also noteworthy that TL renditions can differ widely from the wording of SL phrases:

[891] . . . Why you might just as well say that . . .
[893] Das ist/wäre ja genauso/gerade so, wie wenn man sagen würde . . .

[899] . . . it may be just as well to tell you that . . .
(900) . . . kann ich Euch gleich sagen, dass . . .

Such divergence is, of course, again due to markedness relative to specific contexts. It can be considered to be interlingual corroboration of the claim made previously that idiomatic phrases have "an overall meaning that is not necessarily predictable from the individual meanings of the lexemes." Also the phrase IT WILL BE AS WELL in (901) has such an idiomatic meaning, which becomes evident when seen in the light of its German equivalent in (902):

(901) It will be as well for her to know it. =
(902) Es schadet ihr gar nichts, es zu wissen. (*Langenscheidts Enzyklopädisches Wörterbuch*, Vol. 1, Part 2, p. 1645)

Finally, the phrase IT WOULD BE AS WELL can serve as the rendition of the covertly modal construction ES WÜRDE ANGEBRACHT SEIN (Wildhagen and Héraucourt 1972: 56).

6.4.1.2 Modals and Other Cotextual Elements

The examples in the previous subsection featured MAY and MIGHT in what may be referred to as *fixed phrases*. In addition to these syntagmas are others, the elements of which are not invariably fixed. However, for the sake of adequate translations, these other syntagmas must nevertheless be considered as a whole. Such syntagmas are to be found in the field of negation.

In our section on negation (3.1.5) we focused on CAN and MAY. It was shown that negation is an important revision factor in that it modifies the rendition patterns valid for the affirmative use of these modals. But negation also affects other modals' renditions. A case in point is MUST.

What immediately comes to mind as a rendition for MUST is MÜSSEN. Yet all contrastive grammars and textbooks point out that rendering *must not* requires use of *darf nicht* (or some other form of DÜRFEN). This correlation certainly holds for the following sentence pair:

(903) I must not go swimming.
(904) Ich darf nicht (*muss nicht) schwimmen gehen.

Now consider the following examples:

(905) A translator *must not only* be able to translate a particular number of words per hour or per day, but *must* do so accurately and *must* create readable, natural prose in the target language. A simultaneous or consecutive interpreter *must not only* be able to keep pace with a speech for a certain number of minutes, but *must not* tire, *must not* miss words or phrases and *must not* misinterpret what the speaker is saying. (Chriss 1994: 3; our italics).

These lines, written by an experienced professional translator and interpreter as part of an essay titled 'Translation as a Profession,' also lend themselves for an interesting analysis to be carried out for the sake of translating them.

As suggested earlier, the two affirmative uses of MUST can straightforwardly by rendered by *muss*. Also the three final instances of *must not* (. . . *must not tire* . . . , etc.) conform to the rule outlined previously in that they are all rendered by *darf nicht*. But the two instances of *must not only* are an exception to this rule because it would not be correct to say:

(906) *Ein Übersetzer darf nicht nur in der Lage sein, eine bestimmte Anzahl von Wörtern pro Stunde oder pro Tag zu übersetzen . . .

(907) *Ein Simultan- oder Konsekutivdolmetscher darf nicht nur in der Lage sein, mit einer Rede soundsoviele Minuten lang schrittzuhalten . . .

The pertinent revision factor ruling out DÜRFEN in these cases is another cotextual element of MUST, namely, ONLY. The important point to note is that this adverb, not the modal MUST, is modified by NOT. Therefore ONLY forms a semantic unit with NOT, leaving MUST in its affirmative status. In this respect it corresponds to the second instance of MUST, which is affirmative anyway. Numbering may help to demonstrate the affirmative nature of both *musts*:

(908) A translator must
    1. not only be able to translate . . .
       but must
    2. do so accurately . . .

The nonnegative status of MUST in *must not only* thus being proven, MUST in this syntagma can now regularly be rendered by MÜSSEN:

(909) Ein Übersetzer *muss nicht nur* in der Lage sein, eine bestimmte Anzahl von Wörtern pro Stunde oder pro Tag zu übersetzen, sondern *muss* auch eine korrekte, lesbare und natürliche Prosaübersetzung vorlegen. Ein Simultan- oder Konsekutivdolmetscher *muss nicht nur* in der Lage sein, mit einer Rede soundsoviele Minuten lang schrittzuhalten, sondern *darf* auch *nicht* ermüden, ihm *dürfen keine* Wörter oder Wortgruppen entgehen, und er *darf* das, was der Sprecher sagt, auch *nicht* falsch interpretieren.

This will suffice for having shown that it is vital to take into account the entire syntagma *must not only* to do justice not only to collocative meaning but even to conceptual meaning.

Note that the word ONLY brings about this enlargement of relevant translation unit for MUST. Interestingly, the addition of ONLY also accounts for a similar change with respect to another modal, COULD. Consider the perfective construction *could only have been* in the following statement made by Leech.

(910) In hindsight, we can perhaps say that the performative analysis was an attempt to incorporate situational factors into grammar, and *could only have been* seriously entertained by linguists whose view of language and meaning excluded pragmatics. (Leech 1981: 329; our italics).

The remarkable thing about the syntagma *could only have . . . −en* in (910) is that it denotes neither counterfactuality as in (911) nor present or past epistemic modality as in (912) or (913):

(911) He could have been given the first prize but the jury decided otherwise.

(912) He could have been given the first prize but I doubt it.

(913) Seeing him in such a joyful mood I thought he could only have been given the first prize.

Here the renditions *hätte . . . können, könnte . . . haben*, and *konnte . . . haben* are appropriate:

(914) Er hätte den ersten Preis erhalten können, aber die Jury traf eine andere Entscheidung.

(915) Er könnte den ersten Preis erhalten haben, aber ich bezweifle es.

(916) Als ich ihn so fröhlich sah, dachte ich, er konnte nur den ersten Preis erhalten haben.

For rendering (910), however, all these constructions are ruled out because this sentence does not conform in meaning to any of the three constructions. Which meaning does it express, then? It presupposes the factuality of the said attempt having been entertained and emphasizes the necessity of its having been entertained by persons belonging to the kind of group of those who in fact entertained it. To render this meaning German allows of no perfective construction such as *konnte nur . . . unternommen worden sein*, formally paralleling the English one in (910) but inevitably taken to denote epistemic modality (which is obviously *not* intended in English). Instead the past-tense construction *konnte nur unternommen werden* has to be used:

(917) Rückblickend kann man vielleicht sagen, dass die performative Analyse einen Versuch darstellte, situative Faktoren in die Grammatik zu integrieren, und dass ein solcher Versuch ernsthaft *nur* von solchen Linguisten *unternommen werden konnte*, deren Vorstellung von Sprache und Bedeutung die Pragmatik ausschloss.

The *konnte* construction in (917) undoubtedly has root meaning, which contrasts not only with an epistemic but also with a counterfactual interpretation and rendition of COULD along the lines of (911) and (914). Yet the counterfactual rendition *hätte nur unternommen werden können* is not completely far-fetched; it would, however, require prior statement of factuality and might read like this: *Dieser Versuch wurde von Linguisten unternommen, deren Vorstellung von Sprache und Bedeutung die Pragmatik ausschloss, und er hätte überhaupt/auch nur von solchen Linguisten ernsthaft unternommen werden können.* The crucial second—modal—part of this 'rendition' *presupposes* the characteristic of linguists as stated in the relative clause. The SL original (910) does not, however, state that the attempt *was* in fact entertained by such linguists; it is a case of explicit modality/*implicit* factuality conveyed by one expression, not of explicit factuality followed by explicit modality/counterfactuality (of *other* members of the same kind of linguists having entertained said attempt). This is why we would prefer (917) as a rendition of (910).

The parallel between the construction *konnte nur . . . werden* in (917) and *could only have been . . .* in (910) may be made more transparent syntactically by equating the latter to *had to be . . .* (being nonperfective as is the German construction), which corresponds to *musste . . . werden* or *konnte nur . . . werden.*

Two similar instances of this use of COULD occur in Leech (1983: 20; italics ours):

(918) The performative hypothesis was an apparently inadvertent attempt to 'grammaticize' pragmatic phenomena (i.e., illocutionary forces), and *could*, I believe, *only have* been entertained by those for whom the grammatical paradigm of generative grammar was considered all-sufficient. *Only* in this way *could* they *have* tried to ignore the obvious: viz., that language takes place in situations.

Note that the two instances of ONLY differ in scope. In the first sentence ONLY syntactically modifies the verb phrase (*only have been entertained*) but semantically refers to the agent (*only by those*); in the second sentence it appears in initial position, thus modifying the specification of manner (*only in this way*) in terms of both syntax and semantics. So it is only in one out of four respects that ONLY actually modifies the verb phrase in the two sentences. Nevertheless the *could have* construction must in both cases be rendered as exemplified in (917) above. The reader is invited to apply this knowledge and translate (918).

In conclusion, we can say that in certain cotexts of seemingly negative MUST and affirmative COULD the adverb ONLY has the effect of necessitating a larger translation unit to be taken into account for the purpose of rendering the modals in German correctly.

6.4.2 Modal Adjectival, Participle, and Nominal Constructions

In Sections 6.3.3, 6.3.4, and 6.3.6 we dealt with modal adjectives, participles, and nouns, respectively. These can also be used as part of modal constructions such as BE LEGITIMATE TO, BE PERMITTED TO, THERE'S A POSSIBILITY THAT. As mentioned in Section 3.2.1, such 'near synonyms' of the modals are typically treated as mere paraphrases of the modals, but are only rarely considered in their own right. It is true that modal constructions such as BE PERMISSIBLE TO can "illuminate the meanings of the modal auxiliaries that are the primary focus of interest" (Perkins 1983: 2):

[229] He may go.
[230] It is permissible for him to go.

As we can see, BE PERMISSIBLE TO may indeed be used to explicate that MAY is used in the root sense. But then we must not forget that Perkins was able to demonstrate subtle differences between the modals and other modal expressions, each of which has a unique semantic contribution to make (see Section 3.2.1.1).

Moreover, the expressions that are the subject of this section are actually indispensable because they take the place of the missing forms of the modals:

[48] Er muss kommen können.
[46] *He must can come.
[47] He must be able to come.

Due to its lacking nonfinite forms, CAN is completely ruled out as a rendition of KÖNNEN here. This being so, however, it would not be correct to refer to BE ABLE TO as being a paraphrase of CAN in this case, let alone being a 'mere paraphrase.' This example gives an idea of the significance of other modal constructions, three kinds of which will now briefly be dealt with.

6.4.2.1 Modal Adjectival Constructions

As in (47), BE ABLE TO is a valuable suppletive form of CAN for a rendition of nonfinite forms of KÖNNEN, see also

[45] Er wünschte sich, Gitarre spielen zu können.
[44] He wished to be able to play the guitar.

[42] Reiten (zu) können war Peters Wunsch.
[41] To be able to ride a horse was Peter's wish.

See further (46)–(63) and (70)–(74). In addition to these cases, where BE ABLE TO must be used for formal reasons, it must also be used for pragmatic ones:

[665] Hans konnte seine Disseration rechtzeitig einreichen.
[667] Hans was able to submit his dissertation in time.

COULD is ruled out here due to the factuality of Hans's submitting his dissertation (see Section 4.3.3).

The modal adjectival expressions dealt with by Perkins (1983: 77 ff.) include BE POSSIBLE TO/THAT, BE NECESSARY TO/THAT, and BE LEGITIMATE TO. In choosing any of these as a rendition for a German modal, care must be taken to make it match with context, because the specific meaning intended is not indicated by the modal itself.

6.4.2.2 Modal Participle Constructions

Also modal participle constructions such as BE ALLOWED TO and BE PERMITTED TO can take the place of the missing nonfinite forms of the modals:

[74] Er hat(te) gehen dürfen.
[73] He has/had been allowed to go.

[314] Er durfte nach Hause gehen.
[316] He was permitted to go home.

The same is true if German prefixed modals are to be rendered—also when they are used in elliptical constructions:

[105] Ob wir da durchgehen dürfen?
[106] Ob wir da durchdürfen?
[104] I wonder if we will be allowed to pass there.

For the preceding English sentences no suppletion would be required in present tense; here CAN or MAY may be used in their finite form (but see the next subsection).

However, as pointed out in Section 3.2.1.2, there are cases in which a German modal cannot be rendered by an English one under any circumstances whatsoever:

[321] Er soll in London gewesen sein.
[322] He is said to have been in London.

To render the quotative (see Palmer 1986: 73 f.) expressed by the modal in (321), English modal participle constructions such as BE SAID TO, BE ALLEGED TO, BE BELIEVED TO, BE REPORTED TO have to be used.

Also, certain anthropomorphic uses of the German modals cannot be expressed by means of an English modal:

[628] Dieses Faltblatt möchte Sie . . . informieren.
[632] This leaflet . . . is designed to/is meant to give you information . . .

6.4.2.3 Modal Nominal Constructions

Modal nouns were said to represent "the ultimate stage in the objectification of modality" (Perkins 1983: 87; see our Section 6.3.6):

[823] Hier können Sie in einen anderen Bus/in andere Busse umsteigen.
[824] (Die nächste Haltestelle ist) 'Hauptpost'; hier haben Sie (die) Um-
       steigemöglichkeit in einen anderen Bus/in andere Busse.
[822] Hauptpost—Umsteigemöglichkeit.

Whereas (823) denotes something the hearer can personally do, (824) presents an objective fact—an objective possibility, an object that the hearer literally *has* (see the verb HABEN); and in (822) nothing but the object remains.

This means that the modal nominal construction UMSTEIGEMÖG-LICHKEIT HABEN represents an intermediate stage between subjective and objective reference to a modal situation. This also explains the relation existing between the following sentences:

[233] Er darf gehen.
[235] Er hat die Erlaubnis zu gehen.

If the level of abstraction on the subjective-objective scale of "permission" is to be an invariance factor, then the elements in the correlations must not be exchanged for each other: (233) ↔ (229) and (235) ↔ (400):

[229] He may go.
[400] He has permission to go.

This requirement applies equally to other suppletive forms such as modal adjectival and participle constructions.

6.5 CLAUSE

We conceive of a clause as one of two or more parts of a bigger syntactic unit: a complex sentence. Phenomena discussed in this section are such that it is not the whole complex sentence that has to be taken into account for rendering modals. This, of course, does not mean that all clauses are syntactically or semantically independent—on the contrary, most clauses to be dealt with are subordinate in nature.

6.5.1 Main Clauses and Subordinate Clauses

There are uses of the German modals that can occur in main clauses only, not in subordinate ones. Remember modal *and*-coordination as presented in Section 3.3.5.2. Usually clause type is no blocking factor for it:

[465] Ich kann und darf morgen nach München fahren.

(919) . . . , weil ich morgen nach München fahren kann und darf.

Modal coordination in clause-final position as in (919) is no common phenomenon, but can occur. There are exceptions, however,

(920) Die Tür will und will nicht zugehen.

(921) * . . . , weil die Tür nicht zugehen will und will.

So autocoordination of WOLLEN in subordinate clauses is impossible. Note that this is not due to this particular type of modal coordination itself because *will und will* in (921) is the same as in (920).

Instances of modal *and*-coordination are referred to by Luelsdorff as *modal freezes* (see Section 3.3.5.2). In case of autocoordination, freezing seems to have encroached even upon cotext (more precisely, the full verb ensuing the modals). As a result the whole verb phrase *will und will nicht zugehen* presents itself as one inseparable 'frozen' unit.

6.5.2 Conditional Clauses

Neither in English nor in German need a conditional clause be explicitly indicated as such by a conjunction (IF or WENN/FALLS):

(922) Should you be interested let me know.

(923) Solltest du interessiert sein, lass es mich wissen/sag mir Bescheid.

However, if WOLLEN is used instead of SOLLEN only German can do without a marker of conditionality:

(924) Wollten wir das anstreben, müssten wir eine andere Strategie wählen.

(925) *Wanted we to aim at that, we would have to adopt a different strategy.

(926) If we wanted to aim at that, we would have to adopt a different strategy.

Now let us assume sentence (926) is to be translated into German. As regards the factor of conditionality, the relevant translation unit in this clause is merely the conjunction IF, because it is a sufficient identification factor for a conditional clause. But if the task is to translate (924), the whole subordinate clause has to be taken into account for correctly identifying the conditional function of *wollten*. It might even be argued that the relevant translation unit is the whole complex sentence, because the *wollten* clause may turn out to be a simple sentence:

(927) Wollten wir das anstreben?
(928) Did we want to aim at that?

The observation that fronted *wollten* in (924) has no syntactically congruent English equivalent is in accordance with Hawkins's (1986: 199) remark that "in conditionals, SHOULD (which expresses a rather remote possibility) is the only auxiliary to undergo inversion"—a process that, in his view, is triggered by the deletion of IF. "This process," he continues, "is considerably more limited in English than it is in German . . ." He illustrates this restriction with reference to the ungrammaticality of COULD in a counterfactual verb-first structure, as opposed to the grammaticality of KÖNNEN in an equivalent structure:

(929) ?*Could I only sleep longer, I would feel better. (Hawkins 1986: 199)
(930) If I could sleep longer . . . (Hawkins 1986: 213)
(931) Könnte ich nur länger schlafen, ich würde besser arbeiten können. (Hawkins 1986: 205)

Another example of an ungrammatical conditional clause starting with a modal (other than SHOULD) is

(932) *Can he behave himself, he will be invited. (Hawkins 1986: 199)
(933) If he can behave himself . . . (Hawkins 1986: 213)

Hawkins's qualification that IF deletion is "considerably more limited in English than it is in German" invites the inference that also in German it is not completely unlimited. Some evidence for such an assumption comes from considering (934) as a rendition of (933):

(934) Kann er sich benehmen, wird er eingeladen.
(935) Wenn er sich benehmen kann, wird er eingeladen.

The slight reluctance felt with the conditional clause in (934) may be due to *kann* being indicative, which mood in inversion is typically associated with questions. (A similar observation could be made with respect to (924) and the possible noncontinuation of its conditional clause in the form of the simple sentence (927).) At any rate *könnte* in (931) is a better candidate for non-overtly marked conditionality.[47]

6.5.3 Object Clauses

Different kinds of phenomena relating to object clauses are relevant to the translator.

First, English object clauses can sometimes be reduced to German infinitival constructions:

[82] He declared he wanted to come soon.
(936) Er erklärte, er wolle bald kommen.
[81] Er erklärte, bald kommen zu wollen.

If (81) is to be translated into English no such reduction would be possible:

(937) *He announced to want to come soon.

It must be emphasized, though, that also the shorter German version (81) is subject to certain constraints. It is marked for formal style. In colloquial language (936) would be preferred. In spoken language, a *dass* clause with an indicative form of WOLLEN would be even more customary:

(938) Er kündigte an, dass er bald kommen will/wollte.

The choice between present or past tense will depend upon the time of utterance. If 'his' coming refers to a point in time subsequent to the time of utterance *will* can be used. In such cases a still more colloquial wording would be

(939) Er hat gesagt, dass er bald kommen will.

or even

(940) Er hat gesagt, er will bald kommen.
(941) Er hat gesagt, er kommt bald.

In the last three sentences, the performance of the reported illocutionary act of announcing can be inferred only from the verb group.

A syntactic reduction similar to that of (936) → (81) is the following one:

(942) Er schlug ihnen vor, dass sie mit ihm gehen sollten.
(943) Er schlug ihnen vor, mit ihm zu gehen.

Wildhagen and Héraucourt (1972: 1319) render (943) by (944):

(944) He suggested they should go with him.

A reduction of (944) analogous to that of (942) is, however, also possible:

(945) He suggested to them to go with him.

The reason why (945) is grammatical whereas (937) is not is that in (945) there are two pronouns, *he* and *them*, which are not coreferential, whereas in (937) the sole pronoun involved is *he*.

Second, in (81), German offers a syntactic contraction of the object clause in (936). English does not permit a corresponding contraction (cf.

(937)); but there are other English object clauses—*wh*— clauses—that can be contracted to nonfinite constructions whereas corresponding German clauses cannot:

(946) I will tell him what he should do.
(947) I will tell him what to do.

(948) Ich werde ihm sagen, was er tun soll(te).
(949) *Ich werde ihm sagen, was zu tun.

The grammaticality of (947) in contrast to the ungrammaticality of (949) shows that English allows for deletion of the modal and for covertness of the subject of the infinitival complement but German does not.

Third, English object clauses can not only be reduced to infinitival constructions (see (944) → (945)) but also to the gerund involving suppletion of a modal by expressions such as BE ABLE TO:

[60] Er schätzte es, dass ich ihn besuchen konnte.
(950) He appreciated that I could visit him.
[59] He appreciated my being able to visit him.

Sentence (59) can also be arrived at by starting from another *that* clause:

(951) He appreciated that I was able to visit him.

As is familiar from Section 4.3.3, the difference between COULD and *was able to* is that the former denotes 'mere' possibility but the latter indicates that the possibility was actually made use of. Interestingly, this distinction is carried over to subordinate clauses such as those in (950) and (951). It is, however, blurred in (59), where the use of a suppletive as BE ABLE TO is a must in any case. Because (60) is equally ambiguous between mere possibility and the invited inference of an actual visit having taken place, (59) is in fact a fitting rendition of it.

Fourth, a passive *that* clause as the object of a wish may be shortened to a noun plus the past participle of a full verb:

(952) Er wollte, dass das Problem gelöst würde.
(953) He wished that the problem (should) be solved.
(954) He wanted the problem solved.

In German no such contraction is possible,

(955) *Er wollte das Problem gelöst.

unless WISSEN is added:

(956) Er wollte das Problem gelöst wissen.

According to Wildhagen and Héraucourt (1972: 1366) *etwas getan wissen wollen* is equivalent to *to wish a thing to be done*. This means that (956) should be equated not with (953) or (954) but with (957):

(957) He wished the problem to be solved.

If the agent of a desired action is identical to the 'wisher,' an infinitival clause may be used in both English and German:

[45] Er wünschte sich, Gitarre spielen zu können.
[44] He wished to be able to play the guitar.

Fifth, in the preceding clauses (919), (81), (938), (939), (942), (948), and (60) the modal appears in final position. Hawkins (1986: 132) explains that "the verb is final in German subordinate clauses." (For exceptions, see his Chapter 10.2 as well as the subordinate clauses in our examples (923), (924), (931), and (934), where the modals serve a conditional function and therefore appear in initial position.)

Also infinitive clauses such as those in (45) and (81) have a modal-final structure (see also Section 2.6).

Sixth, in reported object clauses the present subjunctive of the modals must be used (see Section 3.6):

[569] Yesterday he said it could/might rain.
[570] Gestern sagte er, es könne regnen.

Seventh, the syntactic reductions presented in Section 6.5.2 and points one to four in this subsection consist of merely shortening and restructuring object clauses. In German there also exists the possibility of completely deleting the main clause preceding an object clause:

(958) Ich frage mich/dich, ob es dir etwas ausmacht, die Tür zu schliessen.
[611] Ob es dir etwas ausmacht, die Tür zu schliessen?

In general, English does not allow for such clausal ellipsis:

[606] I wonder if you'd mind shutting the door?
(959) *If you'd mind shutting the door?

Correctly valuing the modal WOULD in (606) would, by the way, require choosing the past subjunctive of WERDEN in (958) and (611), respectively:

(960) Ich frage mich/dich, ob es dir etwas ausmachen würde, die Tür zu schliessen.
(961) Ob es dir etwas ausmachen würde, die Tür zu schliessen?

But just as the main clauses in (958) and (960) are highly unlikely to occur (at least for the purpose of performing indirect directives), so (961) including *würde* is less likely to be heard; it would be chosen only in case the speaker wished to be particularly polite.

Deletion of whole clauses is also possible in certain exclamatory utterances containing modals, see Section 6.5.8, point two.

6.5.4 Subject Clauses

First, the final position of German modals found in object clauses (see previous subsection) is also found in subject clauses:

[79] Es war klar, dass er sich würde anstrengen müssen.
[80] It was evident that he would have to make an effort.

It must be emphasized that the infinitive of MÜSSEN is due only to *würde*, which can be demonstrated by its omission:

(962) Es war klar, dass er sich anstrengen musste.

Also a rendition of (962) requires a suppletive:

(963) It was evident that he had to make an effort.

Second, in Section 6.5.3, point three, an object clause reduced to a gerund construction was found blurring the distinction between factuality and nonfactuality of modal expressions. A similar phenomenon exists for subject clauses. Take the German sentence

[54] Dass er an der Prüfung teilnehmen konnte, machte ihn glücklich.

This sentence can theoretically be rendered by (964) and (965):

(964) That he could sit for the exam made him happy.
(965) That he was able to sit for the exam made him happy.

The subject clause in (964) merely denotes the possibility of sitting for the exam (which made him happy); in contrast, his happiness in (965) originated from his actually sitting for the exam. Both these sentences can be converted to a gerund version:

[53] His being able to sit for the exam made him happy.

Again, (54) also being ambiguous between factuality and nonfactuality, (53) can be considered to be an adequate rendition of it (and vice versa).

6.5.5 Relative Clauses

In Section 6.3.8, relative infinitives were rendered by a German prepositional phrase, transposition being justified by an equally unspecific degree of modality:

[332] Here is a book to settle your dispute.
[336] Hier ist ein Buch zur Lösung deines Problems.

In case a definite degree of modality is clearly intended, a relative clause containing a modal also may be used, see Beilhardt and Sutton (1954: 44):

(966) First the colonists had to find ships to take them across the ocean.
(967) Zuerst mussten die Siedler Schiffe zur Überquerung des Ozeans finden.
(968) Zuerst mussten die Siedler Schiffe finden, die sie über den Ozean bringen konnten.

(969) He built a house with thick walls to protect him from cold weather.
(970) Er baute ein Haus mit dicken Wänden zum Schutz vor kaltem Wetter.
(971) Er baute ein Haus mit dicken Wänden, das/die ihn vor kaltem Wetter schützen sollte(n).

Past nonfactuality also permits use of counterfactual modal constructions:

(972) At first they had no houses to sleep in/in which to sleep.
(973) Zuerst hatten sie keine Häuser zum Schlafen.
(974) Zuerst hatten sie keine Häuser, in denen sie schlafen konnten.
(975) Zuerst hatten sie keine Häuser, in denen sie hätten schlafen können.

The choice between one of the three German versions will depend on different factors of the modal situation. Sentence (973) is only covertly modal, with emphasis on the purpose of the desired houses. The final two versions are overtly modal, with (975) focusing on counterfactuality, a factor that is, of course, also present in (974); but here it is only inferred from the negative quantifier *keine* in the main clause, whereas in (975) it is explicitly expressed by means of a subjunctive construction.

6.5.6 Adverbial Clauses

Generally speaking, German adverbial clauses have to be marked for their type—adversative, consecutive, temporal, causal, and so on—whereas this is not required for corresponding English gerund constructions:

[63] Da er fliessend Englisch sprechen konnte, verstand er mich gut.
[62] Being able to speak English fluently, he understood me well.

Lack of a causality marker in (62) indicates a semantic asymmetry between the English and the German versions, in addition to the syntactic one. Nonetheless, such pairs of equivalents are quite common because each clause type represents a popular way of expression in its language. The relevant compensation factor in such equivalence pairs is that the overtly lacking semantic information in English is usually evident from co(n)text. This applies equally to adverbial clauses other than causal ones.

6.5.7 Active and Passive Clauses

In Section 3.4 we dealt with voice, showing that the meaning of a modal can differ according to its being used in an active or in a passive clause. Here we would like to continue observations by pointing out characteristics of the two clause types themselves. Consider the following sentences taken from the BASF leaflet enclosed with audio cassettes (see Section 6.3.10.2; italics ours):

(976) Den Fortschritt, den die Chromdioxid-SM-Cassetten beinhalten, *können Sie* jedoch auch schon auf Ihrem bisherigen Gerät nutzen. . . . Eine mögliche Überbetonung der hohen Frequenzen *können Sie* am Höhenregler wieder ausgleichen . . .

(977) But the progress inherent in the Chromium Dioxide SM Cassettes *can* already *be utilized* on conventional recorders. . . . A possible over-accentuation of high-pitched notes *can be balanced* with the aid of the treble control . . .

It is striking that the SL writer chose two active clauses with KÖNNEN that were transformed into two passive constructions containing CAN. The subject of the German active clauses is the reader, which gives them a personal tone. Their transformation into passive voice involving (optional!) deletion of *by you* referring to the hearers-as-agents makes the English versions sound much more impersonal. Formulations such as *can be utilized* and *can be balanced* present possibilities as somewhat objective realities existing independent of the individual user. Active KÖNNEN, on the other hand, informs about these possibilities as personal courses of action. The factor accounting for this change in perspective may be the intention of the translator to create a more object-oriented text. We will return to this topic in our discussion of text classes (Section 6.8).

For ellipsis in passive *that* clauses, see Section 6.5.3, point four; suppletion in English passive clauses is mentioned in Section 2.5, point (cb).

6.5.8 Exclamations

First, exclamatory clauses can involve subject-auxiliary inversion such as

(978) They thought they were going to a party, and were they surprised. (*Fortune* magazine, no. 29, 1990, p. 4, first sentence of "Editor's Desk")

Hawkins (1986: 198) points out, however, that "on closer inspection, the inversion is more limited. In particular, many modals are not fully grammatical when inverted . . . although corresponding periphrastic modals . . . are fully grammatical . . . " His examples include (p. 198)

(979) ?*Boy, must I work hard!
(980) Boy, do I have to work hard!

Later on he comments: "Verb-first exclamations are still very productive, but certain modals no longer undergo the rule, for reasons I do not understand" (Hawkins 1986: 212).

German has no such restrictions on the modals, which is why here "the fronting of modals is more productive than in English" (Hawkins 1986: 204); for example,

(981) Mann, muss ich hart arbeiten!

As (980) shows, exclamations can be transposition factors, but they need not be:

(982) Kann er aber Klavier spielen! (Hawkins 1986: 204)
(983) Boy, can he play the piano! (Hawkins 1986: 198)

So for CAN, no suppletive is required. Hawkins also offers a periphrastic version, however:

(984) Boy, is he able to play the piano! (p. 198)

But he gives no clues for differentiating between (983) and (984).

Second, in Section 6.5.3, point seven, we reported on the possibility of deleting whole main clauses of German complex sentences. This possibility extends to exclamations:

(985) Ich bin erstaunt darüber, dass er das kann.
(986) Dass er das kann!

Sentence (986) is derivable from (985). The deletion factor accounting for complete loss of the main clause in (985) can be assumed to be the tendency of the speaker to be brief when emotionally moved.

Even though English has its own ways of formulating exclamations, emotional involvement giving rise to constructions shorter than (985) can be traced here, too:

(987) What? He can do that?
(988) And he was able to do that?
(989) Oh, gee, he could manage that!

6.6 SENTENCE

As stated in the introduction of Section 6.5 several clauses make up a complex sentence. In this section we intend to show that it can be necessary to take into account both clauses of a complex sentence to arrive at a satisfactory rendition of modals. Also the uniclause counterpart of complex sentences, the *simple sentence*, deserves our attention. In Chapter 3, we discussed cases where syntactic mood of simple sentences was a sufficient identification factor for meanings of modals (see Section 3.1.2). Pragmatic implications of syntactic mood were dealt with in Chapter 4. Both these topics will be taken up again in the present context of translation units. We will end this section with a semantico-pragmatic factor relating to the sentence level: proverbs and sayings.

6.6.1 Simple and Complex Sentences

The subordinate clauses in Sections 6.5.2 and so forth were all considered to be self-sufficient translation units for the modals contained in them. But there were one or two exceptions, such as the German sentence

[924] Wollten wir das anstreben, müssten wir eine andere Strategie wählen.

For an unambiguous identification of the first clause as a conditional one (i.e., not a question, in spite of inversion), the whole complex sentence must be taken into account.

6.6.2 Syntactic Mood

Syntactic mood can be understood in terms of what Leech (1981: 335) refers to as "the three sentence-types of declarative, interrogative, and imperative."

Considering semantic factors we found that syntactic mood can be a reliable identification factor for excluding meanings of the modals. Figure 3.7 sums up two relevant findings:

- in questions about epistemic possibility, MAY cannot be used;
- in nonnegated statements of epistemic possibility, CAN cannot be used.

In German, KÖNNEN may invariably be used.

Turning to pragmatic factors, we found that, for indirect speech acts, the relation of syntactic mood and illocutionary force can be an indirect one. Consider again the following example discussed in Section 4.1.1:

[585] Can you finish your thesis?

Syntactically this sentence is a question, yet the point of uttering it may be to give an order. The term *whimperative* captures both these syntactico-pragmatic aspects. (For other kinds of indirectness, see Leech's (1981: 335) three-level diagram.)

Because English and German are basically alike as regards the possibility of correlating syntactic and pragmatic categories (see Section 4.1.1), pragmatic considerations of syntactic mood do not constitute major change factors comparable to the semantic ones implied by the English-German differences mentioned earlier (i.e., the constraints on CAN and MAY vs. the 'free' use of KÖNNEN).

Minor changes relate mainly to punctuation serving as an indicator of syntactic mood. As was mentioned in Section 5.3, punctuation may reflect an indirect illocution, thus being an unmistakable identification factor for 'indirect syntactic mood':

[785] Will you listen to me and stop interrupting!

Here English differs from German in that the exclamation mark is more often replaced by the period:

[778] Will you belt up.
[780] Wirst du wohl ruhig sein!

In spoken language, syntactic mood is correlated to stress and intonation (see Section 5.2).

6.6.3 Tag Questions

First, tag sentences or tag questions consist of a declarative and a shortened interrogative clause, which may contain a modal:

[38] He can go there, can't he?
(990) He can't go there, can he?
(991) He can go there, can he?
(992) He can't go there, can't he?

Regarding the two parts of tag sentences, Quirk et al. (1972: 391) state that "it is important . . . to separate two factors: an *assumption* (expressed by the statement) and an *expectation* (expressed by the question" (italics as in the original). If, as in (38) and (990), these two aspects differ in polarity (i.e., presence of a negative element), the sentences are referred to as *reversed-polarity tags*; if, as in (991) and (992), they do not differ in this respect, they are called *constant-polarity tags* (see König 1977: 45).

The very fact that German has no modals in tags is an important transposition factor. For reversed-polarity tags the conjunction ODER suggests itself because it invites the hearer's reaction. For underlining the assumption expressed by the statement, the modal particle DOCH can be used. Thus the renditions for (38) and (990) would be

[39] Er kann doch dorthin gehen, oder (etwa nicht)?
(993) Er kann doch nicht dorthin gehen, oder (etwa doch)?

Note that the tag in (993) serves to disambiguate the main clause, which by itself could be interpreted as a definite statement with primary stress on DOCH, in the sense of

(994) He can't go there, after all.

But even though (993) itself is unambiguous, its semantic structure appears a bit complicated. Moreover, the sentence sounds clumsy. We therefore propose to integrate the components contained in the tag into the main clause, the result being

(995) Er kann doch nicht etwa dorthin gehen?

A slightly more positive version would be

(996) Kann er etwa dorthin gehen?

The positive-negative orientation evident from the parenthesized elements in (39) and (993) corresponds to that of the English sentences. Because these elements are optional, ODER itself is good enough for signaling the speaker's readiness to receive an answer that differs from his or her own assumption.

König (1977: 50) points out that different degrees of confidence regarding an assumption may be expressed by different intonation contours of the tag. He adds (p. 47) that O'Connor (1968) mentions more than eight intonation patterns occurring in reversed-polarity tags.

Sentences with constant-polarity tags, on the other hand, almost invariably show a low rise (König 1977: 47). They are restricted to informal discourse situations (p. 53). Here the speaker does not hold an opinion but attempts to verify the truth of his or her inferences drawn from the hearer's utterances, nonverbal actions, or situations in which the hearer is involved (p. 55).

To convey the inferential nature of nonnegative constant-polarity tags, we suggest using interpolated ALSO plus the postpositive modal particle JA or fronted *das heisst (also)*. Sentence (991) could thus be rendered by

(997) Er kann also dorthin gehen, ja?
(998) Das heisst (also), er kann dorthin gehen?

For rendering negative constant-polarity sentences such as (992) the negation of the declarative sentence can be supplemented by the German interrogative tag *nicht wahr?*

(999) Er kann also nicht dorthin gehen, nicht wahr?

Second, tags can also be appended to orders (see König 1977: 58 ff.):

(1000) Come here, will you?
(1001) Come here, won't you?

(1002) Don't do this, will you?
(1003) *Don't do this, won't you?

Reversed-polarity tags serve to soften orders (Nehls 1986: 206). The modal particle DOCH often being part of suggestions (as a less strict form of directive), we propose to render (1001) as (1004), and (1002) as (1005):

(1004) Komm doch her!
(1005) Mach das doch nicht!

Orders followed by constant-polarity tags such as (1000), however, express curt commands (see Nehls 1986: 206). To render them we recommend using the modal particle WOHL (see Section 6.3.9.6):

(1006) Kommst du wohl her!

As far as the modals in the previous English tags are concerned, integration of the German modal particle into the imperative clause itself is no disadvantage to interlingual congruence because German modals do not appear in tags anyway. The same is true of modal particles incorporated into declarative sentences such as (995) and (996). This shows that the relevant translation unit for tags as SL or TL items is indeed the sentence, not just the (tag) clause.

Third, tags are *shortened* clauses. Full interrogative clauses can be attached to indirect orders containing modals. Elgin (1992: 94) observes in this connection: "People frequently soften the effect of their modals by putting a question after them, like this:

(1007) You should leave, don't you think?"

Here German does offer a rendition that is largely congruent:

(1008) Du solltest gehen, meinst du nicht auch?

6.6.4 Proverbs and Sayings

As is evident from comprehensive dictionaries, numerous idioms, proverbs, and stock phrases used in certain communicative situations in English and German are expressed by means of the modals. Because proverbs typically come in (simple and complex) sentences, these are the relevant translation units for them.

Gläser (1986: 111) observes that one of the characteristic features of proverbs is their modality manifested as modals. They are used in phrases geared to influence behavior such as *you cannot*; *you may . . . but*; *(you) should not*; *(you) must*, as in

(1009) You may lead a horse to the water, but cannot make it drink.

Gläser (1986:167) considers pairs of SL-TL idioms as being completely equivalent only if not just the conceptual meanings but also the emotional-expressive and stylistic connotations correspond to each other in both languages. This sounds as if equivalence of conceptual meaning were the minimum requirement of bilingual pairs of sayings. But it is easy to show that conceptual meaning cannot necessarily be expected to be (fully) congruent; such as in Gläser's (1986: 135) politeness clichés used on the telephone:

(1010) May I ask who is calling?
(1011) Wer ist bitte am Apparat?
(1012) Wer spricht da bitte?

and by the sales assistant in a shop:

(1013) Can I help you?
(1014) Werden Sie schon bedient?
(1015) Was darf es sein?

Wilss (1983b: 251) juxtaposes the following sayings used for the opening of a sales talk:

(1016) What can I do for you?
(1017) Was kann ich für Sie tun?
(1018) Sie wünschen, bitte?

He characterizes (1018) as the former standard German expression being pushed out by (1017), which corresponds to (1016) in terms of syntax and semantics. This change "probably owing to heavy English-German film-dubbing" (1983b: 251) is seen as a sociocultural phenomenon.

The coexistence of the two variants (1017) and (1018) is no isolated phenomenon, see (1011)–(1012) and (1014)–(1015). From the translational point of view it shows that conceptual meaning is not a factor to be taken too seriously in this type of sentences. The most we can say is that they share reference to the same communicative situation, but they differ with regard to choice of its elements. These examples are thus similar to those discussed in Sections 4.4.1 and 4.4.2 regarding the factor of situation. In all such examples the factor of unilingual standardization overrules all other considerations. This suggests that wordings determined by standardization relative to situations may well be referred to as (modal) 'freezes' as discussed in Section 3.3.5.2 in connection with modal conjunction.

As to the extent of 'freezing,' there seems to be a gradient, however:

- In modal *and*-conjunctions (*can and may* vs. **may and can*) only the sequence of the modals is fixed;
- in modal autocoordination (*. . . will und will nicht zugehen* vs. **. . . nicht zugehen will und will*, see Section 6.5.1) the sequence of conjoined modals and the full verb is fixed;
- in the sayings dealt with in the present subsection, whole sentences are invariable 'frozen' units, and hence 'en bloc' translation units. So whereas it is true that, as already mentioned, modals appear in "phrases . . . such as *you cannot*; *you may . . . but . . . ,*" consideration of these phrases alone will not suffice as translation units for sayings. They will not even suffice as translation units for the modals contained in them because their renditions sometimes do not contain any modal: see (1011), (1012), (1014), and (1018)! This clearly shows the relevance of the whole sentence (considered in the light of its typical communicative situation) as the required translation unit for proverbs and sayings. This truth will finally be illustrated with reference to the German proverb

(1019) Wer A sagt, muss auch B sagen.

The Globalink machine-translation program, based on the translation unit *word*, can produce only

(1020) *Who A says, must also say B.

Wildhagen and Héraucourt (1972: 1) suggest the following two renditions:

(1021) He who calls the tune must pay the piper.
(1022) In for a penny, in for a pound.

The second English version again shows that the presence of a modal in the German version is not the ultimate criterion for translation; rather it is a matter of finding a proverb adequate for use in a similar kind of situation.

6.7 PARAGRAPH

Up until recently, the sentence used to be the traditional unit of description in linguistics. Also, in translation studies, focus has characteristically been on sentences. This is justified to a certain extent because "it is sentence by sentence that the translator translates," as we said in the introduction to this chapter. But it must be borne in mind that sentences uttered in a sequence are not completely isolated from each other; an 'intersentential dynamism' connects sentences by such means as articles, adverbs, pronouns, tense, and conjunctions. In other words, sentences enter into a bigger unit, the paragraph, and ultimately into a whole text. Let us first consider the paragraph as a relevant translation unit for sequences of sentences containing modals.

Just like a sentence or the whole text, a paragraph may be considered to be a whole characterized by a specific information structure. Information substructures exist with respect to various parameters such as tense. There are rules regulating the sequence or concord of tenses. If some ongoing process is described in present tense, everything that happened before will be told in past tense (or even past perfect), and for what is still expected future tense will be used. But there are verb phrases that are unspecific in terms of tense:

(1023) John may have arrived.

Butler (1972: 29) observes that this sentence containing a modal corresponds to any of the following three sentences each indicating a specific tense:

(1024) John had possibly arrived (by some time in the past).
(1025) John has possibly arrived (by now).
(1026) John will possibly have arrived (by some time in the future).

Whereas each of the latter three sentences is restricted in reference to a specific point in time relative to the present, (1023) is not. This can be shown by placing it into the three contexts suggested by (1024)–(1026):

(1027) John may have arrived before 9 o'clock because at that time I saw that his lights were on.
(1028) John may have arrived by now because I can see that his lights are on.
(1029) John may have arrived by the time I reach his house this afternoon.

German shows a similar time-tense structure:

(1030) John kann angekommen sein.

(1031) John war (damals/zuvor) vielleicht angekommen.
(1032) John ist (jetzt) vielleicht angekommen.
(1033) John wird (dann) vielleicht angekommen sein.

Paralleling English, the unspecific modal-verb construction in (1030) can be used in all three contexts, each of which can otherwise be verbalized only by one of the mutually exclusive tense-specific constructions in (1031)–(1033);

(1034) John kann vor 9 Uhr angekommen sein, weil ich um die Zeit gesehen habe, dass bei ihm Licht war.
(1035) John kann jetzt angekommen sein, weil ich gerade sehe, dass bei ihm Licht ist.
(1036) John kann angekommen sein, wenn ich heute nachmittag zu seinem Haus komme.

If identity of tense and time reference is taken to be an invariance factor, interlingual correlations are completely unproblematic. Tense-specific sentences (1024)–(1026) and (1031)–(1033) are equivalents of one another (in that sequence), as are (1027)–(1029) and (1034)–(1036); finally, unspecific (1023) and (1030) correspond to each other.

This analysis can be considered satisfactory on the sentence level. Which factor could modify it on the level of the paragraph? We said earlier that sentences in a paragraph are connected with one another and that a paragraph has a specific information structure. If a sentence is followed by other sentences, these will often contain elements already present in the first one. This is one way of connections between sentences being created. Another one is by taking up information only implied in preceding sentences. One by-product of both kinds of connections being established by reference to 'old' or given information is the creation of redundancy. Avoiding such redundancy in the process of translation is the purpose of Kussmaul's (1986: 213 ff.) interlingual *maxim of the necessary degree of differentiation.* Its principle is that information already expressed or implied in cotext preceding an SL sentence need not be expressed again in a TL rendition of that sentence. In other words, renditions need not be as precise and differentiated as possible but only as *necessary*—necessity arising only in case of new information. Accordingly, Kussmaul attempts to show that a rendition that is apparently 'imprecise' on the lexical level can nevertheless be precise *enough* by virtue of being embedded in a text. We will now try to show how this maxim could be applied to modality occurring in a text paragraph.

Consider the following paragraph, which could be part of a letter or diary entry:

(1037) We expect John to return from his journey today. When I looked out of my window half an hour ago I saw that the lights in his flat were on. Of course it might have been Paul who was there—I know he has the key. But since I'm not sure if Paul is in town *John had possibly arrived.*

Someone translating this paragraph into German on the level of the individual sentences might come up with the following rendition:

(1038) Wir erwarten John heute von seiner Reise zurück. Als ich vor einer halben Stunde aus dem Fenster geschaut habe, sah ich Licht in seiner Wohnung. Das kann natürlich auch Paul gewesen sein, er hat ja den Schlüssel. Aber da ich nicht sicher bin, ob Paul z. Zt. da ist, *war John vielleicht schon angekommen.*

Now let us have another look at the SL paragraph to probe into the possibility of an alternative rendition. The use of the past perfect in the final (italicized) main clause in (1037) is noteworthy because as far as the speaker's *present* situation is concerned he or she might equally well have said something corresponding to (1025)

(1039) . . . John has possibly arrived (more than half an hour ago).

But the use of past tense in the same paragraph of (1037)—. . . *When I looked* . . .—becomes the perspective from which John's possible *prior* arrival is seen. This is why backshift to the past perfect in the final main clause of (1037), and correspondingly of (1038), is necessary.

This second shift in time and tense is inevitable and cotextually obvious, however; so its marking in terms of TL tense may be considered to be redundant. In terms of Kussmaul's maxim of the necessary degree of differentiation, such a marking can therefore be regarded as unnecessary. Rendering (1037), a translator may accordingly feel entitled to employ a TL construction the final clause of which is unspecific for tense, something along the lines of (1034) containing the modal KÖNNEN:

(1040) Wir erwarten John heute von seiner Reise zurück. Als ich vor einer halben Stunde aus dem Fenster geschaut habe, sah ich Licht in seiner Wohnung. Das kann natürlich auch Paul gewesen sein, er hat ja den Schlüssel. Aber da ich nicht sicher bin, ob Paul z. Zt. da ist, *kann John schon angekommen sein.*

As practical and elegant a panacea for heaving semantic ballast it may seem, there are two caveats against this kind of TL 'minimalist' approach.

First, redundancy reduction by means of jettisoning given information is no strategy that could be adopted only in TL. In other words, not only the translator but even the SL speaker could (have) use(d) a construction lacking double marking of tense, having as the final clause a modal-verb construction such as (1027)

(1041) We expect John to return from his journey today. When I looked out of my window half an hour ago I saw that the lights in his flat were on. Of course it might have been Paul who was there—I know he has the key. But since I'm not sure if Paul is in town *John may have arrived.*

We may ask the legitimate question, If even the SL speaker can thus use the minimalist maxim as exemplified in (1041), why should it be left to the translator to scavenge redundancy? The SL speaker who wants to avoid it will do so. This disenchanting insight proves Kussmaul's maxim to be no privilege of translation theory and practice but to be applicable to (unilingual) speech in general. It could thus be turned into a conversational maxim à la Grice: *Avoid redundancy.* But language-in-use is not free of redundancy; on the contrary: it abounds with redundancy. This is true of SL as it is of TL. Why then should the translator unrealistically and unnecessarily subdue it?

The second reservation against (translational) minimalism is that not all given information can be considered unnecessary to mention again, even though this may appear to be so at first sight. In terms of our preceding examples, for instance, one should be aware that the 'tense-neutral' TL version including a modal—(1040) . . . *kann John schon angekommen sein*— leaves open whether the SL version was the past perfect construction, (1037) . . . *John had possibly arrived*, or the present perfect one, (1039) . . . *John has possibly arrived* . . .

When we say this it should not be taken to imply that we revoke what we said earlier about the two backshifts in time inevitably leading to the use of past perfect (*had . . . arrived*) in (1037). But, consider the following SL version constructed along the lines of (1039):

(1042) We expect John to return from his journey today. When I looked out of my window half an hour ago I saw that the lights in his flat were on. Of course, it might have been Paul who was there—I know he has the key. But since I'm not sure if Paul is in town *John has possibly arrived.*

This construction does not invalidate the statements made about the past-perfect version (1037). It is definitely true that past tense (*when I looked*) is the perspective necessitating use of the past perfect in the final main clause (provided a specific tense marker is deemed advisable). But, more fundamentally, it is not necessary to adopt the past tense as a perspective in the first place. When reading (1042) you will have noticed that the perspective from which *John has possibly arrived* is seen is the speaker's situation at the time of speaking, as mentioned in our description of (1039). John's possible arrival is no longer seen with reference to the speaker's previously having looked out of the window but with reference to the speaker *presently* being unsure about Paul being in town (see . . . *I'm not sure* . . .). And precisely this distinction of viewpoints gets blurred when either (1037) or (1042) is rendered as (1040). To do justice to the distinction it is advisable to render (1037) . . . *John had possibly arrived* as (1038) . . . *war John vielleicht schon angekommen* and (1042) . . . *John has possibly arrived* in conformity with (1035) as (1043)

(1043) . . . ist John vielleicht schon angekommen.

So the net result of our whole analysis is that the tense-neutral English sentence containing a modal should be rendered by only a correspondingly tense-neutral German sentence containing a modal: (1041) → (1040). This should actually come as no surprise: It is just another corroboration of our repeated finding that modals should preferably be rendered by modals, because they correspond to each other in terms of various kinds of non-specificity. In the present connection such nonspecificity of tense is shared by epistemic MAY and KÖNNEN. But this we have known ever since we compared sentences (1023)–(1036) to one another, correlating (1023) with (1030); that is, even before entering detailed considerations of the translation unit *paragraph*. Does this mean that the paragraph is no relevant translation unit for the modals? Not necessarily—consider the following sentence:

(1044) I shall here deal with the poet's late work.

In the spoken language or in informal written language (1044) may well be rendered as

(1045) Ich behandle hier das Spätwerk des Dichters.

But if (1044) appears in one of the introductory paragraphs of an academic work, the well-versed translator may shift to a different rendition:

(1046) Die vorliegende Arbeit behandelt das Spätwerk des Dichters.

Formulations of this kind, that is, announcements lacking reference to the author, were found by Kussmaul (1978: 54 f.) to be typical of German treatises in the field of the humanities. Comparable English texts predominantly showed personal constructions such as (1044). What this means is that the sentences by themselves are not sufficient as translation units but their being part of a specific, namely, introductory, paragraph in a specific kind of text. This finding also has implications for rendering the German modals. A translator faced with (1046) will, for instance, not necessarily come up with an impersonal formulation containing WILL such as

(1047) The present work will deal with the poet's late work.

but prefer a personal construction with WILL or SHALL such as (1044).

However, Kussmaul's findings are not restricted to instances of modals in specific paragraphs of a text. Speech acts other than programmatic announcements such as the preceding ones may occur anywhere in a text. Therefore differences in the use of the English and German modals can generally be found when certain kinds of text are considered. This is our next topic: text classes determining whole texts and their characteristics in terms of the modals.

6.8 WHOLE TEXT

In the introduction to the previous section we said that sentences enter into a bigger unit, the paragraph, and ultimately into a whole text. Equivalence of SL and TL items may be found on the level of morpheme, word, phrase, clause, sentence, paragraph, and the whole text. Obviously equivalence on different levels may differ. As regards the consideration of the whole text, Neubert (1991: 20 f.) says: "This view transcends the concept of meaning as a sentence-bound phenomenon. It locates equivalence in the whole text. What is actually carried over into the target text is the composite semantic/ pragmatic function of the source text. With the *global* meaning of original as main determining factor the translation is reconstructed as a new semantic/ pragmatic totality redesigned within the textual universe of the target language community" (our italics). This approach is based on the text as the translation unit, so it may be referred to as *text linguistic*; because it is based on the entire text it may be called *holistic* (see Neubert 1991: 21).

An example par excellence of text-based translation is the rendition of book titles. Even an SL book title is no isolated syntagma or sentence but the expression of the *entirety* of that book. So, to fully understand and value the title, the whole contents of the book must be known first. This knowledge is equally important for the translator in producing an adequate rendition. This qualifies translation of book titles as one of the most time-consuming endeavors; it requires that the translator read the whole book first before being able to translate its title. Because, however, book titles are not typically translated in isolation but only as one aspect of translating a whole book, the activity of reading its entire text will constitute no extra activity for the translator.

Now it might be assumed that, because the SL book title was adequately chosen by the SL author, the translator can afford to just take the title as it is and translate it literally. Empirical evidence shows, however, that many book titles are not translated this way, that reference or predication in the TL title even differ widely from that of the SL title. To explain this, it might be argued that the particular TL factors such as TL hearers and TL culture are seen by the translator as constituting obligatory change factors. True as this may be in many a case, it does not replace the necessity of *also* knowing the contents of the whole book for coming up with a title rendition which is adequate in this respect, too.

Nord (1993), who wrote a whole book on translating (book) titles, looks upon them as one text class with varieties such as nonfiction titles (p. 300 f.). Just as there are conventions for the formulation of (sub)classes of book titles, there are also conventions regarding the actual book texts and other kinds of texts.

Remember that the dimensions of socio-stylistic variation listed by Leech (1981: 14) and quoted in Section 3.3.3 include

- *Province* (language of law, science, advertising, etc.);
- *Modality* (language of memoranda, lectures, jokes, etc.).

The term *modality* is used here in a way very different from that common in linguistics; but this is so evident as not to require any further comment. To avoid a clash in terminology we propose to subsume these two style dimensions under the general notion of *text classes*. The idea is that different texts of each of the categories mentioned in parentheses (and many others) share certain characteristics, and these characteristics justify membership of the respective texts in a specific text class.

As regards literary texts, for instance, "the factors of situation and function are infinitely more complex than in pragmatic texts; and . . . the factor of style, which in literary translation is so important, has in nonliterary translation theory barely been considered" (Snell-Hornby 1990: 84).

Not only do text classes vary in this way, that is, as regards the factors relevant or dominant in each; but from the translational point of view it is also important to note that those factors that are different for different text classes can also differ in different languages. We are going to demonstrate this with reference to conventions regarding use of the modals in treatises from the humanities (Section 6.8.1) and legal texts (Section 6.8.2). Finally we will deal with reductive language, especially in the form of Nuclear English (Section 6.8.3).

6.8.1 Texts in the Humanities

By researching into the different linguistic means employed for expressing several kinds of speech acts in English and German texts from the humanities, Kussmaul (1978) aimed at setting up a contrastive stylistics for this text class. He based his investigation on a 120,000-word corpus of texts from the fields of linguistics and literary science. It consisted of 365 German and 362 English speech acts of the following kinds: statements, announcements, anaphoric references, directives, and conjectures. Having dealt with announcements in the last part of the previous Section (6.7) we will focus here on the other kinds of illocutionary acts.

As regards *statements*, the following German examples represent a scale in terms of frequency of constructions occurring in the corpus researched into (Kussmaul 1978: 55):

(1048) Wir können darin eine Motivation erkennen. (*wir* constructions, 36 percent)

(1049) Darin wird eine Motivation erkennbar. (passive constructions, 19 percent)

(1050) Man kann darin eine Motivation erkennen. (*man* constructions, 17 percent)

(1051) Darin lässt sich eine Motivation erkennen. (reflexive constructions, 15 percent)

(1052) Darin ist eine Motivation zu erkennen. (infinitive constructions, 9 percent)

This scale shows that, for the expression of modality in German, stylistic choices are between constructions with modals ((1048) and (1050)) and other modal expressions: modal adjectives in –*bar* in passive constructions (1049), reflexive LASSEN (1051), and modal infinitives (1052). As regards constructions with modals, there is the further choice between different pronouns: personal WIR in (1048) and impersonal MAN in (1050).

The latter possibilities are also used in English sentences containing modals—see (1054) and (1056), with *I* in (1055) as a further option. In contrast to (1049), the English passive construction (1053) contains a modal:

(1053) His later work cannot be seen as typical. (passive constructions, 31 percent)

(1054) We cannot see his later work as typical. (*we* constructions, 28 percent)

(1055) I do not see his later work as typical. (*I* constructions, 26 percent)

(1056) One cannot see his later work as typical. (*one* constructions, 15 percent)

As regards the factor of frequency, in English, passive constructions dominate, whereas in German, formulations including the pronoun WIR are most popular. Because the percentage of formally corresponding *we* constructions is also fairly high, it appears to be acceptable to render (1048) as (1057) and (1054) as (1058):

(1057) In this we can recognize a motivation.

(1058) Wir können sein späteres Werk nicht als typisch betrachten.

Mutual correspondence can also be said to hold between impersonal *man* and *one* constructions. Sentence (1050) could be rendered as (1059), (1056) as (1060):

(1059) One can recognize a motivation in this.

(1060) Man kann sein späteres Werk nicht als typisch betrachten.

Even though passive constructions in German are not as predominant as they are in English, their frequency is still high enough to warrant their use as a rendition for English ones and vice versa: (1053) ↔ (1061), (1049) ↔ (1062):

(1061) Sein späteres Werk kann nicht als typisch betrachtet werden.

(1062) In this a motivation is recognizable.

Note that both (1049) and (1062) are not syntactically overt passive constructions, because they lack a past participle such as *erkannt* or *recognized*. Passive voice enters into the picture only if semantic paraphrases such as (1063) or (1064), which are syntactically congruent with the genuine passive construction (1053), are introduced:

(1063) Darin kann eine Motivation erkannt werden.
(1064) In this a motivation can be recognized.

We may suppose that Kussmaul had in mind sentences such as (1063) when he referred to *passive constructions*. It must be added that (1049) would be semantically more congruent with (1048) and (1050)–(1052) if the auxiliary SEIN had been used instead of WERDEN:

(1065) Darin ist eine Motivation erkennbar.

This lexical substitution at the same time reveals even more clearly that WERDEN in (1049) is no marker of passive voice but of a process (of recognition) taking place.

So far we have found it justifiable to set up pairs of formally equivalent constructions because they do not differ very much in frequency in the two languages. For the remaining constructions, however, frequencies are so different that the translator should hesitate to go by formal correspondence alone. Whereas, for instance, personal constructions with the pronoun *I* occurred 41 times in 160 statements, *ich* was found to occur only 7 times among 201 German statements. This is a ratio of 26 percent to 3.5 percent! Hence (1055) should be rendered by (1066) only when the impression is created that the evaluation is really a subjective one:

[1055] I do not see his later work as typical.
(1066) Ich betrachte sein späteres Werk nicht als typisch.

Otherwise we would recommend choosing one of the two kinds of German constructions that themselves do not have direct English equivalents in the present text class but that express a high degree of objectivity: reflexive constructions such as (1051) and (1067) or modal infinitives such as (1052) and (1068):

(1067) Sein späteres Werk lässt sich nicht als typisch betrachten.
(1068) Sein späteres Werk ist nicht als typisch zu betrachten.

Vice versa, if these two types of German constructions occur in a text, equally impersonal constructions such as (1053) or (1056) suggest themselves as renditions. If such renditions involve a change in word-class, objectivity of the modal source may be regarded as a transposition factor. Regarding the modals themselves, in all their preceding occurrences in SL statements TL modals were found, so that for them no transposition was needed.

In the illocutionary act of *anaphoric reference* personal constructions in English predominated even more than in statements (93 percent!), whereas in German this personal style is much less popular (27 percent). Kussmaul's examples in this speech act category do not contain modals, so we will go on to *directives*, where the same tendency can be observed:

(1069) Es ist dabei zu beachten/dabei ist zu beachten . . . (infinitive constructions, 36 percent)

(1070) Dabei muss beachtet werden . . . (passive constructions, 23 percent)

(1071) Man beachte dabei . . . (*man* plus imperative constructions, 23 percent)

(1072) Wir wollen dabei beachten . . . (*wir* constructions, 18 percent)

(1073) Let us consider . . . (*we* imperatives, 41 percent)

(1074) . . . should be considered. (passive constructions, 28 percent)

(1075) Consider . . . ('pure' imperatives, 25 percent)

(1076) One should consider . . . (*one* constructions, 6 percent)

Note that the use of the two different modals in (1070) and (1072) makes a semantic difference: MÜSSEN suggests a(n objective) modal source external to the sentence subject, whereas WOLLEN collocates with deliberate acts of the subject. The modal infinitive in (1069) belongs to the same category as MÜSSEN. This distinction is paralleled by (1073) vs. (1074) and (1076), which is why these two English-German groups of expressions are suitable renditions of each other. Particularly the first-person plural constructions (1072) and (1073) translate each other well, because (1073) rendered by the completely congruent structure *Lassen Sie uns . . .* sounds old-fashioned. Furthermore, the imperatives in (1071) and (1075) parallel each other in form and frequency of occurrence.

The last type of speech acts, *conjectures*, showed a high ratio for epistemic modals: 51 percent in the German and even 59 percent in the English texts:

(1077) . . . dürfte typisch sein. (modal auxiliary, 51 percent)

(1078) . . . ist wahrscheinlich/vermutlich etc. typisch. (modal adverb, 31 percent)

(1079) . . . ist, wie ich glaube, typisch. (modal lexical verb, 18 percent)

(1080) There may be more than one conclusion . . . (modal auxiliary, 59 percent)

(1081) There is, I think, more than one conclusion . . . (modal lexical verb, 27 percent)

(1082) There is probably more than one conclusion . . . (modal adverb, 14 percent)

Not only the quantitative predominance of the modals but also their formal equivalence in English and German suggests repeated application of our familiar formula: *render SL modals by TL modals*:

(1083) . . . will be typical.
(1084) Es mag mehr als eine Lösung geben . . .

We prefer rendering epistemic MAY in (1080) by MÖGEN in (1084) because KÖNNEN in (1085) might be mistaken for conveying root modality in the sense of CAN in (1086):

(1085) Es kann mehr als eine Lösung geben . . .
(1086) There can be more than one solution . . .

As regards the other four sentences, (1078)–(1079), (1081)–(1082), it appears to be most reasonable to go by form and membership to kind of modality, namely, objective or subjective epistemic modality. This would suggest correlating SL and TL modal adverbs ((1078) ↔ (1087), (1082) ↔ (1088)), as well as SL and TL modal lexical verbs ((1079) ↔ (1089), (1081) ↔ (1090)):

(1087) . . . is probably typical.
(1088) Es gibt wahrscheinlich/vermutlich mehr als eine Lösung . . .
(1089) . . . is, I think, typical.
(1090) Es gibt, glaube ich/wie ich glaube, mehr als eine Lösung . . .

Frequency of occurrence would suggest the opposite correlation, but because the differences are not overwhelmingly great, going by form and subkind of modality expressed is surely justifiable.

With the exception of conjectures, a general feature of the researched speech acts in the English treatises is predominance of personal *I* and *we* constructions. In addition to *wir* constructions in statements, in the German texts passive, reflexive, and *man* constructions are preferred, none of which clearly dominates. All of these constructions do, however, share one feature: In contrast to the English ones they keep writer and reader in the background and give the text an objective tone (Kussmaul 1978: 56). The latter evaluation is echoed by Panther (1981b: 233), who points out that impersonal constructions create an impression of greater authority and expertise and are designed to evoke the image of an 'objective scientist' (1981b: 258). Kussmaul (1978: 57) adds that it would be interesting to find out whether content corresponds to linguistic form, that is, whether objective formulations in German treatises of the humanities really parallel objectivity of thought; and whether the personal tone of English texts really mirrors personal points of view, or whether expressions such as *I find*, *I suggest* do not in reality hedge objective facts that are completely established. In terms of the modals we have to ask if their epistemic use as in (1077), (1080), and (1083)–(1084) can be said to represent *objective* epistemic modality by virtue of the mere fact that these sentences occur in scientific texts;[48] see our discussion on subjective and objective epistemic modality in Section 3.2.4.2.

As regards the application of his findings in the field of translation, Kussmaul (1978: 57) himself points out that it is not enough to find translation equivalents in the areas of lexis, syntax, phraseology, and so on; rather it is necessary to ask which conventions are most common for a certain speech act relative to a given text class. He suggests that listing communicative conventions pertaining to various text classes could be part of a context-sensitive translation training.

6.8.2 Legal Texts

As mentioned in the introduction to this section (6.8), Leech includes as an example within his socio-stylistic dimension *province* the category *language of law*. Levi (1986: 260) emphasizes the value of this language variety for linguistics: "linguists should be interested in examining the language of the law for their own professional purposes, that is, to further their understanding of the structure, organization, and use of natural language." Vice versa, the knowledge of linguistics is seen by her to be relevant to legal questions and problems: "linguistics can be applied to solve real-world problems and to assist individuals who must deal with the legal system to work more successfully towards their own objectives."

A promising angle for the mutual study and benefit of linguistics and the law is speech act theory. Hancher (1980: 254) explains: "Speech act theory and the law are made of much the same stuff. Pragmatic concepts such as authority, verifiability, and obligation are basic to both. Each elaborates and refines ordinary language behavior, the one descriptively and the other prescriptively. Such compatibility argues for a lasting marriage . . ."

When Hancher says that speech act theory *describes* acts of obligation and so on whereas the law *prescribes* them it must not be forgotten that also in ordinary language an obligation may be *laid*, that is, action be prescribed. Of course speech act theory can describe such 'performative' use but as far as its status is concerned it is just as prescriptive as it is in legal language (albeit not necessarily that binding and universal in scope). Ever since we became familiar with the concept of discourse-oriented modality (see Section 3.2.4.4), that is, deontic modality used performatively, we have known that CAN and MAY are used for giving permission and MUST is used for laying an obligation:

[354] You may/can go now. (permission)
[356] You must be very careful. (obligation)

SHALL may be used for promising and for giving an order:

[355] You shall have it. (promise)
(1091) You shall do as you are told. (order—Nehls 1986: 205)

This performative use of the modals also occurs in legal texts; see Quirk (1982: 50), who refers to *"deontic* or 'root' modality expressing constraint, whether imposed by the speaker . . . or by some other agency (such as the law) . . . "* (italics as in the original).

Legal language most typically manifests in general provisions such as

(1092) Except in the United States of America, this book is sold subject to the condition that it *shall* not, by way of trade or otherwise, be lent, re-sold, hired out, or otherwise circulated without the publisher's prior consent in any form of binding or cover other than that in which it is published and without a similar condition including this condition being imposed on the subsequent purchaser. (Leech 1981: iv; italics ours.)

(1093) All rights reserved. No part of this book *may* be reprinted or reproduced or utilized in any form or by any electronic, mechanical, or other means . . . without permission in writing from the publishers. (Baker 1992: iv; italics ours.)

Such copyright notes including modals are usually rendered in different ways in German, the rendition being idiomatically 'frozen' in terms of this text class; such as the following example, discussed in Section 6.3.10.3:

[886] No part of this magazine may be reprinted without the express permission of the publisher.

[885] Nachdruck auch auszugsweise nur mit ausdrücklicher Genehmigung des Verlages.

Lawlike rules such as these are also found in ordinary language use, such as the following two signs spotted by Nehls (1986: 191):

(1094) Ice cream may not be brought into this store.

(1095) Bicycles must not be placed against this building.

These parallels between ordinary and legal language might suggest identity of use of the modals in the two varieties. But there are noteworthy differences.

Maley (1987: 29 f.) first observes that in legislative texts MUST and SHALL are used for performing *mandatory* speech acts, by which an obligation (not) to act is imposed; MAY is used for the performance of *discretionary* speech acts conferring a power the exercise of which is optional.

Nehls (1986: 49 ff.) states that the use of SHALL to express the imposition of a strict obligation first occurred in Early Modern English and is to be found in contracts and official provisions to this day. He quotes Coates (1983: 190), who remarks that this use of SHALL is restricted to formal legal contexts. Noteworthy though the synonymy of SHALL and MUST in specific text classes may be, the following observation is even more remarkable. Maley (1987: 30) argues that the expression *shall be treated* in a legislative text *appears to* create a rule with the (illocutionary) force of a command. He justifies this interpretative reservation by pointing out that SHALL—as well as MUST and MAY—are notorious sources of ambiguity in legislative interpretation. In certain cases, that is, one may argue that the legislature intended SHALL to be not mandatory, but only discretionary. This may have the following consequence: "In such cases, courts in effect, if they agree with the argument, decide that *shall* means *may* or vice versa"! (1987: 30).

Maley continues: "Such apparent reversals of semantic common-sense are forced upon courts" in cases where the wording of the law seems absurd or inconsistencies arise when other contextual evidence is taken into account. Because the text itself cannot be changed by the courts they can only give it the meaning presumably intended by the legislature.

To identify the actually intended meaning of modals in such legal contexts, the translator can only try to follow the legal specialist's strategy just outlined and aim at achieving a correct interpretation of the modals consistent with their co- and contexts. It is as if the translator were declaring: "Instead of SHALL the speaker should have used MAY," which amounts to an actual restructuring of the SL text. Because the translator thus goes far beyond the usual task of 'merely' translating what is presented, he or she enters a new professional field, and it is fitting to acknowledge this new status by referring to the person as a *translator-editor* (inspired by Juhel's (1982: 109) expression *traducteur-rédacteur*, see Gutknecht 1987: 241).

On an international scale, the situation becomes even more complex because the legal systems of several nations must be taken into consideration. Stellbrink (1987: 32) gives the example of a license contract "which, negotiated in English by a German and an Italian party, is entered into under Swiss Federal Law with arbitration proceedings in accordance with the provisions regulating composition and arbitration proceedings as issued by the International Chamber of Commerce in Paris, with auxiliary application of the procedural law of the Canton of Zurich" (our translation).

Stellbrink even adds that "this construction, complicated though it may seem, is quite common and will be found in the same or in a similar form in far more than half of all international contracts made under private law" (our translation).

In view of such complexity, which can only increase the semantic indeterminacy of how to interpret the modals, there seems to be an urgent requirement for intervention and the setting up of binding guidelines for the use of the modals, at least in the field of language for special purposes. This would alleviate the translator of the burden of an unduly great amount of 'editing' activity.

A general proposal in this direction was made by the internationally known Canadian draftsman Dr. Elmer Driedger (quoted by Meredith 1979: 63) when he said: "A Draftsman should not . . . indulge in unnecessary variation . . . ; and he must use the same words or phrases over and over again if he means the same thing . . ."

In terms of the English modals, this would call for a standardization of the use of MAY and SHALL by assigning each modal only one degree of modality. At the same time those uses of the modals could be dispensed with that, according to modern standards, appear to be obsolete and hence unjustified on objective grounds.

In his own proposals Meredith fulfills these postulates. First he makes two general "principal points to remember in translating" juridical acts; one of them reads: "Legal jargon is out. The trend today is toward keeping legal documents, whether in translation or in their original drafting, clear, comprehensible, and uncluttered by legal gobbledygook" (1979: 63). He then proceeds to propose improvements in the use of the English modals in legal texts along these lines. The present indicative is to be used after *if*, obviating the use of SHALL and SHOULD:

(1096) "If there shall be no child of mine alive at that time"

should read

(1097) "If no child of mine is alive at that time."
(1098) "If the testator should leave no issue . . ."

becomes

(1099) "If the testator leaves no issue . . ." .

As a solution to Maley's paradox of the interchangeability of SHALL and MAY Meredith proposes: "In many cases, SHALL, to the surprise of many, is contraindicated, particularly after a negative subject: *No debtor shall* should become *No debtor may*. SHALL should always be replaced by the present indicative in giving a definition: *"Debtor means . . .* is preferable to *Debtor shall mean . . .* The only case in which SHALL is admitted is that where someone is actually commanded to do something. This situation is rare indeed in juridical acts" (1979: 63).

Use of the modals is also shown to be an alternative for 'surplus words and phrases' to be avoided. Meredith (1979: 64) argues: "As long as surplus words can be deleted *without altering the meaning of the text*, this should be done" (italics as in the original). He maintains that

(1100) "The lessor hereby directs that the lessee is fully authorized to"

means

(1101) "The lessee may . . ."

As we know (see Section 3.2.6.2), such a change from source- to goal-oriented modality does entail loss of semantic content, namely, information about the modal source (here, *the lessor*). Furthermore, it involves a change in modal perspective (see Section 3.2.6.3). When Meredith still ascribes synonymy to the two preceding sentences he will be of opinion that, by virtue of the semantic relationship holding between the lexemes LESSOR and LESSEE, the modal source of (1101) will be evident (in a way analogous to the 'permittor' of (407) being evident in (408), see Section 3.2.6.1) and that change in perspective is immaterial. For the translator it is, however, safer to have source or goal orientation as an invariance factor to optimize congruence of SL and TL sentences.

Our proposal would be to replace (1100) by (1102):

(1102) "The lessor permits the lessee to . . ."

and to translate accordingly. This use of a source-oriented lexical verb would allow preservation of all the factors mentioned and still permit surplus words to be jettisoned.

The other steps suggested by Meredith—restricting SHALL to commands, banning it from conditionals—amount to a reduction of the expressive possibilities of the language. He nevertheless sets up the following general postulate for a translation into English: "The construction should be as English as possible" (1979: 63). These two aspects taken together imply that what is aimed at is the creation of a *reductive* version of the (now common) English (legal) language. Its purpose is "clear, comprehensible" language (see earlier), and the measures suggested to be taken for SHALL and MAY show that it can help avoiding ambiguity.

6.8.3 Reductive Language

Elimination of ambiguity as aimed at by the proposed measures just referred to is not the goal in the legal domain only. There are also other fields of life where unmistakable formulation and interpretation of utterances is required. And also in these other fields the means for a reduction of ambiguity is often the reduction of expressive possibilities of (ordinary) language, resulting in a reductive language. One such example is the work of the CEN/CENELEC team (1984) commissioned to set up rules for formulating European norms. They tried to lay down guidelines for an adequate translation of the modals in English, German, and French. In their recommendations, SHALL is again confined to one degree or modality (of unrestricted necessity, "it is necessary"); in normative expressions, *may not* (as a prohibition) is not to be used in lieu of *shall not* (1984: 25). SOLLEN, on the other hand, is recommended not to be used any more because of its lack of precision (1984: 32). MUST is to be used only for the description of an unavoidable situation (1984: 25).

These two approaches, restricting the meanings of a modal and not using it at all, correspond to two out of Quirk's (1982: 51) three proposed possibilities of how various kinds of modality might best be expressed in *Nuclear English*. Nuclear English may be seen as an attempt of "adapting English . . . to constitute a nuclear medium for international use" (1982: 43). "The emblematic consumers of Nuclear English should . . . be seen . . . as Italian and Japanese company directors engaged in negotiating an agreement" (p. 44). This concept can therefore be seen as an undertaking just right for solving the problem of 'international modal proliferation' inherent in the situation described by Stellbrink (see Section 6.8.2). Nuclear English could be considered as a project of "language design" (Quirk 1982: 42) promising to offer our proposed "intervention and setting up of binding guidelines for the use of the modals . . . " as postulated previously (see Section 6.8.2). Only that Quirk opts for the "sharply radical proposal" of "banning the use of all modals altogether" (p. 51).

His aim is understandable and laudable: "In repudiating the claims of 'frequency of occurrence,' we would achieve the objective of avoiding the ultimately far greater disadvantages of extreme polysemy" (p. 51). This approach seems to be suitable for achieving nonambiguity in scientific language, but for ordinary language it seems to be problematic for the following reasons.

Quirk (1982: 51) sets up "the requirement that Nuclear English must provide *full* communicative adequacy" (italics ours). Elsewhere he defines: "Communicative adequacy is to be understood as providing the learner with the means of expressing, however periphrastically, an indefinitely large number of communicative needs (in principle, *all*), with the minimum of ambiguity . . . " (p. 43; italics ours).

Now how can *full* communicative adequacy providing for *all* communicative needs be compatible with "the minimum of ambiguity"? We hold that a great amount of ambiguity, and indeed also of all the other aspects of linguistic indeterminacy, is an integral part of language. Quirk points out that Nuclear English "is not (but is merely related to) a natural language" (p. 44), and this entitles him to freely exclude from it whatever he likes to. But, if he really wants to fulfill *all* communicative needs (as he proclaims), there seems to be no way around the modals, for the following reasons.

In our sections on indeterminacy (3.1.4, 4.1.4) it was shown repeatedly that indeterminacy is available with the modals but not with their paraphrases, which rather bear discrete meanings. This determinacy of modal paraphrases ties in well with Quirk's (1982: 51) postulate of the speaker's intentions having to be determinate for the use of Nuclear English: "In requiring paraphrase, we would be insisting on a speaker's clarifying his own intention in advance."

But what if it is the speaker's intention to be deliberately indeterminate?

Leech (1980: 85) provides examples of modals in indirect utterances that "are not *meant* to be determinate" (italics as in the original; see Section 7.1.2.1). How are we to convey them if not by means of the modals? It should not be assumed that such situations are fringe phenomena and hence negligible. Leech (1981: 336) points out that "illocutionary force is *very often* a matter of degree rather than kind" (italics ours), and shortly after he adds: "Politeness, like the factors of truthfulness, informativeness, and relevance . . . , is a matter of degree, and is variable according to situation of utterance" (1981: 339 f.; see our Section 4.1.4.2).

More basically, it must not be forgotten that paraphrases of the modals cannot generally be used even for 'determinate' indirect speech acts, which can be performed only by means of the modals (see Section 4.1.1).

All this shows that in Quirk's concept of Nuclear English not only "is the language . . . carefully and explicitly restricted" (1982: 52) but so are its expressive possibilities—contrary to his tenets.

But also the various aspects of semantic indeterminacy exclusive to the modals (see Section 3.1.4) are a communicative reality not be neglected. If Quirk intends to provide full communicative adequacy it is indeed wise to "retain the full range of modalities" (p. 51) but it is doubtful whether it is viable to "restrict their expression to carefully prescribed and maximally explicit paraphrases" (p. 51); that is, without use of the modals that are often indeterminate in terms of different modalities. All in all it is questionable if Quirk's "sharply radical proposal" (p. 51) can hope to be compatible with communicative reality.

These brief reflections about a possible universe of discourse without the modals have shown that the object of our case study is indeed an important one, indispensable in normal communication.

If in legal language or in the formulation of norms the range of meanings of the modals is restricted for the sake of nonambiguity, this is of course something the translator must know to be able to produce adequate renditions and arrive at a correct understanding in the first place. So the special semantic rules of restrictive languages are important revision factors to be taken into account when it comes to translating texts formulated in these languages.

7. ESSENTIAL FACTORS OF THE TRANSLATION SITUATION

In Section 4.4.2 we dealt with several aspects of the situation of utterance; that is, the SL speaker's situation. This includes factors such as time and place of utterance, the speaker's own dispositions, and those toward the targeted SL hearer, all of which give rise to the speaker's intentions manifesting in his text.

Next in the process of communication comes reception of this text by the intended (group of) SL hearer(s), also in a situation defined by time, space, and dispositions of action and understanding.

From the SL perspective, the translator is but another hearer. From the point of view of that individual's function, however, understanding the SL text is one of several essential factors constituting the translation situation. The others include working instructions from the client, characteristics of the prospective TL hearer, the translation direction, as well as the translator's own disposition of understanding and how to carry out his or her job.

Chronologically the translation situation originates in the SL speaker, so we will deal with this factor first.

7.1 THE SL SPEAKER

In Section 4.4.2.1 we dealt with different social relationships of speaker and hearer, giving rise to different ways of interpreting and rendering a sentence. In the present section we will focus on the speaker and his or her direct relevance to the translator. There are relatively permanent speaker-related factors such as age, as well as 'short-lived' ones such as intentions, varying with speech act or text.

7.1.1 The SL Speaker's Identity and Speech Act Authority

Werth (1981: 23), taking (1103) in the epistemic sense of (1104),

(1103) Bert should have finished the painting by now.
(1104) It is probable that Bert has finished the painting.

asks the question, "how does the listener decide whether Bert has finished or not?" He gives different answers relative to the possible identity of the speaker:

• If the speaker is Bert's wife, who can be assumed to know his working habits, then the utterance of (1103) can be taken "with great confidence."
• If the speaker is a casual acquaintance of Bert's, the hearer "would view the possibility of (1103) being true as rather dubious"; he or she might even be tempted to interpret SHOULD in the root sense.

If SHOULD is actually intended to bear the root meaning of "obligation" then it is again the speaker's identity influencing the interpretation of (1103):

• If the speaker is Bert's supervisor, the utterance of (1103) can be viewed as authoritative, "and the corresponding probability that Bert does indeed have such an obligation is very high."
• If the speaker is a seven-year-old child, lack of speaker authority is likely to be assumed; Bert's indeed being obliged has a low probability.

Werth applies the notion of a scale of speaker authority to both root and epistemic senses of SHOULD. This means that the degree of modality stated need not coincide with the degree of modality actually representing the objective state of affairs. Accordingly, Werth says that "the actual probability of an epistemic modal is to be assessed using the degree of authority possessed by the speaker to make the statement in question" (p. 22).

The degree of speech act authority will be obvious to the SL hearer if he or she considers the identity of the speaker, which in turn may be evident from co(n)text.

The translator qua (another) SL hearer is basically in the same situation. But there are two subsituations:

• If speaker identity and authority is revealed by the SL *co*text it will also be revealed by TL cotext. No additional information is required in the TL text.
• If speaker identity or degree of speech act authority can be retrieved only on the basis of (nonverbal) *con*text, then mere cotext will be insufficient as an identification factor for it in the TL text. If this contextual information is not available, the translator can only go by what he or she knows. If it

is, the question arises whether it should be passed on to the TL reader (see Section 7.4.3.2).

7.1.2 The SL Speaker's Intentions

All aspects of a speech act performed by an SL speaker are a matter of intention. Using certain strings of words the speaker intends to convey propositions, illocutions, and to produce perlocutions in the hearer.

Just like any SL hearer, the translator has to understand the speaker's intentions. Identification factors for all the levels just mentioned help accomplish this task.

7.1.2.1 Determinacy and Indeterminacy

The speaker's intentions can be said to be determinate because speech acts are generally performed with something specific in mind. In the field of modality, the SL speaker can intend to have a modal carry root or epistemic meaning and any of the submeanings as introduced in Section 3.2.4. In certain contexts he or she may intend to deviate from common usage by exchanging the meanings of MAY and SHALL (see Section 6.8.2). The speaker may further intend an utterance containing a modal to be a direct or an indirect speech act. Questions starting in *Can you*, for instance, may be intended as literal questions or as indirect orders (see Section 4.1.4.1). All such semantic and pragmatic intentions of the SL speaker are determinate.

A speaker can, however, be determined to be indeterminate about certain aspects of the speech act. Consider the factor of illocutionary acts that can be performed by means of the following two sentences:

(1105) How would you like to come outside and look at my squash?
(1106) Would you like to type this letter for me?

Leech (1980: 85) remarks that a sentence like (1105) is "poised between invitation and suggestion," and (1106) is "poised between request and invitation." He adds: "Surely an essential point about such indirect utterances is that they are not *meant* to be determinate." Leech's italics underline the point made in this section: that indeterminacy can be speaker based. His examples of illocutionary gradience could be supplemented by others showing ambiguity and merger created deliberately by the speaker, for instance:

(1107) You will visit her, won't you?
(1108) English transitive verbs may be active or passive. (Leech 1987: 76)

Our sections on semantic and pragmatic indeterminacy (3.1.4 and 4.1.4) show, however, that indeterminacy can also be hearer related. Remember that the first topic dealt with in both these sections was strength of identification factors. In some cases the specific (sub)kind of modality or illocutionary force intended was "not clear" (Coates 1983: 142) due to lack of unmistakable identification factors. To take Coates's own examples illustrating the gradient between permission and possibility (1983: 143):

[217] It is subject to the final prerogative of mercy of the Home Secretary who may recommend a reprieve.

[218] But assuming that the distinction is maintained one may ask which is to be analytically prior?

Coates categorizes these sentences as "intermediate examples . . . where it is not clear if rules and regulations apply or not . . ." (1983: 142). Now it is legitimate to ask, 'Not clear' to whom? Not necessarily to the speaker, who will definitely know what he or she is talking about. So locutionary gradience may be purely hearer related. But even the hearer may know exactly what the speaker is alluding to, provided there are sufficient co(n)textual clues. Where then is indeterminacy located? Perhaps only in the mind of the analyzing linguist, whose corpus sentences lack the context necessary for disambiguation.

As a result of these brief reflections the assumption emerges that much of what is presented by linguists in the way of indeterminacy is in fact merely hearer related or even exists only for the linguist whose reception situation differs from that of the original hearer.

What then are the implications for the situation of the translator? If the translator is part of the original utterance situation, for instance, in the capacity of interpreter, there are fewer chances of his mistaking speaker determinacy for indeterminacy. He will thus be able to present as definite in TL what is definite in SL.

Cases of indeterminacy genuinely intended by the speaker and recognized as such by the translator, on the other hand, can be attempted to be kept indeterminate in TL also. For (1105) and (1106) this means that illocutionary gradience must also be a characteristic of the German renditions. We suggest

(1109) Wie wär's, wenn du mal nach draussen kämst und dir meine Kürbisse ansehen würdest?

(1110) Würdest du diesen Brief für mich tippen?

Another facet of the speaker's intentions is the fact that not all modality stated is also modality intended. A speaker of English who says

[624] I can see two ships

intends to refer to actually seeing two ships, not just to the possibility of his doing so (see Section 4.3.1, where we used the expression *point of utterance* to denote speaker intention; see also Table 4.2). In examples such as these, the translator has to be awake to the real intention of the speaker. This would entail skipping overt modality in a German rendition of (624), because in the TL there is no idiomatic constraint to having modality.

7.1.2.2 Creating an Image

A speaker may wish to convey a certain image, personal or of the subject matter in question, by choosing certain modal constructions. Remember that in German scientific writings impersonal constructions are preferred to give the proposition uttered an objective tone and thus to evoke the image of an 'objective scientist' (see Section 6.8.1). This differs from English where personal formulations are more dominant. In American and English scholarly writing, *we* is considered impersonal and editorial. It seems that American and English scientists feel they do not need to use 'objective constructions' when they present objective facts.

The lesson to be learned by the translator is this: In those cases where one realizes that the English speaker, even though using tentative-subjective formulations, presents objective facts, one should employ German constructions conveying objectivity. This principle would apply to both colloquial and scientific English.

7.2 THE SL TEXT

The SL text is the product of the speaker's intentions. Intervening factors may cause the text not to reflect these intentions fully. They include choice of inappropriate linguistic means and unavailability of the whole text produced.

If the speaker can be interviewed on open questions then his or her intentions will become more fully transparent to the translator. But if the text itself is the only point of reference, then the likelihood of intentions being opaque is greater. Such a translation situation exists with historical texts. Here only the knowledge of the modals' forms, meanings, and other characteristics at a particular time will help in ascertaining the SL writer's intentions.

7.3 THE CLIENT

Translation of a text is always performed relative to a specific target. A text cannot be translated 'as such' but only with respect to a specific audience in a specific situation. Reiss (1984: 80) points out that "the factor dominating the respective decisions in translating is the *purpose* of a translation" (our translation, her emphasis). Purpose or target factors are usually preset by the translator's client placing the order.

Suppose the client wishes an English legal text to be translated into German. The text contains the following sentence:

(1111) The judge ruled that this was a case of a debt that must be discharged on the creditor's premises.

Now the client telling the translator that the TL reader is not familiar with legal language, the translator cannot make use of his or her knowledge that the English relative clause containing a modal can be condensed into the German compound BRINGSCHULD (see Section 3.2.5.1) as in the following rendition of (1111):

(1112) Der Richter entschied, dies sei ein Fall von Bringschuld.

Instead a construction would have to be employed that is structurally akin to the English one:

(1113) Der Richter entschied, dies sei ein Fall, bei dem der Schuldner das Geld dem Gläubiger an dessen Wohnsitz übermitteln müsse.

In the previous example the client's instruction resulted in making the SL modal an invariance factor. Exactly the opposite would be the case if the translator were told to translate (1113) into Nuclear English as conceived of by Quirk (see Section 6.8.3). This instruction would amount to banning the modals from the English rendition altogether. The concept of Nuclear English thus being a revision factor, the translator would have to use a different kind of modal expression such as the modal participle construction BE OBLIGED TO:

(1114) The judge ruled that this was a case in which the debtor is obliged to discharge the debt on the creditor's premises.

The two examples discussed in this section featured a special language with extended vocabulary (unusable in the given case) and a reductive language with restricted vocabulary. Both examples show that the client's order can have quite an effect on the translator's handling of the modals. In both cases the client's instructions became blocking factors to possibilities that otherwise objectively exist.

7.4 THE TRANSLATOR

Having established the role of the client as that of the ultimate or fundamental factor of any translation, that of being in a position to demand *anything* to be done about an SL text to be translated, we next speak about the second 'human factor' involved in each translation project—the translator.

The translator is certainly expected to just put into practice the factors demanded by the client; yet in view of the complexity of the translation situation this is still an enormous job, as any professional translator will know by experience. The ability or competence to cope with this challenge increases as experience grows. It can also be increased by deepening the necessary knowledge; hence our first subsection deals with the translator's competence. (See Section 5.4 for a strategy to relieve the interpreter's memory.)

Another factor determining the TL rendition relates to a prerequisite to its production; namely, the reception of the SL text by the translator (Section 7.4.2). The quality of the TL product is further influenced by the intentions pursued by the translator (Section 7.4.3).

7.4.1 The Translator's Competence

No doubt the quality of the performance depends upon the translator's competence. It is a different matter whether this competence is so great that the translator feels he or she does not need any translation theory to further improve it. The reflections in Section 7.4.1.1 presuppose a lack of competence in rendering SL modal nouns and hint at a strategy of how to compensate for it by using TL modals. In Section 7.4.1.2 mother-tongue interference and rare uses of the modals possibly escaping the non-native speaker's competence will be dealt with.

7.4.1.1 Competence in the Use of Modal Nouns

Just as linguistic and communicative competence is a prerequisite for any SL speaker to realize his or her verbal intentions, thorough knowledge of the two languages (and cultures) involved in translating is a must for the translator. But just as lack of competence in unilingual communication can sometimes be compensated for by using periphrastic expressions, the same strategy can be employed by the translator who lacks the knowledge of a specific TL expression. Suppose the covertly modal expression STEUERPFLICH-TIGER is used by a speaker of German, and the translator knows what it means but does not know an appropriate English noun. In this case it is very easy to switch to a paraphrase containing a modal:

(1115) Er ist ein Steuerpflichtiger.
(1116) He is someone who must pay taxes.

This procedure of compensating for lack of TL competence by analyzing a modal compound into its semantic constituents as expressed by a set of separate lexemes can also be applied to other modal nouns:

[822] Hauptpost—Umsteigemöglichkeit.
(1117) General Post Office; here you can change (buses).

(1118) Hier haben Sie auch die Durchwahlmöglichkeit.
(1119) Here you can/may also dial direct.

Not only compounds conveying covert modality may be paraphrased by means of the modals. Consider the expression *amphibian vehicle*, which can be shortened to *amphibian*. For a modal paraphrase it is actually possible to use a dictionary entry. In *Webster's New Twentieth Century Dictionary of the English Language* (1983: 60) we find s.v. *amphibian, n.*: "5. a tank or other vehicle that can travel on either land or water." Someone who is unsure about *amphibian* may well translate as follows:

(1120) Sieh mal. Dies ist ein Amphibienfahrzeug.
(1121) Look here. This is a vehicle that can travel on either land or water.

Summing up our reflections so far we can say that insufficient competence of TL modal nouns acts as a blocking factor to their rendition. Here familiarity with the modals as commonly known modal expressions comes to the growing translator's aid as a compensation factor. The combination of both these factors in turn acts as a revision factor for the rendition of the SL nouns that would normally have been rendered as TL nouns. Their modal specificity is split up into a general modal aspect expressed by the modals and a nonmodal aspect conveyed by the rest of the paraphrase used.

7.4.1.2 Competence in the Use of the Modals

Let us now turn from insufficient competence of modal nouns to that of the modals themselves. Lindemann (1990: 243) found out that Norwegian learners of German tended to use only those German modals that showed some formal similarity to the Norwegian ones. Moreover, these modals were used with the Norwegian meanings, so that ungrammatical sentences would result.

The same behavior can be observed with regard to the English-German language pair. Native speakers of English using WOULD in the sense of USED TO tend to render it by *würde* for mere reasons of formal correspondence, projecting into it the said meaning of WOULD. Such interference[49] leads to utterances such as

(1122) *Vor einigen Jahren würde ich manchmal schwimmen gehen.

Lindemann refers to the two factors detected by her—the influence of the native language and the tendency for simplification—as evidence for "die vielfältige Faktorenkomplexion, die den Zweitsprachenprozess begleitet" (1990: 252). She concludes: "Als wichtigste Erkenntnis muss die Existenz von Lernersprachen angesehen werden. . . . Diese Lernersprachsysteme werden von einer ganzen Palette von Faktoren beeinflusst, die es näher zu untersuchen gilt" (1990: 254).

Lack of competence can, however, also be of a more subtle nature. Consider the perfective construction *might have . . . –en*. In his dissertation, Matthews (1979: 154) writes:

(1123) There are in addition many articles with promising but not worked out suggestions that I might have included here . . . , but I think it is more profitable to mention these as and when relevant in the course of later chapters.

The second main clause (*but I think it is . . .*) clearly shows that the first one is counterfactual (in the sense of "I did *not* include those promising articles here"). This in turn shows that the modal perfective construction, even though formally prototypical of epistemic modality (see Section 3.3.8), cannot be epistemic in the present case but must have root meaning. Therefore, only the second of the following two renditions is accurate:

(1124) !Es gibt noch viele Aufsätze . . . , die ich hier berücksichtigt haben könnte, . . .

(1125) Es gibt noch viele Aufsätze . . . , die ich hier hätte berücksichtigen können, . . .

Now the two constructions clearly differ in meaning but most learners of English would probably maintain that of all the German modals KÖNNEN is the only one deserving serious consideration as a rendition for MIGHT in a perfective construction, whether it be root or epistemic in meaning. Translating the following sentence proves this assumption wrong:

(1126) Your son might have been more careful. (Reum 1961: 391)

It is true that renditions of this sentence can be constructed in a way analogous to (1124) and (1125):

(1127) Ihr Sohn könnte vorsichtiger gewesen sein.
(1128) Ihr Sohn hätte vorsichtiger sein können.

Reum gives the following equivalent, however:

(1129) Ihr Sohn hätte vorsichtiger sein sollen.

The use of SOLLEN puts the utterance of (1129) in the direction of a reproach. The same effect can be achieved by uttering (1128), especially if this sentence is 'spiced' with some appropriate modal particles:

(1130) Ihr Sohn hätte ja nun auch wirklich vorsichtiger sein können.

But the use of SOLLEN expresses this aspect more distinctly, and probably this is the factor that prompted Reum to use this modal for a rendition of

MIGHT. Given the two renditions of (1128) and (1129), we can say that MIGHT itself oscillates between possibility and necessity in much the same way as KÖNNEN in (1128). The fact that MIGHT can be rendered by SOLLEN shows that the obligatory element can be present in a sentence such as (1126). This root meaning of obligation, which may be present in the construction *might have* . . . *–en* and its possible rendition by *hätte* . . . *sollen*, is a specialty to be presented to the advanced learner, as is the rendition of epistemic COULD by *sollte* mentioned in Section 3.2.3.1.

Gottwald (1982: 108 f.), who deals with similarly rare uses of the modals, states that these constitute a challenge even to the professional translator. Along the lines of Lindemann (cited previously) he concludes: "Für den Übersetzer heisst dies, dass die eingangs konstatierte weitgehende Übereinstimmung der formalen Möglichkeiten [der Modalverben des Englischen und Deutschen] wirkungslos bleibt: Der lebendige Sprachgebrauch wird durch viele einander überlagernde semantische, stilistische, pragmatische und idiomatische Faktoren modifiziert" (p. 110 f.).

The grand conclusion then is that, in all phases of translation teaching— elementary, intermediate, and advanced—courses on the modals should be designed to include an ever-increasing range of factors. Thus the learner will develop the competence[50] that will ultimately lead to facility in the area of grammar that has been referred to as the perhaps most important and difficult one (see Section 1.2.1).

7.4.2 The Translator's Reception of the SL Text

Applying his or her competence, the translator has to identify speaker-related factors such as the speaker's identity and intentions underlying the production of the text in question (see Section 7.1). The way to achieve this task is looking for and applying identification factors of all kinds.

Recognition of the speaker's intentions is necessary because the correlation of SL and TL modals is not on an invariable one-to-one basis (see Section 3.1.1). It can vary considerably, relative to the intended kinds of modality, illocutionary force, and so forth (see Chapters 3 and so on).

Correct recognition of the speaker's intentions is unnecessary, however, if two heterogeneous readings of an SL modal can both be rendered by the same TL modal. This was found to be the case with the gradient of inherency of CAN, where the meanings of ability and possibility as well as each intermediate point on the gradient between them can all be rendered by KÖNNEN (see Section 3.1.4.2, point (ba)).

The same situation holds for ambiguity. A sentence containing MUST can be ambiguous between a root and an epistemic reading. Disambiguation may be necessary for the sake of an appropriate understanding on the part of the 'nontranslating' SL hearer; but if MUST can invariably be rendered by

MÜSSEN, there is no need *for the translator* to pinpoint which reading may have been intended (see Section 3.1.4.3).

This privilege of translational irrelevance of disambiguation in case of a unified rendition extends to the third kind of semantic indeterminacy, that is, merger, and also to illocutionary indeterminacy (see Sections 3.1.4.4, 4.1.4.4, and 7.1.2.1): If both readings of "direct question" and "indirect order" associated with an utterance starting with *Can you* can be rendered by means of KÖNNEN there is no need for the translator to find out which of these readings was intended by the speaker.

All this shows that, even though the SL hearer targeted by the SL speaker may in many respects be in a better position to understand the speaker's intentions, the translator's job of text analysis is sometimes easier than that of the targeted SL hearer.

7.4.3 The Translator's Intentions

The SL speaker and the translator share one factor: They create texts. Yet the respective status of each is entirely different. From the point of view of translation, the creator of the original is completely free to say whatever he or she likes, whereas the creator of the rendition is bound by a number of factors due to being merely a re-creator. Yet loopholes seem to allow the translator to display personal creativity and intentions. These appear whenever there seem to be chances of 'improving upon' the SL text. We will here deal with three purposes of possible 'improvements': enabling understanding, facilitating understanding by making additions to, and avoiding redundancy by making subtractions from the original text.

7.4.3.1 Enabling Understanding

If the SL text is formulated in 'standard' language, the question of the translator's enabling understanding does not arise. Of course, in a very basic sense, the translator's whole activity is one of enabling understanding because without his or her work the TL hearer unfamiliar with the SL would not understand the SL text. What we mean is that if the translator of a text in standard language just goes by established SL-TL correlations then the TL text will 'speak by itself,' and the TL hearer will understand it without any *further* help.

Things are different if modal usage deviates from commonly established standards. Dialects and regionalisms (see Section 4.5.1) cannot be rendered 'unedited,' that is, by mere application of principles suitable for rendering standard language. Legal language with its occasional permutations of the meanings of MAY and SHALL (see Section 6.8.2) also constitutes a revision factor. Here, it is only by using KÖNNEN (in contrast to SOLLEN) that

SHALL intended to have the meaning of possibility or permission can be done justice to in a German rendition. And it is only by this special measure that the translator actually enables the TL hearer to understand the legal text properly.

7.4.3.2 Facilitating Understanding

On the basis of results obtained by experiment, Levý (1965: 78 f.) was able to establish that translators have a tendency to qualitatively modify and differentiate an SL text while transforming it into TL. One way this was found to be done is explaining in TL logical relations not expressed in the SL text.

An example of this kind of obvious 'revision' of the SL original was detected by Jumpelt (1961: 95) in the translation of H. S. Truman's memoirs. When asked at a press conference, "Do you expect to see Mr. Molotow?" the president gave the following answer:

(1131) Yes, he is going to stop by and pay his respects to the President of the United States. He should.

In the German translation the sentence *He should* reads:

(1132) Das ist internationale Gepflogenheit.

To evaluate this rendition properly let us first review the semantic potential of the original sentence *He should*.

SHOULD in (1131) can be understood alternatively in the root or epistemic sense:

(1133) He is obliged to.
(1134) I suspect he will.

Accordingly, (1131) could have been rendered as (1135) or (1136):

(1135) Er ist (eigentlich) gehalten, es zu tun.
(1136) Ich nehme es (zumindest) an.

But just like the English paraphrases, these German ones are semantically more specific than the original, which is, after all, ambiguous between root and epistemic modality due to its containing a modal.

Equally ambiguous German versions containing a modal are, however, also available:

(1137) Er müsste/sollte es eigentlich (tun)./ Das müsste/sollte er eigentlich (tun).

These sentences can be understood in terms of both (1135) and (1136). Why was one of them not chosen as a rendition? To approach this question let us review the functions of root and epistemic modality in the context of (1131):

- When SHOULD is interpreted epistemically (as in (1134), and rendered by (1136)), the degree of certainty of the unconditional forecast expressed before by BE GOING TO is *revised* towards a careful conjecture. Certain doubts arising may be the cause of this modification of the degree of epistemic modality. (This revision is emphasized by the use of ZUMIN-DEST in (1136).)
- When SHOULD is interpreted in the root sense (as in (1133), and rendered by (1135)), it fulfills a completely different function: it *justifies* the use of predictive BE GOING TO by alluding to an existing obligation of the agent to be, while tacitly referring to the presupposition that a person who should take a certain action is going to do so. The actual status of the obligation, however, is left unspecified in (1131), and also in (1133) and (1135)—a feature typical of goal-oriented sentences.

This is precisely the point that the translator of (1132) intended to amend. He wanted to reveal to the hearer the modal source of (1133) and thus of the root reading of (1131). Interestingly though, the translator's rendition (1132) represents also the modal source of the epistemic reading of (1131), that is, (1134): If a specific international habit is relevant in the present case, then it is natural for the speaker to suspect that it will be adhered to. This might lead to the conclusion that the translator of (1132) did not necessarily intend to yield to any specific kind of modality by keeping the rendition as ambiguous as (1137). The reason for not choosing (1137), which contains a *goal*-oriented modal, is that the translator intended to go one step further, toward the modal *source* of both its interpretations.

This modal source is a 'social law' at the basis of both root and epistemic modality, thus confirming Perkins's (1983: 28 f., 58, n. 16) tenet that the use of modals is relative to laws. In the present case an international protocol convention incurs the relatively strong deontic obligation to act in accordance with it and determines the epistemic conjecture by the speaker that the person referred to by the sentence subject is indeed going to act accordingly.

And yet (1132) does not seem to be so completely ambiguous as is (1131) or (1137): representing a 'deontic rule,' it might suggest a deontic, that is, root interpretation. It must not be overlooked that an epistemic reading would only exist *on the basis of* (1132)—it is by no means expressed by it. An epistemic interpretation would indeed require versions such as (1136) or (1137).

The causal nature of (1132) for both the root and epistemic reading may be nicely demonstrated by conjoining (1132) and (1137):

(1138) Das ist internationale Gepflogenheit, deshalb müsste/sollte er es eigentlich tun.

This complex sentence at the same time shows that the translator of (1132) did not in fact translate the SL sentence itself but its cause or reason—as if the SL speaker had said:

(1139) This is an international custom.

Furthermore (1132) is more specific than the original by virtue of expressing the modal source of *He should* in (1131). But here another caveat must be entered. The translator seems to have taken it for granted that the modal source is to be identified with a specific international habit. But who says it really is? Could there be no other motive for 'stopping by . . .' such as the great image the president had of himself, the advisability of the visit in view of the current political situation at the time of speaking, or a prior arrangement? These reasons for a visit are equally possible. So it seems that rendition (1132) was produced on the basis of guesswork—not a very sound basis of a rendition.

But whatever modal source might have been chosen, if it is stated as in (1132) the rendition becomes more overt regarding the elements of the modal situation that are mentioned.

Even so it indicates modality itself much more covertly than each of the two modals in (1137). In (1132) modals such as *müsste* or *sollte* as the literal equivalents of SHOULD remain behind the scene until inferred by the reader.

All these findings taken together reveal that (1132) after all tangibly deviates from its original (1131).

Summing up, explication of alleged implicit 'logical relations' undertaken by the translator can have its price in making overt modality covert, at the same time reducing the range of interpretive potentials in terms of the modal source and even the kind of modality intended.

In *not* containing the modal source and *not* suggesting a specific interpretation, (1131)—and likewise (1137)—have a certain charm of their own: Indeterminacy of modal source and oscillation between root and epistemic modality create an 'openness' of interpretation and reflect the noncommittal characteristic of diplomatic behavior. The puzzling rhetoric is even increased by the fact that, on the other hand, what is talked about is positive committal to a certain behavior!

So the very intention of the translator—building a bridge for the reader who may not be familiar with the world of international diplomacy—defeats its own purpose. Had the translator conformed to the structure of the original he or she would have rendered this diplomatic speech act more adequately.

The idea of facilitating understanding of the reader is laudable, but we believe the translator has a right to actually alter the SL text only if understanding would otherwise be completely blocked or misled, as could occur if nonstandard language were rendered by 'standard' means (see the previous subsection).

Our perspective can thus be captured by the following formula:

- SL alterations for the sake of enabling understanding, yes;
- SL alterations for the sake of facilitating understanding, no. Our veto accrues from the finding that, in rendition (1132), facilitating understanding fell short of our expectations in several respects. If it is not based on reliable knowledge, the translator had better abstain from it (unless expressly asked for it by the client, see Section 8.4).

And what if it is based on reliable knowledge? Suppose the translator were explicitly told that a certain text to be translated was produced by a seven-year-old child. As is well-known, children's understanding and reasoning differ from those of adults. So the information about the speaker's identity is relevant to an adequate understanding of the text (see Section 7.1.1). But suppose it is not contained explicitly in the text itself. Should the translator somehow add it to the TL version?

We would say that the cutter of the Gordian knot in this and similar cases is the client placing the order. It is up to him or her to decide whether the respective additional information should be taken into account and, if so, whether it should be written or spoken in a foreword or be integrated into the text itself; and the way the latter should be done is again a matter of the client's instructions.

7.4.3.3 Avoiding Redundancy

In Section 6.7 we discussed Kussmaul's (1986: 213 ff.) *maxim of the necessary degree of differentiation*. His idea was that information already expressed or implied in the cotext preceding an SL sentence need not be expressed again in the TL rendition of that sentence. The purpose of this principle was the intentional avoidance of redundancy. We argued that, if redundancy had been intended to be avoided by the SL speaker, he or she would have done it. If the speaker did not do it, why should the translator? This line of reasoning exactly corresponds to Friederich's (1990: 159) argument regarding a German rendition unnecessarily deviating from the English original: "Hätte aber [die englische SL-Sprecherin] nicht auch so etwas formulieren können wie im Deutschen . . . , wenn sie das *so* gewollt hätte? Sie hat es eben nicht gewollt . . ." (italics as in the original).

The same comment is appropriate for the strategy of facilitating understanding discussed in the previous subsection, and indeed for all intentional but strictly speaking unnecessary changes in the SL text made by the translator. Any additions, subtractions, or other modifications in the SL text are generally out of place.

Things are different, of course, if the translator is expressly asked by the client to make such changes (see the end of preceding subsection).

7.4.3.4 Being Faithful

In the introduction to this chapter we referred to the translator as "but another hearer." Although this is basically correct, the translator is nevertheless a special kind of hearer, one whose understanding the SL text is in view of translating it for others. What this unique role implies is described by Hatim and Mason (1990: 224) as follows:

> Now, each reading of a text is a unique act . . . , a process subject to the particular contextual constraints of the occasion, just as much as the production of the text is. Inevitably, a translated text reflects the translator's reading and this is yet another factor which defines the translator as a non-ordinary reader: whereas the ordinary reader can involve his or her own beliefs and values in the creative reading process, the translator has to be more guarded. Ideological nuances, cultural predispositions and so on in the source text have to be relayed untainted by the translator's own vision of reality.

In other words, the translator has to be faithful to the SL text. But we have to bear in mind that a text cannot be translated 'as such' (see Section 7.3): The TL rendition is expected by the client to conform to his or her wishes. If the SL text is inevitably to be translated relative to the client's wishes, how can there be 'mere' fidelity to the text itself or to the SL speaker's intentions? Seen this way, it seems to be necessary to expand the notion of the translator's fidelity to encompass also the client: The translator who conforms to the client's wishes can be said to be faithful or loyal.

But even the translator who is asked to be faithful just to the SL speaker's intentions must be guarded not to overshoot the mark. In an attempt to uncover the 'real' meaning of the SL text the translator must not go so far as to unearth hidden intentions of the speaker. To illustrate this point let us return once again to Sir Harold and his intention to finish his talk with his visitor (see Section 6.3.10.2). To convey this intention to the latter he says:

[881] . . . I mustn't keep you . . .

Uttering this sentence, his hidden intention might be to dismiss his visitor, so he might as well have said:

(1140) Away with you!/Be off!

Being a polite, diplomatic person, however, he prefers to express himself in a more distinguished way. Now the question arises of whether the translator has a right to render Sir Harold's 'real' intention, that is, to translate (1140) instead of (881), and to say thus

[883] Machen Sie, dass Sie rauskommen!

It may even be obvious to the SL hearer that the speaker, uttering (881), *means* (1140); but because the former sentence was uttered, the translator has to go by its characteristics and keep as an invariance factor its high degree of politeness. The rendition might be

[884] Jetzt will ich Sie aber nicht länger aufhalten.

So here the point of reference is the overt(ly expressed) intention of the SL speaker, not the covert one. And this is also the yardstick for the notion of translational fidelity: The translator has to go by what is overtly expressed (unless demanded otherwise). But this is no drawback to the possible implicatures of the SL utterance: (884) may pragmatically implicate (883) just as well as (881) may (1140)!

There is another reason why the translator in his or her quest for truth must be careful not to overdo it. Uttering (881), the SL speaker may not have in mind the covert intention (1140) at all. Sir Harold may in good earnest think in terms of his interlocutor's precious time, which he may feel he must not claim any longer. Choosing (883) as a rendition would in this case amount to be the result of overinterpretation. The same is true if (1131) is rendered as (1132) (see Section 7.4.3.2):

[1131] . . . He should.
[1132] Das ist internationale Gepflogenheit.

We have to ask, Who would *warrant true* the interpretations expressed by (883) and (1132)?

In all such cases of overinterpretation we find the limits of the translator legitimately being a 'translator-editor' (see Section 6.8.2). As suggested in Section 7.4.3.2., alterations in the SL text made for the sake of enabling understanding are the only justification for leaving the beaten track of standard renditions. Otherwise any translator could defend any rendition in the name of having found the allegedly 'ultimate' truth of the SL text.

The unwarrantableness of these two examples corroborates Hatim and Mason's postulates quoted at the beginning of this subsection. It also confirms the appropriateness of the *ten elements of good translation* set forth by Fuller (1984: 157–59); the first one on meaning (in international conference translating) says that good translation "attempts first and foremost to render the meaning of the original, the whole meaning and nothing but the meaning, as far as the inherent limitations of language will allow. It guards against the possible accusation that it merely paraphrases the sense; and it neither omits significant elements nor adds explanatory or other matter not included or very strongly implied in the original."

Now again consider our two examples in the light of these statements. Rendition (1132) *Das ist internationale Gepflogenheit* represents added explanatory matter, while (883) *Machen Sie, dass Sie rauskommen!* is not necessarily very strongly implied in the original.

So in addition to fidelity to any factors preset by the client, what counts in translation is the SL text as conceived by its author. This point is important because a TL rendition not properly reflecting the SL author's intention might be rejected on the basis of the TL hearer falsely thinking: "What? This is what the author said?" So the translator has a great responsibility towards the SL speaker or author, and this is why "he must have the author's intent firmly in mind as he translates. The translator should read the source text several times asking himself, 'What was the intent of the author as he wrote this particular text? What information does he want to communicate, what mood, and what response did he expect from the readers?' A translator who is oblivious to such questions will not be able to produce a faithful translation" (Larson 1984: 421 f.).

So being faithful is geared toward representing the SL author properly; this in turn is geared toward presentation to the TL hearer: "The goal of the translator is to communicate to the receptor audience the same information and the same mood as was conveyed by the original document to the original audience" (Larson 1984: 421). This takes us to the consideration of the next essential factor of the translation situation: the TL hearer.

7.5 THE TL HEARER

Nord (1991: 51) points out that "in almost all approaches to translation-relevant text analysis, the recipient is considered to be a very important, if not the most important, factor." It will not do, however, to make global reference to 'the' TL hearer(s) or reader(s); we have to further ask: "Which factors characterize the 'average readers' of the target text . . .?" (Florin 1993: 127). They include level of education, age group, occupation, previous knowledge of the subject, degree of bilingualism, and language attitudes. Larson (1987: 69–72) deals with all of these under the heading "Factors which Affect the Translation Project."

Rather than go into these characteristics in detail here, we will expand on a point already touched upon—deference to the TL hearer. In Section 3.3.2 we said that, when permission is granted, MAY may be used in English, but DÜRFEN, otherwise corresponding to MAY in terms of formality, must not be used:

[439] Visitors may ascend the tower for 50p this summer.
[440] !Besucher dürfen den Turm diesen Sommer für 50p besteigen.
[441] Besucher können den Turm diesen Sommer für 50p besteigen.

The reason why DÜRFEN is out of place was said to be the connotation of speaker authority associated with it.

Let us try to find out why English does not have a comparable restriction on MAY, which is, after all, used to grant permission and might be assumed to evoke similar connotations in the hearer.

One point distinguishing MAY from DÜRFEN is its ability to express root possibility, as in

[187] Cader Idris, however, may be climbed from other points on this tour.
(1141) !Cader Idris darf jedoch von anderen Punkten dieser Tour aus bestiegen werden.
[189] Cader Idris kann jedoch von anderen Punkten dieser Tour aus bestiegen werden.

Sentence (1141) has not been marked as ungrammatical because it could be used to express permission (evoking said connotation); it could, however, not be used at all to express root possibility as does MAY. Now root possibility does not carry any implications of authority associated with permission. So if MAY is used in the sense of root possibility (as in (187)), this association is excluded. Drawing upon our knowledge of *reflected meaning* (see Section 3.3.4), we may hypothesize that this meaning 'rubs off' on the permission use of MAY and makes it appear much less authoritarian or not authoritarian at all.

One semantic justification of this neutralization of associations may be said to be that *permitting* means "making possible," so the result of giving permission is a certain action being possible—a modal state devoid of associations of authority. DÜRFEN, on the other hand, has no root possibility meaning that could neutralize its connotation. This is why it has to be replaced by KÖNNEN if permission is to be expressed to hearers who might be offended by an authoritarian tone.

This is the case if the hearer is addressed individually (435) or as a member of a certain group (441), and even if there is no specific reference to that person, as in (1142) addressed to prospective participants of a contest:

[435] Wenn der gewünschte Platz ausverkauft ist, können Sie nach Belieben umdisponieren.
[441] Besucher können den Turm diesen Sommer für 50p besteigen.
(1142) Teilnehmen kann jeder, ausgenommen Mitarbeiter des Verlages M. & H. Schaper sowie deren Angehörige. (*Gesund leben*, no. 6, 1994: 16)

However, if the subject is not the hearer—as is the case in passive constructions—the 'distance' from the speaker is felt to be great enough to warrant use of DÜRFEN; for example,

(1143) Kinder dürfen mitgebracht werden.

Another exception occurs if the hearers are children for whom overt display of authority may not be considered disadvantageous:

(1144) Du darfst jetzt gehen.
[193] Ihr dürft jetzt gehen.

This fact corroborates inclusion of age group as a translation factor relating to the hearer.

The factor *previous knowledge of the subject* on the part of the TL hearer was discussed in Section 7.3 with reference to the translation of sentence (1111).

7.6 TRANSLATION DIRECTION

Some factors put the translator in a different working situation as the translation direction changes; we refer to them as *unidirectional change factors*. In contrast, *bidirectional invariance factors* are constant under a change of translation direction. We will briefly illustrate both kinds of direction factors, starting with the latter one.

7.6.1 Bidirectional Invariance Factors

Let us consider two formal examples of these factors that are identical in SL and TL.

- Linkage of a modal is always to the bare infinitive of a full verb; that is, one lacking TO/ZU (see Section 2.3). This means that for each of the two translation directions the rendition will show a modal plus a bare infinitive.
- Verbal nouns can be based on all the German modals but not on all the English ones; for example, *das Können/*the can(ing)*, see Section 6.3.6. Nonetheless, English nouns are used for a rendition, albeit nonverbal ones such as *the skill* for *das Können*, *the intention* for *das Wollen*, and so forth. Similarly, German nominal forms of the modals lacking the plural, *musts* can be rendered by a German nonverbal noun: *Erfordernisse*. Third, in the singular there are even two modal-based nouns corresponding to each other: *a must—ein Muss*. What is common to all three kinds of correspondence is that in each case SL nominal forms are rendered as TL nomi-

nal forms, whatever the translation direction. This feature can therefore be looked upon as a bidirectional invariance factor.

7.6.2 Unidirectional Change Factors

These occur when elements in a certain category give rise to changes that are different for each translation direction. In the second of the two examples just given the morphological source of nominal expressions was such a factor. Let us review three more.

Remember the richness of forms of the German modals in contrast to the English ones (see Section 2.1), such as

[19] CAN → *kann, kannst, können, könnt, könne, könnest, könnet.*

Of course, also here we find an invariance factor, namely, the word class *modal verb*; but what is of special importance is the big contrast in the number of forms, which thus becomes a change factor. It plays a different role for each translation direction, however:

- For translation into German it is a divergence factor,
- for translation into English it is a convergence factor.

This phenomenon of different roles played by different translation directions also exists in the field of pragmatics. As discussed in Section 4.3.3, implicativeness entails the use of a suppletive for COULD, such as *was able to*. Because its equivalent KÖNNEN is not subject to such a restriction, divergence of forms occurs when moving into English, while convergence is found in the opposite translation direction.

As regards unilingual semantico-syntactic restrictions, we found that the epistemic use of CAN and MAY is bound to specific modes of syntactic mood: In interrogative sentences only CAN is possible, in affirmative statements only MAY (see Section 3.1.2, Figure 3.7). Again KÖNNEN is more flexible in that it can invariably be used in each construction. Therefore, a change in translation direction has the same consequences as those just sketched for pragmatics.

8. FACTORS IN TRANSLATION THEORY

One of the tasks of a scientific translation theory is "to explain the phenomenon of translation" (Delisle 1988: 32, 34). Explaining translation amounts to specifying the causal factors of renditions because "the basic function of translation factors is to bring about renditions" (Section 1.1.2). In systematizing translation factors in Chapters 2–7 we pursued the stated objective of translation theorists "to make systematic what is most general in the work of the translator, to extract from it those elements that lend themselves to analysis" (Etkind 1967: 23, quoted by Delisle 1988: 34 f.)

Up to this point we have dealt with various factors largely one by one.[51] The idea was to focus on each factor individually to demonstrate its relevance as a translation factor. This isolation of factors, even though expedient for an introductory survey, does not, however, represent the translation situation as it is in practice. Any text to be translated shows syntactic, semantic, as well as pragmatic factors of all kinds; it belongs to a specific text class, is embedded in a situation, and expresses a certain culture; its translation is determined by the intentions of the speaker, the client, the competence and intentions of the translator, and the characteristics of the TL recipient—or, as Neubert and Shreve (1992: 45) put it: "Linguistic system, pragmatic constraints, world knowledge, and meaning systems all converge in the act of translation. Translation is a synthetic process in which the translator dynamically matches semantic, syntactic, textual, and pragmatic fields to create a unitary whole, the L_2 [TL] text." In short, a realistic theory of *translating by factors* requires a multifactor approach involving whole sets of factors to be taken into account simultaneously (see Section 8.1).

This immediately raises the question about the relationship between different factors in a set and between different factor sets. Remember that in Section 4.6 it was shown that cultural norms can be a revision factor overruling purely linguistic equivalents. This corroborates Toury's tenet that linguistic rules and laws "are merely one set of factors operating on the translation process"; he postulates "a new set of factors which may be more powerful than other factors. The eventual goal of Toury's theory is to establish a hierarchy of interrelated factors (constraints) which determine (govern) the translation product" (Gentzler 1993: 129 f.). The notions of factor hierarchy and factor entailment will be dealt with in Section 8.2.

Having established the interrelatedness of certain factors it next comes to ask which SL and TL factors are actually relevant for translating (Section 8.3).

Another objective of translation theorists is "to develop rules and recipes for translators" (Delisle 1988: 34). This normative aspect leads to the consideration of translation principles (Section 8.4).

Other topics central to translation theory are the notion of equivalence (Section 8.5) and the distinction between translation and adaptation (Section 8.6). In our concluding section (8.7) we will argue for focusing on integrative factor sets rather than marking off translation from adaptation.

8.1 SETS OF FACTORS

In the introduction we said that translating by factors requires a multifactor approach involving whole sets of factors to be taken into account simultaneously. But what does *take into account* mean?

The simplest answer would be that all factors of the SL text would have to reappear in the TL text. If translation factors are compared to objects and the two languages involved to the colors red and green, this reappearance would amount to repainting all red objects green.

Now some might object that no two languages are congruent in structure, so the idea of factors being objects just appearing in a guise different in SL from TL but otherwise being identical is at least doubtful. To examine this claim let us focus on the factors *form* and *meaning* in the following SL-TL sentences.

[48] Er muss kommen können.
(1145) *He must come can.
[47] He must be able to come.

'Rendition' (1145) would be a perfect formal and semantic equivalent of (48). All the German word forms, their meanings, as well as syntax would miraculously have been 'turned into English'—were it not for its ungrammaticality, for which there are two obvious reasons:

- Since English modals lack an infinitive, a suppletive form is obligatory. Hence one of the modals 'gets lost' in TL.
- In contrast to German, English requires the 'logical' sequence of verbal elements, that is, immediate prepositioning of elements modifying other elements (*must* modifies *be able to*, which in turn modifies *to come*). Thus, the formal factor of 'illogical syntax' is also missing in TL.

Even this simple example has shown that it can by no means be taken for granted that *all* SL factors are kept on their way to the TL, not all of them can be 'taken into account,' as we put it earlier. In our previous example, for instance, the translator cannot help abandoning the factor of syntactic form if the task is to produce a TL sentence that is grammatical. So syntax in terms of word order differs in the two languages. But note that active voice as such is an invariance factor, because both (47) and (48) are grammatical active sentences. The same is true of passive voice in (445) and (447):

[445] The same point can be made about borrowing as was made about analogy . . . (Lyons 1981: 206)
[447] Über Entlehnung kann dasselbe gesagt werden wie über Analogie . . .
[446] Über Entlehnung lässt sich dasselbe sagen wie über Analogie . . . (Lyons 1992: 189)

As is previously the case with (47), (447) differs from the original in terms of word order (*. . . kann . . . werden . . . gesagt . . .* would be the congruent but again ungrammatical rendition). In each case this is due to obligatory change factors. So that aspect of syntax differs. Another one, however, does not. Both (445) and (447) show the syntactic structure of passive voice (albeit each in its unilingual way). To this extent the factor of form *is* invariant. Because meaning is also being preserved, we can say that in this sentence pair both factors of form and meaning are (largely) identical, (447) thus being an apparently satisfactory solution.

But in the published German version (445) was rendered by (446). In terms of conceptual meaning this sentence is practically identical to (447). As regards stylistic meaning, however, two factors prompted the translators to prefer (446) over (447): the "natural tendency for variation of expression," and the fact that reflexive LASSEN "sounds a bit more elaborate" than the modal verb construction (see Section 3.3.3).

So the predominance of elevated stylistic meaning has an effect on form. In (446) the passive voice is replaced by a reflexive construction. This is why a translator who has been instructed to create a rendition in which syntax is retained to the largest possible extent cannot use (446). The overall translation situation described can thus be depicted as in Figure 8.1.

This figure actually represents two partially intersecting translation situ-

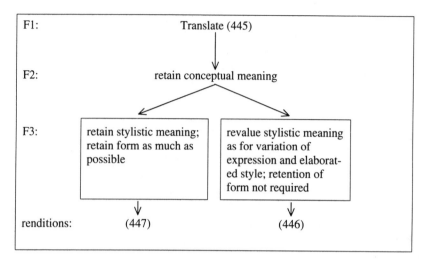

FIGURE 8.1.
The Translation Situation of Sentence (445)

ations, one for instructions leading to (446), and one for those leading to (447). This means that Figure 8.1 in its entirety is relevant only to a translator who is not given one of the alternative sets of instructions and may therefore wish to balance one alternative against the other.

The general principle to be inferred from the example is this: The more detailed instructions a translator is given, the less need there will be to compare possible renditions. This is why bifurcation models of the translation process such as that in Figure 8.1 are in fact unnecessary if the translator has clear-cut instructions. In this case factors may be presented as a set, for instance in the following way: "Please translate sentence (445). Its conceptual and stylistic meaning should be maintained, and also its form as much as possible." Usually such instructions will pertain not just to an individual sentence but to an entire text to ensure a homogeneous rendition. Hence the order for the translation of the book by Lyons (1981) where (445) is contained might have been as follows: "In translating the book conceptual meaning should, of course, be retained. But it would be good to follow the German tendency to avoid repetition of expressions. So do not hesitate to make use of linguistic variation. And since the book is directed to educated readers, it would be appropriate to translate it in an elevated style."

Whether such a set of factors is preset by the client or by the translator, its definiteness will relieve the translator of continually vacillating between partially alternative renditions. This presents a clear picture of the benefits of working on the basis of a set of factors as a whole, of pursuing a holistic multifactor approach.

Even though translating has repeatedly been referred to as a decision process by various authors, it will be obvious by now that the number of genuine decisions to be made in translating is inversely proportional to the number of factors given; the greater is the number of preset factors, the smaller the number of necessary decisions to be made by the translator. This situation is illustrated in Figure 8.2.

Now let us verify this principle with reference to sentence (445). Is the factor set *invariance of conceptual and stylistic meaning, and largest possible invariance of form* really sufficient for unambiguously arriving at rendition (447)? Let us see if other German sentences are not also eligible for a rendition on this basis. Here is the first candidate:

(1146) Dasselbe kann über Entlehnung gesagt werden wie das, was über Analogie gesagt wurde . . .

Remember that the instruction was to retain the factor of form as much as possible. Source sentence (445) contains an elliptical relative clause (. . . *as* [*that which*] *was made* . . .). This clause is explicated in the TL version (1146). Because in German such ellipsis is not possible, (1146) represents the closest syntactic equivalent of this aspect of (445) discussed so far. Also its syntax in terms of subject-predicate structure is more similar to (445) than that of (446) and (447): *Dasselbe* syntactically corresponds to *The same point.* This formal factor is connected with a semantic one. In contrast to the last two sentences, (1146) also corresponds to (445) as regards a type of meaning neglected so far, thematic meaning (see Section 3.3.6), as conveyed by the order of its noun phrases. On the other hand, by virtue of its partial repetition of words (*gesagt werden/gesagt wurde*), its style is clumsy; conventions are different in English in this respect (*can be made/as was made* is perfectly acceptable).

For another possible rendition of (445) the relative clause in (1146)

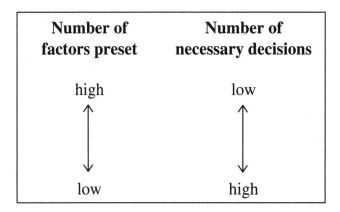

FIGURE 8.2.
Relationship of the Numbers of Factors and Decisions in Translating

could be deleted entirely except for its prepositional phrase, giving us a structure identical to that of (446) and (447) in this respect:

(1147) Dasselbe kann über Entlehnung gesagt werden wie über Analogie
    . . .

Compared to (1146), the ellipsis here increases syntactic deviation from the original but at the same time improves stylistic meaning by avoidance of the aforementioned repetition. Sentence (1147) does not, however, reflect that good style of (447) or even (446) because, like (1146), it starts with new information or the rheme. It is true that in this respect it is congruent with the English original; but again conventions in the two languages differ, especially in cases such as the one under consideration where the rheme is the first point of reference within a comparative construction. Table 8.1 lists the characteristics of the four renditions of sentence (445) discussed here.

Let us now resume our initial question of whether sentence (447) is really the only rendition possible of (445), given the factor set to be taken into account. Table 8.1 shows that the requirement of invariant conceptual meaning is fulfilled by all four German sentences; but only (447) is invariant as regards stylistic meaning. Yet also the requirement of invariant form is to be considered. This has at least two aspects to it. As regards voice, all German sentences except for (446) show passive voice, but only (1146) and (1147) have an invariant subject-predicate structure.

Summing up, whereas in terms of stylistic meaning (447) is indeed the winner, formal aspects are most similarly represented by (1146) and (1147). Moreover only these latter sentences are also invariant as regards thematic

Renditions / Factors	(446)	(447)	(1146)	(1147)
1. Meaning				
1.1 Thematic	changed	changed	invariant	invariant
1.2 Conceptual	invariant	invariant	invariant	invariant
1.3 Stylistic	changed (more elaborate)	invariant	changed (clumsy)	changed (less elaborate)
2. Form				
2.1 Elliptical relative clause	changed	changed	slightly changed	changed
2.2 Subject-predicate structure	changed	changed	invariant	invariant
2.3 Syntax, voice	changed (reflexive)	invariant (passive)	invariant (passive)	invariant (passive)

TABLE 8.1.
Factor Analysis of Four German Renditions of Sentence (445)

meaning. But, because invariance of stylistic meaning was expressly demanded, whereas only the largest *possible* invariance of form was called for, this factor set suggests rendering (445) by (447).

This finding as well as all the others summed up in Table 8.1 are remarkable for several reasons. First, they demonstrate that the notion of equivalence, defined in terms of invariance, is a quantitative notion in that it can refer to different numbers of invariance factors. In (446) only one factor, namely, conceptual meaning, is equivalent to those of (445); in (447) three factors are equivalent; and in (1146) and (1147) there are as many as four. Second, our comparison of all these sentences in terms of their correspondence to a particular factor set demanded by the client has just shown that *instead of the largest number of invariance factors being decisive for selecting a particular rendition, it is compliance with the client's wishes that counts.*

This principle can also be shown to be true with reference to the printed translation of (445), where (446) was taken as a rendition. This was done even though this is the German sentence that shows least equivalence in terms of the number of invariance factors. But it conforms to the demand "to translate . . . in an elevated style." It was shown previously that of all the sentences compared, sentence (446) is indeed the one meeting this requirement best. But it remains to be examined whether this is tenable with reference to the factor of conventions of the text class in question and whether there is no further relevant translation factor.

Sentence (445) is contained in Lyons (1981), which is a textbook in linguistics. Remember that authors of English and German texts from the humanities pursue different lines of writing (see Section 6.8.1). In English, statements are preferably made by way of passive constructions, whereas for statements of modality in German, stylistic choices are between *wir* constructions containing modals and other expressions such as modal adjectives in *−bar* in passive constructions, as well as reflexive LASSEN and modal infinitives:

(1148) Über Entlehnung können wir dasselbe sagen wie über Analogie . . .

(1149) Über Entlehnung ist dasselbe *sagbar/!feststellbar wie über Analogie . . .

(1150) Über Entlehnung ist dasselbe zu sagen wie über Analogie . . .

The first adjective in (1149) is to be rejected because the suffix *−bar* does not go together well with the stem *sag−*; use of the alternative expression *feststellbar* leads to an undesirable ambiguity (*can be said* vs. *can be discovered/found*). A different kind of ambiguity is created by the modal infinitive in (1150), one between permission and necessity (*können sagen* vs. *müssen sagen*). This type of construction ranks last in Kussmaul's frequency list anyway.

So what remain as serious alternatives are the modal-verb construction

(1148) and the one with reflexive LASSEN, sentence (446). According to Kussmaul's statistics, the frequency of the former kind of construction is much higher than that of the latter one (see Section 6.8.1). Why then was (446) preferred by the translator?

It seems that consideration of text-class conventions as such will not lead us any further. What will help is Kussmaul's (1986: 209) observation that a text is ultimately conditioned by culture. Kussmaul (1978: 56 f.) himself suggests relating his findings about communicative conventions in English and German scientific treatises (see Section 6.8.1) to "the style of scientific speaking and writing as it is generally practiced in the two cultural areas, that is, to juxtapose them within a sociocultural frame of reference" (our translation). He mentions the personal style of English lectures and treatises as opposed to 'bald' and 'academic' German lectures and concludes that, for the presentation of scientific research results, there appear to exist quite different habits and traditions in England and Germany.

Whereas Kussmaul refers to cultural conventions in relation to certain academic text classes, we would like to extend his reflections to cultural aspects of the two languages in general. In our section on culture (4.6), we quoted Snell-Hornby's finding that on English public signs "prohibition can be expressed by everyday modal verbs" (1984: 209) whereas German signs feature more 'sophisticated' expressions such as *verboten* that are more symptomatic of official language.

Generalizing from these observations, we would maintain that the use of 'simple' language (at least as far as modality as expressed by the modals is concerned) is more widespread in English than in German. In German, texts with a *public* readership—be it public signs or publications, especially those geared toward a more pretentious readership—tend to contain more elaborate formulations for the expression of modality. Hence the modal verb in (445) and the choice of the stylistically more sophisticated LASSEN construction in (446).

Note that the factor of cultural conventions thus found to be relevant was not expressly contained in the factor set suggested for translating Lyons's (1981) book; but the competent translator will be aware of its inevitability and hence take it into account.

So in the case of rendition (445) → (446) equivalence holds on the level of culture, which factor may be said to override all other factors. This superiority of one factor suggests that factors in a set do not just coexist but enter asymmetric relationships of one dominating the other. This phenomenon will be focused on in the next section.

8.2 RELATIONSHIPS BETWEEN FACTORS

Factors are taken as a set—this formula has just been shown to be a handy key to TL renditions. The concept of a factor set has been presented as the sum of factors the combination of which, if specific enough, is so unique as to lead to a unique TL rendition. For instance, given the factors *sentence (445)* and *invariance of conceptual and stylistic meaning,* rendition (447) will naturally follow. Let us now turn to a consideration of the internal structure of a factor set and see if there is any relationship among its factors as elements.

In a very basic sense it may be said that actually *all* the factors in a set are related to one another because their unique combination determines a particular rendition. So the very notion of a set acts as a unifying bond for its factors.

On a second level of consideration we might ask if there are also correlations between individual factors contained in a set. This line of investigation will lead us to two kinds of relationships between factors: entailment and hierarchy.

8.2.1 Factor Entailment

To explore this relationship between two factors let us reconsider sentence (445) and two of its possible renditions:

[445] The same point can be made about borrowing as was made about analogy . . . (Lyons 1981: 206)
[447] Über Entlehnung kann dasselbe gesagt werden wie über Analogie . . .
[446] Über Entlehnung lässt sich dasselbe sagen wie über Analogie . . . (Lyons 1992: 189)

Sentence (447) formally corresponds to the original (445) in terms of the passive voice. Now the translator whose task is to attach importance to an elevated style may use sentence (446) fulfilling this requirement. This step taken cannot be seen in isolation, however, because "the predominance of elevated stylistic meaning has an effect on form. In (446) the passive voice is replaced by a reflexive construction" (Section 8.1). So improving style seems to entail a change in voice. But other renditions of (445) expressing an elevated style do not, like (446), involve a reflexive LASSEN construction. The following sentence, for instance, contains a modal in a passive voice construction similar to (447):

(1151) Über Entlehnung kann dieselbe Aussage getroffen werden wie über Analogie . . .

Does this mean that, considered in a broader framework, the assumed correlation of the factors of form and style is not inevitable?

Let us approach this question by reversing the order of factors. Suppose a translator were to render (445) by means of a reflexive LASSEN construction. Coming up with (446) he or she inevitably produces a stylistically improved rendition. But again, there are also other possible versions with LASSEN:

(1152) Es lässt sich über Entlehnung dasselbe sagen wie über Analogie . . .
(1153) Es lässt sich dasselbe über Entlehnung sagen wie über Analogie . . .

Due to their marked syntax, which deviates from that of (445), these sentences are stylistically inferior to (446). Unless this additional formal factor is expressly intended to be included in the factor set, these renditions will not be chosen anyway. Therefore, it seems to be pretty safe to say that LASSEN constructions corresponding to our factor set do entail a more elevated style.

A similar form-style correlation can be found in the following sentence:

[1146] Dasselbe kann über Entlehnung gesagt werden wie das, was über Analogie gesagt wurde . . .

Due to nonellipsis of the relative clause in this sentence, that is, "by virtue of its partial repetition of words (*gesagt werden*/*gesagt wurde*), its style is clumsy" (Section 8.1).

So, in both cases discussed, a particular level of style is entailed by a specific formal value; in more general terms, one factor entails another one.

But then what about our unfinished comparison between (446) and (1151)? Elevated style in the latter sentence was found *not* to entail a change of voice. This is certainly true, but again the tacit assumption that German tends to avoid 'everyday modal verbs' in public texts (see Section 4.6 and final part of 8.1) suggests going for rendition (446), which does entail a change in voice. Only if this 'culture factor' were neglected would (1151) be acceptable as a rendition of (445), which indeed would not involve factor entailment in the sense discussed.

8.2.2 Factor Hierarchy

The concept of entailment just dealt with denotes the nonarbitrary order of two factors. As soon as more than two factors come into play, repeated entailment (F1 → F2 → F3 . . .) may be assumed, giving rise to a factor hierarchy.

To fathom this possibility out, let us return to Figures 3.2–3.7, 3.9–3.14, 3.17 and 3.19, all of which highlighted sequences of factors. Their overall purpose was that of flowcharts for arriving at correct renditions. These were reached after going through a series of steps, following factors that were set up as signposts at a number of bifurcations of the translation paths. Although created on the basis of specific English and German sentences, the charts were designed to be utilized for any SL sentence containing the modal mentioned as their first factor, F1, namely, SL form(s), and conforming to all the other factors, that is, F2 and so on.

To link our more recent ideas to those expressed in Chapter 3 let us translate CAN in (445)

[445] The same point can be made about borrowing as was made
    about analogy . . . (Lyons 1981: 206)

on the basis of Figure 3.13 (reproduced for convenience on p. 284).

Under F1 we find the relevant modal: CAN. F2 is devoted to SL syntax and negation; sentence (445) belongs to the first category, *affirmative statements*. The arrow pointing from there to "root meaning" under F3 indicates a factor entailment between these two categories of syntax and semantics. As discussed in greater detail in Section 3.1.3, the "justification for organizing factors this way is that sentence mood and negation actually *determine* the root meaning . . ." Next we have to find out which subkind of root modality is intended. The co(n)text of CAN in (445) is most closely related to the following set of features listed under F4:

- no necessary association with an agentive subject function;
- unmarked with respect to human restriction;
- possibility not determined by inherent properties of the subject.

These features are identification factors for "root possibility" listed under F5. A final step takes us to the corresponding TL rendition KÖNNEN as F7.

We may now ask how all this relates to Figure 8.1, which is, after all, a flowchart for sentence (445) under consideration, albeit a much smaller one.

F1 in Figure 8.1 is not merely a modal as in Figure 3.13 but the whole sentence (445). F2 is the instruction *retain conceptual meaning*. As we have just ascertained when we arrived at F5 of Figure 3.13, CAN in (445) has the meaning of root possibility. Now instead of immediately pointing the way toward just one corresponding rendition, as does F5 in Figure 3.13, F3 in Figure 8.1 offers some further criteria, which relate to stylistic meaning and to form. Note that the single German rendition KÖNNEN as suggested by Figure 3.13 is only one of two possible renditions supplied by Figure 8.1, the other one being a LASSEN construction; namely, sentence (446).

The net result of this juxtaposition of the two flowcharts is the finding that Figure 8.1 comes in where Figure 3.13 ends; that is, F2 and F3 of Figure 8.1 could be added as two final translation factors to Figure 3.13. This finding should come as no surprise. A closer look at both charts reveals that Figure 3.13 contains a series of SL factors, whereas Figure 8.1 offers some TL factors. Of course, the translator has to know both kinds of factors to be able to translate the sentence. Figure 3.13 gives all sorts of identification factors for finding out the different conceptual meanings of the SL modal CAN in different contexts. Once SL identification is achieved, Figure 8.1

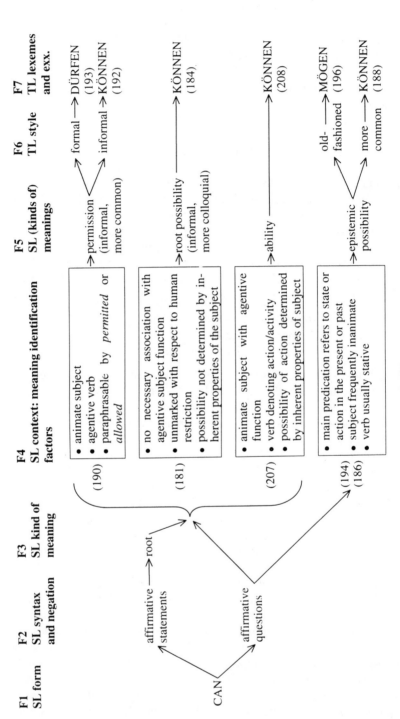

FIGURE 3.13.
German Renditions of CAN (5)

takes over and tells the translator some formal and semantic factors determining two renditions of one of these meanings ("root possibility") in TL. This shows that both figures complement each other and are required for a more comprehensive survey of translation factors in the two languages.

Let us now return to our initial question about the possibility of factor hierarchy. What we find at first glance in the originally cited figures is just a numbered series of factors. A hierarchy, however, is more than a mere numerical ordering; it is defined as "an organization of . . . things arranged into *higher or lower* ranks, classes or grades" (*The World Book Dictionary* 1992: 998; italics ours). Where in our charts do we find this aspect of asymmetry and irreversibility of factors, of one factor ranking higher than another one, that is, determining it?

An obvious example of this kind of relation is that between F2 and F3 in Figure 3.13. Here sentence mood and negation actually *determine* that CAN has root meaning (see earlier). Such a unilateral implication (of one factor by another one) was referred to as *factor entailment*. We assumed that repeated instances of factor entailment give rise to a factor hierarchy. This would require that the entailment between F2 and F3 extend to *all* the instances of factor linkage found in (the combination of) Figures 3.13 and 8.1. The important question to be asked is whether the order of each step toward the subsequent factors in these charts is indeed a necessary, irreversible one. To find the answer let us go through the factor links in Figure 3.13 one by one.

F1 and F2 connect CAN with categories of syntax and negation; namely, affirmative statements and affirmative questions. It is a truism that CAN must of necessity appear in a sentence showing some kind of syntactic mood and some value of negation, therefore the step from F1 to F2 is necessary. As repeatedly mentioned, step F2–F3 from affirmative statements to root meaning is one of entailment. It would therefore make no sense to place F3 before F2. This means that, after all, the entire factor sequence F1–F2–F3 is an organic whole, one whose sequence it would be unwise to change. Note also that it would make no sense to have CAN itself as F2 or F3 instead of F1 because the question of how to translate this modal was the motivating force for setting up this translation chart in the first place. So the initial position of CAN is indeed very purposeful.

Because affirmative questions under F2 do not by themselves entail a specific meaning of CAN, as do affirmative statements, the chart user is immediately led on to F4. Here one finds contextual features grouped in sets, each of which is correlated with a specific subkind of root modality or with epistemic modality. These feature sets serve as identification factors for the (kinds of) meanings listed under F5, so it would be absurd to permute F4 and F5. Similarly, it would be futile to put them before F3 because these meanings can be determined only on the basis of (major) kinds of modality having been identified before. Factor F6, that of style, refers only to "permission" in Figure 3.13. It features two possibilities, which make sense only with prior reference to the notion of permission, because this meaning is expressed in a formal or an informal way. Therefore, this factor also seems to be well placed.

In our discussion up to this point we have found different reasons for keeping the factor sequence in Figure 3.13 in the arrangement proposed. One of them is entailment, which holds between two items under F2 and F3. It also holds between all the feature sets under F4 and the corresponding (kinds of) meanings under F5. Its symbol is the single arrow originating in each set of F4, and in affirmative statements under F2. All the other, 'nonentailment' connections between factors show more than one arrow directed toward factor categories to their right. Here an unconditional one-to-one correlation of entailment between factors does not exist; hence the bifurcation in these cases.

Even though the last kind of factor correlation cannot be referred to as *entailment*, its order of factors was repeatedly shown to be reasonable nonetheless. This qualifies their structure as another nonarbitrary, irreversible positioning of factors. So the overall picture emerging is indeed that of a logical series of factors at different levels within a factor hierarchy.

As already observed, continuation of Figure 3.13 by Figure 8.1 slightly modifies the final structure of renditions in the previous figure: Due to additional differentiating factors for "root possibility" provided by Figure 8.1, the alleged unitary rendition of KÖNNEN in Figure 3.13 is expanded by the alternative of LASSEN. But this does not invalidate the principle of factor hierarchy: The factors of style and form determining each of the two renditions in question are meaningful only in the light of prior reference to the notion of root possibility (F2). This is evident from the fact that the LASSEN construction would not necessarily be a possible rendition for a different meaning of CAN; compare the possibility of rendering (445) as (447) *and* (446) with the impossibility of translating CAN in the sense of "permission" by means of LASSEN:

(1154) The tower may be ascended for 50p.
(1155) Der Turm kann für 50p bestiegen werden.
(1156) *Der Turm lässt sich für 50p besteigen.

8.3 IDENTITY OF FACTORS

We have just detected a hierarchy of all the factors determining the move from an SL modal to its TL renditions. We found that the order of factors listed in Figures 3.13 and 8.1, our points of reference, is indeed a purposeful one. Having established the nature of these factor connections we will now turn to the topic of factor identity. Our question is this: Why should it be necessary for translation charts such as Figures 3.13 and 8.1 to contain just those factors decided upon by us? Could there not be others that, to the same extent, would build upon one another and finally lead to TL renditions? We will first consider SL factors, then TL factors.

8.3.1 Identity of SL Factors

On closer inspection, F2, F3, and F4 in Figure 3.13 constitute a series of identification factors for the possible meanings of F1, which is the modal CAN. Knowledge of the meaning intended for a modal in a given case is essential, because different meanings may lead to different renditions (see Sections 3.1.1 and 3.1.2).

In Section 3.1.3 we listed identification factors for meanings that Coates (1983) discovered on the basis of empirical research. But in Section 3.1.4.1 we pointed out that not all such factors invariably co-occur with a specific meaning of a modal; different factors have varying degrees of strength so that "not all of the identification factors are *definite* determinants." Take, for instance, the third feature set under F4, which indicates "ability" under F5. The first feature listed there is *animate subject with agentive function*; yet 2 percent of the Survey sample and as much as 23 percent of the Lancaster sample have an inanimate subject (Coates 1983: 91). So the features given under F4 can at best be referred to as the most typical identification factors for the various meanings of CAN (see Section 3.3.8). Being the *most* typical factors, however, makes them (and not any others) the most reliable identification factors. This answers the question about optimum identity of SL factors.

Also it must not be forgotten that utterances with modals can show ambiguity, gradience, or merger (see Sections 3.1.4.2 and those that follow; 4.1.4.2 and those that follow). This makes the application of identification factors for meanings or illocutions less imperative than in the determinate cases. With merger, for instance, identification factors for root and epistemic meaning are unnecessary, provided there is a unitary rendition for both of them in TL to allow for the same phenomenon of merger.

In the introduction to this subsection we raised the question of whether any other factors could be organized hierarchically. Up to now we have restricted our attention to Figure 3.13. It should be clear, though, that this chart represents merely some syntactico-semantic factors for identifying several meanings of CAN. Remember that, in the introduction to this chapter, we said that any text to be translated has syntactic, semantic, as well as pragmatic factors of all kinds. Indeed all the factors and subfactors dealt with in this book—and many more—can come to mold the interpretation of an SL unit and its rendition.

We also said that all the factors involved need to be taken into account simultaneously. When we say *simultaneously* we do not exclude the possibility of all these factors being organized hierarchically. But for the SL hearer and for the translator it is not so much a matter of these factors being organized 'as such,' it is more a matter of approaching comprehension of them in an organized way. There emerges the picture of a hearer-related hierarchy, one that is suitable for an economic understanding of the relevant factors. The basic principle of interpretation can be assumed to be the tendency to find these factors in the minimum number of steps. This means that the clearest and most important identification factors should come first. This principle was applied in Figure 3.13 when F2, syntax and negation, was given top ranking because in one specific item in this category, affirmative statements, this enables us to know *immediately* that CAN can have only root meaning. The logical sequence of factors in Figure 3.13 as explained in Section 8.2.2 in fact reveals that all these steps conform to the principle of economic identification of relevant factors. What remains to be done is to incorporate into the chart any other factors that may be relevant to the understanding of a modal in various contexts. Where should we start?

The most basic point of reference seems to be that element which is all-pervasive and hence all-determining. It is traced by Kussmaul (1986: 209), who observes that a text passage is to be interpreted with reference to the whole text, which itself is part of a situation, which in turn is determined by culture. So culture is considered to be the most general SL factor at the top of a hierarchy of interpretation factors. What does this mean in practice? Suppose an SL speaker reports on a prohibition that only exists in the SL culture, for instance, by speaking about railway journeys in India as follows:

[748] Passengers must not travel on the roof.

The dominance of the culture factor means that no factor other than culture will help to explain the nature of the prohibition stated and thus enable full understanding of sentence (748). Note, however, that the negative modal form *must not* here is the same *must not* also used for prohibitions reported to be expressed in other cultures, for instance British or American. It is true that the way of prohibiting may itself be culture specific, as can be seen from the public sign at Old Delhi railway station (see Section 4.6):

[746] Passengers are kindly requested not to travel on the roof.

But this cannot distract from the fact that in a reported version of any prohibition *must not* can invariably be used. So even though the factor of cultural knowledge is a necessary condition for making sense of the concept of *traveling on the roof of trains* as expressed in (748), it does not, strictly speaking, touch upon the modal used for reporting. This does not, however, invalidate the sequence of interpretive factors laid down by Kussmaul. Sentence (746) is a short text presented in a specific situation embedded in a specific culture, and certainly only by reference to these two factors can it be interpreted properly.

Nonrelevance of the culture factor for the modal in (748) does not mean that culture never influences the use of a modal. At the end of Section 4.6 we saw how a speaker familiar with two cultural worlds felt that verbalization is completely different in each of them—see the modal forms in example (752). In this sense it is certainly valid to award culture the highest rank also in an SL hierarchy of factors for the modals.

As regards the factor of *situation* (embedded in a culture) we found that the relationship between speaker and hearer as well as the identity of the speaker are also basic to the understanding of an utterance containing a modal (see Sections 4.4.2.1 and 7.1.1).

Let us now consider another SL factor hierarchy for interpreting the modals as suggested in the literature. Glas (1984: 270) proposes a method of analysis involving a stepwise approach to identifying the meanings of polysemous expressions such as the modals. He considers intrasentential cotext to be relatively unproductive for disambiguation and makes a case for also referring to textual information. Nevertheless his first and third steps of analysis pertain to intrasentential cotext.

Glas suggests first checking if the polysemous expressions are part of a fixed sequence of words that are given a translation equivalent in the lexicon. This approach seems to be a very practical one because modal phrases, for instance, can thus be identified correctly as a whole in one step. It must be emphasized, though, that not all such phrases are unambiguous by themselves: MAY/MIGHT (JUST) AS WELL may have root or epistemic meaning (see Section 6.4.1.1). We feel that the holistic approach proposed is especially promising in the case of even longer idiomatic units, such as proverbs. Because they consist of a whole sentence, they are typically unambiguous as regards the kind of modality expressed by the modal they contain.

If the modal is not part of a fixed expression, the question arises if certain interpretations of it are ruled out by virtue of the text class in which it occurs. As an example, Glas (1984: 265) reports that he found no examples of the epistemic use of the German modals in the legal regulations of the European Community. He adds that it is inconceivable that this use occurs in these texts. This would make this text class a reliable identification factor for root modality.

In other cases, where there is the possibility of several interpretations of a modal occurring in a given text class, Glas (1984: 270) suggests passing on to his third step of identification, applying criteria for disambiguation related to the closer cotext, as listed in the lexicon. Such criteria include co-occurrence with certain adverbs, anaphoric relationships, and time reference:

- As regards co-occurring adverbs, Glas (1984: 269) mentions that GRUNDSÄTZLICH identifies the deontic sense of SOLLEN by modifying demands being made by means of this modal.
- As regards anaphoric relations, deontic SOLLEN is indicated by a preceding verb or noun of saying that contains a prescriptive meaning component (1984: 270).

Summing up, Glas's hierarchy of identification factors for SL modals is as follows:

1. cotext in terms of a fixed sequence of words;
2. (im)possible readings relative to text classes;
3. cotextual factors other than that under 1.

As regards the sequence of factors 2 and 3, Glas (1984: 270) says he ranks text-class information higher than cotextual information because the former has a stronger selective effect in disambiguating the modals and related expressions. This decision seems to be a wise one when we remember that MAY and SHALL can exchange their root meanings in legal texts (see Section 6.8.2). The easiest way to detect such a semantic reversal is by first focusing on the text class in question and asking if there are any peculiarities about it.

When we compare the SL factor models proposed by Kussmaul, Glas, and ourselves (Figures 3.13 and so on) we see no contradiction between them. Each model postulates a hierarchy of factors, but all of them may well be integrated into one another because they are complementary. Each model is eclectic anyway. Note, for instance, that none of them takes into account the factor of word class. Before trying to pinpoint the meaning of a modal in a given case it is necessary to ascertain whether it is used as a verb, a noun, or an adjective (see Section 2.8.1). Even prior to that, it is essential to make sure that what we have before us in a given instance is indeed a modal and not a homonym of a modal (see Section 2.8.3).

Here is a brief comment on each of the factor models presented:

- Kussmaul's model just contains the elements of culture, situation, whole text, and text passage. It was not developed specifically for the modals, identification factors of which would have to be added to the model. These are provided by Glas.
- But in Glas they pertain mainly to some German modals. Complete factor models for each modal are not provided by Glas. And, because he looks at the German and the French modals and some other modal expressions, the English modals would have to be considered separately.

- This is done in our Figures 3.2–3.7, 3.9–3.14, 3.17, and 3.19. But note that in these charts we dealt with only the modals CAN and MAY. Moreover, what is missing in our charts is several of the factors referred to by Kussmaul and Glas and all the other factors dealt with and not dealt with in this book.

On the other hand, it must be emphasized that not all the SL factors are relevant in a given case (see the factor of culture with reference to the modal in sentence (748) discussed earlier). Just to give a fuller account of what is involved in identifying the *relevant* factors in a given case let us once more take a sentence containing CAN and see what more can be said about it:

[190] You can go now.

First, it is necessary to identify word class. CAN in (190) is preceded by a pronoun and followed by a full verb, therefore it can be neither a noun ("container") nor a full verb ("to preserve"). Occupying the initial position in a verb phrase it can be only a modal verb. Having arrived at this word class, we can now continue with Figure 3.13. The modal CAN (F1) is part of a sentence that is an affirmative statement (F2). This factor is decisive for the major kind of modality it reflects, root modality (F3). The cotextual features (animate subject, agentive verb) and its being paraphrasable by *are permitted* or *allowed to* (F4) further narrow down its meaning potential to deontic modality; that is, "permission (informal, more common)" (F5).

At this point we must leave Figure 3.13 and add some pragmatic factors. With all its semantic disambiguation achieved, sentence (190) is still in three ways ambiguous pragmatically. Its utterance could count either as the direct speech act of stating the hearer's having permission to go or as an indirect speech act, namely, either as that of giving the hearer permission to go or as an order for the hearer to go (see Section 4.1.4.3). In Sections 4.1.2 and 4.1.4.1 we dealt with a criterion for distinguishing between CAN in direct statements and indirect directives, namely, (non)givenness of the proposition expressed. In (190) the temporal adverb NOW indicates that the proposition *you can go* cannot possibly be considered to be given; it must be new information. This is why the interpretation of stating permission is ruled out from the start. Situational criteria help distinguish between the other two readings. If it can be assumed that the hearer has been waiting some time for permission to go, uttering (190) will count as giving permission. As regards the third possible interpretation, Leech (1987: 71) says: "Condescension . . . intervenes to make the *can* of *You can go now* . . . into something approaching a command . . ." (see Section 4.1).

At this point we can return to Figure 3.13, which has in stock another facet: the style factor F6 with its bifurcation into *formal* and *informal*. It is important to note that passing from F5 to F6 we have crossed the 'border' from SL to TL. The reason is that CAN itself has already been characterized as informal in F5, so the dichotomy formal vs. informal can pertain to only the TL part of the translation path toward German renditions. Accordingly, TL factors will be our next topic. Before entering into it let us just say by way of conclusion that the analysis of sentence (190) given as an example was to provide an idea of what it can be like to consistently follow the factor approach for sequentially unfolding various aspects of an SL sentence. Its systematic step-by-step progression lends itself to machine translation also. But in order to make it really a FAST (factor analysis in sequential translation) procedure, SL analysis must be complemented by TL synthesis. This we will turn to now.

8.3.2 Identity of TL Factors

At first glance you may wonder why TL factor sets should have to be set up as an extra category. After all, it might be argued, once all the relevant SL features have been identified, why not simply 'transfer' them into TL? Proof of the feasibility of this suggestion may be adduced with reference to sentence pairs such as the following:

[364] John can swim.
[619] John kann schwimmen.

Here the English factor set—modal verb with "ability" meaning; affirmative statement; syntactic sequence of subject, auxiliary, and full verb; present tense indicative—might seem to be exactly what reemerges in the German sentence. And yet a closer look reveals that the German version requires knowledge of two more factors: person and number. It is not that the English sentence does not conform to these features; but here they are not *relevant* factors for suffixation of the modal for the simple reason that there is only one form of CAN. But without explicit reference to third person singular in German it would not be clear which of the following forms of KÖNNEN is intended: *kann, kannst, können,* and *könnt* (see Figure 3.4). This shows that, even in simple-looking cases, there is no complete identity of relevant SL and TL factors. In most cases, divergence of factors is even greater. Reconsider the following sentence pair (from Section 8.1):

[48] Er muss kommen können.
[47] He must be able to come.

What the two versions have in common is conceptual meaning: MÜSSEN/ MUST are both ambiguous as regards root and epistemic modality, and KÖNNEN/BE ABLE TO both cover the semantic gradient of inherency ranging from ability to possibility. Yet English must have a suppletive form where German can use a modal, and a change of word order is another must in English.

In other words, different TL rules are obligatory change factors. But there are also optional change factors, in the sense that they are not required by the TL language system. This brings us back to the point where we left off in the previous subsection. Having arrived at F5 in Figure 3.13—permission (informal, more common)—we faced an option under F6—formal vs. informal. We said that this dichotomy cannot be taken to refer to SL CAN because this modal has already been characterized as informal. Immediately questions arise, How can informal CAN be turned into anything formal in German? Does not fidelity to the style dimension demand adherence to informality, which is, after all, the SL characteristic?

Asking these questions we have arrived at a crucial point because we have to give two different answers:

- With reference to the SL factor as a yardstick, the answer is clear: The criterion of equivalence demands that style in SL and TL be identical.
- With reference to the purpose of translation determined by the client in a given case, style need not necessarily be kept invariant. He or she may demand *any*thing to be done about any SL text that is to be translated into TL—any factor may be added to or subtracted from those present in the SL text.

This is the fundamental twofold answer to the question about identity of TL factors. This may come as a surprise because, after all, it is the SL text that is supposed to be translated and that therefore can be held to determine the TL rendition. But we are by now well acquainted with the phenomenon of deliberate TL variation. In Sections 8.1 and 8.2.1, for instance, we presented as many as ten German renditions of the English SL sentence

[445] The same point can be made about borrowing as was made about analogy . . . (Lyons 1981: 206)

Note that none of the German renditions we proposed is a mere 'variant' of any other one; each is characterized by specific features that, if preferred by the client, become translation factors leading to the appropriate TL sentence.

To show that there is really nothing unusual about a client wishing factors of the SL text to be modified for its rendition in TL, let us again quote the possible task description for translating Lyons's book (1981), where (445) is contained: "In translating the book conceptual meaning should, of course, be retained. But it would be good to follow the German tendency to avoid repetition of expressions. So do not hesitate to make use of linguistic variation. And since the book is directed to educated readers it would be appropriate to translate it in an elevated style." Such task specifications are the legitimate right of the client and can therefore be expected to be adhered to by the translator. Rendition (446), which appeared in the printed German version of Lyons (1992: 189), did conform to these factors.

8.4 TRANSLATION PRINCIPLES

In our two answers to the question of fidelity given in the preceding subsection, addition of translation factors by the client was contrasted with 'mere' adherence to the factors as found in the SL text. But it must not be overlooked that even this SL orientation does not come about 'by itself,' it is also on the basis of a corresponding translation order. This suggests that the two answers given have to be restructured. In each case it is the client that determines what is to be done about the text. He or she can ask the translator

- to go by the factor set of an SL text and carry over into TL as much of it as possible, or
- to go by whatever (additional) factors he or she prescribes.

The preceding remarks have far-reaching implications for the understanding of key terms in translation theory, such as *equivalence, fidelity,* and, more fundamentally, the notion of *translation* itself.

Equivalence can, strictly speaking, be said to exist only between factors equally present in an SL and a TL text. Those TL factors requested that are not contained in the SL text can hardly be said to be equivalent because there is no textual basis of comparison; it does not make much sense to speak of 'equivalence of SL factors and TL factors' in these cases. Here *adequacy* seems to be a better term. The notion of *fidelity* or *being faithful,* however, seems to make sense in both translation situations referred to. If so wished, the translator can be faithful to SL-text factors, as well as to any factors not present in the SL text itself. In each case he or she will be faithful to the wishes expressed by the client if conforming to the factors laid down (see Section 7.4.3.4).

The third term said to be affected by the optional SL-TL orientation is *translation.* The impression might be created that the more factors (not present in the SL text) are included in the client's task description, the more translation loses its genuine character and slides into the field of adaptation, that is, modified translation made suitable for a specific purpose. The supposition that added translation factors deprive translation of its genuine character is lent force by the guiding principle that "good translation . . . neither omits significant elements nor adds explanatory or other matter not included or very strongly implied in the original," as tentatively postulated by Fuller (1984: 157), see Section 7.4.3.4. On the other hand, some scholars go so far as to make the addition of explanatory matter a necessary condition for certain renditions to be good. A case in point is the following example (partly) supplied by Hönig and Kussmaul (1984: 53 f., 58).

(1157) When his father died his mother couldn't afford to send him to Eton any more.

(1158) Als sein Vater starb, konnte seine Mutter es sich nicht mehr leisten, ihn nach Eton zu schicken.

(1159) Als sein Vater starb, konnte seine Mutter es sich nicht mehr leisten, ihn auf eine der teuren Privatschulen zu schicken.

(1160) Als sein Vater starb, konnte seine Mutter es sich nicht mehr leisten, ihn nach Eton zu schicken, auf die teure englische Privatschule, aus deren Absolventen auch heute noch ein Grossteil des politischen und wirtschaftlichen Führungsnachwuchses hervorgeht.

Sentence (1158) matches the original (1157) most closely. Yet to a German-speaking reader unfamiliar with the synecdoche *Eton*, rendition (1158) will not be fully intelligible. The semantics of the verb group *couldn't afford* merely tells one that the referent of the subject's son still being sent to Eton would have exceeded his mother's financial capacity; but full information about the culturally determined modal source is not supplied. To do justice to such readers, the translator-editor may feel called upon to add some explanatory note, for instance by providing the background knowledge contained in (1160). Hönig and Kussmaul (1984: 58), however, maintain that this sentence 'overexplains' the concept of Eton; a mere hint at the fact that it denotes an expensive private school would do. This is exactly what (1159) offers (albeit lacking mention of the word *Eton* itself). So whereas (1158) and (1160) present information that for the ignorant is under- or over-differentiated, (1159) represents the 'degree of differentiation' just necessary, which makes it an optimal rendition.

Newmark (1993: 21), commenting on Hönig and Kussmaul's concept of degree of differentiation, remarks that by its application

> their targeted readership gets no chance to learn anything but the 'message,' as they, the translators, not the authors determine it. Vermeer claims that Thomas Mann consciously wrote for a cultured readership. I doubt it. I think Mann wrote to educate his readers a little, and hoped they would take the trouble to turn to dictionaries and encyclopedias when they read him. Mann taught me and I revere him. I don't want any 'degree of differentiation' coming between me and an author. The duller, the more passive a readership, the more it has to be targeted.

Applying these remarks to our previous example, this means that if the concept of Eton is unknown to any German reader it is up to the reader, not to the translator, to clarify it. So, along the lines of Newmark, (1158) would have to be preferred as a rendition, not (1159), which is opted for by Hönig and Kussmaul.

From what we said about the client's authority, we know that he or she is the one to make decisions. It is up to the client whether realia or unique objects such as Eton are to be explained or not. So if Newmark were to order Hönig and Kussmaul to translate (1157) for him, he might specify his commission by adding, "and, you know, I would like to educate my German readers a little, and hope they will take the trouble to turn to dictionaries and encyclopedias in case they do not understand the expression *Eton*"—and Hönig and Kussmaul would have to comply and deliver a rendition along the lines of (1158).

Likewise, if Hönig and Kussmaul wanted Newmark to translate for them a culturally embedded sentence such as (1161),

(1161) Ihre Erfindung ist fantastisch; Sie sollten sie nach München schikken.

he would have to go by their instructions. If, in their function as clients, they insisted on this sentence being made intelligible to *all* native speakers of English, then Newmark would have to hand in something like (1163), because (1162) would not do:

(1162) Your invention is fantastic; you should send it to Munich.
(1163) Your invention is fantastic; you should send it to the (German) Patent Office (in Munich).

Again the modal source of (1161) and (1162) remains opaque for the reader unfamiliar with national institutions. All one can conclude is that Munich must have something to do with inventions but this is, of course, insufficient knowledge for understanding these sentences pragmatically.

Our two examples have shown that *both* Hönig and Kussmaul *and* Newmark are 'right' in their theoretical orientations even though these are contradictory. Their compatibility becomes evident when the authors become clients themselves, thus being entitled to demand *any* factor to be taken into account or to be ignored. So whether a factor is to be highlighted or not, this is the question to be decided upon by the client, not by the translatologist!

Taking this perspective we also find the solution to all the other contradictory translation principles found in translation studies. Savory's (1968: 54) collection includes the following ones:

• a translation must give the words of the original;
• a translation must give the ideas of the original;
• a translation should read like an original work;
• a translation should read like a translation;
• a translation may add to or omit from the original;
• a translation may never add to or omit from the original.

Again the idea underlying these statements is to postulate what is 'right'; but contradictory statements such as these can apparently not all be right at the same time. From what was said previously, however, it will be obvious that each of these postulates can be valid in its own right. To take the first pair of principles as an example, the demand that "a translation must give the words of the original" (a word-for-word translation) is justifiable if the aim is to carry out comparative linguistic research (see Reiss 1989: 115). If, on the other hand, the main purpose of a translation is to describe to the hearer a certain state of affairs as closely as possible, then "a translation must give the ideas of the original." Note the two *ifs* used: Our statements just made are no longer as absolute and unconditional as those quoted by Savory, rather they are made relative to different target factors. In this way the age-old controversy of "whether a translation should be literal ('word for word') or free ('sense for sense')" (Chesterman 1989a: 7) passes off happily. It turns out to be not so much a question of arguments to be adduced for deciding which of the two principles is 'better' or 'right' per se. So, opting for one or the other of the two principles—and, indeed, for any translation principle—is a matter of clear-cut requirements relative to a given purpose or target giving rise to a corresponding commission. Or, put differently, the 'arguments' in favor of each principle turn out to be just factor sets, each calling for application of that principle. Taking these factor sets to constitute 'counterarguments' against (an)other principle(s) is a futile endeavor because it is of no relevance to practical translation work.

Indeed the notion of relevance can be held to account for preferring one principle to another one. Gutt (1991), subscribing to relevance theory as a means of shedding light upon translation theory, says that "the different 'translation principles' do reflect differences in what different readers consider to be relevant. . . . Thus the contradictions can be resolved when each principle is not stated in absolute terms, but qualified by the condition: '. . . when required for consistency with the principle of relevance'" (p. 121).

8.5 EQUIVALENCE

Relativizing translation principles in this way entails relativizing the notion of equivalence. Reiss (1989: 113, 115) correlates word-for-word translation with equivalence on the word level. For bigger translation units, she cites equivalence on the sentence level and equivalence on the text level. And if "all the factors of the communication situation [are to] be brought into account", then "the aim . . . is a communicatively effective translation . . . with equivalence not only of content and meaning but also of effect" (p. 114).

Baker (1992) devotes each of her chapters to one kind of equivalence: equivalence at word level, equivalence above word level, grammatical equivalence, textual equivalence—thematic and information structures; textual equivalence—cohesion, and pragmatic equivalence.

Neubert also distinguishes between pragmatic equivalence (1989: 151) and textual equivalence (1989: 154). In another paper, Neubert (1986) establishes a hierarchy of different kinds of equivalence. He argues that the text as a whole influences grammatical-lexical choice and thus relativizes equivalents on the lower level (p. 89). This suggests that not only is equivalence itself a relative concept, but equivalence holding on the level of one translation unit can relativize equivalence holding at another level. It must be emphasized, however, that the direction of this relativization process again depends upon the nature of the commission specifying which factors are to be kept invariant in TL. A word-for-word translation, for instance, would not call for dominance of overall textual equivalence as suggested by Neubert.

8.6 TRANSLATION OR ADAPTATION?

Equivalence proven to be a relative notion, immediately the question arises whether this in any way affects the concept of translation. Is this notion compatible with all kinds of equivalence, or are there varieties of equivalence that, in conjunction with nonequivalent, additional factors, entail such changes as to necessitate speaking of adaptation? To examine these questions, let us return to the Eton and Munich examples in (1157)–(1163). Sentences (1157) and (1161) themselves do not explicitly contain information about an expensive private school at Eton or Munich being the location of the German Patent Office. This information is supplied by (1159) and (1163). It is definitely an addition to the elements explicitly present in the source sentences. This addition may be regarded as natural by those who have in mind optimal understanding of the TL hearer; nevertheless it seems uncontroversial to say that formally and semantically the SL sentences have been adapted to the needs of the TL hearer.

If, on the other hand, Reiss (1989: 113) says that, for establishing equivalence on the sentence level, "the syntax should be *adapted* to that of the TL" (our emphasis), many will feel reluctant to speak of *adaptation* in this case. The reason is that usually a shift to TL syntax must be considered to be part of translation. If it is taken to be adaptation, then all translation except for the—rare—word-for-word translation would be adaptation.

In search of a reasonable criterion for distinguishing between translation and adaptation it seems to be practical to go by an element that actually defines equivalence—*invariance*. Whenever equivalence is said to hold, this is due to the invariance of certain SL-TL elements. In other words, certain SL elements become invariance factors reappearing in the TL text. Equivalence will always exist only to the extent to which specific invariance factors have been taken into account by the translator and will exist only in terms of them, hence the different kinds of equivalence (grammatical, pragmatic, etc.) referred to in the preceding section.

Having recognized that *all* SL factors cannot be kept invariant simultaneously (see Section 8.1), let us next ask about the opposite case—nil invariance. Gutt (1991: 52 ff.) explores this aspect and its impact on the notion of translation in a subsection titled "Translation—When All Is Change?" He illustrates this way of questioning with reference to an example provided by Hönig and Kussmaul (1984: 36 ff.). Its SL version appeared as an ad in the *Sunday Times* and reads like this:

(1164) What's in a Name?

It sounds ordinary on paper. A white shirt with a blue check. In fact, if you asked most men if they had a white shirt with a blue check, they'd say yes.

But the shirt illustrated on the opposite page is an adventurous white and blue shirt. Yet it would fit beautifully into your wardrobe. And no one would accuse you of looking less than a gentleman. Predictably, the different white and blue check shirt has a different name. Viyella House. It's tailored in crisp cool cotton and perfectly cut out for city life. Remember our name next time you are hunting for a shirt to give you more than just a background for your tie.

On women's and children's wear as well as on men's shirts, our label says—quietly but persuasively—all there is to say about our good quality and your good taste.

OUR LABEL IS OUR PROMISE.

Now suppose the English company placing this ad decides to sell its products also in Germany. In this connection there are two possible commissions and ways of translating the ad. Either the point of translation is to show the company's marketing strategy used in England; in this case preservation of the content of the original is called for. Or a corresponding ad to be placed in Germany is what is commissioned, which amounts to preservation of intention or function. So in the first case there is functional change (the SL ad no longer functioning as an ad in TL), in the second there is functional constancy or functional equivalence defined by invariance of function (the SL ad being intended to become a TL ad).

With regard to the last kind of commission, all that matters is the effectiveness of the rendition in terms of boosting sales. This is why there need not be *any* lexical resemblance between the SL ad and the TL ad, as Hönig and Kussmaul (1984: 40) point out. So the question of rendering WOULD occurring twice in (1164) does not arise, in much the same way as CAN in (752) (Section 4.6) was not translated on the word level. And yet, for all the (possible) differences between the English and German versions relating to (1164) and (752), there is one invariance factor, as was just pointed out: function. This is why it is, strictly speaking, not correct to say that *all* is change in this case.

Nevertheless it is legitimate to ask whether it is justifiable to speak of *translation* if there is not any formal or semantic resemblance between the SL and the TL texts. This question is all the more appropriate because, as

Gutt (1991: 56) observes in this case, "there is no *necessary* relationship between the source-language and the target-language texts" (emphasis as in the original). The reason is that "the success of the German version would not be measured in terms of its resemblance to the original." (1991: 55); this is why "the German advertisers might set the English advertisement aside and come up with a completely different advertisement . . ." (1991: 55 f.).

Hönig and Kussmaul (1984: 40) themselves concede that theoreticians as well as practicians would prefer terms such as *modulation* or *adaptation* to *translation* in such cases. Yet in their own opinion functional constancy and functional change constitute two basic types of translation of completely equal rank. Later in their book they add that, due to the possibility and necessity of functional changes, they are not in a position to draw a sharp dividing line between the notions of translation and adaptation or modulation (1984: 132). Does this, then, mean that these notions are fluid concepts?

Schreiber (1993), who devotes a whole book-length account to this question, indeed starts out by saying that the boundary between translation and adaptation is apparently fluid. Nevertheless, he considers research into the possibility of differentiating these notions worthwhile, because in his opinion it is not just a terminological issue (one of mere labeling) but one of different phenomena to be distinguished (1993: 3).

Schreiber's comment on Hönig and Kussmaul's example of a function-preserving ad entailing an entirely different TL wording parallels that of these authors (see previously): He points out that in such cases some translation theorists would prefer the term *adaptation* to *translation* (1993: 68). Later on he defines *adaptation* as preserving at least one complex individual textual feature such as identical topic indicating the dependence of the TL text upon the SL text (1993: 104). In the TL version of example (1164), however, *topic* is not necessarily an invariance factor. Hönig and Kussmaul (1984: 40) remark that it might even be agreed upon to present in the TL ad children's clothing instead of shirts (as was done in the SL ad (1164)). Such departure not just in terms of wording but even in terms of topic would truly place the 'translators' in a position to "set the English advertisement aside and come up with a completely different advertisement." In this situation there would definitely be no more "relationship between the source language and the target-language texts."

Schreiber takes exactly this point to be criterial for distinguishing adaptation from the notion of a TL text created independently. If even the topic changes, and the TL text is no longer based upon an SL text for its content, he considers this text to be autonomous or original (1993: 102). Exactly this would apply to a German 'version' of (1164) created completely on its own.

Having established the difference between autonomous texts and TL adaptations, the next question is what distinguishes the latter from translations. Here Schreiber states that translation is geared toward preserving as much as possible[52] except for the source language, whereas adaptation is a matter of changing certain textual features more or less 'arbitrarily' (except for said feature relating to the SL text) (1993: 104 f.).

Preservation denoting invariance and change denoting variance, both these factors can be demanded in a commission. Schreiber goes on to say that translation is based primarily upon invariance demands, whereas adaptation is based primarily upon variance demands (1993: 105).

Schreiber mentions as an example of a variance demand the commission to change a difficult SL text into a simple one (1993: 105). Applied to the field of modality this could mean choosing a simple TL expression (such as a modal auxiliary) for an SL special or technical term, as was illustrated by the following translations (see Section 7.4.1.1):

[1115] Er ist Steuerpflichtiger.
[1116] He is someone who must pay taxes.

[1120] Sieh mal. Dies ist ein Amphibienfahrzeug.
[1121] Look here. This is a vehicle that can travel on either land or water.

Both renditions involve transpositions; that is, changes in word class (here in the area of modality). As is well-known, there are two kinds of transpositions: obligatory ones that must occur due to the difference of linguistic systems (e.g., modal auxiliary *musste* → semi-auxiliary *had to*) and optional ones (e.g., constructions involving the modal auxiliaries MUST and CAN in (1116) and (1121) instead of the modal nouns TAXPAYER and AMPHIBIAN (VEHICLE), which in principle would be equally possible).

Schreiber (1993: 127) traces obligatory transpositions back to what he refers to as the *hierarchy of invariance demands*; that is, the superiority of the demand for invariance of the textual feature *grammaticality* over the demand for invariance of word class. Such dominance of grammatical correctness is evident from preference of (47) over (1145) (see Section 8.1):

[48] Er muss kommen können.
[1145] *He must come can.
[47] He must be able to come.

But Schreiber then points out that superiority of grammaticality is by no means an invariable phenomenon. In the case of word-for-word translations, it is surpassed in priority by the demand for invariance of word class and word order (as fulfilled by (1145), for instance). Therefore, he concludes that the so-called obligatory changes are not ultimately obligatory at all (1993: 127). This does not, however, invalidate the principle of demand for some superior invariant, because in each of the two cases just referred to some factor is given higher priority.

This principle might also be assumed to hold for apparently optional transpositions. It is true that nonobligatory changes in word class may be due to, say, the factor of style given highest priority.[53] But, when Schreiber suggests that optional transpositions *invariably preserve* the level of style (1993: 127), this seems to be justified only in terms of one of two aspects involved. Take as an example of optional transpositions in the field of modality our familiar example, (445) *The same point can be made . . .* rendered as (446) *. . . lässt sich dasselbe sagen . . .* Given the express instruction: "since the book is directed to educated readers it would be appropriate to translate it in an elevated style" (see Section 8.1) it may be wondered what kind of readers the SL original was supposed to have. If both (445) and (446) appear in a book on linguistics, after all, it should be taken for granted that the English readership is educated. Why then is there an additional demand for elevated style to be used in the German rendition?

Again it seems to be most sensible to refer to the habit of Germans to use an elaborate style in certain public utterances, as opposed to the habit of using more 'ordinary' language in English (see Sections 4.6, 6.8, and the end of Section 8.1). This means that even a sophisticated English readership expects a more unpretentious style, whereas the German readership expects a more elevated style. Now if each expectation is fulfilled *in its own right*, then in this sense the dimension of style can indeed be said to be invariant. As regards its actual quality, however, style is different in SL and TL. The existence of these two aspects should be borne in mind when the question is considered whether optional transpositions are style preserving or not.

JAnother angle from which the preceding example may be seen is the factor of quality demands, defined by Schreiber (1993: 129) as demands made on the TL text irrespective of the SL text. Because elaborate style is demanded irrespective of what was written in the English original, it might well be referred to as a quality demand.

8.7 COEXISTENCE OF CHANGE FACTORS AND INVARIANCE FACTORS

To conclude our investigation let us now focus on the possible relations of different kinds of factor demands. Translation was characterized by Schreiber as being based on invariance demands (see Section 8.6). He distinguishes the notion of *invariance* (the fact of invariableness) from that of *invariant* (that which is demanded to be invariable) (1993: 30). He further differentiates between *intratextual* and *extratextual* invariants (p. 32), subspecifying them as follows: "As regards the intratextual invariants I distinguish between formal and semantic factors, whereas regarding the extratextual factors . . . I make a basic distinction between intention (of the sender) and effect (on the receiver)" (p. 33, our translation). Because certain invariants are mutually exclusive and others are interdependent, Schreiber postulates the need for setting priorities within a hierarchy of invariance demands

(p. 33 f.). Depending on whether the superior invariant demanded is intratextual or extratextual in nature Schreiber distinguishes between the methods of *text translation* and *context translation* (pp. 66 ff.).

But this latter distinction must not be overstated. Schreiber (1993: 34, 67) expressly points out that for different parts of a text to be translated the superior invariant may well change. It may be added that, if such a change is from intratextual to extratextual invariants (or vice versa), this would amount to a change from text translation to context translation (or vice versa).

But even the theoretical distinction between translation and adaptation may collapse in a similar way. Schreiber (1993: 131) remarks that in practice there are complex texts involving dominance of invariance demands in certain passages and dominance of variance demands in others. Depending upon the overall dominance of one kind of demand over the other, Schreiber suggests speaking of *translation approaching adaptation* or *adaptation approaching translation* (p. 131).

Now it is perfectly possible to take the argument another step further and say that the dominance of the two kinds of demands in a text is not restricted to different text passages: In many texts there may be found invariance demands as well as variance demands (i.e., demands for invariance factors as well as change factors) *coexisting throughout*. To test this claim let us again refer to the possible task description for translating Lyons (1981): "In translating the book conceptual meaning should, of course, be retained. But it would be good to follow the German tendency to avoid repetition of expressions. So do not hesitate to make use of linguistic variation. And since the book is directed to educated readers it would be appropriate to translate it in an elevated style." Retention of conceptual meaning is an invariance demand, linguistic variation of expressions is a variance demand. But why on earth should one of these two demands be considered to be superior to the other? The client may consider each one to be important *on its level*. Invariance of conceptual meaning is important as far as types of meaning (see Section 3.3) are concerned; variation or variance of expression is important in the stylistic dimension; and the notion of elevated style was shown to have both an invariance and a variance aspect anyway (see the final part of Section 8.6). Of course, it may happen that certain demands—be they variance or invariance demands—are more important to the client than others. However, it is equally possible for that client to make a list of factor dimensions (meaning, style, etc.) and specify variance demands relating to some of them and invariance demands relating to others, giving equal importance to all of them, thus demanding coexistence of change factors and invariance factors being of equal rank. So we see no reason to speak of a dominance of variance demands over invariance demands or vice versa in such a rendition. Therefore it is futile trying to label each factor set (demanded to be followed by the client) according to its membership to (a subkind of) translation or adaptation.

We consider it to be a more worthwhile endeavor of translation theory to do research into the ways and means of creating optimum TL renditions of (different kinds of) SL texts in the light of different factor sets. This would amount to postulating that, for the sake of accumulating practical knowledge and experience, both translation theory and translation practice should be oriented toward translating by factors.

8.8 RETROSPECT AND PROSPECT

In this final section we would like to briefly recap what we consider to be the most important theoretical points we have made and indicate what more could be said and done.

First, translation and adaptation have in common preservation of at least one feature indicating dependence of the TL text upon the SL text (see Section 8.6). This invariance factor gives rise to SL-TL equivalence regarding this factor. Any additional invariance factor(s) demanded by the client give(s) rise to further (aspects of) equivalence. So different invariance demands will give rise to different kinds of equivalence. This is why *equivalence is a relative concept*, whose content ('what is equivalent') cannot be defined without reference to the nature of the invariance factors contained in the factor set demanded in a given case. The only general statement that can be made about equivalence is that it "will always exist only to the extent to which specific invariance factors have been taken into account by the translator and will exist only in terms of them . . ." (see Section 8.6).

Second, factors are the guidelines for translation. Such guidelines are necessarily to be expressly given by the client for each translation being commissioned[54] because no one a priori translation principle could be said to be invariably valid for every commission (as evidenced by the conflicting principles listed in Section 8.4).

True, there were times when certain standards ("A translation must . . .") were postulated to be (applied) universal(ly); but even these may in hindsight be referred to as specific—although rigid—factors as guidelines for translating.

Times have changed, and dogmatic statements by translatologists have given way to multifarious factor demands made by clients according to different needs on different occasions.

But the principle has remained the same: No translator can translate without reference to a particular factor set that he or she is expected to go by in a given case.[55] This leads to the grand conclusion that *translating by factors is in fact inevitable*; throughout the ages each translator has invariably been doing it. Translating means translating by factors.[56]

Third, success of any translation may be gauged in terms of the extent to which the translator has successfully taken into account the factors demanded by the client. Thus, *translation factors turn out to be the felicity conditions for each act of translating.* Just as there is a set of felicity conditions defining a particular kind of monolingual speech act, different sets of translation factors will characterize different kinds of translation acts. And just as felicity conditions can be turned into rules for performing speech acts, factor sets can be made the rules according to which the act of translating is to be performed. Because each commission involves its own factor set, each act of translating will follow its individual combination of rules (see Section 8.4).

As for monolingual speech acts, there is the knowledge of how to implement speech act rules by finding the appropriate linguistic means for performing the speech act in question. Likewise there should be the knowledge of how to felicitously turn factor sets (including the factor *SL text*) into TL renditions; that is, of how to arrive at felicitous renditions. *This* knowledge of felicity in terms of adequacy to the respective factor set demanded we consider to be the relevant object of translation studies. The whole perspective can be summed up in the one formula: factors for felicity.

Researching into TL speech-act felicity relative to different kinds of factor sets potentially demanded by the client seems to be a promising path toward a theory of translating successfully.

NOTES

1. The full bibliographical information on these titles is contained in the References.

2. We classify this paper as belonging to the second category because Straight (1981: 50) says of it: "Upon reflection, it has become apparent to me that *evaluation* of the quality of translations was the topic of that paper" (emphasis as in the original).

3. Translation didactics will, of course, have to include factors specific to didactics; but if "it is the goal of translation didactics to render teaching and learning of translating and interpreting more effective" (Königs 1981: 333; our translation) then the knowledge of factors relevant to translating will be very helpful, as will become obvious as we go along; see further notes 4, 6, and 50.

4. When Wilss (1978: 351) says, "Only those factors which can be systematized are teachable and learnable," this is consistent with our initial claim about factors determining translation and factors to be applied in translation didactics being (partially) identical.

5. Critics are thus expected by Senn to go by the desired translation criteria. This confirms our initial claim that "the very same factors determining translation . . . may also be drawn upon as criteria for judging the adequacy of translation" (see previously); cf. also Neubert (1991: 18) who, presenting the retrospective, evaluative, or critical model of translation, says that "there are many variations of the *critical model* of translation, depending upon the historical, social as well as individual factors playing more or less distinct roles in the evaluation process" (emphasis as in the original).

6. Commenting on her factor model, Nord (1992: 44) says: "This model includes all the relevant extratextual factors, offering the advantage of a practical formula which is easy to be remembered and can be used as a checklist in translator

training." Here again the value of the factor approach for its didactic application is expressed, "allowing a systematic approach for both teachers and students" (p. 48).

7. Stolze (1992) is a treatise on the hermeneutics of translation. Elsewhere Stolze (1994: 183) points out that hermeneutic thinking does not involve reference to factors. Nonetheless in the introduction to her *categories of reception* she repeatedly states that she is going to deal with factors: "So sollen in der vorliegenden Studie zunächst für den Bereich der Interpretation als Vorbereitung auf das Übersetzen die Kategorien der Rezeption dargestellt werden. Unter der Kategorie der Thematik werden v.a. verstehensrelevante textexterne Faktoren wie Umfeld, Situation, Kommunikationsbereich, Textaufbau abgehandelt werden" (1992: 85). Also her *categories of production* are described by her in terms of factors: "Bei der Verbalisierung als dem produktiven Teil des Übersetzungsprozesses werden dann andere Faktoren wichtig" (1992: 85). Later she adds: "Diese Ausführungen deuten schon an, dass das Übersetzen als produktive Sprachverwendung keineswegs nur durch textinterne Phänomene der Sprachstruktur bestimmt ist, sondern dass hier ganz wesentlich auch aussersprachliche Faktoren eine Rolle spielen, worauf im Nachfolgenden näher eingegangen werden soll" (1992: 194) (repeated emphasis omitted).

8. This is the reason why the predecessor of this book was titled, 'The Multifactorial Translation Situation of the Modals of the German-English Language Pair' (Gutknecht and Rölle 1988; in German). The present work is a modified and greatly enlarged, though not translated, but newly written successor of that article.

9. The modal auxiliaries share the following characteristics with the primary auxiliaries BE, HAVE, and DO (cf. Palmer 1979a: 9):

(i) Negative form with -*n't*, see (5);
(ii) Inversion with the subject, see (3);
(iii) 'Code' (reduced anaphoric constructions), see (4);
(iv) Emphatic affirmation: *He* ‖*will be there.*
    Huddleston (1976: 333) acronymically refers to these functions as the NICE properties.

Several verbs do not exhibit all the NICE properties characteristic of the modals proper (or modal auxiliaries or modal verbs listed at the end of this subsection), but are still called *modals* by some authors. Coates (1983: 4f.), for instance, states that, apart from the TO infinitive, OUGHT has all the formal characteristics just mentioned. Neglecting this small difference, she considers OUGHT to be a modal auxiliary.

Quirk et al. (1985: 137) present an *auxiliary verb—main verb scale* containing different sets of verbs related to the modals in different formal or semantic ways. Even though DARE, NEED, OUGHT TO, and USED TO are considered by Quirk et al. as modals, we will not focus on them in this study since none of them satisfies all the preceding criteria of the modals.

10. For a table of the present and past tense indicative forms of all German modals, see Hammer (1991: 229).

11. This corresponds to Malone's (1988: 17) concepts of divergence and convergence: "Divergence . . . holds where an element of the source text . . . may be mapped onto any of two or more alternatives in the target text . . ." With convergence "two or more distinct source text elements . . . may each be mapped onto one and the same target element . . ."

12. See Hammer (1991: 229, 261 f., 329 f.).

13. Modal-compatible prefixes include *hin–, her–; (d)ran–, (he)ran–, fort–, weg–, ab–; hinüber–, (he)rüber–; hinauf–, rauf–, hinunter–, (he)runter–; hinein–, (he)rein–, hinaus–, (he)raus–; (hin)durch–; (aussen)rum–, (aussen)herum–; längs–, vorbei–, (ent)lang–; voran–, zurück–; vorneweg–, hinterher–, zusammen–, auseinander–; voreinander–, hintereinander–, nebeneinander–, übereinander–, untereinander–; höher–, tiefer–; (oben)drüber–, (d)rüber–; (unten)drunter–, (d)runter–; drüber(hin)weg–, drunterdurch–, untendurch–; auf–, zu–;* . . .
Not all of these are equally well-suited for combinations with each modal.
Note that no prefixes denoting a state are possible here: **obenkönnen, *untenkönnen;* but: *oben hinkönnen* or *obenhin können.*
For the same reason prefixes that may denote both a state and a motion, such as *links–* and *rechts–*, can be combined with the modals only in their latter function, as in *rechts hinmüssen* or *rechtshin müssen* (but *nach rechts hin müssen*). Thus the direction element *hin–* is implied in (i) . . . *weil wir jetzt rechts müssen.*

14. This strategy is not possible if the modals are used metalinguistically. For reasons to be explained in Section 3.3.9, language philosopher J. L. Austin's paper 'Ifs and Cans' could not be rendered as (i) *Bedingungen und Möglichkeiten.*
Computerized translation programs cannot even be expected to recognize the plural form *ifs* and the modal nature of the expression *cans*. The *Globalink* translation program tested by us for its rendition of *Ifs and Cans* took the *–s* of *cans* to be indicative of the plural form of the *noun* CAN. But, because it did not have a plural form of *if* in its memory, it refused further processing. The result was this: (ii) **Ifs und Dosen.*

15. Here we will not go into the question of whether these meanings are to be attributed to the modals themselves or to context; that is, we will not attempt to determine whether the modals are essentially monosemous or polysemous. The term *polysemy* will be used to refer to the phenomenon of different meanings related to each other occurring when a word occurs in different instances. For the sake of simplicity we will refer to the modals as being polysemous.

16. This is the first of five general types of translation equivalence as given by Koller (1983: 158) (without reference to the modals).

17. *Probability* refers to a piece of knowledge (being true). Because, as Lyons (1977: 793) explains, the term *epistemic* is derived from the Greek word for "knowledge," it appears to be adequate for characterizing the notion of probability; for a more differentiated view, see Section 3.2.4.9.
In Section 3.2.4.1, the labels *root* and *epistemic* will also be applied to the notion of necessity and will be characterized as two *kinds of modality.*

18. For reasons of space, we will no longer specify (the individual forms for) the factors *person* and *number*.

19. (1) We leave out, for the moment, the category of negative statements because it involves different rendition patterns not yet dealt with. We will take up this point in our section on negation (3.1.5). (2) Negative questions containing epistemic *can't* can be rendered only by KÖNNEN, not by MÖGEN; for example,

(i) Can't he be in Los Angeles?
(ii) Kann er nicht in Los Angeles sein?
(iii) !Mag er nicht in Los Angeles sein?

(3) Note also that MÖGEN as a rendition for epistemic CAN in affirmative questions is restricted to *wh*– questions, such as (196) and (v) and would be ruled out in *yes-no* questions, such as

(iv) Where can the keys be?
(v) Wo mögen die Schlüssel sein?

(vi) Can the keys be in the car?
(vii) Können die Schlüssel im Wagen sein?
(viii) *Mögen die Schlüssel im Wagen sein?

20. The following four characteristics are given by Coates (1983: 42) for epistemic MUST. Because, however, she later states that epistemic *can't* "is associated with the same syntactic features as epistemic MUST" (1983: 101), we present these features here. Except for (iv), they are, of course, also valid for affirmative CAN in epistemic questions such as (198).

21. In these and (almost) all of the following examples taken from Coates (1983), we do not include the prosodic information provided by her. Nor do we underline the modals in the examples. Coates (1983: 137) lists two more syntactic cooccurring items—*stative verb* and *negation*—which are, however, no invariable identification factors of epistemic MAY.

22. The numbering of examples was changed to fit ours.

23. This would, in turn, require enlarging Perkins's chart by the category of 'nondeontic' root "possibility," including "circumstantial possibility" as conceived of by Palmer (see Section 3.2.4.5).

24. In (279) we omit the prefix *un*–, in the ensuing English sentences the corresponding negative element.

25. Just as there is a gradient of acceptability for the English sentences listed previously, so several of the following German sentences are on the verge of acceptability. This is especially true of (304), which is better replaced by (i) *Für das Problem gibt es eine Lösung*. See also Mossop (1983: 275) on variable renditions.

26. To do justice to Newmark it must be added that he states one would normally expect (279) to be translated by (282): see Newmark (1981: 102).

27. Hofmann (1979: 3 f.) points out that both root and epistemic MAY can be paraphrased by means of POSSIBLE; for example,

(i) He may be singing. =
(ii) It is possible that he is singing.

(iii) He may go play now. =
(iv) It is possible for him to go play now.

28. Schmid (1966) presents a translational comparison of English, German, French, and Italian modal expressions denoting "necessity," including their negations.

29. Gailor (1983), comparing root SHOULD/OUGHT TO and MUST, emphasizes the inappropriateness of defining the difference between these expressions in 'quantitative' terms such as 'strong' or 'weak' (pp. 347, 349). Discussing various aspects of politeness and authority, he suggests that "there are precise factors of meaning and appropriateness which distinguish these verb-forms" (p. 349).

30. The terms *root* and *epistemic* are by no means the only ones used for referring to this basic dichotomy in the field of modality. Raynaud (1977: 1) lists the following terminological variants accumulated in the linguistic literature:

• *objektiver* vs. *subjektiver Gebrauch* (Schulz and Griesbach) (not to be confused with the distinction *objective* vs. *subjective modality* to be introduced in Sections 3.2.4.2 and 3.2.4.4)
• *ontologisch* vs. *logisch* or *logisch-psychologisch* (Valentin, Schenker, and Zemb)
• *noninferential* vs. *inferential* meaning (Lyons)
• *modulation* vs. *modality* (Halliday)
• *internal* vs. *external* modality (Bach)
• *transitive* vs. *intransitive* (Perlmutter)
• *Modifikation* vs. *Modalisation* (Raynaud)

Perkins (1983: 31) further illustrates this proliferation of terminology by adding a few more pairs of terms:

• *noncomplex* vs. *complex* modality (Anderson)
• *factual* vs. *theoretical* modality (Leech)
• *knowledge* vs. *influence* modality (Young)

For a more detailed comparison of root and epistemic modality, see Collins (1974: 154 ff.).

31. Doherty (1982) gives a brief survey of the wide range of epistemic expressions in English and German. A contrastive description of the epistemic use of the English and German modals is offered by Townson (1981).

32. See Lyons (1977: 787 ff.), Palmer (1979a: 2 f.); as for a logical description of modality in English, German, Spanish, and Hungarian, see Fülei-Szántó (1972).

33. In an August 1994 news broadcast of Deutschlandradio, the all-German broadcasting station, the construction . . . *Fähigkeit,* . . . *zu können* was used.

34. The analysis presented here for "possibility" could be extended to "necessity." Sweetser herself characterizes *muss nicht* as denoting "the absence of the force," whereas *must not* is regarded as "a very forceful prohibition" (1990: 152, n. 6).

Note also that Sweetser uses the term *metaphor* to characterize only the extension of the concept of forces and barriers from root to epistemic modality: "The meaning of epistemic MAY would thus be that there is no barrier to the speaker's process of reasoning from the available premises to the conclusion expressed in the sentence qualified by MAY. My claim, then, is that an epistemic modality is *metaphorically* viewed as the real-world modality which is its closest parallel in force-dynamic structure" (1990: 59, our italics). All the preceding examples involving the notions of *door, key,* and *way* suggest, however, that it is perfectly possible to describe also root modality in terms of metaphor.

35. Leirbukt (1979) seeks to demonstrate that perfective root constructions of the German modals, even though a relatively rare phenomenon, are to be seen as a linguistic regularity (see his p. 50).

36. Direct speech acts are defined by their literal meanings, whereas the meanings of indirect speech acts are more than merely a function of the meanings of the sentences used to perform them (Panther 1977: 227 ff.).

37. Panther (1977: 229) distinguishes between three kinds of indirect speech acts in English, German, and French.

38. As Jacobsson (1980: 47) remarks, HAD BETTER as an auxiliary is usually dubbed by grammarians as 'marginal,' 'semi' or 'quasi.' His own decision to refer to it as *modal auxiliary* is questionable, because it does not fulfill all the criteria mentioned in Section 1.2.2.1.

39. Also in German the use of a modal is possible, as in (i) *Ich kann zwei Schiffe sehen.* Standwell (1979: 253) points out, however, that KÖNNEN is used only if visibility is poor. In such situations also the full verb ERKENNEN would be appropriate.

40. See Taylor (1990: 27) who writes: "Modality . . . is expressed in various ways, e.g., lexical expressions, mood, *even silence,* but principally through modal verbs" (italics ours).

41. Only those aspects of the prosodic information given in Coates's examples that are of relevance to our purposes will be included in this section. For an explanation of the prosodic markings used see *Key to Symbols,* p. xvi.

42. When we refer to *translation units relevant to the modals* we do not extend

the notion of *translation unit* to refer to a *general* translation procedure such as a word-for-word translation where the unit of translation is the individual word; see the following.

43. Leech (1981: 213) states that from (i) the acceptability of (ii) may be predicted and, for many cases, that of (iii):

(i) We can trace new substances by various means.
(ii) New substances can be traced by various means.
(iii) New substances are traceable by various means.

But he adds that for many other cases the rule of conveying the passive meaning through the suffix *–able* does not work; the adjectives **triable*, **findable*, and **gettable* are absent from the regular English lexicon and would convey an air of strangeness, novelty, jocularity, etc. Several modern American and British dictionaries do, however, list the three lexemes as acceptable.

44. For English equivalents of the modal use of ABER in spoken and written language, see Section 5.2.2.2.

45. In addition to its function of strengthening directives, WOHL can also be used epistemically. In this sense Doherty (1978) relates it to full verbs such as DENKEN, ANNEHMEN, SUPPOSE, and THINK.

46. A survey of acceptable combinations of German modal particles is provided by Thurmair (1989: 207–61).

47. CAN and COULD in *if* clauses such as (930) and (933) are a common phenomenon. In contrast WILL as a modal auxiliary rarely appears in conditional clauses, as Gallagher (1990: 162) observes. For WILL in this clause type, he distinguishes between two meaning categories each comprising several meanings (p. 162 f.) and deals with their German equivalents (p. 164 f.).

48. Meyer (1989) researched the use of modals in English physics texts. Whereas a large number of his corpus sentences represent objective modality, cases of subjective modality were found to be of minor importance. Here the modals serve to add the author's comment, particularly in terms of his or her certainty regarding the validity of statements made (Meyer 1989: 132 f.).

49. Kufner (1977: 132 ff.) cites evidence of such mother-tongue interference adduced by means of a test performed at Cornell University. American students who had participated in German classes for at least two years were asked to translate into German ten English sentences containing modals. For nine of these sentences different modal usage in English and German led to mistakes due to interference predicted before.

For the sake of overcoming interference Gutknecht and Panther (1971) seek to provide guidance on the problem of finding a collection of basic English patterns fundamentally different in structure from their German counterparts. The aim is to help teachers understand why certain mistakes keep occurring despite nine years of foreign language teaching. Differences presented with reference to the modals include word order, MIGHT expressing personal feelings, the imperative with question tag, and English infinitive constructions corresponding to German relative clauses. For further reading in the field of contrastive linguistics, see Gutknecht (1978: 14 ff.).

50. See Nord's [1991]1992 factor model, about which she says that it is "particularly suitable for translator training. Intended to guide the fundamental steps of the translation process, it points to the essential competencies required of a translator. . . . Since it comprises the essential factors and dimensions of the translation process, it seems appropriate to identify the priorities of a particular translation task, thus allowing a systematic approach for both teachers and students" (1992: 47 f.).

Nord's model is, however, of a general nature, that is, not 'modal-specific.' For aspects related to teaching the German modals to Americans, see Folsom (1974); see also Fullerton (1977).

51. We say *largely* because in Section 3.1.4.1 it was already suggested that "it seems to be wisest to consider the interplay of several identification factors taken together; see the factor sets in Figures 3.13 and 3.14, under F4." Moreover, discussion of sentence (220) in Section 3.1.4.2 showed that several of its possible modal sources tend to be grouped together. Taking *modal source* to be a translation factor, we concluded that "factors come in sets," an idea to be extended in this chapter because it is true of all kinds of translation factors.

52. In Section 3.2.1.2 we mentioned as a translation principle the tenet that "renditions should resemble their original as much as possible"; cf. "the principle of having maximum equivalence by having as many invariance factors as possible" referred to in Section 3.2.6.4.

53. See Wilss (1982: 105), who states that optional shifts of expression such as transpositions are stylistically motivated.

54. We have repeatedly emphasized the supreme status of the client as the dominating factor of a translation assignment (see, for instance, Sections 7.3 and 8.4). However, Holz-Mänttäri (1984: 96) rightly states that only the translator as an expert will be able to fully survey all the relevant factors.

55. When the translator takes into account or processes a particular factor set, this is a cognitive activity. Therefore, a set of translation factors may be referred to as a *cognitive set*; see Neubert and Shreve (1992: 141), who apply van Dijk's notion of cognitive set to translation theory. With regard to a particular context of discourse processing, van Dijk (1980: 201) himself speaks of "the various factors in a cognitive set."

56. This is true of the practice of translating. But also as a theoretical (translatological) concept, translating by factors is nothing new. Holz-Mänttäri, for instance, sums up her treatise on translational action by saying: "The analytical description of the translator's activity aimed at elucidating the factors guiding his actions" (1984: 162; our translation); see also the titles listed at the beginning of Section 1.1.1. As a matter of fact, the notion of factor may be found in many publications on translation (theory). The authors of all these investigations therefore subscribe to the truism that every translation is motivated in some way or other.

REFERENCES

Allerton, D. J., Carney, E., and Holdcroft, D. (eds.). 1979. *Function and Context in Linguistic Analysis. A Festschrift for William Haas*. Cambridge: Cambridge University Press.

Altman, R. 1986. 'Getting the Subtle Distinctions: *Should* versus *Had Better*.' *Studies in Second Language Acquisition* 8: 80–87.

Antinucci, F., and Parisi, D. 1971. 'On English Modal Verbs.' *Papers from the Seventh Regional Meeting. Chicago Linguistic Society*: 28–39.

Arntz, R. (ed.). 1988. *Textlinguistik und Fachsprache. Akten des Internationalen übersetzungswissenschaftlichen AILA-Symposions Hildesheim, 13.–16. April 1987*. Hildesheim: Georg Olms.

——— and Thome, G. (eds.). 1990. *Übersetzungswissenschaft: Ergebnisse und Perspektiven. Festschrift für Wolfram Wilss zum 65. Geburtstag*. Tübinger Beiträge zur Linguistik 354. Tübingen: Gunter Narr.

Aronoff, M. 1976. *Word Formation in Generative Grammar*. Linguistic Inquiry Monograph 1. Cambridge, Mass.: The MIT Press.

Austin, J. L. 1956. 'Ifs and Cans.' *Proceedings of the British Academy* 42: 109–32.

———. 1975a. '*Falls* und *Können*.' In: J. L. Austin, *Wort und Bedeutung*, pp. 213–44. Munich: Paul List.

———. 1975b. *Wort und Bedeutung*. Munich: Paul List.

Bach, E., and Harms, R. (eds.). 1968. *Universals in Linguistic Theory*. New York: Holt, Rinehart and Winston.

Bailey, C.-J. N. 1980. 'English Verb Modality.' *Arbeitspapiere zur Linguistik* [Berlin] 10: 109–47.

Baker, M. 1992. *In Other Words. A Coursebook on Translation.* London and New York: Routledge.

Bales, K. 1976. 'Factors Determining the Translation of American Belles-Lettres into Hungarian, 1945–1973.' *Slavonic and East European Review* 54, no. 2: 173–91.

Ball, W. J. 1983. 'Might/May as Well.' *IATEFL Newsletter* 77: 14–16.

Barrera-Vidal, A., and Kühlwein, W. 1975. *Angewandte Linguistik für den fremdsprachlichen Unterricht. Eine Einführung.* Dortmund: Lambert Lensing.

Bartsch, R., and Vennemann, T. (eds.). 1973. *Linguistik und Nachbarwissenschaften.* Kronberg, Germany: Athenäum.

Bassnett, S., and Lefevere, A. (eds.). 1990. *Translation, History and Culture.* London and New York: Pinter.

Bastein, F. (ed.). 1987. *Kanada heute. Hamburger Beiträge zu Raum, Gesellschaft und Kultur.* Anglo-American Forum 20. Frankfurt am Main: Peter Lang.

Bausch, K.-R., and Weller, F.-R. (eds.). 1981. *Übersetzen und Fremdsprachenunterricht.* Frankfurt am Main: Moritz Diesterweg.

Beaugrande, R. de 1978. *Factors in a Theory of Poetic Translating.* Approaches to Translation Studies 5. Assen, the Netherlands: Van Gorcum & Co.

Behre, F. 1962. 'The *You Will* Request. A Syntactical Study.' *Gothenburg Studies in English* 14: 119–50.

Beilhardt, K., and Sutton, F. W. 1954. *Learning English, Unterrichtswerk für höhere Lehranstalten. Englische Schulgrammatik.* Stuttgart: Ernst Klett.

Bjarkman, P. C., and Raskin, V. (eds.). 1986. *The Real-World Linguist: Linguistic Applications in the 1980s.* Norwood, N.J.: Ablex.

Blum-Kulka, S. 1985. 'Modifiers as Indicating Devices: The Case of Requests.' *Theoretical Linguistics* 12: 213–29.

Bouma, L. 1975. 'On Contrasting the Semantics of the Modal Auxiliaries of German and English.' *Lingua* 37: 313–39.

Bowen, M. 1980. 'Bilingualism as a Factor in the Training of Interpreters.' In *Georgetown University Round Table on Languages and Linguistics*, pp. 201–7. Washington, D.C.: Georgetown University Press.

Boyd, J., and Thorne, J. P. 1969. 'The Semantics of Modal Verbs.' *Journal of Linguistics* 5: 57–74.

Brünner, G. 1981. 'Zur inferentiellen Verwendung der Modalverben.' In *Sprache:*

Verstehen and Handeln, ed. G. Hindelang and W. Zillig, pp. 311–21. Tübingen: Max Niemeyer.

Bublitz, W. 1978. *Ausdrucksweisen der Sprechereinstellung im Deutschen und Englischen. Untersuchungen zur Syntax, Semantik und Pragmatik der deutschen Modalpartikeln und Vergewisserungsfragen und ihrer englischen Entsprechungen.* Linguistische Arbeiten 57. Tübingen: Max Niemeyer.

Buelens, M. 1981. '*Können, Dürfen, Mögen* and Their English Equivalents.' Diss., Rijksuniversiteit Gent.

Bungarten, T. (ed.). 1981. *Wissenschaftssprache. Beiträge zur Methodologie, theoretischen Fundierung und Deskription.* Munich: Wilhelm Fink.

Butler, C. S. 1972. 'A Contrastive Study of Modality in English, French, German and Italian.' *Nottingham Linguistic Circular* 2: 26–39.

———. 1985. *Computers in Linguistics.* Oxford and New York: Basil Blackwell.

Calbert, J. P. 1975. 'Toward the Semantics of Modality.' In J. P. Calbert and H. Vater, *Aspekte der Modalität*, pp. 1–70. Tübingen: Gunter Narr.

——— and Vater, H. 1975. *Aspekte der Modalität.* Studien zur deutschen Grammatik 1. Tübingen: Gunter Narr.

CEN/CENELEC. 1984. 'Modale Hilfsverben und Europäische Normen.' *Der Sprachmittler. Informationshefte des Sprachendienstes der Bundeswehr* 22: 22–32.

Chesterman, A. 1989a. Introductory section. In *Readings in Translation Theory*, ed. A. Chesterman, p. 7. Helsinki: Oy Finn Lectura Ab.

——— (ed.). 1989b. *Readings in Translation Theory.* Helsinki: Oy Finn Lectura Ab.

Chriss, R. 1994. 'Translation as a Profession. Article Number 3. Teaching Translation and Interpretation.' Ms. (CIS 73543, 2020).

Coates, J. 1980a. 'On the Nonequivalence of *May* and *Can*.' *Lingua* 50: 209–20.

———. 1980b. Review of Palmer, *Modality and the English Modals. Lingua* 51: 337–46.

———. 1983. *The Semantics of the Modal Auxiliaries.* London and Canberra: Croom Helm.

Cole, R. W. (ed.). 1977. *Current Issues in Linguistic Theory.* Bloomington: Indiana University Press.

Collins, P. 1974. 'The Analysis of the English *Modal Auxiliaries* as Main Verbs,' *Kivung* 7: 151–66.

Crandell, T. E. (ed.). 1975. *Translators and Translating.* Binghamton: State University of New York Press.

Crystal, D., and Davy, D. 1969. *Investigating English Style.* London: Longman.

Dasenbrock, R. W. 1987. 'Intelligibility and Meaningfulness in Multicultural Literature in English.' *PMLA* 102: 10–19.

Delisle, J. 1988. *Translation: An Interpretive Approach.* Translation Studies 8. Trans. Patricia Logan and Monica Creery. Ottawa and London: University of Ottawa Press.

Dijk, T. A. van 1980. *Macrostructures. An Interdisciplinary Study of Global Structures in Discourse, Interaction, and Cognition.* Hillsdale, N.J.: Lawrence Erlbaum Associates.

Dirven, R. (ed.). 1989. *A User's Grammar of English: Word, Sentence, Text, Interaction.* Duisburger Arbeiten zur Sprach- und Kulturwissenschaft 4. Frankfurt am Main: Peter Lang.

Doherty, M. 1978. 'Die Übersetzung von deutschen Modalpartikeln ins Englische.' In *Zur lexikalischen Semantik des Englischen,* ed. A. Neubert, pp. 176–87. Berlin: Akademie der Wissenschaften der DDR, Zentralinstitut für Sprachwissenschaft.

———. 1979. 'Zur Äquivalenz von *müssen* im System englischer Modalverben.' *Zeitschrift für Anglistik und Amerikanistik* 27: 133–45.

———. 1982. 'Epistemische Ausdrucksmittel im Deutschen und Englischen.' *Fremdsprachen* 26: 92–97.

Dollerup, C., and Loddegaard, A. (eds.). 1992. *Teaching Translation and Interpreting: Training, Talent and Experience.* Papers from the First Language International Conference, Elsinore, Denmark, 31 May–2 June 1991. Copenhagen Studies in Translation. Amsterdam and Philadelphia: John Benjamins.

Downes, W. 1977. 'The Imperative and Pragmatics.' *Journal of Linguistics* 13: 77–97.

Dückert, J., and Kempcke, G. (eds.). 1984. *Wörterbuch der Sprachschwierigkeiten. Zweifelsfälle, Normen und Varianten im gegenwärtigen deutschen Sprachgebrauch.* Leipzig: VEB Bibliographisches Institut.

Duden. 1985. Vol. 9. *Richtiges und gutes Deutsch. Wörterbuch der sprachlichen Zweifelsfälle,* 3d ed. Mannheim: Bibliographisches Institut (Duden-Verlag).

Duff, A. 1989. *Translation.* Oxford: Oxford University Press.

Edmondson, W., House, J., Kasper, G., and McKeown, J. 1977. *A Pedagogic Grammar of the English Verb.* Tübinger Beiträge zur Linguistik 95. Tübingen: Gunter Narr.

Elgin, S. H. 1992. *The Gentle Art of Verbal Self-Defense.* New York: Barnes and Noble.

Eppert, F. (ed.). 1983. *Transfer and Translation in Language Learning and Teaching.*

Selected Papers from the RELC Seminar on Interlanguage Transfer Processes in Language Learning and Communication in Multilingual Societies, Singapore, April 1982. Anthology Series 12. Singapore: Singapore University Press.

Esser, J. 1984. *Untersuchungen zum gesprochenen Englisch.* Tübinger Beiträge zur Linguistik 228. Tübingen: Gunter Narr.

Etkind, E. 1967. 'La stylistique comparée, base de l'art de traduire.' *Babel* [Budapest] 13: 23–30.

Fawcett, R. P. 1983. Foreword. In M. R. Perkins, *Modal Expressions in English*, pp. ix–x. London: Frances Pinter.

Fillmore, C. J. 1968. 'The Case for Case.' In *Universals in Linguistic Theory*, ed. E. Bach and R. Harms, pp. 1–88. New York: Holt, Rinehart and Winston.

———. 1977. 'Topics in Lexical Semantics.' In *Current Issues in Linguistic Theory*, ed. R. W. Cole, pp. 76–138. Bloomington: Indiana University Press.

Florin, S. 1993. 'Realia in Translation.' In *Translation as Social Action*, ed. P. Zlateva, pp. 122–28. London and New York: Routledge.

Folsom, M. H. 1974. 'Die Modalverben im Deutschunterricht für Amerikaner.' *Deutsch als Fremdsprache* 11: 99–106.

Friederich, W. 1964. *Die infiniten Formen des Englischen. Infinitiv, Gerundium, Partizip.* Schriftenreihe des Sprachen- und Dolmetscher-Instituts. Munich: Studentenwerk.

———. 1990. 'English Nominal Constructions: Noch einmal visitiert.' *Lebende Sprachen* 35: 159–62.

Fülei-Szántó, E. 1972. 'Ein Versuch der logischen und grammatischen Beschreibung der Modalität in einigen Sprachen.' In *Papers from the International Symposium on Applied Constrastive Linguistics, Stuttgart, October 11–13, 1971*, ed. G. Nickel, pp. 141–56. Bielefeld, Germany: Cornelsen/Velhagen and Klasing.

Fuller, F. 1984. *The Translator's Handbook (with Special Reference to Conference Translation from French and Spanish).* Gerrards Cross, Buckinghamshire: Colin Smythe.

Fullerton, G. L. 1977. 'On Teaching the Subjective Use of Modal Auxiliaries.' *Unterrichtspraxis* 10, no. 2: 73–78.

Gailor, D. 1983. 'Reflections on *Should, Ought to,* and *Must.*' *ELT Journal* 37: 346–49.

Gallagher, J. D. 1990. 'Will in Conditional Clauses: A Translation Problem.' *Lebende Sprachen* 35: 163–66.

Geis, M. L., and Zwicky, A. M. 1971. 'Invited Inference.' *Linguistic Inquiry* 2: 561–66.

Gentzler, E. 1993. *Contemporary Translation Theories.* London and New York: Routledge.

Gerhardt, M. (ed.). 1974. *Linguistik und Sprachphilosophie.* Munich: Paul List.

Gerver, D., and Sinaiko, H. W. (eds.). 1978. *Language Interpretation and Communication.* NATO Conference Series 3: Human Factors 6. New York and London: Plenum Press.

Glas, R. 1984. 'Zur maschinellen Übersetzung von Illokutionsindikatoren.' In *Text—Textsorten—Semantik,* ed. A. Rothkegel and B. Sandig, pp. 262–73. Hamburg: Helmut Buske.

Gläser, R. 1986. *Phraseologie der englischen Sprache.* Tübingen: Max Niemeyer.

Gottwald, J. 1982. *Übersetzung Englisch-Deutsch. Texte—Fehlerquellen—Übungen.* Munich: Manz.

Greenbaum, S., Leech, G., and Svartvik, J. (eds.). 1980. *Studies in English Linguistics for Randolph Quirk.* London: Longman.

Gutknecht, C. 1971. 'Präsupposition als Kriterium für Grammatikalität von Sätzen.' *Linguistische Berichte* 15: 32–39.

———. 1978. *Kontrastive Linguistik: Zielsprache Englisch.* Stuttgart: W. Kohlhammer.

———. 1987. 'Kanada—ein 'klassisches' Land des Übersetzens? Anmerkungen zum Stand von Theorie und Praxis der Translation in einer bilingualen Nation.' In *Kanada heute,* ed. F. Bastein, pp. 225–61. Frankfurt am Main: Peter Lang.

———. 1996. *Lauter böhmische Dörfer. Wie die Wörter zu ihrer Bedeutung kamen,* 3d ed. Munich: C. H. Beck; 1st ed., 1995.

——— (ed.). 1977. *Grundbegriffe und Hauptströmungen der Linguistik.* Hamburg: Hoffmann and Campe.

——— and Panther, K.-U. 1971. 'The Role of Contrastive Grammars in Foreign Language Learning (Structural Differences Between English and German).' *The Incorporated Linguist* 10: 105–11, 118.

——— and Panther, K.-U. 1973. *Generative Linguistik: Ergebnisse moderner Sprachforschung.* Stuttgart: W. Kohlhammer.

——— and Rölle, L. J. 1988. 'Die multifaktorielle Translationssituation bei den Modalverben des Sprachenpaares Deutsch-Englisch.' In *Einheit in der Vielfalt,* ed. G. Quast, pp. 154–215. Berne: Peter Lang.

Gutt, E.-A. 1991. *Translation and Relevance. Cognition and Context.* Oxford and Cambridge, Mass.: Basil Blackwell.

Hammer, A. E. 1991. *German Grammar and Usage*, revised by Martin Durrell. London: Edward Arnold; 1st ed., 1978.

Hancher, M. 1980. 'Speech Acts and the Law.' In *Language Use and the Uses of Language*, ed. R. W. Shuy and A. Shnukal, pp. 245–56. Washington, D.C.: Georgetown University Press.

Hanon, S., and Pedersen, V. H. (eds.). 1980. *Human Translation—Machine Translation: Papers from the 10th Annual Conference on Computational Linguistics in Odense, Denmark, 22–23 November 1979*. Odense: Odense University, Romansk Institut.

Hansen, B., Hansen, K., Neubert, A., and Schentke, M. 1985. *Englische Lexikologie. Einführung in Wortbildung und lexikalische Semantik*. Leipzig: VEB Verlag Enzyklopädie.

Hartmann, R. (ed.). 1977. *Contrastive Analysis. Papers in German-English Contrastive Applied Linguistics*. Occasional Papers in Linguistics and Language Learning 3. Coleraine: New University of Ulster.

Hatim, B., and Mason, I. 1990. *Discourse and the Translator*. London and New York: Longman.

Hawkins, J. A. 1986. *A Comparative Typology of English and German. Unifying the Contrasts*. Austin: University of Texas Press.

Hindelang, G., and Zillig, W. (eds.). 1981. *Sprache: Verstehen und Handeln. Akten des 15. Linguistischen Kolloquiums Münster 1980*, Vol. 2. Linguistische Arbeiten 99. Tübingen: Max Niemeyer.

Hlebec, B. 1989. 'Factors and Steps in Translating.' *Babel* [Budapest] 35: 129–41.

Hofmann, T. R. 1979. 'On Modality in English and Other Languages.' *Papers in Linguistics* 12: 1–37.

Holmes, J. S. 1972. 'The Cross-Temporal Factor in Verse Translation.' *Meta* 17: 102–10.

Holz-Mänttäri, J. 1984. *Translatorisches Handeln*. Helsinki: Suomalainen Tiedeakatemia.

Hönig, H. G., and Kussmaul, P. 1984. *Strategie der Übersetzung. Ein Lehr- und Arbeitsbuch*, 2d ed. Tübinger Beiträge zur Linguistik 205. Tübingen: Gunter Narr; 1st ed., 1982.

Høyem, S. 1981. 'Zum Problem der Setzung einer Agens-Phrase bei der Fügung *sein + zu + Infinitiv* in der deutschen Gegenwartssprache.' *Nordlyd. Tromsø University Working Papers on Language and Linguistics* 5: 4–35.

Huddleston, R. 1976. 'Some Theoretical Issues in the Description of the English Verb.' *Lingua* 40: 331–83.

Italiaander, R. (ed.). 1965. *Übersetzen. Vorträge und Beiträge vom Internationalen Kongress literarischer Übersetzer in Hamburg 1965*. Frankfurt am Main: Athenäum.

Jacobson, S. 1975. *Factors Influencing the Placement of English Adverbs in Relation to Auxiliaries. A Study of Variation*. Stockholm Studies in English 33. Stockholm: Almqvist and Wiksell.

————. 1980a. 'Issues in the Study of Syntactic Variation.' In *Papers from the Scandinavian Symposium on Syntactic Variation*, ed. S. Jacobson, pp. 23–36. Stockholm: Almqvist and Wiksell.

———— (ed.). 1980b. *Papers from the Scandinavian Symposium on Syntactic Variation*. Stockholm, May 18–19, 1979. Stockholm Studies in English 52. Stockholm: Almqvist and Wiksell.

Jacobsson, B. 1979. 'Modality and the Modals of Necessity *Must* and *Have To*.' *English Studies* 60: 296–312.

————. 1980. 'On the Syntax and Semantics of the Modal Auxiliary *Had Better*.' *Studia Neophilologica* 52: 47–53.

Jahr, E. H., and Lorentz, O. (eds.). 1990. *Tromsø Linguistics in the Eighties*. Tromsø Studies in Linguistics 11. Oslo: Novus Press.

Jennings, C. B., King, N., and Stevenson, M. (eds.). 1957. *Weigh the Word*. New York: Harper and Brothers.

Johansson, S. 1985. 'Some Observations on Word Frequencies in Three Corpora of Present-Day English Texts.' *I.T.L. Review of Applied Linguistics* 67–68: 117–26.

Juhel, D. 1982. *Bilinguisme et Traduction au Canada: Rôle Sociolinguistique du Traducteur*. Centre International de Recherche sur le Bilinguisme, Publication B-107. Québec: C.I.R.B.

Jumpelt, R. W. 1961. *Die Übersetzung naturwissenschaftlicher und technischer Literatur. Sprachliche Massstäbe und Methoden zur Bestimmung ihrer Wesenszüge und Probleme*. Berlin-Schöneberg: Langenscheidt.

Kade, O. 1964. 'Subjektive und objektive Faktoren im Übersetzungsprozess. Ein Beitrag zur Ermittlung objektiver Kriterien des Übersetzens als Voraussetzung für eine wissenschaftliche Lösung des Übersetzungsproblems.' Doctoral diss., Leipzig.

Kastovsky, D. 1989. 'Word Formation.' In *A User's Grammar of English*, ed. R. Dirven, pp. 171–214. Frankfurt am Main: Peter Lang.

Kątny, A. 1987. *Bibliographie zur Modalität. Modalausdrücke im Deutschen und Polnischen*. Kölner Linguistische Arbeiten Germanistik 14. Cologne: Cologne University, Institut für Deutsche Sprache und Literatur.

————. 1989a. 'Bibliographie zu Modalverben im Englischen und ihren Konkurrenzformen.' In *Studien zur kontrastiven Linguistik und literarischen Übersetzung*, ed. A. Kątny, pp. 165–82. Frankfurt am Main: Peter Lang.

———. 1990a. 'Bibliographie zu den Modalverben des Deutschen.' In *Studien zum Deutschen aus kontrastiver Sicht*, ed. A. Kątny, pp. 181–97. Frankfurt am Main: Peter Lang.

——— (ed.). 1989b. *Studien zur kontrastiven Linguistik und literarischen Übersetzung*. European University Studies. Series 21: Linguistics 76. Frankfurt am Main: Peter Lang.

——— (ed). 1990b. *Studien zum Deutschen aus kontrastiver Sicht*. European University Studies. Series 21: Linguistics 86. Frankfurt am Main: Peter Lang.

Kempson, R. M. 1977. *Semantic Theory*. Cambridge: Cambridge University Press.

Kiefer, F. 1987. 'On Defining Modality.' *Folia Linguistica* 21: 67–94.

Kjellmer, G. 1975. 'Are Relative Infinitives Modal?' *Studia Neophilologica* 47: 323–32.

———. 1980. "'There Is No Hiding You in the House': On a Modal Use of the English Gerund." *English Studies* 61: 47–60.

Kluckhohn, C. 1962. 'The Concept of Culture.' In *Collected Essays of Clyde Kluckhohn*, ed. R. Kluckhohn, pp. 19–73. New York: The Free Press of Glencoe.

Kluckhohn, R. (ed.). 1962. *Collected Essays of Clyde Kluckhohn. Culture and Behavior*. New York: The Free Press of Glencoe.

Kolb, H., and Lauffner, H. (eds.). 1977. *Sprachliche Interferenz. Festschrift für Werner Betz zum 65. Geburtstag*. Tübingen: Max Niemeyer.

Koller, W. 1983. *Einführung in die Übersetzungswissenschaft*, 2d ed. Heidelberg: Quelle and Meyer; 1st ed., 1979.

König, E. 1974. 'Sind Sprachen vergleichbar? Aspekte der kontrastiven Linguistik.' In *Linguistik und Sprachphilosophie*, ed. M. Gerhardt, pp. 240–59. Munich: Paul List.

———. 1977. *Form und Funktion. Eine funktionale Betrachtung ausgewählter Bereiche des Englischen*. Anglistische Arbeitshefte 13. Tübingen: Max Niemeyer.

König, E., and Legenhausen, L. 1972. *Englische Syntax I. Komplexe Sätze*. Frankfurt am Main: Athenäum Fischer Taschenbuch Verlag.

Königs, F. G. 1981. 'Übersetzungswissenschaftliche Terminologie.' In *Übersetzen und Fremdsprachenunterricht*, ed. K.-R. Bausch and F.-R. Weller, pp. 314–38. Frankfurt am Main: Moritz Diesterweg.

Kufner, H. L. 1977. 'Englisch-deutsche Interferenzen am Beispiel der Modalverben.'

In *Sprachliche Interferenz*, ed. H. Kolb and H. Lauffner, pp. 127–37. Tübingen: Max Niemeyer.

Kussmaul, P. 1977. 'Englische Modalverben und Sprechakte.' *Neusprachliche Mitteilungen aus Wissenschaft und Praxis* 30: 202–7.

———. 1978. 'Kommunikationskonventionen in Textsorten am Beispiel deutscher und englischer geisteswissenschaftlicher Abhandlungen. Ein Beitrag zur deutsch-englischen Übersetzungstechnik.' *Lebende Sprachen* 23: 54–58.

———. 1986. 'Übersetzen als Entscheidungsprozess. Die Rolle der Fehleranalyse in der Übersetzungsdidaktik.' In *Übersetzungswissenschaft—eine Neuorientierung*, ed. M. Snell-Hornby, pp. 206–29. Tübingen: Francke.

Langenscheidts Enzyklopädisches Wörterbuch der englischen und deutschen Sprache. 1978. Berlin: Langenscheidt.

Larson, M. L. 1984. *Meaning-Based Translation. A Guide to Cross-Language Equivalence*. Lanham, Md.: University Press of America.

———. 1987. 'Establishing Project-Specific Criteria for Acceptability of Translations.' *ATA. American Translators Association Scholarly Monograph Series* 1: 69–76.

Leech, G. N. 1980. *Explorations in Semantics and Pragmatics*. Amsterdam: John Benjamins.

———. 1981. *Semantics. The Study of Meaning*, 2d ed. Harmondsworth: Penguin Books; 1st ed., 1974.

———. 1983. *Principles of Pragmatics*. London and New York: Longman.

———. 1987. *Meaning and the English Verb*, 2d ed. London and New York: Longman; 1st ed., 1971.

Leech, G. N., and Coates, J. 1980. 'Semantic Indeterminacy and the Modals.' In *Studies in English Linguistics for Randolph Quirk*, ed. S. Greenbaum, G. Leech, and J. Svartvik, pp. 79–90. London: Longman.

——— and Svartvik, J. 1975. *A Communicative Grammar of English*. London: Longman.

Leirbukt, O. 1979. 'Über objektiven Modalverbgebrauch bei Infinitiv II im heutigen Deutsch.' *Nordlyd. Tromsø University Working Papers on Language and Linguistics* 1: 49–96.

Levi, J. N. 1986. 'Applications of Linguistics to the Language of Legal Interactions.' In *The Real-World Linguist*, ed. P. C. Bjarkman and V. Raskin, pp. 230–65. Norwood, N.J.: Ablex.

Levý, J. 1965. 'Will Translation Theory Be of Use to Translators?' In *Übersetzen*, ed. R. Italiaander, pp. 77–82. Frankfurt am Main: Athenäum.

Lewandowski, T. 1975 and 1976. *Linguistisches Wörterbuch*. Vol. 1, 2d ed. (1976), vol. 2, 2d ed. (1976), vol. 3 (1975). Heidelberg: Quelle and Meyer.

Lindemann, B. 1990. 'Wie lernen norwegische Studenten die deutschen Modalverben?' In *Tromsø Linguistics in the Eighties*, ed. E. H. Jahr and O. Lorentz, pp. 239–58. Oslo: Novus Press.

Lodge, K. R. 1974. 'Modality and the Modal Verbs in English and German.' Ph.D. thesis, University of East Anglia.

———. 1977. 'The Modal Verbs.' In *Contrastive Analysis*, ed. R. Hartmann, pp. 46–54. Coleraine: New University of Ulster.

Longman Dictionary of Contemporary English, 2d ed. 1987. Berlin and Munich: Langenscheidt/Longman; 1st ed., 1978.

Longman Dictionary of English Language and Culture. 1992. Harlow: Longman.

Longman Lexicon of Contemporary English. 1981. Harlow: Longman.

Longman Modern English Dictionary. 1976. Harlow and London: Longman.

Luelsdorff, P. A. 1979. 'Some Modal Freezes.' *Anglistik und Englischunterricht* 8: 131–36.

Lyons, J. 1977. *Semantics*. Cambridge: Cambridge University Press.

———. 1981. *Language and Linguistics. An Introduction*. Cambridge: Cambridge University Press.

———. 1992. *Die Sprache*. Trans. C. Gutknecht, H.-P. Menz and I. von Rosenberg, 4th ed. Munich: C. H. Beck; 1st ed., 1983.

Maley, Y. 1987. 'The Language of Legislation.' *Language in Society* 16: 25–48.

Malone, J. L. 1988. *The Science of Linguistics in the Art of Translation. Some Tools from Linguistics for the Analysis and Practice of Translation*. SUNY Series in Linguistics. Albany: State University of New York Press.

Margalit, A. (ed.). 1979. *Meaning and Use. Papers Presented at the Second Jerusalem Philosophical Encounter April 1976*. Synthese Language Library. Texts and Studies in Linguistics and Philosophy 3. Dordrecht: D. Reidel.

Mattern, N. 1974. 'Anticipation in German-English Simultaneous Interpreting.' M.A. thesis, Saarbrücken.

Matthews, R. C. L. 1979. 'The Linguistic Analysis of Modality—with Special Reference to English and German.' Ph.D. thesis, University of Edinburgh.

———. 1991. *Words and Worlds. On the Linguistic Analysis of Modality*. European University Studies. Series 14: Anglo-Saxon Language and Literature 191. Frankfurt am Main: Peter Lang.

———. 1993a. *Papers on Semantics and Grammar*. European University Studies. Series 14: Anglo-Saxon Language and Literature 258. Frankfurt am Main: Peter Lang.

———. 1993b. 'Predicted Possibilities, Necessary Inferences and the Like: *Epistemic Modality*.' In R. C. L. Matthews, *Papers on Semantics and Grammar*, pp. 55–78. Frankfurt am Main: Peter Lang.

———. 1993c. 'Modality Revisited.' In R. C. L. Matthews, *Papers on Semantics and Grammar*, pp. 113–37. Frankfurt am Main: Peter Lang.

Meredith, R. C. 1979. 'Some Notes on English Legal Translation.' *META* 24: 54–67.

Mettinger, A. 1986. 'Comparing the Incomparable: English Adjectives in *–able* and Their Rendering in Modern Chinese.' *Papers and Studies in Contrastive Linguistics* 25: 21–29.

Meyer, H. J. 1989. 'Modality in Science Texts.' *Special Language/Fachsprache* 11: 127–35.

Mossop, B. 1983. 'The Translator as Rapporteur: A Concept for Training and Self-Improvement.' *META* 28: 244–78.

Nehls, D. 1986. *Semantik und Syntax des englischen Verbs. Teil 2: Die Modalverben. Eine kontrastive Analyse der Modalverben im Englischen und Deutschen.* Heidelberg: Julius Groos.

———. 1989. 'German Modal Particles Rendered by English Auxiliary Verbs.' In *Sprechen mit Partikeln*, ed. H. Weydt, pp. 282–92. Berlin and New York: Walter de Gruyter.

Neubert, A. 1986. 'Translatorische Relativität.' In *Übersetzungswissenschaft—eine Neuorientierung*, ed. M. Snell-Hornby, pp. 85–105. Tübingen: Francke.

———. 1989. 'Translation, Interpreting and Text Linguistics.' In *Readings in Translation Theory*, ed. A. Chesterman, pp. 141–56. Helsinki: Oy Finn Lectura Ab.
———. 1991. 'Models of Translation.' In *Empirical Research in Translation and Intercultural Studies*, ed. S. Tirkkonen-Condit, pp. 17–26. Tübingen: Gunter Narr.

Neubert, A. (ed.). 1978. *Zur lexikalischen Semantik des Englischen*. Linguistische Studien, Reihe A: Arbeitsberichte 45. Berlin: Akademie der Wissenschaften der DDR, Zentralinstitut für Sprachwissenschaft.

——— and Shreve, G. M. 1992. *Translation as Text*. Translation Studies 1. Kent, Ohio and London: Kent State University Press.

Newmark, P. 1981. *Approaches to Translation*. Oxford: Pergamon Press.

———. 1993. *Paragraphs on Translation*. Topics in Translation 1. Clevedon, England: Multilingual Matters.

Nickel, G. (ed.). 1972. *Papers from the International Symposium on Applied Contrastive Linguistics, Stuttgart, October 11–13, 1971*. Bielefeld, Germany: Cornelsen/ Velhagen and Klasing.

Nord, C. 1991. *Text Analysis in Translation. Theory, Methodology, and Didactic Application of a Model for Translation-Oriented Text Analysis*. Amsterdamer Publikationen zur Sprache und Literatur 94. Amsterdam and Atlanta, Ga.: Rodopi.

———. 1992. 'Text Analysis in Translator Training.' In *Teaching, Translation and Interpreting*, ed. C. Dollerup and A. Loddegaard, pp. 39–48. Amsterdam and Philadelphia: John Benjamins.

———. 1993. *Einführung in das funktionale Übersetzen. Am Beispiel von Titeln und Überschriften*. Tübingen and Basel: Francke.

O'Connor, J. D. 1968. 'The Intonation of Tag Questions in English.' *English Studies* 36: 96–105.

Palmer, F. R. 1971. *Grammar*. Harmondsworth: Penguin Books.

———. 1974a. *The English Verb*. London: Longman.

———. 1974b. *Grammatik und Grammatiktheorie*. Trans. C. Gutknecht. Munich: C. H. Beck.

———. 1976. *Semantics. A New Outline*. Cambridge: Cambridge University Press.

———. 1977. *Semantik. Eine Einführung*. Trans. C. Gutknecht. Munich: C. H. Beck.

———. 1979a. *Modality and the English Modals*. London and New York: Longman.

———. 1979b. 'Non-Assertion and Modality.' In *Function and Context in Linguistic Analysis*, ed. D. J. Allerton, E. Carney, and D. Holdcroft, pp. 185–95. Cambridge: Cambridge University Press.

———. 1986. *Mood and Modality*. Cambridge: Cambridge University Press.

———. 1987. 'What Is Modality?' In *Studies in Honour of René Derolez*, ed. A. M. Simon-Vandenbergen, pp. 391–401. Ghent: University of Ghent.

———. 1990. *Modality and the English Modals*, 2d ed. London and New York: Longman; 1st ed., 1979.

Pampell, J. R. 1975. 'More on Double Modals.' *Texas Linguistic Forum* 2: 110–21.

Panther, K.-U. 1977. 'Neuere Tendenzen in der linguistischen Pragmatik: Sprechakttheorie.' In *Grundbegriffe und Hauptströmungen der Linguistik*, ed. C. Gutknecht, pp. 206–35. Hamburg: Hoffmann and Campe.

———. 1981a. 'Indirect Speech Act Markers Or Why Some Linguistic Signs Are Non-Arbitrary.' *Papers from the Seventeenth Regional Meeting. Chicago Linguistic Society*, pp. 295–302.

————. 1981b. 'Einige typische indirekte sprachliche Handlungen im wissenschaftlichen Diskurs.' In *Wissenschaftssprache*, ed. T. Bungarten, pp. 231–60. Munich: Wilhelm Fink.

Parkes, G., Cornell, A., Marsden, P., and Fenn, P. 1989. *101 Myths about the English Language. A Guidebook for Foreign Teachers and Learners of English*. Southampton: Englang Books.

Perkins, M. R. 1983. *Modal Expressions in English*. London: Frances Pinter.

Picken, C. (ed.). 1989. *The Translator's Handbook*, 2d ed. London: Aslib; 1st ed., 1983.

Potter, S. 1974. 'Contrastive Linguistics in Action.' *The Incorporated Linguist* 13, no. 1: 1–5.

Quast, G. (ed.). 1988. *Einheit in der Vielfalt. Festschrift für Peter Lang zum 60. Geburtstag*. Berne: Peter Lang.

Quirk, R. 1982. *Style and Communication in the English Language*. London: Edward Arnold.

———— and Greenbaum, S. 1973. *A University Grammar of English*. London: Longman.

————, Greenbaum, S., Leech, G., and Svartvik, J. 1972. *A Grammar of Contemporary English*. London and New York: Longman.

————, Greenbaum, S., Leech, G., and Svartvik, J. 1985. *A Comprehensive Grammar of the English Language*. London: Longman.

Raith, J. 1963. *Englische Grammatik*, 3d ed. Munich: Max Hueber.

Raynaud, F. 1977. 'Noch einmal Modalverben!' *Deutsche Sprache* 5: 1–30.

Reiss, K. 1984. 'Adäquatheit und Äquivalenz.' In *Die Theorie des Übersetzens und ihr Aufschlusswert für die Ubersetzungs- und Dolmetschdidaktik*, ed. W. Wilss and G. Thome, pp. 80–89. Tübingen: Gunter Narr.

————. 1989. 'Text Types, Translation Types and Translation Assessment.' In *Readings in Translation Theory*, ed. A. Chesterman, pp. 105–15. Helsinki: Oy Finn Lectura Ab.

Reum, A. 1961. *A Dictionary of English Style*. Munich: Max Hueber.

Rose, M. G. (ed.). 1977. *Translation in the Humanities*. Binghamton: State University of New York Press.

————. 1981. *Translation Spectrum. Essays in Theory and Practice*. Albany: State University of New York Press.

Ross, S. D. 1981. 'Translation and Similarity.' In *Translation Spectrum*, ed. M. G. Rose, pp. 8–22. Albany: State University of New York Press.

Rothkegel, A., and Sandig, B. (eds.). 1984. *Text—Textsorten—Semantik. Linguistische Modelle und maschinelle Verfahren.* Papiere zur Textlinguistik 52. Hamburg: Helmut Buske.

Rückert, F. 1882. *Gesammelte Poetische Werke* in Zwölf Bänden, new ed., vol. 8. Frankfurt am Main: I. D. Sauerländer's Verlag.

Russ, C. V. J. (ed.). 1981. *Contrastive Aspects of English and German.* Heidelberg: Julius Groos.

Sager, J. C. 1989. 'Quality and Standards—the Evaluation of Translations.' In *The Translator's Handbook,* 2d ed., ed. C. Picken, pp. 91–102. London: Aslib.

Savory, T. H. 1968. *The Art of Translation.* London: Cape.

Schmid, H. 1966. 'Studien über modale Ausdrücke der Notwendigkeit und ihrer Verneinungen. Ein Übersetzungsvergleich in vier europäischen Sprachen.' Doctoral diss., University of Tübingen.

Schreiber, M. 1993. *Übersetzung und Bearbeitung. Zur Differenzierung und Abgrenzung des Übersetzungsbegriffs.* Tübinger Beiträge zur Linguistik 389. Tübingen: Gunter Narr.

Seiler, H. 1971. 'Abstract Structures for Moods in Greek.' *Language* 47: 79–89.

Senn, F. 1986. 'Literarische Übertragungen—empirisches Bedenken.' In *Übersetzungswissenschaft—eine Neuorientierung,* ed. M. Snell-Hornby, pp. 54–84. Tübingen: Francke.

Shuy, R. W., and Shnukal, A. (eds.). 1980. *Language Use and the Uses of Language.* Washington, D.C.: Georgetown University Press.

Silverstein, M. 1973. 'Linguistik und Anthropologie.' In *Linguistik und Nachbarwissenschaften,* ed. R. Bartsch and T. Vennemann, pp. 193–210. Kronberg: Athenäum.

Simon-Vandenbergen, A. M. (ed.). 1987. *Studies in Honour of René Derolez.* Ghent: University of Ghent, Seminarie voor Engelse en Oud-Germaanse Taalkunde.

Skov-Larsen, J. 1980. 'On the Establishment of Formalized Transfer Rules Based on Cotextual and Contextual Factors.' In *Human Translation—Machine Translation,* ed. S. Hanon and V. H. Pedersen, pp. 69–71. Odense: Odense University, Romansk Institut.

Snell-Hornby, M. 1984. 'The Linguistic Structure of Public Directives in German and English.' *Multilingua* 3: 203–11.

———. 1986a. 'Einleitung: Übersetzen, Sprache, Kultur.' In *Übersetzungswissenschaft—eine Neuorientierung,* ed. M. Snell-Hornby, pp. 9–29. Tübingen: Francke.

———. 1988. *Translation Studies. An Integrated Approach*. Amsterdam and Phila-delphia: John Benjamins.

———. 1990. 'Linguistic Transcoding or Cultural Transfer? A Critique of Transla-tion Theory in Germany.' In *Translation, History and Culture*, ed. S. Bassnett and A. Lefevere, pp. 79–86. London and New York: Pinter.

——— (ed.). 1986b. *Übersetzungswissenschaft—eine Neuorientierung. Zur Integra-tion von Theorie und Praxis*. Tübingen: Francke.

Soomere, K. 1989. 'A Statistical Analysis of Rhythm as One of the Key Factors of Adequacy of Literary Translations of Prose (from English into Estonian).' *Lin-guistica* [Tartu]: 131–39.

Standwell, G. J. B. 1979. 'A Contrastive Study of the Modals in English and Ger-man.' *IRAL* 17: 251–64.

Steele, S. 1975. 'Is it Possible?' *Stanford University Working Papers in Language Universals* 18: 35–58.

Steiner, A. 1991. *Englisch wie es nicht im Wörterbuch steht*, 10th ed. Bergisch Glad-bach: Bastei-Lübbe; 1st ed., 1981.

Stellbrink, H.-J. 1987. 'Der Übersetzer und Dolmetscher beim Abschluss interna-tionaler Verträge.' *Textcontext* 2: 32–41.

Stolze, R. 1992. *Hermeneutisches Übersetzen. Linguistische Kategorien des Ver-stehens und Formulierens beim Übersetzen*. Tübinger Beiträge zur Linguistik 368. Tübingen: Gunter Narr.

———. 1994. *Übersetzungstheorien. Eine Einführung*. Tübingen: Gunter Narr.

Straight, H. S. 1975. 'Translation: Some Anthropological and Psycholinguistic Fac-tors.' In *Translators and Translating*, ed. T. E. Crandell. Binghamton: State Uni-versity of New York Press. Reprinted in *Translation in the Humanities*, ed. M. G. Rose. Binghamton: State University of New York Press, 1977.

———. 1981. 'Knowledge, Purpose, and Intuition: Three Dimensions in the Evalua-tion of Translation.' In *Translation Spectrum*, ed. M. G. Rose, pp. 41–51. Al-bany: State University of New York Press.

Strawson, P. F. 1979. 'May Bes and Might Have Beens.' In *Meaning and Use*, ed. A. Margalit, pp. 229–38. Dordrecht: D. Reidel.

Sweetser, E. E. 1990. *From Etymology to Pragmatics. Metaphorical and Cultural Aspects of Semantic Structure*. Cambridge Studies in Linguistics 54. Cambridge: Cambridge University Press.

Sykes, J. B. 1989. 'The Intellectual Tools Employed.' In *The Translator's Handbook*, ed. C. Picken, pp. 35–41. London: Aslib.

Taylor, C. 1990. *Aspects of Language and Translation. Contrastive Approaches for Italian/English Translators.* Udine: Campanotto Editore.

Temmerman, D. 1981. 'Some Aspects of Verbal Necessity: A Contrastive Study of German and English.' Diss., Rijksuniversiteit Gent.

Thurmair, M. 1989. *Modalpartikeln und ihre Kombinationen.* Linguistische Arbeiten 233. Tübingen: Max Niemeyer.

Tirkkonen-Condit, S. (ed.). 1991. *Empirical Research in Translation and Intercultural Studies.* Selected Papers of the TRANSIF Seminar, Savonlinna 1988. Language and Performance 5. Tübingen: Gunter Narr.

Tottie, G. 1980. 'Negation and Ambiguity.' In *Papers from the Scandinavian Symposium on Syntactic Variation,* ed. S. Jacobson, pp. 47–62. Stockholm: Almqvist and Wiksell.

———. 1985. 'The Negation of Epistemic Necessity in Present-Day British and American English.' *English World-Wide* 6: 87–116.

Toury, G. 1980. *In Search of a Theory of Translation.* Tel Aviv: Porter Institute for Poetics and Semiotics (Tel Aviv University).

Townson, M. 1981. 'Epistemic Modality in English and German.' In *Contrastive Aspects of English and German,* ed. C. V. J. Russ, pp. 159–80. Heidelberg: Julius Groos.

Vermeer, H. J. 1986. 'Übersetzen als kultureller Transfer.' In *Übersetzungswissenschaft—eine Neuorientierung,* ed. M. Snell-Hornby, pp. 30–53. Tübingen: Francke.

Walther, W. 1990. 'Faktoren für die Übersetzung von Metaphern.' In *Übersetzungswissenschaft: Ergebnisse und Perspektiven,* ed. R. Arntz and G. Thome, pp. 440–52. Tübingen: Gunter Narr.

Wekker, H. C. 1987. 'Points of Modern English Syntax 69.' *English Studies* 68: 456–63.

Werlen, I. 1985. *Gebrauch und Bedeutung der Modalverben in alemannischen Dialekten.* Zeitschrift für Dialektologie und Linguistik. Beihefte 49. Wiesbaden and Stuttgart: Frank Steiner.

Werth, P. 1981. 'Tense, Modality and Possible Worlds.' *Rapport d'Activités de l'Institut de Phonétique* [Brussels] 16: 17–30.

Wertheimer, R. 1972. *The Significance of Sense. Meaning, Modality, and Morality.* Ithaca, N.Y., and London: Cornell University Press.

Westney, P. 1995. *Modals and Periphrastics in English.* Linguistische Arbeiten 339. Tübingen: Max Niemeyer.

Weydt, H. (ed.). 1989. *Sprechen mit Partikeln*. Berlin and New York: Walter de Gruyter.

Wierzbicka, A. 1987. 'The Semantics of Modality.' *Folia Linguistica* 21: 25–43.

Wildhagen, K., and Héraucourt, W. 1963 and 1972. *English-German/German-English Dictionary*: Vol. 1 (1963), vol. 2, 2d ed. (1972). Wiesbaden: Brandstetter and London: George Allen and Unwin.

Wilss, W. 1978. 'Syntactic Anticipation in German-English Simultaneous Interpreting.' In *Language Interpretation and Communication*, ed. D. Gerver and H. W. Sinaiko, pp. 343–52. New York and London: Plenum Press.

———. 1982. *The Science of Translation. Problems and Methods*. Tübinger Beiträge zur Linguistik 180. Tübingen: Gunter Narr.

———. 1983a. 'Methodological Aspects of the Translation Process.' In *Transfer and Translation in Language Learning and Teaching*, ed. F. Eppert, pp. 175–92. Singapore: Singapore University Press.

———. 1983b. 'The Function of Translation in Foreign Language Teaching.' In *Transfer and Translation in Language Learning and Teaching*, ed. F. Eppert, pp. 243–58. Singapore: Singapore University Press.

———. 1988. 'Übersetzen als Entscheidungsprozess.' In *Textlinguistik und Fachsprache*, ed. R. Arntz, pp. 7–20. Hildesheim: Georg Olms.

———. 1989. 'Towards a Multifacet Concept of Translation Behavior.' *Target* 1: 129–49.

———. 1992. 'Was ist Übersetzungsdidaktik? Versuch einer Faktorenanalyse.' *Lebende Sprachen* 37: 56–60.

——— and Thome, G. (eds.). 1984. *Die Theorie des Übersetzens und ihr Aufschlusswert für die Übersetzungs- und Dolmetschdidaktik. Translation Theory and Its Implementation in the Teaching of Translating and Interpreting*. Akten des Internationalen Kolloquiums der Association Internationale de Linguistique Appliquée (AILA) Saarbrücken, 25.–30. Juli 1983. Tübinger Beiträge zur Linguistik 247. Tübingen: Gunter Narr.

Zlateva, P. (ed.). 1993. *Translation as Social Action. Russian and Bulgarian Perspectives*. London and New York: Routledge.

Author Index

333

Subject Index